The Gilded Age Letters of
E. L. Godkin

The Gilded Age Letters of E. L. Godkin

First Edition

Published by State University of New York Press

99 Washington Avenue, Albany, New York 12210

© 1974 State University of New York

Library of Congress Cataloging in Publication Data

Godkin, Edwin Lawrence, 1831–1902.
The gilded age letters of E. L. Godkin.

1. Godkin, Edwin Lawrence, 1831–1902.
2. Journalists—Correspondence, reminiscences,
etc.   1. Armstrong, William M., ed. II. Title.
PN4874.G5A4   1974   070.4'092'4 [B]   74-6462

ISBN 0-87395-246-4 (clothbound)

ISBN 0-87395-247-2 (microfiche)

Godkin in 1899

The Gilded

E. L. Godl

EDITED BY WILLIAM M. AF

ALBANY, NEW YORK, 1974

STATE UNIVERSITY OF NEW YORK

To Bruce

Contents

Illustrations

Preface

What are the reasons for producing a book of E. L. Godkin's letters, now that time and recent revisionist scholarship have erased some of the stature of the man whom historians long thought one of the most useful citizens of the Gilded Age? The answer lies partly in the question. The partially distorted view that historians until recently had of the later nineteenth century they got in large part from Godkin, which is to say the *Nation,* because Godkin *was* the *Nation.* Now that scholars are aware that their assessment of the Gilded Age was warped by the Mugwump historians who subscribed to the *Nation,* Godkin's personal letters take on significance. To many, including those historians who still cannot resist the urge to quote the Godkin *Nation* with authority, he remains something of a mystery. Not only has he had no real biographer—he has not until now been permitted to speak publicly through his own letters except in censored form. The shortcomings of Rollo Ogden's *Life and Letters of Edwin Lawrence Godkin* in this regard are evident. In 1903, some months after Godkin's death, his son, Lawrence Godkin, set about with Godkin's widow to collect his father's letters, explaining to correspondents that "a volume of his life and letters is contemplated and I am now engaged in collecting material for this purpose." The Godkins were just relaxing from their whirlwind campaign to honor the dead editor's memory by establishing an annual series of lectures bearing his name at Harvard University.

For the next year and a half the family solicited personal letters of Godkin, ignoring, however, correspondents of his such as Grover Cleveland, Theodore Roosevelt, Henry Cabot Lodge, Carl Schurz, and Henry Villard, with whom he had suffered difficulties. At last, in January 1905 Lawrence Godkin advised his old Harvard classmate, William Roscoe Thayer, that he and his stepmother had assembled the material for their intended "memorial" to Godkin, as they called it, and he asked Thayer to edit it. Thayer scanned the material, heard the family's plans, and

declined with the advice that a friend undertake the book. Thereupon the family turned to Rollo Ogden, a former editorial writer
under Godkin and now his successor as editor of the *Evening
Post,* and Ogden consented to compile the volume.

A year and a half later, the two-volume *Life and Letters of
Edwin Lawrence Godkin* was sent to the press. It bore the marks
of its hasty construction; it was neither an accurate biography of
Godkin nor a representative collection of his letters. Most of
the letters, in fact, had been written by others. The *Life and
Letters* is disappointing in part because its editor was also the
busy editor of a metropolitan daily newspaper who did not have
time to search for his subject's letters, and in part for other rea-
sons. Years later Ogden told Allan Nevins that many of the
Godkin letters that the family had collected were unprintable.
This assumes interest in the light of Mrs. Godkin's assertion that
Ogden at first opposed the plan to censor her husband's letters.
As she told Charles Eliot Norton during the compilation of the
Life and Letters:

> Happily [Ogden] seeks, rather than avoids, suggestions from
> L[awrence] and myself [but] one point of difference which I
> foresee, is how far taste and discretion can be stretched in the
> mention of individuals. Edwin's phrases, sometimes caustic,
> are very tempting to quote, and indeed what the public wants.
> . . . Ogden thinks when a man is dead, Greeley, Seward, for
> instance, anything can be said—some he rather hoped might
> die before the book was published, [E. C.] Stedman for in-
> stance, in order that a phrase might be used, (this not quite in
> earnest perhaps). As a journalist, his limit in this respect is
> lower than ours. On the other hand a certain timidity in
> Lawrence . . . points to suppression liberally . . . mine . . .
> is rather a middle voice between L's and Ogden's.

The *Life and Letters* received polite reviews, but some Godkin
admirers, including the family, were disappointed. Fortunately
for them, critics of Godkin—and they were numerous—were
deprived of the knowledge that this memorial to a man of proclaimed integrity lacked basic integrity of its own. Ogden, under
the lax editorial standards of the day, had toyed with his subject's

words; not only did he suppress some of Godkin's most important letters, but he printed others out of context—silently deleting expletives and controversial paragraphs and even rewriting several. Some of the alterations were for the purpose of avoiding libel, but others were meant to improve the image of Godkin. By any editorial standard the Ogden work is unsatisfactory. "How I wish that Mrs. Godkin had intrusted the writing of Mr. Godkin's life to me," lamented the twentieth-century editor of the *Nation*, Oswald G. Villard. "The Ogden book is pathetically inadequate." In 1935 Villard, who in his youth had worked under Godkin, determined to provide a remedy. But before he began to write, Godkin's daughter-in-law stressed to Villard's research assistant the obstacles the biographer would face. "I myself destroyed the letters of E. L. Godkin to his wife," Cornelia Godkin told Thatcher Winslow, "as I felt they were quite too personal for other eyes." Yet, eager to be of assistance, she sent to Villard for his inspection quantities of Godkin's surviving papers.

Villard—who a generation earlier had heatedly rebuffed an attack on Godkin's character by Edward Everett Hale with the rejoinder, "Mr. Godkin's reputation and private life are unassailable"—carefully studied the papers and returned to Mrs. Godkin a bundle of Godkin letters referring, as he put it, "to private family affairs that ought not to remain in existence" with the advice that they, too, be destroyed. Thereupon, Villard gave up his intended biography. In the decades that followed, nearly a dozen aspiring biographers of Godkin turned up, but none of them completed the task.

It was obvious to me, as I undertook my own study of Godkin some years ago, that a competent treatment of the Gilded Age editor would require years of labor in locating surviving letters that were now widely scattered. A professor of English who had given up a projected biography of Godkin assured me that the search for letters would be fruitless. True, Harvard University owned the Godkin Papers, a collection based on the papers assembled by Lawrence and Katharine Godkin between 1903 and 1905. But of the nearly 2,000 letters in the collection, barely two hundred were Godkin's, the family having screened the collection for controversial letters of his before transferring it to Harvard. To do a critical study of the editor would entail a search for personal letters elsewhere as well as a careful backtracking on Ogden's scholarship, a task made difficult by the fact that a large number of the letters quoted in the *Life and Letters* were missing —obviously destroyed by the family—including most of Godkin's sprightly correspondence with women.

A search, employing the excellent facilities of the Houghton Library at Harvard, disclosed many unpublished Godkin letters in other collections of the University. A check of vital statistics, genealogical records, and social registers, revealed the existence and whereabouts of relatives of Godkin by marriage and of descendants of friends and acquaintances. Manuscript dealers aided me in the search, and advertisements placed at home and abroad brought helpful responses. The Union Catalog Division of the Library of Congress joined me in circularizing manuscript depositories, many of which I visited in person. A search of one of these, the Manuscript Division of the Library of Congress, disclosed more than two hundred unpublished Godkin letters. Hundreds more were found at the Johns Hopkins University, Cornell University, Columbia University, Yale University, the University of Pennsylvania, and the University of Vermont; and there were scattered letters at Trinity College, Swarthmore College, Vassar College, Duke University, and the University of Rochester.

In addition, state and private historical societies, as well as public libraries, proved important sources of Godkin letters, among them the New York Public Library, the Massachusetts Historical Society, the Hayes Memorial Library, the Historical Society of Pennsylvania, the Stockbridge (Massachusetts) Library, the library of the Boston Athenaeum, the New-York Historical Society, the Maryland Satte Historical Society, and the State Historical Society of Wisconsin. Scattered letters were found in the Huntington Library, the library of the American Academy of Arts and Letters, the Pierpont Morgan Library, and the Barrett Collection of American Literature. Finally, from private hands and from the Bodleian Library of Oxford University and other depositories in the British Isles came nearly one hundred unpublished Godkin letters.

Happily, as the letters flowed in, a composite picture of Godkin emerged, one that etched him in all his frailties as well as his virtues. He could at last be returned to the human race.

Acknowledgments

The persons who, in the course of more than a decade of collecting the letters of E. L. Godkin, gave me helpful assistance are many. Among the relatives or friends of persons mentioned in this book to whom I am especially indebted are Cornelia Godkin, Frederick Law Olmsted, Jr., Edith Perkins Cunningham, Mrs. Henry D. Sedgwick, Ellery Sedgwick, Jr., Rosamond Gilder, Mrs. Ward Thoron, Marian Hague, Susan Norton, Susan Sedgwick Hammond, Frederick Bonham-Carter, and Margaret V. Bryce. Among the scholars whom I wish particularly to thank are Leon Edel, Gordon Milne, Allan Nevins, George Arms, Morton Keller, Elizabeth Wallace, Hans Trefousse, Alan P. Grimes, Arthur R. Hogue, John K. Reeves, Richard B. Hovey, J. Albert Robbins, Richard E. Welch, Jr., Robert Muccigrosso, and, with a special word of appreciation for their many kindnesses, Martin B. Duberman and James M. McPherson.

This volume could not have been assembled without the cooperation of archivists and librarians throughout the United States and the British Isles. I especially wish to express my gratitude to the Houghton Library of Harvard University and the Bodleian Library of Oxford University for providing me with microfilm copies of their Godkin holdings, an indispensable aid because of Godkin's hard-to-read handwriting. Besides Miss Bryce, Mr. Bonham-Carter, and the Bodleian Library, those in England to whom I am especially indebted are D. Flanagan of the Cooperative Union Library in Manchester, Marjorie Plant of the British Library of Political and Economic Science, E. Taylor of the John Rylands Library in Manchester, W. D. Coates of the National Register of Archives, Anna Hackel of the British Association for American Studies, and D. S. Porter of the Bodleian Library. To Mr. Porter I owe a particular debt of gratitude for his assistance.

In the United States I received courtesies from so many archivists and librarians that I cannot suitably thank them all here. I especially wish to express my appreciation to John Alden of the

Boston Public Library, Ruth E. Ballenger of the Rutherford B. Hayes Library, T. D. Seymour Bassett of the Wilbur Library of the University of Vermont, W. E. Bigglestone of the Oberlin College Archives, Alice H. Bonnell of the Butler Library of Columbia University, Dorothy W. Bridgewater of the Yale University Library, Kimball Evans of the Harvard University Archives, Margaret Hackett of the Library of the Boston Athenaeum, John E. Buchanan and John Wertis of the Mann Library of Cornell University, Herbert Cahoon of the Pierpont Morgan Library, Marian Clarke of the Watkinson Library of Trinity College, Josephine L. Harper of the State Historical Society of Wisconsin, James J. Heslin of the New-York Historical Society, Robert W. Hill of the New York Public Library, William A. Jackson and Carolyn E. Jakeman of the Houghton Library of Harvard University, Mrs. Matthew Josephson of the American Academy of Arts and Letters, Stephen T. Riley of the Massachusetts Historical Society, Angela Rubin of the University of Chicago Library, George A. Schwegmann, Jr. of the Library of Congress, Frieda C. Thies of the Johns Hopkins University Library, Mrs. Graham D. Wilcox of the Stockbridge (Massachusetts) Library, and Clifford K. Shipton.

Finally I wish to thank the American Philosophical Society, the National Endowment for the Humanities, and the Research Division of Clarkson College of Technology for providing me with the research grants that made this volume possible and Mrs. Angie Ely for lending it her admirable typing and editorial skills. Thanks of a very special kind are due my former wife Norma C. Armstrong for her unselfish help during the embryonic stages of this book.

A Note on the Editing

Faced with the tyranny of rising printing costs, I have had to exercise a high degree of selectivity in editing Godkin's letters so as to keep them within the bounds of a single, compact volume. Most of the letters that I have selected for inclusion in the volume are manuscript letters never before published, but for balance I have included a quantity of letters published elsewhere, such as in the *Life and Letters*, for which manuscripts no longer exist. Most of the last are reprinted without change except that (1) I have added elliptical dots wherever internal evidence shows that Ogden or another omitted something, including the salutation or a concluding sentence. (Sometimes Ogden used ellipses for omissions he made in the text; sometimes he did not. Occasionally a comparison of the Ogden text with surviving replies to Godkin's letters reveals the fact of an omission.) (2) I have corrected typographical errors, and, in some instances, restored Godkin's British spelling to the original. (3) Where my study of the Ogden text and the replies to Godkin's letters in my possession show that Ogden misdated a letter or threw two or three letters together under a single date, I have restored these letters to their correct dates.

In regard to the above-discussed previously printed letters and copies of letters for which there are no surviving originals—mainly those published by Ogden—the question arises: How reliable are they? Fortunately, enough of the Godkin letters that Ogden printed survive in manuscript to allow a study of Ogden's editorial method. Besides revising punctuation, spelling, syntax, and capitalization, he silently deleted adjectives and controversial passages from his subject's letters, but only infrequently did he alter Godkin's meaning. Although the reader cannot know precisely what sins of omission Ogden and the Godkin family committed in editing these letters, he may be confident that most of the words that remain in them are Godkin's.

The letters in this volume are arranged in chronological order according to periods of Godkin's career, beginning with the first letter in 1859. Dates that I have editorially supplied are bracketed; undated letters for which only the year may be conjectured are grouped at the end of each year. The full name of the recipient of the letter is given at the top—except where such a designation is superfluous—together, on occasion, with the recipient's title such as "Lord," "Senator," "Professor," and the like. Besides omitting detailed passages of the text in the interest of space—which I have indicated with ellipses—I have, in deference to the publisher, made certain technical changes. They are: (1) the substitution of a colon for the comma that Godkin customarily placed after his salutation, (2) the occasional combining of several paragraphs into one, (3) the elimination of underscored superscription in the use of abbreviations such as "th" and "rd" and the bringing of the letters down to the line; (4) the streamlining and, frequently, relocation at the top of the letter of the place and date—such as printed letterheads—with their punctuation, capitalization, and indentation altered to conform to a uniform style.

To avoid distracting the reader, I have kept to a minimum editorial finger-pointing at Godkin's mistakes of syntax and spelling. For example, words that he regularly misspells, such as his "canvas" (for votes), "edite," and "enterprize," I have refrained from labelling *sic* after their first appearance in the text.

Besides the deletions from the text denoted by ellipses and the above-noted technical alterations, the editorial changes that I have made in the body of the text are: (1) the supplying of periods, apostrophes, and question marks that Godkin omitted or where the text is faded; (2) the elimination of unintentionally duplicated words; (3) the completion of quotation marks and parentheses; (4) the replacement of ampersands with "and" or "etc.," whichever is appropriate; (5) the conjectural addition in brackets of a word unintentionally omitted; (6) the conjectural replacement in brackets of words or phrases missing from the manuscript owing to torn corners or faded text; (7) the italicization of all periodicals, ships, and uncommonly used foreign phrases. Lastly, although I have tried to resist tampering with Godkin's wretched punctuation, I have given him the benefit of the doubt when a mark resembling a comma appears where a period ought to be, and vice versa.

Changes below the text of the letter consist of compressing the complimentary close into one line above the signature, and, in most cases, deleting the name of the recipient in the lower left corner. Godkin customarily signed his letters "E. L. Godkin," but for brevity the signature has been changed to ELG.

Key to Letter Source Citations

Codes used in the citation notes of manuscripts are from *Symbols of American Libraries,* 10th ed. (Washington, D.C.: Library of Congress, 1969).

CSmH   Henry E. Huntington Library, San Marino, California.
CtHT   Trinity College, Hartford, Connecticut.
CtY   Yale University, New Haven, Connecticut.
DLC   Library of Congress, Washington, D.C.
ICU   University of Chicago, Chicago, Illinois.
IHi   Illinois State Historical Library, Springfield.
MdBJ   Johns Hopkins University, Baltimore, Maryland.
MH   Harvard University, Cambridge, Massachusetts.
MH-Ar   Harvard University Archives, Cambridge, Massachusetts.
MHi   Massachusetts Historical Society, Boston.
MStoc   Stockbridge Library Association, Stockbridge, Massachusetts.
NHi   New-York Historical Society, New York City.
NIC   Cornell University, Ithaca, New York.
NN   New York City Public Library.
NNC   Columbia University, New York, New York.
NNPM   Pierpont Morgan Library, New York, New York.
NPV   Vassar College, Poughkeepsie, New York.
NRU   University of Rochester, Rochester, New York.
OFH   Rutherford B. Hayes Library, Fremont, Ohio.
OO   Oberlin College, Oberlin, Ohio.
PHi   Historical Society of Pennsylvania, Philadelphia.
PSC   Swarthmore College, Swarthmore, Pennsylvania.
PU   University of Pennsylvania, Philadelphia.
ViU   University of Virginia, Charlottesville.
VtU   University of Vermont and State Agriculture College, Burlington, Vermont.
WHi   State Historical Society of Wisconsin, Madison.

Published Sources (referred to in text by author's last name)

Bigelow, John. *Retrospections of an Active Life.* 2 vols. New York: Baker and Taylor, 1909.

Cortissoz, Royal. *The Life of Whitelaw Reid.* 2 vols. New York: Charles Scribner's Sons, 1921.

Ogden, Rollo. *The Life and Letters of Edwin Lawrence Godkin.* 2 vols. New York and London: Macmillan, 1907.

Roosevelt, Theodore. *An Autobiography.* New York: Macmillan, 1919.

Tansill, Charles C. *The Foreign Policy of Thomas F. Bayard, 1885–1897.* New York: Fordham University Press, 1940.

Wilson, Woodrow. *The Papers of Woodrow Wilson.* Edited by Arthur S. Link et al. 16 vols. to date. Princeton: Princeton University Press, 1966– .

1. Prologue, 1831–56

Few letters survive from the first three decades of Godkin's life, but the details of his youth are well established. He was born in Ireland in 1831, the son of a Congregational clergyman who left the pulpit in 1848 to devote his full time to journalism. Both father and mother claimed descent from early English settlers in Ireland, and young Edwin was educated both in England and at Queen's College, Belfast. In 1851 he went to London with the intention of studying law but instead gave most of his time to writing for *The Workingmen's Friend*, a penny weekly started by John Cassell and aimed at the artisan classes. It boasted among its contributors Harriet Beecher Stowe, Frederika Bremer, and the young Jules Verne.

The liberal revolutions of 1848, especially the Kossuth movement in Hungary, fired the imagination of many young middle-class Britons, and in 1851 Godkin commenced a series of articles on Hungary for *The Workingmen's Friend* that two years later he published in refined and expanded form as *The History of Hungary and the Magyars*. A laudatory treatment of Kossuth and democracy and a denunciation of Austrian tyranny, the book was reprinted on both sides of the Atlantic and earned its twenty-two-year-old author the thanks of a group of Hungarian patriots. (Later Godkin would dismiss *The History of Hungary* as a work of misplaced juvenile enthusiasm.)

The same year that Godkin published his *History of Hungary* the smoldering Eastern Question reignited when Europe's perennial invalid, Turkey—egged on by England and France—sent an army to oppose Russian encroachments along the Danube. In the fall of 1853 Godkin wrote a letter on the Eastern Question to the liberal *Daily News* of London that opened the way for an invitation to him to serve as the special correspondent of that paper with the Turks. Uncritically supporting the war at its outset, he spent a year with the Turkish army on the Danube and accompanied it when it joined the Allied expeditionary army in the Crimea in 1855. At first high in his praise of the Turkish soldiery, like most of the special correspondents he soon became censorious of the Allied effort, especially British mismanagement of the war.

Returning to the British Isles at the close of the war, Godkin lectured for a few weeks in Belfast on his experiences in the East and then in the spring of 1856 settled down to a position as a contributing editor to the thrice-weekly Belfast *Northern Whig*, a moderately liberal paper owned by Frank D. Finlay.

2. Godkin Discovers America

In 1850 a newly-ordained young American clergyman, Charles Loring Brace, in company with Frederick L. Olmsted and his brother, visited Belfast on the last leg of their walking tour of the British Isles. There Brace met and subsequently married Letitia Neill, one of several daughters of Robert Neill who earlier had entertained in his home the Abolitionists William Lloyd Garrison and Frederick Douglass. Returning with Letitia to Belfast for a visit in 1856, Brace encountered Godkin, a close friend of Letitia's brother William. Godkin was dissatisfied after almost six months on the Belfast *Whig*, and young Neill recommended a trip to the United States. Getting assurances of help from Neill, Brace, and Olmsted, the twenty-five-year-old journalist quit his job and in the fall set out for America.

Arriving in New York just before the presidential election of 1856, Godkin spent a few days with Olmsted, then boarded a train and, taking with him copies of Olmsted's widely-read *A Journey in the Seaboard Slave States*, set out to follow the older man's previous trail and gather information on the cotton crop for the firm of Neill Brothers. His written impressions of the lower South were published in a series of letters to the *Daily News*; although colorful, they contain little information about the region that Olmsted had not already supplied.

Returning to New York from New Orleans early in 1857, Godkin decided to remain in the United States. He got permission to study in the office of legal reformer David Dudley Field and once more set about preparing for the law. He was admitted to the bar in New York the following February, but, finding his practice time-consuming and unrewarding, he gradually abandoned it in favor of becoming a contributor to the recently-founded *New York Times* and the *Knickerbocker* as well as serving as the New York correspondent of the *Daily News*. In 1859 he married Frances ("Fanny") Foote of New Haven and Cincinnati, the attractive cousin of Harriet Beecher Stowe. Conveniently, the marriage provided the leisure-loving and somewhat hypochondriac Godkin with financial security at a time when he felt himself yielding to emotional and physical illness. Shortly after the wedding he dropped all work and in the summer of 1860 recrossed the Atlantic. Fanny and their infant son joined him in the fall, and for the next two years they lived a life of leisure in Europe, wintering in Paris and summering in Switzerland. Meanwhile, the American Civil War had begun; Godkin's American acquaintances such as Olmsted, George E. Waring, Jr., and the Woolseys of New Haven and New York were immersed in the Northern war effort. In Paris late in 1861 Godkin rediscovered his pen and set about in the columns of the *Daily News* to support the Lincoln government. His letters to that London paper, although somewhat lessened in effectiveness by captiousness, helped marshal middle-class opinion in England behind the Union cause.

In 1862 Godkin returned to the United States where he resumed contributing to the *New York Times* as well as serving as New York correspondent of the *Daily News*. In 1863 he carried to Boston a letter of introduction from Olmsted to Charles Eliot Norton, the frail Cambridge Brahmin who, with James Russell Lowell, was resuscitating the moribund *North American Review*. The object of his visit—to obtain financial help from Norton and his friends for a proposed weekly of independent views was not realized, but in the course of the visit Norton invited Godkin to contribute to the *North American Review*, beginning a life-long friendship between the two men.

To John Bigelow [1]

82 Broadway [New York] Friday [1859] (Bigelow 1: 110–11)
Private

DEAR SIR: There is a great number of subjects coming under the head of "social sciences," such as labour, charity, taxation, exchange, insurance, the province of governments, and a hundred others that will readily suggest themselves to you, which there is no means of discussing with any care, and which are imperfectly understood. I might add free trade and the various questions arising out of it—to the number. There is in this city, and in fact in this country, no means of getting a hearing upon them, for any one who gives them any thoughtful consideration. The *Post* has done more for them than any newspaper, but no newspaper can do much. The legislature does still less, as few of the legislators have ever *thought* on any question in their lives.

Would it not be possible to get up an association for their discussion, somewhat like that for the "Advancement of Social Science," which Lord Brougham recently inaugurated in England, but possibly with a larger mélange of statistics than that is likely to have? [2] I belonged to an association of this kind before coming to this country, and as I feel a deep interest in most of these questions, would be glad to see one formed here.

I am still so much of a stranger in New York that I hardly like to do anything which would wear the appearance of taking the initiative in the matter. But possibly you can say what you think of the scheme, and whether you would feel disposed to aid in carrying it out.

I am writing under the impression that you know who I am, and consequently dispense with the ceremony of an introduction. I am

Yours truly
ELG

1. John Bigelow (1817–1911) was managing editor and part owner of William Cullen Bryant's New York *Evening Post*, to which Godkin contributed one or two articles during 1858.

2. The writer Lord Brougham (1778–1868) was instrumental in the founding of the National Association for the Promotion of Social Sciences. Nothing at once came of the proposal in this letter, but a few years later the American Social Science Association was founded, with Godkin as a member.

To Charles L. Brace [1]

Paris, January 7, 1862 (Ogden 1: 202 [2])

. . . I want you, as far as your means go, to urge on the news-paper men in New York attention to the fact that there is a large party in England composed of dissenters, democrats, reformers of all shades—if not a majority at least quite large enough to render interference with the war against the South impossible—who strongly sympathize not only with Northern anti-slavery principles but Northern theories of government, whose feelings of nationality the North ought to *ménager*. The abuse of England has been so *indiscriminate* that these have all been driven over to the Tory side. They sympathize with you, did so very much at the outset, but won't bear being kicked and called names. The Southerners have beaten us hollow in the management of public opinion on this side of the water. You know how much more of the work of diplomacy is done in social intercourse than by note writing; and yet no member of our Legation here *speaks one word of French*. Dayton goes to see Thouvenel with a hired interpreter! And the story goes that the interpreter sells the conversations to the Southern Commissioners! I don't vouch for this, but it's funny. The secretary of Legation is a common, New Jersey horse-jockey, who can't speak English decently. As to French, I am told he and his teachers both despair. This, at such a time as this, really seems a defiance of Providence. However, I don't despair; a great battle won, or three months of successful operations in the field, will change the face of everything, and change everybody's opinion on a variety of subjects. . . . I expect to be, by the time I get to New York, perfectly well; in fact, better than I was before my breakdown. I wrote to Raymond some time ago as to my connection with the *Times*, in answer to a letter of his offering me a permanent connection with the paper as partner, etc.[3] I said I should like it and shall accept it if I can muster money enough to buy any shares; in fact, I don't see, if I settle in New York, that I could do a better thing. There is only one point that troubles me and I should like to hear your opinion of it. How would my being a foreigner affect my position if I were prominently and openly an editor? There is a sort of feeling, I fancy, in America, against foreigners connected with the press, as if they were meddling in other people's business and were simple *condottieri*. What is this worth, do you think, as it would affect me socially? You see if Raymond were away a good deal, I would become to a certain extent identified with the *Times*, and responsible for it, and I dare say would often displease some of its readers; in fact, I should feel it my duty to do so, but it would be very disagreeable not to get credit for writing conscientiously, or for not writing under the influence of sympathy with the country and the people.

We are well here, enjoying Paris, particularly the theatres, in a moderate way. Like all the rest of the world we are obliged to look carefully after the *sous*. Things, I think, are looking up here. There are signs of political revival and men are getting over the shock of 1848, and the example of Italy is begetting a return of admiration for self-government. . . . Louis Napoleon is really a great man, wise as well as shrewd. . . .

Weed has been denouncing you over here for saying Seward wanted to escape from the Southern imbroglio by a war with England. I was not present, and so did not knock him down. . . .[4]

1. Charles Loring Brace (1826–90), the philanthropist and pioneer social worker, was the earliest of Godkin's American friends.

2. A flattering reference to Louis Napoleon that Ogden deleted has been reinstated.

3. Henry J. Raymond (1820–69) was the proprietor of the *New York Times* from its founding until his death. For Godkin's association with him, which was slighter than this letter intimates, see William M. Armstrong, "The Writings of E. L. Godkin," *Bulletin of the New York Public Library* 72, no. 5 (May 1968): 294.

4. Thurlow Weed (1797–1882), the editor of the *Albany Evening Journal* and a power in national Republican circles, had reacted to the charge that Secretary of State William H. Seward (1801–72) had proposed a foreign war to Lincoln in order to forestall Southern secession. Weed and Seward were friends.

To Frederick Law Olmsted [1]

Felsenegg, Zug, Switzerland, June 15, 1862 (Olmsted Papers, DLC)

MY DEAR OLMSTED: The war has now lasted a year since I last wrote to you, and I want to know once more, what you think of the future. . . .

Let me say at the outset, a few words about things here as they affect you in America. . . . The last three months tide of success has affected a total revolution in the feeling as to the military ability of the North, and has completely dumbfounded the sneerers. But I must add, that on the other hand, the total absence of any appearance of Union feeling as the Northern army advances, had confirmed the vast majority of people in France and England, including those most friendly to you, that a reconstruction of the Union is impossible, supposing resistance in the field were at an end tomorrow. To hold the South down by military force, will, it is also said, be either physically impossible or can only be achieved by the sacrifice of your own liberties. What is the theory of men like yourself on this point? You are surely none of you prepared to surrender liberty for the sake of power. How long, I should also like to know, will slavery continue to be held more sacred than everything else in America?

Let me add also that Banks' defeat, insignificant, as it is militarily, has been a great moral disaster, on this side of the water. It has been a stupendous blunder, and has completely neutralized the effect of the capture of New Orleans. The friends of the South say, that since after a year of war, the capital of the United States is still in danger, it is absurd to suppose that there is any immediate prospect of the rebellion being crushed, and a movement is on foot both in London and Paris at this moment for a joint offer of mediation, the penalty in case of its rejection, being a recognition of the Confederacy. I am satisfied that nothing will prevent this except a victory in the field. Military men say, and say with reason that for the conquest and subjugation of so vast a territory nothing is done, as long as two huge armies are still untouched. This, in the present case may not be true, but it is near enough to the truth to support a foregone conclusion or to be used in defence of a policy already worked out. I have defended McClellan all along, but I am getting to feel that just now, considering the state of feeling here, and the state of the finances at home that slowness is something closely approaching incapacity. Do I take too gloomy a view of things? . . .

Yours as ever
ELG

1. Frederick Law Olmsted (1822–1903), the landscape architect and pioneer environmentalist noted as the creator of Central Park and the author of *The Cotton Kingdom*, was the closest of Godkin's early friends in the United States.

To Charles Eliot Norton [1]

New York, January 4, 1864 (Ogden 2: 32–33)

. . . The book arrived on Saturday, and gave me great pleasure, all the greater I need hardly say, for the kind message I found accompanying it. . . . Clough will always be a very agreeable reminder of some very agreeable hours.

I knew little or nothing of him or his works, and so devoted the greater part of Sunday to him. The *Bothie of Tober na-Vuolich* [*sic*] I knew, and relished already, but some of the shorter pieces have, I think, even greater power and greater depth, except that their charm is somewhat diminished to me, by the sad impression which is always made on me by the protests against social wrongs of Englishmen who feel them as strongly as he seems to have done. Even Mill's "Political Economy," not a sentimental book, leaves this behind it. It looks like such hopeless dreary work to anybody who is familiar with the views of life entertained by the middle and upper classes, and with the tenacity with which they cling to them. . . .

1. Charles Eliot Norton (1827–1908), the fervent New England "apostle of culture" was, with Olmsted, the closest of Godkin's early American friends. He had just sent Godkin a copy of the collected *Poems* of Arthur Clough (1819–61).

To Frederick Law Olmsted

37 East 19th St., New York, February 24 [1864]
(Godkin Papers, MH)

MY DEAR OLMSTED: . . . You ask, "Can I hope to have you here?" [1] I answer yes; but with divers distinctions and limitations. The attractions are two in number and both strong. In the first place, my present employment leads to nothing, and I have a good many rather sad half hours—between ourselves—in the reflection that I am slowly frittering my best years away in what is for the writer certainly the most unprofitable of all literary labour. I am winning neither fame nor money. My income is not large enough to save much, (if any in these times) and I am conscious all the while, that I am not stimulated to do my best in writing. My letters to the *Daily News* are the only things that really rouse me, because I know they *tell;* I receive now and then very complimentary letters from the editor about them, and then it is a better channel and reaches a better public than the papers here.[2]

My health is not good enough, though very good, for ordinary purposes, to permit of my going back to the law. To succeed at the bar here, needs *for one thing,* the capacity to stick at a desk twelve or fourteen hours a day; this I have not got, and never expect to have it. Something may turn up in the newspaper line that may suit me, such as an opening in the *Ev. Post,* or some other evening paper; but for the moment I see no sign of anything. Consequently my prospects are by no means so brilliant as they seemed when I first determined to settle in this country. My illness has knocked me off the track, and if I were not now sincerely attached to the country, and deeply interested in its future, married and so forth, I would go back to England. The competition in expense in New York is getting to be frightful, and as long as I live here, I do not see much chance of my gratifying the second object of my ambition—getting sufficient exemption from *daily* [labor] to write for the *reviews,* etc., in a way that would really give me a chance of saying what I have to say, in the best way.

Moreover I miss *you* very much. I have met no one in America who has the same hold on me and with whom I sympathize so strongly, and certainly I should always feel amply compensated by your friendship alone for having come here. Leading the unsettled life that I have led since I was twenty two, leaving my country at twenty five; my intimate friends are few in number, and I value those I have all the more for that reason. Your quitting the east was therefore a great blow to me, greater than I cared to say when you were going. I looked forward to your settling down somewhere within my reach so that we could grow old, and grumble over the ways of the world together. Since then both Fanny and I have fallen in love with your wife, and I feel all the more strongly how much your departure has cost me.

Lastly, I have a brother now about 20, who has been educated at one of the government agricultural schools in Ireland, and very thoroughly educated, a most accurate painstaking fellow, who since leaving the school has been in a bank in Dublin, and for whom I should very much like to do something. I should therefore be to some extent tempted to go to California on his account, as I should hope, if there to be able to find some opening in which his special training in agricultural matters could be brought into play.

The foregoing would be my principal reason for going. I may add as a secondary one the fact that I am by nature and temperament rather fitted for an outdoor than an indoor life. I have not got the *literary temperament*, and in fact, in so far as I have ever done any work well, it has been rather due to bodily activity than any thing else.

On the other there are many and weighty reasons for my *not* going. I am rather fastidious about many things, which in a new country it does not do to be fastidious about. I am not popular in my manners and could never become so. I am not pushing; I am not a natural orator. I am not sympathetic; and I am too old to change now. Then my wife is not strong, and would be ill fitted to any kind of hardship, and though she would behave "like a brick," under any circumstances, I think she would feel it very hard to leave all her friends and break up all her associations, and I should be very reluctant to urge her to do so, *unless for a very certain gain.* You see, you went out under brilliant auspices; with a place ready to pop into. I should go out very differently. And I see by your letter that it is pretty hard to make rapid fortunes in California as well as every where else. I should have to count upon spending the best years of our life in a wild place, and losing all hold on that part of the world which is now everything to us. So it would be for us a very serious step;—it was so to you though you had $10,000 a year etc. before you. As regards climate, I doubt if I could bear exposure to the sun in August, but otherwise it would suit me admirably.

I want very much, however, to hear from you more fully about the place and your prospects, and what you think my chances would be, and whether you think you could work my brother into any of your great plans, whether I go or not. What are your vaulting schemes? Amongst the things of which I have often dreamed are sheep raising on a great scale, and this I could use my brother in. I want you also to tell me whether you could now and then invest $200 or $300 dollars for me in a safe way, and at a good interest. I hoped last summer to be able to lay up about $1000 a year; at the present cost of house keeping, I doubt if I can save $500; but whatever it may be, you would do me a great service, if you could put [it] into something that would either grow in value, or yield a good interest. . . .

Ever yours
ELG

1. Olmsted had gone to California to seek his fortune in a mining enterprise.

2. Between 1854 and 1871 Godkin wrote weekly letters for the *Daily News* of London. As with the *New York Times*, the cordiality of his relations with that paper varied according to its editors.

To Charles Eliot Norton

37 East 19th St., New York, March 10 [1864]
(Norton Papers, MH)

MY DEAR SIR: I have taken a day or two to think over your proposal that I should write the preliminary article on Amendments to the Constitution. . . .[1]

The result of my cogitations is that I think I may promise to be ready by the time you mention. I think about 40 printed pages will be the probable length of the article. I propose to discuss the matter somewhat in this way—

1. The singular and unprecedented reverence with which the Constitution has been regarded, considering that it was not either the growth of ages, or the result of great suffering; the untrue

and probable cause of this feeling—and its value as a conservative force.

2. The dangers it now runs, and is likely to run from the changed character of the American population, since the foundation of the government, such as the want among the foreign element of the Anglo Saxon respect for *forms* and legal traditions; the consequent necessity for great caution in meddling with it, both as regards the nature of the changes and the manner of making them.

3. The points on which it has failed to answer the expectations of its framers, with regard to difficulties which they foresaw; and the points on which the present generation has found it defective, owing to difficulties which the founders did *not* foresee.

4. The exact nature of the purpose which it serves; considered as a guide in amending it, and under this head—the purposes which it is *not* intended to serve and ought not to be made to serve.

. . . The keynote of my whole argument would be found in my notion that the future changes to the Union will mainly arise out of the tendencies to disintegration caused by distance, numbers, difference of manners and habits and of thought caused by difference of climate, soil, and situation and origin, and that therefore the aim of all changes in the organic law ought to be the promotion of assimilation, without, however, underrating the value of state organization, both for the security of liberty and for experimental legislation.

Very truly yours
ELG. . . .

1. Norton, with James Russell Lowell, coeditor of the *North American Review*, had solicited an article from Godkin.

To Charles Eliot Norton

37 East 19th St., New York, May 10 1864 (Norton Papers, MH)

MY DEAR NORTON: The accident of which I spoke which prevented my sending my M.S. yesterday, consisted in the loss of the last ten pages, through the blunder of a servant. I have had to

write them over, and I am having them copied out, and hope to
send the whole article on tonight. . . .[1]

This is glorious news from the army, but we must not hallo
too much before we are out of the wood. Lee, I am confident
will "die game." He is the only man in the Confederacy whose
fate I should regret if they were all at the bottom of the James
River.

Yours very truly
ELG

Charles Eliot Norton Esq.

1. E. L. Godkin, "The Constitution and Its Defects," *North American
Review* 99 (July 1864): 117–45.

To Frederick Law Olmsted

37 East 19th St., New York, May 31 [1864] (Godkin Papers, MH)

MY DEAR OLMSTED: . . . I was very sorry to read Jenkins's
letter from you about your health. But he and Van Buren both
think your San Francisco doctor mistaken as to your symptoms.
And I suppose, I may myself after what I have gone through,
claim the honors also of an expert, and I add my testimony to
theirs. I have had every symptom you describe, with palpita-
tions so violent as to keep me awake at night. I have been *six*
times examined for disease of the heart, and once blistered for
inflammation of the pericardium. There never was anything the
matter with my heart except functional derangement caused by
the state of my nerves. I am not conscious now that I have a
heart; Doctors are constantly mistaken on this point, often for
want of knowledge of the patient's antecedents. I would have
wagered 100 to 1 anytime these four years, that your mode of
life would end in laying you up with your present ailments. I
offer the same odds that two years hence if you avoid fatigue
—especially mental, do no work in the afternoon, go to bed at
10 p.m. and totally abandon tea and coffee, you will be as well
as ever.[1]

There is nothing very new amongst the people you know.
The Sanitary Commission is working well. . . . The Christian
Commission is very fierce and vindictive. Its agents abuse the

Sanitary wherever they go all over the country, and lie like sinners of the lowest grade. They find at last that spiritual consolation is not much needed by wounded men on the battlefield, so they are working might and main to get hold of the supplies as well.

Brace is off fishing and I think is growing rich. He says the life of man is divided into two ages,—the *amorous* and the *acquisitive*, and he has now entered on the acquisitive. We are all in a state of trembling anxiety about Grant's campaign. The chances so far are I think evenly balanced. The toughest part of the job, the capture of the fortification at Richmond has still to be done; but the advantage so far rests with Grant. No Union general before has ever been so well seconded, I think by his subordinates. Gold continues high and rising, owing to the great uncertainty which still prevails, and prices of course rise with it. Beef has almost got to be a luxury confined to the rich. You may thank your stars you are living on a specie basis. The market is full of gold mining enterprizes—in Sonora. The Elliotts have got one on foot, which seems to promise very well. They say they get $1000 out of a ton of quartz, with some new machine. Goodbye.

Yours as ever
ELG

1. Olmsted was beginning to receive warnings of the mental illness that later would overtake him.

To Charles Eliot Norton

Athenaeum Club   New York, October 12, 1864
(Norton Papers, MH)

MY DEAR NORTON: . . . I propose . . . that you . . . take from me now, a paper of which my brain is rather full, and which I propose to call, "On Some Popular Errors about Democracy." It would be a criticism on all the delusions,—as I conceive them to be—current at present both amongst democrats and aristocrats here and in Europe, as to the real nature, requirements, and consequences of a democratic form of government.—Such as, that democracy *necessarily* involves the direct appointment of all officials by the people; that the power called universal suffrage can only work through one kind of machinery; that it is *necessarily* fatal to the highest order of excellence in art, or science, or literature or statesmanship; that it is the only security for liberty; that it is the cheapest kind of government; that the defects of *taste* so much complained of in America are mainly due to it, etc., etc. Some of these are American, and some English notions. I should try to deal with them impartially, and would ask for about forty pages. . . .

The news from the elections is good, but might be better. Those rascally Pennsylvanians have not done as well as I hoped, but in any case "George B." is consigned for a little while longer to the classic shades of Orange, New Jersey. This is hard for "the most accomplished soldier of the age," but such is life.[1]

Yours very cordially
ELG. . . .

1. A reference to the former commander of the Army of the Potomac, General George B. McClellan (1826–85), who had accepted the Democratic nomination for President.

To Charles Eliot Norton

37 East 19th St., New York, October 14 [1864]
(Norton Papers, MH)

MY DEAR NORTON: . . . I am very glad you are so well satisfied with my subject. I only wish I had more time for it, as there is a good deal in it. . . .

Tell Professor Smith I am sorry he will not be in New York during the election or before it, as the great horrors of Yankee life at such periods, may be witnessed in greater perfection here than in New England.[1]

Yours ever
ELG

1. The pamphlets of Professor Goldwin Smith (1823–1910) helped swing upper middle-class opinion in England away from the Confederate cause. Later, historian Smith threw up a brilliant career at Oxford University to migrate to North America.

To Frederick Law Olmsted

New York [(?) November 1864] (copy, Godkin Papers, MH)

DEAR OLMSTED: . . . Goldwin Smith, Professor of Modern History at Oxford has been here, and been a good deal fêted. He has been writing very ably on the American side in England. I have seen a good deal of him, and he has been asking much about you. He has been a diligent reader and is a great admirer of your books. He says you are the "Arthur Young of America." Pray make your fortune quickly and come back to civilization.

Yours
ELG

To Frederick Law Olmsted

37 East 19th St., New York, December 25 [1864]
(Godkin Papers, MH)

MY DEAR OLMSTED: . . . We have been back in town for about two months and are leading our old uneventful life. I have been busy ever since in writing an article about democracy for the *North American Review,* which I will send you when it appears (Jan. 1st). . . .[1] There is a tremendous libel suit going on here between Weed (Thurlow) and Opdyke, from which it plainly appears that one is as great a scoundrel as the other. . . . I am sorry to say I [am] perfectly satisfied that the leading Republican politicians are worse rogues than the Democrats, inasmuch as they are fully as corrupt while making far more pretensions to honesty. Opdyke is, I consider a consummate rascal, to whom politics is a branch of his trade, and nothing more.

Public affairs look very well, except the finances. . . . If this government avoids bankruptcy, and meets all its liabilities honestly, it will in my opinion, be due to the astounding resources of the country, and not either to Congress, or the Secretary of the Treasury. My reason for thinking so, is partly the recklessness, haste, and confusion of all the financial legislation; the tariff, as well as the internal revenue law, is a model of confusion, passed in haste, and in excitement, and amended last year in panic, by men to whom the whole subject of raising revenue was entirely new; and partly the extraordinary ignorance, presumption, and absence of study or reflection displayed in the debates on these subjects. And this is a difficulty, which I see little prospect of overcoming. The class from which our public men are drawn are perhaps less given to study or reflection than any other in the community. They are generally men of quick sympathies fond of crowds, fond of moving audiences, and to whom readiness of tongue is the highest of gifts. And it is one of the peculiarities of political economy that all its problems *seem* simple, because they concern affairs with which every man is familiar, while the laws which solve them are exceedingly complex. So that I see no prospect of getting the people who go to Congress to know much about it except what they learn by experience, which is I think the way in which Americans learn nearly everything. But experience in this case, may be awfully costly. And what is most provoking is that these fellows scoff at the experience of other countries and will not profit by it. There is just now an unusual disposition to rely on the "mineral wealth" of the country to carry the government out of its difficulties, as if the government either owned the mineral wealth, or as if the working of mines was a business that would bear taxation very much better than any other.

I think the conduct of the War, however, ever since Grant took the command, has been admirable, something of which the country may well be proud, and which to my mind for the first time, has made the subjugation of the South not only seem possible, but *near*. I think Sherman has real genius, and of the first order, but how he compares with Grant, I cannot tell, till I know how much of his operations Grant has planned. . . . Give Sherman an object, and his way of reaching it is extraordinarily brilliant, but to decide what the object shall be, and decide it rightly, requires a higher order of talent than he has yet displayed. Grant I think has it. And in this age and in this country there is to me something very impressive in the way in which Grant lies quiet, leaving it to others to make the great *coups,* and produce the dazzling effects. . . . But I do not look for any submission on the part of the South. They will I think fight as long as they can keep an organized force together; then fight as guerillas and then assassinate; until they are gradually improved off the face of the earth, and their places taken by northern settlers—a process which I expect to see lasting a great portion of my lifetime.

. . . I don't see the Sanitarians as often as I used, as I have no longer the *Bulletin* on my hands. It has been moved to Philadelphia. The *World* is attacking the Commission very fiercely in its usual truculent style, owing I think to Bellows' rampant Republicanism. . . .[2]

All your old friends are much as ever. Brace is busy making money. . . . Vaux is "the same old two and sixpence"—jolly, happy, and careless of the morrow.[3] Green of the Central Park, I met last winter one evening, and he almost kissed me, he was so affectionate. Raymond goes to the next Congress; the *Times* being edited in the usual shilly shally way, though on some points vastly improved. But I am satisfied that there is no security for the independence or honesty of the press, but the impersonality of the editor. When a newspaper becomes, as all the leading newspapers are here, the mouthpiece of a well known man who is occupied in making a career for himself, it becomes utterly worthless, either as a critic, or exposer of abuses. The *Times* can say nothing that seems likely to damage Raymond's fortunes, or impair his relations with any of the thousand brother politicians to whom he is under obligation, or from whom he expects something. . . .

Ever affectionately yours
ELG

1. E. L. Godkin, "Aristocratic Opinions of Democracy," *North American Review* 100 (January 1865): 194–323.

2. A reference to the Sanitary Commission, the service organization to aid Union volunteers of which Olmsted was general secretary until his departure for California and whose *Bulletin* Godkin briefly edited in 1864. The Unitarian clergyman Dr. Henry W. Bellows (1814–82) was president of the Sanitary Commission.

3. The Anglo-American landscape architect Calvert Vaux (1824–95) was a partner of Olmsted in the development of Central Park.

To Charles Eliot Norton

37 East 19th St., New York, January 6 [1865]
(Norton Papers, MH)

MY DEAR NORTON: . . . Public affairs are looking well. I cannot help thinking [that] the feelers which are being thrown out at the South about the abolition of slavery come from the leaders, who care more for power than for the precise nature of the political organization over which they exercise it, and that the split whenever it occurs, will be between them and the main body of the slaveholders on this question. Independence with emancipation as long as there was a good excuse, which the pressure of the North would always furnish—for keeping up a large standing army, would answer Davis's purpose just as well as independence with slavery, or at all events nearly as well. But in the eyes of the rank and file of slaveholders I think the revolution would seem worthless if it did not establish the model "slave society" on a sure and lasting foundation. I would give a great deal to be able to spend the next year in the South, and hear them talk. There is probably nothing in history more curious and interesting than the workings of their minds just now. . . .

Very cordially yours
ELG. . . .

To Charles Eliot Norton

January 18, 1865 (Ogden 2:33)

. . . I have begun on "Democratic Errors" as you suggested, and you shall have the article at the time fixed, Feb 20. The subject has much more attraction for me than Abbott, but I feared that perhaps you or your readers had had enough of my political disquisitions. I single out Abbott for special hostility, not because I think he is himself or his books worth half a page, but because his "histories" are fair specimens of a kind of literature of which there is an immense quantity issued every year, and which the half-educated look on as "solid reading." [1] I suppose neither you nor I have any idea of the enormous number of respectable people who think his history of Napoleon and his history of the rebellion solid works, and it is sickening to see him treated in the newspapers with great deference as "Abbott the historian." You have, I think, fewer of these charlatans in Boston than we have here and you may be thankful. New York swarms with quack poets, quack novelists, and quack historians, if I may use the phrase, and they are all doing a roaring trade, and enjoy the greatest consideration. So I shall turn to him at some more convenient season. . . .

1. A reference to the popular historical writer J. S. C. Abbott (1805–77).

To Charles Eliot Norton

37 East 19th St., New York, February 21 [1865]
(Norton Papers, MH)

MY DEAR NORTON: There is an allusion in the article which I sent you yesterday, to the "Veteran Observer", of the New York *Times*, of the good taste of which I am doubtful. . . .

I used him as an illustration, because I am told at the *Times* Office that his letters are the most popular things that appear in the paper, although the majority of them are excellent specimens of the conceit, folly, half knowledge, of which so much of the political talk of the day is composed.

Yours very cordially
ELG

To Charles Eliot Norton

February 28, 1865 (Ogden 2:45)

. . . If my article conveys the idea that I argue from a denial of the natural-right theory, against the doctrine of universal suffrage, it certainly needs revision, for nothing was further from my thoughts. What I sought to show was:—

(1) That there is no natural right to share in the government, and that the precise form of government in any given country is purely a question of expediency.

(2) That the state has, therefore, a right to say who shall vote

and who shall not vote, and has in all ages and countries exercised this right. The possession of it is deducible from the right of self-preservation.

(3) The natural-right theory has, however, been and is preached in this country, and especially by the Democratic party, to such an extent as to lessen or destroy the feeling of responsibility necessary to a proper exercise of the suffrage, especially amongst ignorant voters. The theories of government supported by orators and newspapers are part of the popular education, and are therefore in democratic countries of the highest importance.

(4) The natural-right theory, therefore, is not "a shadow," as you seem to consider it, but a positive and powerful obstacle to the establishment even of that educational test which you acknowledge to be necessary to the security of a government resting on the intelligence of the people. In how many States does any such test exist? Is it not rendered a farce, in practice, in Connecticut, for instance, where it does exist, by the general indifference? In how many States is any good system of popular education provided?

(5) The dangers arising out of this error or neglect are aggravated by the enormous influx of ignorant foreigners which is now taking place, and by the proposed addition to the constituency of a million of liberated slaves at present in the lowest state of ignorance and degradation. There, therefore, has in my opinion never been a time when it was more necessary to assert boldly the value of education, and the authority of training and culture in matters of government.

I do not oppose the admission of such negroes as shall prove their fitness. On this point we thoroughly agree. What I ask, and meant to ask, was not that the blacks shall be excluded *as blacks*, but that they shall not be admitted to the franchise simply because they are blacks and have been badly treated. I want to have the same rule applied to them that I would, if I could, have applied to white men. But let me say that I think there ought to be in the case of *liberated slaves* a moral as well as an educational test, such, for instance, as proof of disposition to earn a livelihood, or support a family by honest labor.

On the whole I really do not think I differ from you materially on any point except as to the importance (practical) of arguing against the natural-right doctrine. But I think I can make out a good case for this. I am in favor of as broad a basis as possible for the suffrage in this country, and for precisely the same reason as you,—that it is a good thing; in other words, on the ground of expediency. And I am willing to admit all blacks *at once* who comply with the conditions I have mentioned.

It is evident, however, from your objections, that I have not conveyed myself with anything like sufficient clearness. Of this you are, of course, the better judge, and if you will send me the article back, I will rewrite the portions you object to. [Governor] Andrew, Lincoln, and Governor Morton are, I admit, good men. So is Mr. Fenton. But you surely will not maintain that the State legislatures, for instance, are composed of as good men as can be had, and these are very important bodies. The intellect and education of this country have for three generations run into law, divinity, or commerce. Ought we not to try to do something to turn the tide into politics? . . .

To John Stuart Mill

37 East 19th St., New York, April 1 [1865] (Mill Papers, MdBJ)

Sir: I took the liberty of forwarding you a week ago a copy of the *North American Review*, for January last, containing an article by me, on "Aristocratic Opinions of Democracy."

The explanation there offered of some of those defects of American society and government, which European observers commonly ascribe to the working of democratic institutions, and you yourself, if I am not mistaken, to the growth of the commercial spirit—is, so far as I know, novel. I should be very much flattered by learning that you had discovered in it any other merit than that of originality, and shall venture to hope that you will, at all events, deem the article worthy of your perusal.[1]

I am, Sir, your obedient, faithful servant
ELG. . . .

1. The English philosopher politely responded to Godkin that he found Godkin's article a contribution to the understanding of democracy because of its elucidation, said Mill, of the extent to which unattractive American

qualities can be blamed not on democracy but on "the mental type formed by the position and habits of the pioneers." Godkin's thesis, which had developed out of his discussions with his friend Olmsted, precedes by a generation the Frontier Thesis of Frederick Jackson Turner. The major difference between the Godkin Thesis and the Turner Thesis, to which it has been compared, is that Godkin finds no value in the frontier experience.

To Frederick Law Olmsted

37 East 19th St., New York, April 2 [1865] (Godkin Papers, MH)

MY DEAR OLMSTED: . . . I think I told you that John Forbes of Boston had written to ask me, whether I thought you would come back [to] take the Superintendentship of the Freedmen['s] Bureau. Curtis has asked me the same question. . . .[1] The country needs such men as you near the centre of political and social influence more now than it did. Still, I confess frankly that I am more and more satisfied, the older I grow, that no man can do his best, with his brains, who is not free from pecuniary anxiety; which means that you ought to make money first, if you can and therefore stay where it can be made best. . . .

I sent you the January number of the *North American Review*, containing an article by me on "Aristocratic Opinions of Democracy." Did you ever get it? I want you to read it, and let me have your opinion. . . . A great battle is going on at Petersburg while I write. Things look favourably so far, and I am satisfied that however it may result, the end is near, and that this campaign is the last. The change of tone during the late debate on American affairs in the House of Commons was very remarkable. If people here had only had the dignity to let events wring this from the English, instead of scolding, how much better it would have been.

Yours
ELG

1. The prominent Unionist John M. Forbes (1813–98) helped to organize the New England Loyal Publication Society and to recruit black regiments in Massachusetts during the Civil War. George W. Curtis (1824–92) was the influential editor of *Harper's Weekly*.

To Charles Eliot Norton

37 East 19th St., New York, April 10 [1865] (Norton Papers, MH)

MY DEAR NORTON: . . . I have received the article, but have only time to say today, that I shall write again about it during the week. I have not been able to look over it yet, so that I cannot tell, whether we are nearer being of one accord than we were. I have read Mr. Lowell's article on "Reconstruction," but think that portion of it relating to the negro suffrage, has several weak points, of which "more anon."

Yours as ever
ELG

To Frederick Law Olmsted

37 East 19th St., New York, April 12 [1865] (Godkin Papers, MH)

My DEAR OLMSTED: First and foremost let me congratulate you on the great events of the last fortnight. They are I think the most momentous the modern world has seen. I was quite overcome by Lee's surrender, and sat dumfoundered [*sic*] for an hour. It has been so long and eagerly and vainly desired, that strong as my faith in Grant and in the people has always been, it had taken the shape in my mind of a wild dream. All difficulty, is I think now over: I mean all serious, alarming difficulty—military, political, and financial. Though I confess I should be very anxious about the terms of reconstruction, if Lincoln were not to be president for the next four years.

I think you are right about the 5/20s; but I would not go in very deeply, as I do not believe they will rise much higher than they are now for some time. . . .

As regards the newspaper, I can only say, that with my ignorance of men and things in California, I can of course form but a poor judgment of how suitable or agreeable, newspaper work there, would be to me. I could not undertake night work, so that an evening paper would be the only thing I could touch. No salary would tempt me which did not secure me, *considerably* more than the means of living comfortably in San Francisco. In other words, my main object in going—apart from the desire of doing something with you, which would influence me strongly—would be to make money, so as to secure me at an early period what I have always longed for—leisure and liberty to choose my own work. . . .

About petroleum [this] business of getting up companies, for the mere purpose of floating off the shares, and without the intention of working the wells, has been so overdone in the New York market, that it is now very difficult indeed to get capitalists, or investors to touch them. Of the thousand companies in the field, I do not believe five per cent, from all I hear, are working their lands. Their main business seems to be puffing them in the newspapers.

I am satisfied that as matters now are your only chance, unless you can enlist commercial men of high standing, of setting your petroleum going is to begin there and work it, even on a small scale. That is what will make the impression. But can you compete at that distance in the eastern and European markets with the Pennsylvania oil? . . .

I have between $4000 and $5000 now invested in Western railroad stock and paying 8 per cent. Does anything occur to you in California, or are there any of your enterprizes in which, as a prudent man, with due regard for the fact that the loss of it, would be a serious one for me, you would advise me to invest it? . . .

I am sorry to find the *North American* of January, with my article has not reached you. The article would interest you, as it discusses a subject on which we have often talked, on a theory which I think you hold yourself. I will send another copy, as I fear that one may have miscarried. It has been very well spoken of here, and excited some attention. . . .

Yours ever
ELG

To Charles Eliot Norton

April 13, 1865 (Ogden 2:47–48)

. . . I have gone through my article, and shall adopt your suggestion with regard to the discussion of the "natural-right" theory.

I agree with you, on reading it over again, in thinking much, if not all, of it unnecessary, as it really does not render much, if any, aid in establishing the positions subsequently taken up, which can be made, and, in fact, are just as strong without it. I shall therefore, either modify it, or leave it out. I have read Mr. Lowell's article attentively.

Read what he says at p. 546, beginning "Wise statesmanship," and ending "yet refusing to go." It seems to me that in advocating negro suffrage *because* this is a democracy and negroes are men, he adopts that very "French method" which he condemns. The Anglo-Saxon method which he commends is not bound by logic, nor does it feel obliged to push any political principle to its extreme consequences. Therefore, for it, it is not enough to prove the negro's age, sex, and humanity in order to establish his right to the franchise or the expediency of giving it to him. He has to rebuke the presumption of his unfitness for it, raised by his origin —his ancestors having all been either African savages, or as nearly beasts of the fields as men can be made; by his extreme ignorance —having been kept in darkness by law; by his defective sense of social obligations—never having enjoyed any rights, not even the commonest. It would, therefore, not confer the franchise on him without being satisfied as to the effect his exercise of it would have on the material and moral condition of the society in which he lives, or, in other words, on his own highest interests.

The mistake which, in my eyes, the radical democrats make— and I call those who support the bestowal of the franchise on the negro, merely *because* it would be an act of justice or of kindness to *him*, by this name—lies in their denial or forgetfulness of the fact that the highest allegiance of every man is due to liberty and civilization, or rather civilization and liberty. The possession of the suffrage by anybody, black or white, is but a means to these ends. If the majority in the United States were to vote for the establishment of a despotism or a community of goods, I should feel as much bound to resist them sword in hand as I would a foreign invader. We have put down the Southern insurrection not simply because the insurgents were a minority, but because their aims were dangerous to the very objects for which in our view civil society exists. And for the very same reason that we would resist the decisions of negro voters, if they appeared to threaten our highest interests, we would be justified in withholding the suffrage, until we had satisfactory assurance that they would not abuse it. Slavery surely cannot be a bad school if it fits the negro slave to share immediately in the conduct of a species of government, for which only one of the civilized races has hitherto shown the necessary qualifications.

"The objections to the plan are, of course, the same which lie against any theory of universal suffrage" (p. 555). Surely this is not a correct statement. Do they not differ by the whole interval which separates slavery and free labor, in regard to their respective influence on the character of the laborer?

I entirely agree with you and Mr. Lowell, however, as regards the expediency of giving the blacks the franchise, but I hate logic in politics, and all I ask is that they be subjected to a test, which in their case, ought, I think, to be somewhat different from that imposed on the white man, for I think the latter also should submit to it. All voters ought to know how to read at least—not a bit of the Constitution or the Lord's Prayer—but a piece of the newspaper of the morning of election day, both as an indication, however slight, of intelligence, and because the newspaper in modern democracies has taken the place in the formation of public opinion which was filled in the ancient ones by the habit of assembling in the Agora. In addition to this, the negro voter ought, for at least, I should say, ten years after emancipation, to prove himself to be earning a livelihood by regular labor, or supporting a family in the same way (of course the last involves the first) as a test of that moral fitness against which his having been bred in slavery raises a presumption. And I think the present affords an excellent opportunity of raising the value and importance of the franchise in the eyes of the whole community and especially in those of foreigners. The display of some care and caution in bestowing it on the blacks could not but impress others with a sense of its importance, and prepare the way for a wide understanding of its fiduciary character.

I shall recast all that I have said about the negroes, and put it in a shape which will not clash with your own opinions and those of the *Review.* . . .[1]

1. E. L. Godkin, "The Democratic View of Democracy," *North American Review* 101 (July 1865): 103–33.

3. Launching a New Weekly, 1865–66

As the Civil War moved rapidly to a conclusion in the spring of 1865, it became apparent to anti-slavery men that the ends for which the *Liberator* and the *Anti-Slavery Standard* had come into being were soon to be realized. Anticipating the post-war demise of these Abolitionist newspapers, several men in Philadelphia and Boston began planning a national weekly to perpetuate the hard-won goals of freedom and nationality. The sponsors of the scheme, chief among them James M. McKim, intended that the new paper should stand astride the divisions that had split the American Anti-Slavery Society and should work unitedly for the well-being of the freedmen. To achieve this, McKim, a Garrisonian Abolitionist, welcomed the support of George L. Stearns of the Wendell Phillips wing of the disrupted American Anti-Slavery Society as well as the support of the Unionist publicist Charles Eliot Norton. Unlike the other two, Norton, although friendly to the anti-slavery movement, was not an Abolitionist.

After giving the paper a name, the *Nation*, and receiving successive refusals from George W. Curtis and Whitelaw Reid to serve as editor-in-chief, the sponsors, on the advice of Norton, offered the post to Godkin. Several years before, Godkin had assisted Olmsted in a scheme to start a New York weekly paper, which Godkin wanted to call *The Week*, but the scheme fizzled out for lack of funds. After making certain that he would have to assume only a token share of the financing of the *Nation* but would enjoy full editorial power, Godkin accepted McKim's, Norton's, and Stearns's offer. His employers stipulated that his engagement be on a trial basis for two years.

While the others were busy raising $75,000 for the paper in anti-slavery circles in Boston, Philadelphia, and Baltimore, Godkin quietly avoided Abolitionists in his fund-raising efforts in New

York City. After intensive preparations during May and June in which Norton decisively participated, the first number of the *Nation* appeared in July 1865. Its Anglo-Irish editor, although a doctrinaire laissez faire liberal and utilitarian of the Bentham-Mill school, was preeminently a critic, and he set about without delay to stamp the *Nation* with his own vigorous personality. Acceding to the wishes of its sponsors, he paid lip service to the Radical Republican program in Congress, but he did not hesitate editorially to attack Radical leaders, while privately he opposed Negro suffrage.

Within a few weeks of the appearance of the *Nation*, it became apparent that divisions among the stockholders over editorial policy were colliding with Godkin's determination to control the weekly. His letters during 1865 and early 1866 deal chiefly with his struggles in getting the *Nation* established, especially his altercation with its principal proprietor, Stearns, over Stearns's allegations that Godkin had diverted the *Nation* from its intended purpose to aid the freedmen.

To Frederick Law Olmsted

37 East 19th St., New York, May 5 [1865] (Godkin Papers, MH)

DEAR OLMSTED: I write in some haste to say that there is a strong probability—almost a certainty that I shall start the weekly paper on the 1st of July, with ample capital.[1] I have not time to go into details now, as I will write again in a few days. What I want now is to get you to secure from Mr. Ashburner, any articles or series of articles that he may have written or be about to write on gold or other mining operations in California, or on petroleum.[2] You told me he was preparing something of the kind. I will pay him rather better and give him more publicity than any other paper he is likely to send them to, and they are just what I want.

I also want you to write something if you can and as often as you can. I shall take the liberty in the meantime of advertizing your name as a contributor. The plan is substantially the same as that which we have projected. I want to make *trustworthy* discussions of financial and economical matters a prominent feature in it.

Pray help me in the matter in any way you can, either by suggestions, fishing up contributions, writing yourself or getting subscriptions. I want to try the experiment fully and fairly, and see whether the best writers in America cannot get a fair hearing from the American public on questions of politics, art and literature through a newspaper.

I will write at greater length in a day or two. In the meantime, get Mr. Ashburner to go to work, and let me have what he produces.

Yours ever
ELG

1. A reference to the *Nation*. For a detailed account of its founding see William M. Armstrong, "The Freedmen's Movement and the Founding of the *Nation*," *Journal of American History* 53, No. 4 (March 1967): 708–26.

2. William Ashburner, brother of the Ashburner sisters of Stockbridge and Cambridge, Mass., friends of Godkin.

To Charles Eliot Norton

37 East 19th St., New York, May 6 [1865] (Norton Papers, MH)

MY DEAR NORTON: Herewith I send the article. I have re-written all the paragraphs about which we seemed to differ in opinion. . . .

The passage on negro suffrage will not, I think, clash with Mr. Lowell's views. . . .

I have had a note from McKim, stating that "the prospectus met with the heartiest approval of his friends," and that "funds enough would be forthcoming." Nordhoff refuses even a temporary engagement for the summer. It seems as if I should have to rely entirely on Garrison.[1] I have had some talk with him and he impresses me very favorably. He seems modest, zealous, has apparently a gentleman's turn of mind, and has apparently also that foundation of all usefulness, a willingness to obey "lawful orders". . . .

Ever yours
ELG

1. James M. McKim, (1810–74), the Philadelphia Abolitionist who traveled to Harper's Ferry with Mrs. John Brown to claim the body of her husband, was the original progenitor of the *Nation*, and Charles Nordhoff was the anti-slavery managing editor of the New York *Evening Post*. Wendell Phillips Garrison (1840–1907), the youngest son of the Abolitionist leader William Lloyd Garrison, was a recent Harvard graduate hired at the stipulation of his father-in-law, McKim, to help edit the *Nation*.

To Charles Eliot Norton

37 East 19th St., New York, May 12 [1865]
(Godkin Papers, MH)

MY DEAR NORTON: I find since writing to you yesterday that the law provides that *a majority* of the trustees must be citizens of *this* state. They must not be less than three or more than nine. The difficulty there usually is in these cases in getting a quorum suggests I think, the propriety of having nine, five from New York, two from Boston and two from Philadelphia. Not half of them would probably ever attend a meeting.

I am going, on Mr. Stearns suggestion to draft an agreement between Richards and myself and the trustees, and send it on for the consideration of the Boston stockholders. You can make your corrections, and emendations, and it can then be all settled before the meeting of the Trustees is held here.[1]

Yours very sincerely

ELG. . . .

1. The Massachusetts Abolitionist George L. Stearns (1809–67) was the principal shareholder of the forty investors in the *Nation*, Godkin contriving to take only a small interest. A friend of Emerson, Whittier, and Charles Summer, Stearns belonged to the Wendell Phillips faction of the disrupted American Anti-Slavery society in opposition to William Lloyd Garrison. Joseph H. Richards was the publisher of the anti-slavery *Independent* of Brooklyn when he accepted the invitation to become publisher of the *Nation*.

To James M. McKim

37 East 19th St. New York, May 19 [1865]
(Godkin Papers, *Nation* Business Records, MH)

MY DEAR SIR: I have $17,000 here, and Howard Potter guarantees me the remainder "more if necessary," early next week.[1] We should have it all in hand now, but that he met with an accident which has confined him to his house for two days. He authorizes me to inform Boston and Philadelphia that the New York quota may be considered ready. Everybody he has seen on the subject takes it up so warmly that he thinks double the amount might be raised if it were wanted, and all those I have seen are desirable of putting it through at any cost.

I am going on to Boston tonight, and hope to complete the organization there before my return.

I have received your note of yesterday. There is one serious difficulty about waiting till July 1st for the subscriptions, and it is this. Until the capital is all *paid in in cash*, the company cannot be organized under the laws of this state or trustees be elected, or any money called for, or any corporate act performed. In fact we can do nothing until this is done, and a certificate and affidavit of the fact filed with the county clerk. Neither Mr. Richards nor

I could make any agreement with anybody, or perform any act whatever, except on our personal responsibility. It is, in fact, essential that the organization should be completed at once. Our subscribers here are ready with their money at any moment; and I think if you explain all this to our Philadelphia friends, they will be disposed to waive their privilege and come down at once.

In haste, very truly yours

ELG

I saw Mr. White and had quite a pleasant chat with him.[2]

1. Godkin is mistaken. Later, months after the Boston and Philadelphia investors had paid over their agreed-upon $75,000, he had not yet collected all of the $25,000 in New York that he promised to raise as a condition of being appointed editor. Howard Potter was a New York business man.

2. Manufacturer Samuel S. White (1822–79) was one of the financial backers of the *Nation* in Philadelphia. Some of the *Nation*'s Philadelphia backers were really Baltimore men.

To Charles Eliot Norton

37 East 19th St., New York, May 28 [1865]
(Godkin Papers, MH)

MY DEAR NORTON: I am going to Philadelphia tomorrow morning to close matters up there, and get some writers. I shall be back on Tuesday.

Mr. G. C. Ward will act, as Trustee, and I have arranged with him to have the meeting on Wednesday forenoon, either his office or that of the paper in Nassau St.[1] He is engaged in the afternoon and Thursday is the fast day. I shall expect you here either on Tuesday evening or Wednesday morning, and shall secure a room for you either at the *Hoffman House* or *St. James*. . . . The list of trustees is full. S. S. White and J. M. McKim represent Philadelphia. I am rather glad McKim is in, as he will be in a measure impressed and controlled by the official action of the others. . . .

Very truly yours

ELG

1. George Cabot Ward was a partner in the New York banking firm of Ward, Campbell & Co.

To Charles Eliot Norton

37 East 19th St., New York, June 6 [1865] (Godkin Papers, MH)

MY DEAR NORTON: . . . I enclose an advertizement which will appear on Thursday morning. What do you think of it? I have on reflection added Garrison's and Tilton's name to the list of contributors.[1] I do not think they will repel anybody, and they are certain to attract a good many. . . .

Yours very truly

ELG

1. The Abolitionist William Lloyd Garrison (1805–79) and Theodore Tilton, editor of the anti-slavery *Independent*. Neither man seems directly to have been consulted about being listed as a contributor, and neither approved of Godkin or the *Nation*. The intimate connection of Garrison's youngest son, Wendell, with the *Nation* was one of the later sorrows of Garrison's life.

To James Parton

37 East 19th St., New York, June 6 [1865] (Parton Papers, MH)

SIR: I enclosed the advertizement which will appear on Thursday, and which explains itself. The project has been for some time under discussion, and is now fully matured and starts with a large capital.

Mr. Chas. E. Norton has mentioned you to me as one on whom I could probably count as a contributor. If so, will you please drop me a line at your earliest convenience, as I should wish to add your name to the list, and arrange with you for some assistance during the coming year.

Our rates of remuneration have not as yet been definitely fixed, but I can say that they will be higher than have yet been paid in this country.[1]

Respectfully yours

ELG

1. James Parton (1822–91), the most sought-after popular biographer of the day, did not avail himself of Godkin's invitation.

To C. C. Hazewell

Nation Office   New York, June 21 [1865]
(Autograph File, MH)

DEAR SIR: Your note to Mr. Richards has been handed to me.

I propose to have in the *Nation* about three pages of paragraphs, somewhat in the style of the London *Spectator,* containing not news, but comments on anything and everything of interest, and varying in length from ten lines to half a column.[1] There is a little danger in this kind of paragraphing of sinking into mere smartness, which I should like to avoid. What I have in mind as the objects to be kept in view are either *force,* or brilliancy, or both. From what I hear of you I think you can probably attain them oftener than most people.

I should be glad to have you furnish us every week with from a column to a page (never more) of this sort of thing, the MS. to be here not later than Friday in each week. We shall pay at the rate of $10 a page for it, the page being the same size as that of the *American Artizan,* in leaded bourgeois.

Very truly yours
ELG

1. A reference to the lead section of the *Nation* captioned "The Week," in furtherance of the name Godkin had hoped to give the weekly.

To Charles Eliot Norton

Nation Office   New York, June 30 [1865]
(Godkin Papers, MH)

MY DEAR NORTON: The first number is gone to press. I think it is good, but we shall do better.

I hope you will follow up your labours in the literary department. "Carlyle" and "Arnold" I thought exceedingly good. Won't Henry James do something for [the] next number? . . .

Everything is working well here. Richards sometimes gets into the dumps lest the paper should be too literary and heavy; the news agents come in and frighten him by telling him he must not rely on Merit, and that he will surely fail, that "our people" won't read such a paper as he proposed. . . .

If you have amongst your acquaintance a good writer on social questions of the light kind, I wish you would put him in communication with me. We want more entertaining matter. The article on "Club Life," is a step in the right direction though not perfect. We run some little risk of being "heavy," though I do not acknowledge this to Richards. I fancy the public trouble him somewhat about my being an Englishman, and therefore imbued with English notions about newspapers etc., and that an Englishman can "understand" the American public no matter how long he lives here, is something which some people, you know will never admit. . . .

We are still $2000 short in New York, and the delay weighs on my spirits. People are going or gone out of town; the weather is hot, I am so occupied by editorial matters, that I have no time for money raising, and nobody else attends to it, and in fact, I have to console myself some times, Mohammedan fashion, by the reflection that "God is great!" I have already put into it myself all I can afford to risk, but as a last resource I may do more.

Yours ever
ELG. . . .

To James M. McKim

Nation Office   New York, July 10 [1865]
(Benjamin F. Butler Papers, DLC)

MY DEAR SIR: If Mr. Pierce supposes that the *Nation* is anybody's "organ," in the sense that it is not to notice or allude to an illegal act, or an act on its face illegal, because committed by somebody who has done much for the freedmen, he is very much mistaken both with regard to it and to me.

The *Nation* has expressed no opinion about General Butler's conduct in the Hudson case.[1] It has simply reviewed a published pamphlet containing serious charges against him, which were he twice as great a friend of the freedmen as he is, I think he owes it to himself and the public to answer. I hope it may be well understood everywhere that the *Nation* will take no man of any party under its wing, or be his organ.

> Yours very truly
> ELG. . . .

1. General Benjamin F. Butler (1818–93) of Massachusetts was a favorite target of the *Nation*, in which he had declined to take stock.

To Charles Eliot Norton

> *Nation* Office   New York, July 11 [1865]
> (Godkin Papers, MH)

MY DEAR NORTON: Many thanks for your letter. I am delighted to find that you like the *Nation*. The second number does not satisfy me, it is heavy. . . . The "Bohemians" here are of course all in arms against us, and are abusive. The notice in the *Times* was probably written by one of them. I had a note of apology about it from Raymond yesterday expressing his extreme "mortification" that it should have appeared. . . .

> Ever yours
> ELG

To Frederick Law Olmsted

> [ca. 15 July 1865]
> (Ogden 1: 239)

. . . I should consider that I had treated you badly in not having replied sooner to your last long letter, if I had not been for some weeks busy to a degree of which I have never in my life known anything before.

We have got the first number of the *Nation* out, after the struggle and agony usual in such cases, and are now fairly afloat. I forget whether I told you the particulars, but the whole story of how it all came about I must reserve till I see you. It is a joint stock company, capital $100,000—shares $1,000 each, and what is most wonderful—we *have got the money paid up*. I am engaged, as is the publisher—a very good man, late of the *Independent*,

—at a salary of $5000 a year with 12 per cent of the profits after the payment of 6 per cent on the stock. $50,000 were raised in Boston, $25,000 in Philadelphia, and the rest in New York. The only great difficulty I have had has been in preventing the thing being torn to pieces between the free traders and protectionists. Can you not make some arrangements, before you leave California, with some one in San Francisco, to get subscriptions for us there, $3 a year and postage? It is dirt cheap, but we want to get an audience at the outset. The first number, of which I have ordered six copies to be sent to you, has been received with general satisfaction. . . .

To Edward Atkinson [1]

Nation Office   New York, July 17 [1865]
(Printed Letter, Godkin Papers, MH)

My dear Sir: I have received your two articles. The first one on "Free Trade and Protection" I like very much, and have kept it by me thus far without writing to you, in hope that I should be able to make up my mind to publish it in its present shape. But I fear I cannot, and for reasons in no way affecting its merit. The fact is, I am rather awkwardly situated as respects free trade. A large amount of stock was subscribed in Philadelphia, and some here, in the understanding that the *Nation* was not to be a free trade paper. I pledged myself in fact to discuss the tariff *for the present* as a question of revenue, and to advocate that adjustment of it that would produce most money to the government with least burden to the tax payers. This, of course, leaves me very free as far as the letter goes; still, although I could not be induced to say a word in favor of protection, I feel bound in honor to some of the gentlemen who subscribed, not to come out at present in favor of free trade.

This is an unfortunate state of things I admit, but this is better than no paper at all.

Now if you could retouch your article, so as to make it more of a summing up or statement, and less of an expression of an opinion on the part of the paper, I should be very glad to have it. I shall wait till I hear from you.

Your second article I shall use. Further contributions will be very acceptable. The paper is doing very well: we are selling 5000 a week, which is considered an unusual success.

Very truly yours
ELG

1. Boston businessman Edward Atkinson (1827–1905) was a stockholder in the *Nation* and an occasional financial contributor to its columns. An ardent free trader, he later was active in the Anti-Imperialist movement in the United States.

To Charles Eliot Norton

July 18, 1865 (Ogden 1:244–45)

. . . Jessup writes from Philadelphia in a rage because Jay Cooke was twitted in the first number; a luminary named Pierce writes in a great rage from Boston because Butler was criticised, he being "a friend of the freedmen." Friend Stearns informs me this morning that No. 2 has not "been well received in Boston, as the political articles have an air of being written to suit somebody." This insinuation is rather hard to bear, but I am going to bear it. A Richmond paper declares that Wendell Phillips is the presiding genius of the concern, but that "the working editor is an Englishman," and it suggests that the capital is probably "British gold" supplied for the purpose of "overthrowing our glorious," etc.

I am firmly resolved in this matter to do my best, and to persevere to the end. If the thing fails, or I fail, I shall try to fall with honor, but in the meantime I shall, owing to the rotten condition of the press and the fixed belief of the public that no paper can be conducted with purity and independence, have a great deal to endure. I should never have gone into it if I had not counted on your confidence and support, because you are the only man of the whole body of projectors with whom I know I am in thorough sympathy. I shall not return to this subject again, and I only mention it now to let you know how much I count on your support hereafter, as well as on your frankness in giving me your opinion about everything. . . .

To Charles Eliot Norton

Nation Office   New York, July 22 [1865] (Godkin Papers, MH)

MY DEAR NORTON: . . . The *Round Table* is coming out in September, and I am told they rely for success as against us, on their freedom from any responsibility with regard to the Negro, and on being more "sprightly." I think, I confess, the *Nation* is not quite as *light* as it ought to be, but I still preserve my faith in the American public. I am trying hard to lighten it a little, but it is very hard to get men of any calibre, to do this kind of work. Your article on the "Paradise of Mediocrities" excited a good deal of attention, and called out plenty of abuse, which is just what we want. It was good, was the kind of article of which we need a great deal, though perhaps some of its statements might be called a little sweeping. The *Evening Post* attacked it, and there is an editor in Yonkers, who has devoted four columns to it, and announces that he will return to this subject.

The Free trade difficulty is coming upon me. Edward Atkinson forwards free trade articles, which I dislike publishing just yet, as I fear Detmold and others will think I have set a snare [for] them.[1] Atkinson has reported that my "hands are tied" by the New York and Philadelphia protectionists, and Forbes and S. G. Ward protest vigorously.[2] If the thing can only be left to me to manage, I will get out of the difficulty, but it is one which needs to be managed with some tact, and I wish our Boston friends, as they know I agree with them, would not press me in this matter, till I get fairly into my seat. If you are writing to any of them, won't you urge this view of the matter upon them? . . .

Yours ever
ELG

1. Christian Detmold (1810–87), the German-American civil engineer who built New York's Crystal Palace, was the president of the *Nation* Association.

2. Banker Samuel G. Ward (1817–1907) was the brother of George Cabot Ward. The one-time member of Brook Farm was called the "good Sam Ward" to distinguish him from the so-called "wicked Sam Ward" of New York society.

To Frederick Law Olmsted

Nation Office   New York, July 23 [1865]
(Copy, Olmsted Papers, DLC)

MY DEAR OLMSTED: I enclose you a letter from Norton received a day or two ago. They propose to establish a sort of propagandish bureau in New York for the evangelization of the South, by subsidizing the press, distributing publications, etc., at the head of which they propose to place you. John Forbes highly approves of the idea, and as he has for some time been anxious to get you back, will I think carry the thing through. It will probably be brought before the Committee of the Loyal Publication Society this week.[1] They propose to give you $2000. a year for this, and the work I imagine would not be very hard. Norton also says that he will give you $500. for your articles for the *North American Review* for one year at least. I cannot yet say what I will give you for the *Nation,* but I will promise to pay you handsomely, or make some arrangements with you that will be satisfactory. Then the Central Park has reappointed you and Vaux architects, at $5,000. a year. This I earnestly trust you will at once accept. It gives you an excuse for coming back, and distracts public attention from the fact of your enterprize in California having proved a failure. . . .

You have plenty of friends who have the utmost faith in your capacity, and there never has been a time, I think, in the history of the country when there were so many openings. I think we are here entering on an era of unparalleled business activity. So I earnestly urge upon you to come on in September without fear or hesitation. . . .

The paper is doing well, far better than we ventured to hope. We reached 5000 circulation by the third number, and it is rising steadily. It has been so far rather heavy, and I find it very difficult to lighten it. Your suggestions about what such a paper ought to contain are admirable, but it is very difficult to find a man to do the work of gossiping agreeably, on manners, lager beer, etc., who will bind himself to do it, whether he feels like it or not. In fact it is very difficult to get men of education in America to handle any subject with a light touch. . . .

My engagement is for two years, with complete control over the editorial department, payment of contributors, etc. The publisher is a good fellow, very competent, but a sensationist, bred in the *Independent* school, with unbounded faith in *names* and puffing, and not much, though it increases every day, in quality. Our leading political aim is to secure equality before the law in all parts of the Union; all others are open questions, but I seek to have everything discussed more temperately and accurately than is usual. "Social articles" however are my great need. We have begun at a low price, but shall raise it in January.

Yours ever

ELG

1. The New England Loyal Publication Society, of which Charles Eliot Norton was secretary, was a private Unionist propaganda organization formed by John M. Forbes and others.

To Charles Eliot Norton

Nation Office   New York, July 25 [1865] (Godkin Papers, MH)

MY DEAR NORTON: . . . We continue to do very well. Subscribers come in at an average of 40 a day which astonishes Richards. My private opinion is, that the paper so far is rather heavy, and didactic. I am doing everything I can think of to lighten it up; but "specific gravity" seems to be a general or almost general failing. I got a man of whose "levity" I felt almost sure, to review the "Army Correspondence," and he has sermonized over it for two numbers; yet the Chicago *Tribune* has engaged him to travel in the South at $6000 a year! [1] Is it so difficult for men of culture to touch things lightly. . . .

I shall be very glad to come up and spend a day with you. . . . I am a little nervous about leaving as Garrison is a little too ready to assume responsibility, and has not yet quite judgment enough to be trusted. He is afflicted with some of the old newspaper vices, gives the lie (à la Greeley) in print, if he is let, and has an unpleasant and alarming tendency to small and rather pitiful jokes. But I think I can arrange matters so as to come up soon. . . .

I am very glad to hear that Curtis is shaken, and that Dana be-

lieves.[2] They are both excellent judges, but I think Dana the better. . . .

Ever yours
ELG

1. A reference to the German-American journalist and financier Henry
Villard (1835–1900). The brother-in-law of Wendell P. Garrison, Villard
subsequently became owner of the *Nation*.

2. The now cynical one-time trustee of Brook Farm, Charles A. Dana
(1819–97), had recently resigned as managing editor of the New York
Tribune over differences with Horace Greeley. Later, as proprietor of
the New York *Sun*, he would incur the opprobrium of his old admirers by
adopting sensational journalism.

To Charles Eliot Norton

Nation Office   New York, July 27 [1865] (Godkin Papers, MH)

MY DEAR NORTON: Mr. John Forbes and Mr. S. G. Ward
called today in a very friendly way to tell me of the way Stearns
is behaving. They read me a letter from him to Mr. Ward, in
which he announced that either he or I must quit the concern,
and that if I do not, he will sell his share in open market, and
publish the reasons. The reasons are the mild tone of the paper
on the slavery question; the expression of an opinion in No. 2.
that there was greater danger from the disaffected Southerners
in the local legislatures than in Congress; and lastly my having
given an "underhand pledge," which I concealed from him, not
to present free trade. . . .

In the first place if anything was well understood at the outset, it was that the *Nation* was to discuss questions evenly and
moderately, and not in the slangwhang abolitionist style. . . .

In the second place all I have to say is, Wendell Phillips to the
contrary notwithstanding, I still believe that inasmuch as in the
state legislatures the rebels will hold in their grasp the whole
social system of the South, and the fate of the Negro [,] while in
Congress, they will be able to exercise little or no influence on
anything or anybody except the tariff and taxation. I still hold
that their being kept [out] of the former is of more importance
than their being kept out of the latter, and I am not such an un-

utterable ninny as to be driven from a position of this sort by simple abuse.

In the third place the only "*pledge*" I have ever given to anybody on any subject connected with the *Nation* was contained in the letter which I wrote to Mr. McKim in your house, and read to you. It declared that the *Nation* would be neither a free trade nor protectionist organ, but would discuss the tariff on revenue grounds. Whether this was "underhand" you can judge. . . .

I need hardly say I have not the least intention of succumbing to this sort of pressure. I have induced persons here to put $20,000 into the paper, and I owe it to them at least to remain firm, and prevent its degenerating into a mere ranting organ of the "radical wing." Most of this feeling which is getting up against me is due, I am satisfied, to the utterly false impression that I am in the hands of the Garrisonians.

I need hardly assure you that there is nobody more Antislavery than I am; no one more filled with abhorrence of the whole southern system, and southern ideas, and nobody more anxious to make the paper do good service in the cause. But I will not do it in the Wendell Phillips way, and I cannot be bullied and abused into it. . . .

How I wish I could have a few hours talk with you!

Yours ever

ELG

To Charles Eliot Norton

Nation Office   New York, July 29 [1865]
(Godkin Papers, MH)

MY DEAR NORTON: You have probably heard of the rumpus the "Belligerent Rights" article has created in Boston. Many think, it has seriously injured the paper, Quincy for one. It was written by Torrey of Cambridge, the person whom you may remember, you recommended for this class of question. . . .[1]

I thought the article a good one, although I did not entirely agree with it, but I was glad to have Bemis rapped over the knuckles.

The adulation of which he has been the object in Boston is ridiculous.

Probably the matter would not have excited much notice, but it afforded an opportunity of raising the cry of "Englishman!" against me, which I imagine they are doing very thoroughly in Boston. I hear no complaints from any other quarter. Coming on the top of the row about the paragraph on Wendell Phillips, it is unfortunate and my last week has been a troubled one. John Forbes has been very kind, but advises me to let international law alone, and let Torrey, and Bemis fight it out among themselves as correspondents. Am I right or rather should I be right in shutting out such a man as Torrey, however, through fear of laying myself open to the charge of foreign feeling?

As regards myself personally, I cannot and never will give in to an outcry against me on the ground of my foreign origin. . . . My children have been born here. I mean to die here, and I protest in these days of Negro suffrage, against being cried down on this score. But the question is, if people get into this way of assailing me, ought I in justice to the stockholders to remain at this post? Can such a thing be "lived down?" Is it possible for an editor with forty stockholders at his back, ever to get over the smallest mistakes committed at the outset?

The paper is doing very well pecuniarily.[2] Our unpopularity seems confined to Boston.

Yours ever
ELG. . . .

1. Edmund Quincy (1808–77) was the editor of the *Anti-Slavery Standard*. Harvard professor Henry W. Torrey (1814–93) was under criticism for his alleged wartime Copperhead views, and Boston readers of the *Nation* objected to Godkin's employing him to debate United States charges that England had adopted an "unneutral" course during the War.

2. The *Nation*, contrary to Godkin's assurances, was losing nearly $5,000 a month, partly because of (1) its expensive format and its excessive size; (2) its lack of advertising revenue; (3) its low price; and (4) Godkin's largesse toward contributors.

To Charles Eliot Norton

July 31, 1865 (Ogden 1:245–46)

. . . On consultation with my friends here, I have concluded that I had better meet this cry of "Englishman" against me now, once for all. If I don't, or appear to cower under it, it will be kept up and I shall be persecuted with it. And there is no man in the community who need less fear a charge of foreign sympathy. So I have written a very strong letter to Edmund Quincy, expressing the indignation which I feel at my being assailed on such a ground as this, by people who are clamoring for *negro* suffrage, and also at the countenance which seems to be given in Boston to the semi-barbarous practice of taking the editor by the throat when anything objectionable in matters of taste and opinion appears in his paper, and digging into his private life in search of unworthy motives. Anything more illiberal or *un-American*, it would be hard to conceive of.

I expect no quarter hereafter from the Stearns and Wendell Phillips set. They are, I think, bent on my destruction. If the fever does not spread, however, I shall not be disturbed by it. I have feared trouble from that quarter ever since he took the liberty of forwarding me an offensive insinuation on the appearance of the second number. He has never been able to rid himself of the idea that I am under the influence of McKim and the Garrison wing . . . whom he seems to hate with true sectarian ferocity. . . .[1]

1. A reference to the factionalism in the disrupted American Anti-Slavery Society.

To James M. McKim

Nation Office   New York, August 2 [1865]
(Godkin Papers, *Nation* Business Records, MH)

DEAR MR. McKIM: I return Judge Bond's letter.[1] As a general rule a man who writes or talks in this way is never nearly [*sic*] right. He may be an exception. It is the old newspaper style, and bears about the same relation to truth and accuracy, as a showman's scene painting does to a topographical survey. No doubt in Baltimore people feel very strongly, but we cannot write up to their feelings. It would be an entire departure from our original plans, and would ruin our influence with the public at large. The *Standard* and *Commonwealth* do this sort of thing, but who reads them? [2]

Again, I wish you would call the attention of our friends in that quarter to the following which was printed in an advertizement for some weeks before the *Nation* started.

> This journal will not be the organ of any party, sect, or body. It will, on the contrary, make an earnest effort to bring to the discussion of political and social questions a really critical spirit, and to wage war upon the vices of violence, exaggeration, and misrepresentation by which so much of the political writing of the day is marred.

Now they constantly assume that it is the "organ" of the freedmen's associations. It is nothing of the kind. All the New York money at least was raised on the understanding that it was to be nothing of the kind. It is morally bound in the strongest way to help the Freedmen's Cause in the way in which its conductors consider most judicious, but if its opinions do not always satisfy every "friend of the freedmen" there is no breach of contract as they seem to suppose. They must put up with it, and learn to place a little more value on free discussion than they now seem to do. Of course, I do not as you know object to temperate or friendly advice. But it is mere waste of paper to write me wild, extravagant, and abusive harangues. I have long learned to estimate this sort of thing at its real worth, and so has, in my belief, the American public.

Yours very truly
ELG

I say the *Nation* "*does suit*"—the public—for whom it was intended.

1. Judge Hugh L. Bond (1828–93) was one of the *Nation's* original anti-slavery backers in Baltimore.

2. A reference to the *Anti-Slavery Standard* (q.v.) and to the *Commonwealth*. The *Commonwealth* was an antislavery weekly established in Bos-

ton in 1862 with the backing of George L. Stearns. Under the working editorship of reformer Frank B. Sanborn, it opposed the *Nation* because of Godkin's conservatism on Freedmen's rights and other social issues.

To Charles Eliot Norton

Nation Office   New York, August 3, 1865
(Godkin Papers, MH)

MY DEAR NORTON: . . . It is quite evident that the row is confined to Boston. There has not been a whisper of complaint from any other part of the country, and I cannot help thinking that two thirds of the uproar there was due to the shock caused by the irreverence shown for the local idol. Bemis has become something of this sort, and I can really only account for the position he has attained there by the intensity of the popular ignorance as to the subjects he has treated of. Whipple has treated us to some rant in the *Transcript,* and asks with amusing donkeyism, how can the claims for *Alabama* damages be considered "without enquiry into the fatal question of belligerent rights." The two things have about as much connection as the Monroe Doctrine and the Pragmatic Sanction. . . .

It is quite certain, that no such paper as we have in our minds, will ever be established here, without encountering this sort of thing. I myself do not care one straw for it, as long as the stockholders remain firm. It is the fire in the rear that demoralizes me.

Yours till Saturday
ELG

To James M. McKim

Nation Office   New York, August 10, 1865
(Godkin Papers, *Nation* Business Records, MH)

DEAR MR. McKIM: The outcry against me in Boston, though ostensibly due to my supposed "pledge" with regard to the tariff, is, I think really due to something else. . . .

From the very first number, the *Nation* has been very snappishly received in Boston, on various grounds. Mr. Stearns I think expected to be consulted more. . . .

Mr. Atkinson has written a good deal. There are three articles of his in the last number. But I have given great offence by disagreeing with him as to the propriety of submitting the construction of the phrase "republican form of government," to the Supreme Court. I think,—and a good many good lawyers agree with me—that the Supreme Court would be obliged to define this as it was understood in the last century, and this would not give us negro suffrage. Moreover, I dislike dragging the Supreme Court into the arena at crises like this, whenever it can be avoided. My theory is that Congress has the power under the Constitution to decide what is, and what is not a republican "form of government," and I think it is not tied up, as the Supreme Court is, by rules of construction. But Mr. Sumner, it appears thinks differently and accordingly he writes abusive letters against me in the Boston papers, and Mr. Stearns sets to work to try and break my contract with the trustees, and all this because I have conscientiously, calmly, and in respectful language uttered an opinion different from theirs on a point of law. Now there is no doubt that Mr. Sumner's opinion is a much more valuable one than mine, but you know I could not, and nobody could edit a paper in New York if I had before taking ground on any question, to write on to Boston, to find out what Charles Sumner and Professor Parsons thought. . . .

Yours very truly
ELG

To Daniel Coit Gilman [1]

Nation Office   New York, August 11, 1865
(Gilman Papers, MdBJ)

MY DEAR SIR: I had hoped to have seen you in the train yesterday to have said, amongst other things, that I have since seeing you, looked into the book of which you sent us the review and find it rabidly proslavery, besides being the work of a confirmed fool. Considering the ground we take on the Negro question, it would hardly do to notice it at all without calling attention to this feature of it, and I think he deserved to have the lash laid over his back pretty severely.

I have therefore laid your notice aside. If you should feel disposed to take it up in this sense I shall be glad to have you. If not, I shall get it done elsewhere. . . .

Yours very truly
ELG

Prof. D. C. Gilman

1. Daniel Coit Gilman (1831–1908) at this time was a professor in the Sheffield Scientific School of Yale College. In 1875 he would become the first president of the Johns Hopkins University. His wife had known Godkin since Godkin's New Haven days of the 1850s.

To Charles Eliot Norton

Nation Office   New York, August 15, 1865 (Godkin Papers, MH)

MY DEAR NORTON: . . . My letter to Atkinson was a private letter, written in haste, in confidence, and without reflection to him as a contributor. His handing it around for perusal always struck me as an extraordinary proceeding, but his giving it to Stearns to print is still worse. My permission he has never asked. At Stearns' printing it, I am of course not surprized. I am mortified to think that I should ever have sat at the table of such a fellow or he at mine. . . .

Yours ever
ELG. . . .

To Charles Eliot Norton

Nation Office   New York, August 16, 1865 (Godkin Papers, MH)

MY DEAR NORTON: . . . That such a plan of ousting me, should have entered into the heads of two middleaged business men, seems to me to indicate mental unsoundness. . . .

G. C. Ward says that the struggle which is now going on in the *Nation*, is the same which has gone on in the Union, the Sanitary Commission, and is now going on in the Freedmen's Aid Union.

An effort is being made to get diverse localities to unite in national objects, and in doing so to sacrifice various local prejudices and opinions on minor matters. Boston, *he said*, is earnest, intelligent, but narrow and intolerant. It is clear that the radical set there expected to supply the *Nation* with its opinion, not only with regard to its main objects—but with regard to most matters of law, criticism, and politics. It has become clear from my rejection of one or two of Atkinson's articles, and my failure to consult and be guided by Stearns, that I am not the man, they took me for, and that the paper, is not the thing they looked for. *Hinc illae irae sic.* . . .

Now pray don't you be worried about this matter. My position is impregnable. I shall not resign. I shall conduct the paper "on this line," and no other, come what may. . . . The paper is doing very well. The public evidently appreciates it and I know we are reaching a class of people, who would not let a paper edited by Geo. L. Stearns and Co. into their houses, and who listen to our views on political questions for the sake of the other good things the paper contains.

Pray keep your mind easy. Mine is perfectly so. Give my kindest remembrance to the ladies and believe me

Ever cordially yours
ELG

To Charles Eliot Norton

Nation Office   New York, August 19, 1865 (Godkin Papers, MH)

MY DEAR NORTON: . . . McKim has letters from the Philadelphians this morning. They are unanimous against Stearns. White, the largest Stockholder there, says, if he "attempts to break the *Nation* down he will hurt his own fingers." The assault on me was too *brutal*, for any civilized community to stand it. . . .

Yours ever, in haste
ELG

To The *Nation* Stockholders

Nation Office New York, August 23, 1865
(Printed circular, Godkin Papers, MH)

SIR: You have doubtless received a circular from Mr. George L. Stearns, making certain charges against me as editor of the *Nation*.

If the letter to Mr. Atkinson, which he prints, had been intended for publication, it would have been more carefully worded. To interpret it fairly, it ought to be understood that I have been long known to be a free-trader. All that it reveals is the fact, that, in order to secure unanimity with regard to the great object for which the paper was established among persons differing widely on other subjects, I thought it expedient to avoid making *The Nation* the "organ" (properly so called) of any particular school of economists. . . .

Yours respectfully
ELG

To Charles Eliot Norton

Nation Office New York, August 24, 1865 (Godkin Papers, MH)

MY DEAR NORTON: . . . I am very much dissatisfied with Atkinson's behaviour. . . . He has been intriguing against me, and actually trying to destroy my independence, while clamouring for it.

Nothing will induce me to print what I conceive to be bad in law, or in logic, or in morals, in the *Nation*, as the utterance of the paper, to help either Chas. Sumner, or Parsons, or any other man or body of men, or to advance the interests of any party whatsoever. If the Republican party can only attain its ends, by humbugging the public, it must look for help from some other quarter. They must get their "bunkum" done in some other establishment than this. . . .

I am placed in an awkward position as regards Atkinson. He sends me a great many contributions. There were three of his in that admirable "No. 7," but my self respect will hardly allow me any longer, I think, to receive articles from a man, who, whenever they are rejected, has no hesitation in renouncing me behind my back as incompetent, and agitating for my removal. . . .

Yours
ELG

To Charles Eliot Norton

Nation Office   New York, August 24, 1865 (Godkin Papers, MH)

MY DEAR NORTON: . . . Atkinson has written me a long letter this morning, which I must consider an *amende,* so pray dismiss his case from your mind. He talks a great deal of the dissatisfaction with me which prevails among the Boston Stockholders. Pray tell me frankly how general this is. I was led to think it was confined very much to Stearns' set.

   In haste

Yours ever
ELG

To Charles Eliot Norton

Nation Office   New York, September 1, 1865
(Godkin Papers, MH)

MY DEAR NORTON: . . . Tuckerman deluges me with trash, though I have never asked him for a line, and send him back a package nearly every week.[1] What do you do with a contributor, or rather bore of this sort, whom you do not wish to treat unkindly? . . . The last week has been one of great calm. I had on Monday one or two foolish letters from Atkinson to which I made no reply. What is the use? He goes on ranting about the Supreme Court and the Constitution apparently without even a glimmering of what a court is, or in what its duties consist, but as regards me personally, is mild, suave, and repentant. It seems to me the rest of the country is more metropolitan in its tone, than Boston. I would say this, *pace vestrâ,* but you deny that you are a Bostonian. The criticisms of this set, at all events, on the *Nation,* have been exceedingly provincial, and the spirit is provincial—

narrow, intolerant, fond of personalities. I do not know how to reconcile this with the intellectual preeminence to which the place is, I think, really entitled. . . .

> Ever cordially yours
> ELG

1. Author Henry T. Tuckerman and Godkin both contributed to the New York literary periodical, *The Knickerbocker*, during the late 1850s.

To Charles Eliot Norton

> *Nation* Office   New York, September 7, 1865
> (Godkin Papers, MH)

MY DEAR NORTON: I met Mrs. Stowe last summer and spoke to her about writing for us, and she said she would be glad to do so, but was bound by contract to the *Atlantic Monthly* for the present year. . . .[1]

What do you think of engaging her *exclusively*, as the *Atlantic* did, for the year 1866? I do not like, as you know, to do anything clap-trap, and I don't much like this kind of arrangement, and don't think *everything* Mrs. Stowe or anybody else writes very valuable. But her name, and her writings have an immense attraction for a large number of people, whom we have as yet not reached, and it might assist powerfully in placing the paper on a paying basis, if it were known to be for a whole year, the only channel through which she reached the public. . . .

> Yours ever
> ELG

1. Harriet Beecher Stowe.

To Edward Atkinson

> *Nation* Office   New York, September 9, 1865
> (Atkinson Papers, MH)

MY DEAR SIR: . . . I was going to write last week, to suggest your writing on the "eight hour movement" in Massachusetts, but waited in order to find a copy of the *Spectator* (London) in which it was strongly denounced. I cannot lay hands on it, but the substance of it was this—"You say that the working classes in England, would not, if they got the suffrage, vote *as a class* for their own benefit, without reference to the rest of the community. See what has happened in Massachusetts. The workmen are there engaged in a movement to secure the shortening of the hours of labour by legislative enactment. The result will be that the production of the state will be greatly reduced, manufacturers will be unable to compete with those of other places and capital will be driven to places, where industry is free, and employers and employed are left to make their own bargains."

I was when I read this very anxious to have the point met, if it can be met, and I intended to forward it to you for that purpose. I want to make the *Nation* a good exponent of democratic ideas abroad as well as here, and if you can take this up, I should be glad to have you do so. There is probably no one better fitted.

Yours very truly
ELG

To Charles Eliot Norton

Nation Office   New York, September 19, 1865
(Godkin Papers, MH)

MY DEAR NORTON: Many thanks for your kind letter. I can assure you the thought of replying to Stearns or taking any further notice of him has never entered my head. . . . Stearns I believe to be a very unscrupulous and unprincipled man, though sincere enough in his anti-slavery zeal. How often do we see zeal for "a cause" vented with private rascality! He knows just as well as you or I do, what parts of his circular are false and what true, but he has used lying as a weapon so long that when he thrusts it into an opponent's ribs, he is so occupied with the effect of the blow on the fortunes of the fight, that the moral complexion of the matter does not trouble him.

Then he is a *low-bred* man. A whole class of motives and restraints which act strongly on you are entirely unknown to him. I brought away a very unpleasant impression of himself and his surroundings after my visit to his house, and congratulated and do still congratulate myself from the bottom of my soul, that I had opposed your withdrawal from the Trusteeship.

He is so maddened by the turn things have taken and the impossibility of getting his money out of the concern, that I feel satisfied he will keep working against me day and night, and will leave nothing undone to damage my reputation. . . .

I enclose a pleasant note from Prof. Cairnes.[1] It will be well if we can give the paper a good circulation amongst that class of men in England.

Many thanks to the ladies for their righteous indignation against the "Major." He is, however, not worth *their* anger.

Mrs. Godkin has come back to town, and joins me in kind regards to you all.

Yours very cordially
ELG

1. John E. Cairnes (1823–75), Irish political economist.

To Charles Eliot Norton

Nation Office   New York, September 26, 1865
(Godkin Papers, MH)

MY DEAR NORTON: I had determined to open up on Johnson, before receiving your last note, and have an article in the forthcoming number on the great "pardon" farce. I am satisfied, and so are the best Republicans here that he is on his way over to the enemy, with arms and baggage, will not trouble himself about the Negro, as long as he can have a "restored union," and a strong party at his back, for the election of [1868]. I am glad to find you share my impression as to the propriety of pitching into him. I *know* that Gilmore is satisfied that slavery will be virtually restored in S. Carolina by the aid of vagrant laws etc. as soon as the state is back in the Union. . . .

Your review of Draper is excellent. I struck out one or two sentences which seemed to me to contain too much *aqua fortis*, and I think on reflection you would agree with me. It will create quite a breeze here, which I shall enjoy. Who is a good person to review the *Life of Sir William Johnson* of New York?

How well Sedgwick writes these reviews! I was sorry he did not make more out of Daganne. I have been looking into White's "Life and Genius of Shakespeare," and think you were too complimentary.

There is no news. We are going on prosperously. The great question of the change of price will shortly come up. . . . Richards thinks by Christmas we can raise the price to the desired point without the least danger. If the thing were once paying its way, I should feel happy, and be ready to "depart in peace." I do not care particularly about pleasing Stearns [,] Hallowell and Company, but I do not want to have it said that I spent $100,000 trying to establish a paper and failed.[1] I think a desperate effort will be made to oust me at the end of the two years, and I shall look forward to its succeeding, but if I leave behind me an established and high class weekly, I shall feel that my work has been done, and the radical dogs may find some one else to snarl over.

Ever yours, my dear friend
ELG

1. Richard P. Hallowell (1835–1904), New England merchant and Abolitionist. The Godkin-Stearns controversy is recounted in detail in Armstrong, "The Freedmen's Movement and the Founding of the *Nation*."

To Charles Eliot Norton

Nation Office   New York, October 3, 1865
(Godkin Papers, MH)

MY DEAR NORTON: . . . Torrey's criticisms are perfectly sound. You know, however, what I have to say on these points. As regards our political as well as other articles, I have felt *morally*, a little discouraged ever since my row with Atkinson and Co. when I found a movement got up to force me to resign because amongst other things, the paper had presumed to differ with Sumner on a point of law, and had lamented the want of *finish* in America, it made me feel, that our notions were too far in advance of our public. And I have thought it best as a matter of policy to avoid rows, till we got a little more character to lean on. This has I think, often unconsciously perhaps interfered with our "spiciness." But the general *heaviness* of writing, and the great preponderance of writers on "reconstruction" and nothing else, is damaging. This Connecticut vote is a heavy blow. What view should you take of that in the *Nation?* I must say I totally despair of Negro suffrage at present. The North will not press for it, though Stearns doubled his issue of pamphlets, and Sumner made two more speeches. I think practically we should accomplish more by pressing furiously for an educational test. Drop me a line to say what you think, before the end of the week.

The Freedmen's union is in a great mess. (This is private) Poor McKim shows in this as in other things his utter want of force and thought, and weight, and is likely to be turned out by abler and more active men. He communicates his sorrow to me, in a way that excites my pity, but also (in the poor man's absence of course) makes me weep with laughter. He is too good and simple for this world. There has been one scene, which as described by himself, almost threw me and my wife into convulsions last week. If he had got hold of the paper, as at first proposed, the public would certainly not have complained of it, as now, for being too *heavy*.

I have had a very kind and pleasant note from Lowell, who is at last coming to the rescue. Howells of Venice is here and is writing well.[1] The paper on Pompeii is his. What do you think of it? When do you go back to Cambridge? Many thanks for the extracts from your English letters. Somehow or other, I cannot be persuaded that if, as the Yankees said—"We could get a look into" Ruskin's "head," we should not find a screw loose.

Ever yours
ELG

1. William Dean Howells at this time was a full-time employee of the *Nation.*

To George P. Marsh [1]

Nation Office   New York, October 11, 1865
(Marsh Papers, VtU)

MY DEAR MR. MARSH: It gave me great pleasure to receive your article on State Rights. I shall use it in an early number of the *Nation*, if not in the next.

Since then your article on "Monumental Honors" has also come to hand. It is very good, and belongs to a class of writing which I find it very difficult to get well or done at all—I mean the *light* treatment of social topics. I shall be very glad indeed to receive from you as many contributions as you may have time or inclination to send. . . .

Very sincerely yours
ELG

Honorable George P. Marsh

1. The Vermont scholar-diplomat George P. Marsh (1801–82) was a frequent contributor to the *Nation*.

To Charles Eliot Norton

Nation Office   New York, October 20, 1865
(Godkin Papers, MH)

MY DEAR NORTON: Stearns' position is very funny. When I see the Boston [*Evening*] *Transcript* also abusing Wendell Phillips for want of confidence in the country, it makes the outburst against me last summer wear a very odd look, and gives me greater and greater disregard of what the heathen say or think. . . .

Olmsted has left California on the 13th. He will reach here in a month. He declines my offer to *write* for the *Nation,* and yours to write for the *North American,* as also the Secretaryship of the Freedmen's Union, on the same ground, want of health. He says it would take him six months to write one article for *N.A.* He says he is "only fit for selection and adaptation now, a sort of memorandic compilation, that is, special editorial business," but doubts whether he can even do that. It is to the Central Park, and similar work that he now looks. Desk work, would, he says risk his life.

I think of making him an offer, such as will be satisfactory to him for the use of his name as editor, and for his counsel, and share in the responsibility. I think it would, if announced give the paper a lift, and enable me to use my arms more freely, and it would be a real pleasure to me to [be] joined with him in any enterprize. Richards is greatly taken by this idea, and I think Olmsted would accept.

I want your opinion as to the probable effect of such a step on me personally. . . .

Would it wear the air of my being superseded, or having failed in any way? . . . I am the more sensitive on this point, as one of the consequences of the Stearns circular has been the circulation of a report here, that I was about to retire.

Ever yours
ELG. . . .

To Charles Eliot Norton

Nation Office   New York, October 24, 1865
(Godkin Papers, MH)

MY DEAR NORTON: Many thanks for your letter. Your views about Olmsted, confirm my own, with which they entirely coincide. We must now wait till Olmsted comes, when I shall state the case to him. Richards suggests, the printing of both our names (Olmsted's and mine) as editors on each number. How does that strike you? Ward's note is very gratifying, particularly as I regard him as the most *sagacious* man of our set.

I had two days ago, a talk with Jones of the *Times*, (the business manager), a very experienced, shrewd newspaper man, which very much assured me about the *Nation*. . . . He said the *Times* did not pay its expenses for three years. Had they lost heart one month sooner, they would have lost all their money. Now $1000 shares sell for $6000. . . . He says the first thing is to make a good paper, whether it be at first a very taking one or not; the second is to *adhere to a fixed line of policy* both literary and financial, and not to be affected by the advice and criticism of droppers in. He says nothing strikes the popular imagination so much as fixity. It is associated in their eyes with strength.

All this struck me as very sound and valuable, coming from such a source, and it makes the same impression on Richards, who is really showing himself to be a very plucky sensible fellow. Jones thinks the *Independent* style of carrying on business—the

essence of charlatanry, and anything but a commercial success.
They give a sewing machine to every new club of 25 subscribers! . . .

> Ever cordially yours
> ELG

Doesn't G[oldwin] S[mith] overrate the bad influence of the
love of military glory? Is it not something to permeate a whole
people, as the French are permeated with a longing ever for
"glory," for something intangible, ideal, something, besides beef
and beer, and new clothes? From all I ever saw of the French
people, I should say their moral condition was far above that of
the English, that is, that though not an admirable condition, it
afforded better ground to start from towards something higher.

To Charles Eliot Norton

> *Nation* Office   New York, November 4, 1865
> (Godkin Papers, MH)

MY DEAR NORTON: . . . Who is Woodman? Is he the luminary
of the *Transcript*, who pooh-poohed Montesquieu as a poor
"Frenchman" who did not know what publicists of the 18th.
Century meant by the phrase, "Republican form of government?"
I am really sorry that you should have to wrangle with such
trashy people. I should think you would sometimes wish that you
had either never heard of the *Nation*, or never heard of me. I am
constantly sensible that your good offices in urging the offer of
the editorship to me has involved you in a summer of trouble, and
worry. But I hope you are as philosophical as you have always
advised me to be. The more I see and hear of the Woodmans and
the Stearnses, the less I am concerned by what they think and
say. . . .

> Yours ever
> ELG

To Henry Wadsworth Longfellow

Nation Office   New York, November 6, 1865
(Longfellow Papers, MH)

DEAR SIR: Although you were kind enough to allow your name to figure on our list of contributors, I have forborne to trouble you for any more substantial evidence of your good will, as I understood from Mr. Norton that you were very much absorbed in other and more important labour.

We have recently raised our price, and are of course anxious that the change should produce no unfavorable effect on our circulation, which has hitherto increased with a steadiness and rapidity for which we did not look. But of course at this juncture stimulants may help us a good deal, and as I have reason to believe that you are interested in the establishment of a first class weekly, and think the *Nation* at least a fair effort towards it, I venture to ask whether you would not lend us a helping hand by a few contributions, either in prose or verse. They would be very valuable if only as an evidence of your good feeling towards the enterprize.[1]

> I am, dear Sir, your obedient Servant
> ELG. . . .

1. Longfellow did not accede to Godkin's request.

To Charles Eliot Norton

Nation Office   New York, November 20, 1865
(Godkin Papers, MH)

MY DEAR NORTON: . . . Stearns has now got up a call for a meeting of the Stockholders, which Atkinson tells me he (Atkinson) has signed, on the ground that the *Nation* is "going under financially." I need hardly say that the report of a meeting having been held for this reason is calculated to injure us seriously. All that there is outrageous and absurd in the proceeding, I cannot well put on paper; you can doubtless imagine it. S. G. Ward, whom I have not yet seen, thinks it desirable I should see Stearns in order to discover whether we cannot come to an understanding with him that will put an end to these freaks of his. Constant rumors kept up by one of the Stockholders, that the paper is failing will of course do something to prevent our getting both advertizements and subscriptions, and in other words depreciate the property of all the Stockholders.

But I really do not see what understanding I could come to with him. I cannot even feign friendly feeling, with my present opinion of him. . . .

Yours as ever
ELG

To Professor William D. Whitney

Nation Office   New York, November 22 [1865]
(W.D. Whitney Papers, CtY)

MY DEAR SIR: I ought to have replied to your note some time ago. I was very much mortified by the way in which the notice of the *North American Review* was done, as I had discovered the blunder you mention, before hearing from you on coming to read the article myself. I had intended writing the notice but found myself unable to do so without waiting another week. The difficulty of getting small things of this kind done conscientiously is very great, but I think I am gradually getting hold of the right men.

Your article on Saadi's *Gulistan* appears in this number. I was going to send you a proof, but it came in rather late, and there did not appear to be anything in it which the MS. left doubtful.

Yours very truly
ELG. . . .

To Charles Eliot Norton

Nation Office   New York, November 29, 1865
(Godkin Papers, MH)

MY DEAR NORTON: . . . I had a long talk with Olmsted last night about the *Nation*. He has come to the conclusion that on the whole, he would rather not go to the bother of buying

Stearns out. He says, that as long as the other Stockholders are
satisfied he thinks it scarcely necessary to beat up for better men
to put in money for the mere purpose of giving a relief to Stearns,
which he does not deserve; and that in fact, he will be all the
more inclined to go in, if Stearns stays in, for the purpose of helping me to put him down. What do you think of this view? . . .

The circulation does not increase as rapidly as we wish, and I
want very much to begin the New Year under the influence of a
legitimate stimulus. Lowell could do everything for us, if he
would. I will send him a check, and write to him tomorrow, and
if you would back me up by a personal interview, I should feel
greatly obliged. I think with some help of this kind we might get
on a paying basis by the end of one year. I am to see Mrs. Stowe
this evening, and I think I shall enlist her also. . . .

Ever yours
ELG

To Charles Eliot Norton

Nation Office   New York, December 13, 1865
(Godkin Papers, MH)

MY DEAR NORTON: There was nothing to be gained by holding
the meeting this week, as McKim found the persons whom he
expected would not be in town. Besides which, it is of prime importance you should be present, in order to represent the "min-
isterial" wing of the Boston Stockholders. I should be very unwilling to have a meeting at which you were not present. So it is
all arranged for next week. I propose to have a social gathering on
Tuesday evening as you suggest, and the formal meeting on
Wednesday at the *Nation* office. We expect you and Mrs. Norton on Monday, and shall be delighted to see you. You shall be as
quiet as you please. You know we live as tranquilly as shepherds.

It is absurd of Lowell to feel under an obligation to be "funny."
I don't care whether he is "grave or gay lively or severe," the
essential is that he should be Lowell. "Nihil tangit quod non
ornate." [*sic*]

Yours ever
ELG. . . .

To Christian E. Detmold

Nation Office   New York, December 19, 1865
(Printed circular, Atkinson Papers, MHi)

DEAR SIR: Mr. Frederick Law Olmsted has, as you are aware, returned from California. I was connected with him in an attempt two years ago to establish a weekly journal somewhat like *The Nation* in this city. The scheme was however dropped, owing to his departure.

He is now engaged to some extent in other pursuits, but is willing, I have reason to believe, to devote a certain portion of his time to assisting me in the editorial management of *The Nation.*

His reputation is such that his connection with the paper would, I am satisfied, materially strengthen it with the public, and there is no person whose judgment and sagacity in journalism as in other fields I esteem more highly. My relations with him are those of old and intimate friendship. I should, therefore, consider myself as well as the paper fortunate in securing his co-operation.

I beg respectfully to request, therefore, that he may be engaged by the Trustees of THE NATION ASSOCIATION to share with me the editorial duties and responsibility; it being understood, however, that beyond this division of the duty and responsibility my own relations with the Trustees, as fixed by my agreement with them, are to be in no way affected by any arrangement that may be made with him.

I remain, dear sir, yours respectfully
ELG

C. E. Detmold, Esq., President of NATION ASSOCIATION

To George P. Marsh

Nation Office   New York, December 26, 1865
(Marsh Papers, VtU)

MY DEAR SIR: . . . I am exceedingly sorry to find that the publication of your initials has been disagreeable to you. I think nobody can be more careful or scrupulous than I am about taking liberty with people's names, which the owners have not authorized, and I did not venture to use yours until I had consulted one of your friends, who concurred with me in thinking you would not object, if my reasons were before you.

The length of the series, and the nature of the subject made me fear that in a paper of such limited circulation as the *Nation*, they would not receive the attention they deserved unless they were known to emanate from some distinguished and respected hand. I did not anticipate the objection you make, arising out of your official position, as I did not and do not regard them as in the ordinary sense of the word political. . . .

I say all this rather to excuse self, than convince you, of course. You are the best judge, and in fact, the only judge of the propriety of using your name, and I have no desire to appeal from your decision. But I think it only just to myself to state the reasons which influenced me in departing from my usual course.

It is quite true the *Nation* has criticized Mr. Johnson occasionally rather sharply, but never factiously, and it has just as little hesitation in praising and supporting him as any of the partizan papers.[1] In fact the course we have pursued in this matter has elicited the warmest encomiums from some of the best men in the country, as something new in American journalism.—What we aim at is in reality not so much to be the exponent of a particular set of views on any subject, but to discuss all subjects in a particular way. For this reason, I do not think that a person's writing in our columns under his own signature commits him to any general agreement with us. . . .

The series of letters being now finished, it only remains for me to thank you for them very sincerely, and to ask you to be good enough to say what you think will be sufficient remuneration on them. I prefer having writers of your standing to fix the value of their own labour. On hearing from you I shall be happy to send you a check for the amount.

Allow me again to express my regret for having been the means of causing you either annoyance or inconvenience and to hope that you may not be deterred by what has happened from continuing your valuable contributions.

Yours very truly
ELG. . . .

1. Marsh, a philologist, had been appointed the first United States minister to Italy by Lincoln, and Johnson continued him in the post; hence Marsh's discomfiture over the revelation that he was writing for a weekly that was critical of the Administration.

To Charles Eliot Norton

Nation Office   New York, December 28, 1865
(Godkin Papers, MH)

My dear Norton: . . . Opposition to the *Nation* has developed in a new quarter. You remember young Dodge,—one of the Trustees—very rich, *good*, a rigid blue Presbyterian, wife ditto—Sabbatarians, great haters of "Romanists," cultivation small, and very narrow in every way. Dodge was active and kind in helping to get the paper up, and I have never had a hint of dissatisfaction from him since, except with regard to a criticism on Bierstadt. It appears, however, that he and his wife have been suffering awfully in secret. They had Olmsted to dinner yesterday, and were very violent in their denunciations of the paper, she for its "vulgarity," and "slanginess" (!!) and he for its generally "sensational" tone. The particular grounds of offense seem to be the critiques on the "Schönberg Cotta Family" on the "Country Parson" and "Timothy Titcomb." He says his friends are laughing at him for having canvassed for it. She says that things appear in it that would disgrace the *New York Herald*. Most of the abuse I have received hitherto has been for our "ridiculous dignity," and "Heaviness," and didactic tone, so this has the merit of producing in my breast a very novel sensation. All this of course proves more clearly than ever the necessity of getting out of reach of the Stockholders. I received a very earnest remonstrance last week from Philadelphia for my irreverent manner of speaking of Jay Cooke the great bond pedlar. I am luckily more thickskinned than I was at the outset, and consequently continue to eat and sleep undisturbed.

But I *am* a little troubled to find that we tread on the corns of the evangelical people. Dr. McClintock of Philadelphia writes a very friendly note this morning, in which he says the "*Nation* is doing nobly," [and] gives me a gentle hint on this point.[1] I have taken some pains to avoid anything of this kind, and I think the tone of the paper has been really religious, in the best sense of the word, but the fact seems to be, and this I did not anticipate, that they will not only not allow you to assail their doctrines, but they will not permit any unfavorable criticism of the literary execution of their books of morality.

All this is in the main very amusing—and Olmsted and I laughed heartily over some of Mrs. Dodge's criticisms this morning. I think after the *Nation* fails, or I retire from it with a fortune, I shall publish a little volume of my experiences. . . .

Yours ever

ELG

1. John McClintock (1814–70), American Methodist theologian. In 1867 he became the first president of the Drew Theological Seminary at the invitation of its promoter, Daniel Drew.

To Charles Eliot Norton

Nation Office   New York, December 30, 1865
(Godkin Papers, MH)

MY DEAR NORTON: . . . We had a very pleasant Christmas,—and it was made all the pleasanter to me by unusually good news from home. My oldest sister with whom I grew up, has been for over a year battling with consumption—the last six months in the South of France, and the doctor at last pronounces her out of danger, and promises to send her home well in the Spring which takes a burden off my mind which has weighed sorely on me for many months.

Our subscription list begins to improve, and we are in better spirits at the office. We have not got the circular to the Stockholders off yet, but shall on Tuesday. Olmsted has begun, and is very useful. He is full of suggestions, and has really a wonderfully sound judgment. I find him already a considerable mental relief to me, as it divides the responsibility, and will of course if we fail, divide the blame of failure.

We are thinking of getting out a circular containing the written opinions of some of the leading men all over the country upon the *Nation*. We have received a great many testimonials of this kind, but have never made any use of them. And we need

something of this kind to give us a push. We have no party backing as we aim to be an independent paper. Radicals, conservatives [,] free traders, protectionists, infidels and evangelicals have
all some reasons for finding fault with us. The cultivated class we
have with us; but the class next below, do not know quite what
to make of us, and are suspicious or hostile. Our criticisms of
books etc., are novel, and outrage them, and so forth. But with
this latter class the opinion of the former is all powerful. Thousands
would declare the *Nation* a very fine paper, if they knew that
Longfellow, Lowell etc., thought so, who do not think so now. So
we propose to collect the opinions of such men and publish them.
What do you think of this? Some of the very strongest testimony
to the excellence of the paper would, for instance, come from
clergymen, which would startle the common run of "evangelicals"; and so on. A happy New Year to you all!

> Yours ever
> ELC

To An Unknown New York Artist

Wednesday [Ca. 1865] (NNPM)

DEAR SIR: Mr. William C. Gilman whom, I believe, you know,
and have met at Mr. Wright's? studio, has lost his only child
this morning, a fine little girl of 3 years old.[1] He and his wife are
of course in great distress. Mrs. Gilman has begged of me to come
and see you in the hope that you can be induced to go to their
house and make a sketch of the child before it is buried. They
have set their hearts on having you do it on your own terms, and
I sincerely trust, that if you can possibly arrange it, you will not
refuse them.

I have called twice at your studio in the hope of seeing you,
and failing, I leave this. The body will remain at their house 182
Lexington Av. today and tomorrow. If I should not succeed in
seeing you before evening, a line sent to my house 37 E. 19.
before seven o'clock with your answer or a call from yourself
would greatly oblige me.

> Yours very truly
> ELG

1. William C. Gilman was one of the trustees of the Children's Aid Society of New York, of which Godkin's friend Brace was general secretary and moving spirit.

To Charles Eliot Norton

[15 January 1866] (Ogden 1:243)

. . . Bowles of Springfield told me last week that he heard the subject discussed at a dinner party in Boston at which it was said that "an Englishman might be fit for the kingdom of heaven, but not to edit an American newspaper." [1] I said the joke was good, but would have more point if the most successful paper in America, in the common low sense of the word, and that whose influence has received the strongest acknowledgment from the public and from politicians, had not been conducted by a blackguard Scotchman.[2] He mentioned also that a paragraph written by Garrison about Mr. Cobden, and put by him at the opening of the "Week," during my absence in the country, was cited as proof of the English direction of my thoughts in editing the paper. The acuteness of some people is wonderful. Olmsted's coming in relieves my mind a good deal, particularly in ridding me of the hateful burden of overcaution. We go over all the editorial matter together, so that he is in fact, as well as in name, responsible for all it contains; but I am amused sometimes to think how little my assistants are likely to gain by the change. Bowles tells me that Emerson took back from here the news, or the idea, that Olmsted had "supplanted" me.[3] This report I care nothing for. The only fear I had about his coming in was that it might seem an endorsement by more respectable men of Stearns's attacks on my character. But there is no danger of this, and you know how little I cared for the *fame* of editing the *Nation*, and how anxious I have always been to remain in the background. So I am well satisfied to have it supposed that Olmsted writes every line of the paper. Fame has to be very well won before I either admire or care for it, and notoriety I abhor.

Let the matter end how it may, I think you and I may always look back on it with satisfaction, and look over our two or three volumes of the *Nation* without any other regret than that it didn't succeed. If it failed to-morrow, I should feel myself abundantly repaid in having by means of it been brought into such close relations with so kind and sympathizing a friend as you have been. The worst charge that has arisen against me out of it is that I am "an Englishman," but I don't think my children will blush over it. . . .

1. Samuel Bowles (1826–78) was the proprietor of the *Springfield Republican*.

2. A reference to James Gordon Bennett (1795–1872), the Scottish-born proprietor of the *New York Herald*.

3. Ralph Waldo Emerson was skeptical of Godkin and declined to contribute to the *Nation*.

To Charles Eliot Norton

Nation Office   New York, January 26, 1866
(Godkin Papers, MH)

My dear Norton: I don't want to send your article back, unless you will promise to recast it; the subject is an excellent one, and your ideas about it are excellent also, and I think you could readily popularize it a little, if you would take the trouble. I think you were born a critic, and you are it seems to me a little too hard on your own pen, and hold yourself in too much. I never read anything of yours except your literary criticisms, which are always admirable, without wishing you would take the bit in your teeth, and run off. There is such a thing, my dear fellow, as having too good a taste, and being too fastidious. Your great charity prevents it, in your case from making you judge others too severely, but it often keep[s] your own fires "banked up," too much.

Olmsted has told me of the "Wise Sayings, or Wisdom of Jonathan." I am enchanted with the idea. If Lowell only could be induced to carry it out, I would consider the *Nation* not only a success but a valuable property, and there is hardly any sum short of the balance of the Capital, I would not recommend his being paid for it. This is the very thing that Artemus Ward, and so many other buffoons, have been trying to do, (and with what success!) and if a man of genius like Lowell only took it up, it would really be one of the literary events of the age, and if done in the *Nation*, would make me happier than anything else that is likely to happen to me, for many a year.

I agree with you about Howells, with certain qualifications. I value him so much mainly because he is by far the best man I have met with for my purpose,—Social experience seems so rare.

In haste, yours ever
ELG

To Edward Atkinson

Nation Office   New York, January 26, 1866
(Atkinson Papers, MHi)

DEAR ATKINSON: I think your letter so valuable, that I am going to use it as an editorial. For this purpose it will need to be somewhat remodelled. I would wait for your permission before doing so, but that your answer would come too late. So I shall risk it.

Yours very truly
ELG

To Charles Eliot Norton

February 6, 1866 (Ogden 2:37)

. . . I shall look for Emerson's article with great interest. But I am myself in a state of fog on the subject of religious worship out of which I fear I shall never get. I am giving up Frothingham *in toto* as an utter failure.[1] He has become more and more a snappish dialectician, and bores one just as much in showing what ought not to be believed as the orthodox in showing what ought. I was drawn to his church by my profound weariness of doctrines, but he discusses nothing but opinions, and I have come to the conclusion that the narrowest of all human beings are your "progressive radicals." They "progress" as I have seen many mules progress, by a succession of kick and squeals which make travelling on the same road with them perilous and disagreeable work. The transition period—supposing Emerson to be right—from

Christianity to the next form of belief or non-belief will be very trying and in many ways a disagreeable period. In fact we are in it now. . . .

1. The Unitarian pulpit orator Octavius B. Frothingham (1822–95) was an occasional contributor to the *Nation*.

To Charles Eliot Norton

Nation Office   New York, February 8, 1866
(Godkin Papers, MH)

MY DEAR NORTON: I am not at all surprized at what you report of Stearns. You may depend upon it, he is, as I told you he was [,] a bad man, with no principle and no honor. Abolitionism has taken with many such men as he, in this country, the place that the strict observance of religious forms does with others, and serves as a cloak for all sorts of moral aberrations. . . .
There is something certainly nauseating in having to consult every few weeks with a man, about his own lies, in order to help him to put a good face on them. . . .
Olmsted sees, and discusses and is responsible for everything that appears in the *Nation* except now and then a book notice. There is nothing merely nominal about his connection with it.

Yours very truly
ELG

To Charles Eliot Norton

Nation Office   New York, February 17, 1866
(Godkin Papers, MH)

MY DEAR NORTON: I enclose you ten copies of a circular which we have drawn up, and propose sending to persons who, we *know*, like the paper, and who, we *think*, would be likely to express a favorable opinion of it. The replies we intend to use as an advertizement. . . .
Stearns has been here and has told a good many lies. If he keeps on in this way, he will certainly be damned, which I should regret

on account of his family. He was to have seen Olmsted but poor Olmsted I regret to say is unwell, and I am afraid will break down completely, unless he breaks off all work for a while. I do not know what had better be done about him. He is greatly run down, does not sleep at night, and is unequal to any care or responsibility, and yet he has a great deal. . . .

In haste, ever yours
ELG

To Charles Eliot Norton

37 East 19th St., New York, February 20 [1866]
(Godkin Papers, MH)

MY DEAR NORTON: . . . I wrote to you yesterday about one or two other books, and the day before about Sedgwick. Howells is going to try doing the "Minor Topics" in Boston, but I do not think he will succeed, nor does he.[1] He will be too much occupied with other things. I shall be glad to have Mr. Sedgwick write once a month either on a "major" or "minor topic."[2] Tell him, for the "minor topics" to avoid as much as possible purely political, and Negro subjects. We have plenty of this in other parts of the paper. His notice of Butler's pamphlet is very good.

The *Commonwealth* opened on me furiously yesterday. I suppose you've seen the article. I am glad to have enraged the rascals so much, but when you read it, and remember that it comes from "Moral reformers," can you blame poor James Gordon Bennett for being what he is?

The Scientific notes *are* capital. Does Prof. Eliot perceive that we are run dry, however, and want a fresh supply?[3] I think it may be said we have decided to reduce the size on the date you mention; but don't talk of it.

I am a little puzzled how to deal with Johnson. Olmsted is very reluctant to have us bear hard on him. He (Olmsted) is afraid of the radicals—afraid that in protecting the Negro, in their wild thoughtless way, they will injure the whole structure of the government, and produce a fatal familiarity with arbitrary processes. This objection however lies rather to their character than their principles. They are, it must be confessed a sad pack to have control of affairs. Read Stevens's and Chandler's speeches—What stuff! Olmsted thinks, and I agree with him, that the first and great duty of the government is to provide thorough protection at the South for all classes in the enjoyment of all their rights, but this ought to be done with care and with as little departure as possible from the normal course of administration. There is a vague notion afloat, that if we only succeed in establishing universal suffrage we shall have the milenium in due course, and need give ourselves little trouble about what comes after. . . .

Ever yours
ELG

1. William Dean Howells had recently resigned his job on the *Nation* staff with Godkin's blessings to take an editorial post on the *Atlantic Monthly* in Boston.

2. Arthur G. Sedgwick (1844–1914), the brother-in-law of Norton, became a friend of Godkin and a leading contributor to the *Nation*, sometimes writing more for it than the editor. A lawyer as well as a journalist, he ended his life by suicide.

3. M.I.T. Professor Charles W. Eliot (1834–1926), soon to become president of Harvard, was an occasional contributor to the *Nation* on scientific topics.

To Charles Eliot Norton

Nation Office   New York, March 20, 1866 (Godkin Papers, MH)

MY DEAR NORTON: . . . To what extent may I draw upon you for assistance for the next three months? I shall need all I can get, but I am always afraid of taxing not your good nature, but your strength too severely. As regards my own health, it continues very good, but I often feel tired, and must get a holiday this summer. However, if the *Nation* succeeds I shan't care even if I am broken down somewhat. After that, perhaps I shall be glad to be removed.

I think you take rather too gloomy a view of the political situation. I have no confidence in Johnson, but I think his little effort to carry things by a *coup de main* has signally failed. I hope you are all well. Give my most cordial regards to the ladies.

Ever yours
ELG

To Charles Eliot Norton

Nation Office New York, April 5, 1866 (Godkin Papers, MH)

MY DEAR NORTON: . . . My father corresponds with the *Times* from Dublin—and has done so for many years on Irish questions of course; so Conway writes to the *Commonwealth* that this is probably the cause of the moderate view I have taken of the first *veto*, in my letters to the *Daily News!* Wonderful fellows—"the progressive friends!" . . . .[1]

1. Moncure D. Conway (1832–1907), the antislavery clergyman and publicist, was in England on extended leave from his post as editor of the *Commonwealth*.

To Professor William D. Whitney

Nation Office New York, April 7, 1866 (Whitney Papers, CtY)

MY DEAR SIR: The fact is that Mr. Welford who has done our "Literary Notes" from the beginning is gone to England. He will resume on his arrival there, but we shall not hear from him before the middle of this month.—He does them in my opinion, admirably, but in the meantime I have had to commit them, *faute de mieux*, to a man in whom on anything but the gossip of the American bookstores, I have very little confidence. I have been expecting from some quarter, some such remonstrance as yours for the last two weeks, and was consequently not surprized by your note. . . . My days and almost my nights are passed in trying to get men to write decently and with care on any subject. . . . As long as the available literary force of the country is so small, of course, we are exposed to occasional mishaps of this kind.

I mention all this rather by way of showing you the difficulties we have to contend with, than by way of defending our lapse on Sanskrit. . . .

Yours very truly
ELG

To Charles Eliot Norton

Nation Office   New York, April 19, 1866 (Godkin Papers, MH)

DEAR NORTON: I heard from Atkinson of the meeting, and judged from what he said, though he gave no particulars, that the tone of the discussion was unfavorable. I presume Stearns lied his way through. I should think also that Atkinson was feeling weak himself. I do not think myself, it is possible for the thing to succeed if bands of stockholders are all the time holding meetings and spreading reports about it, and I am in hopes some crisis will come which will change the whole regime. But I am not troubled at present. They cannot do us any harm. I have got $67,000 independent of the recruiting committee. . . .[1]

Yours most truly

ELG

1. Godkin is referring to the rule of the *Nation* Association that policy changes must have the support of two-thirds of the stock. Godkin wished to convert the *Nation* from a weekly to a twice-weekly publication and was seeking the approval of the stockholders for the change.

To Charles Eliot Norton

Nation Office   New York, April 20, 1866
(Unsigned, Godkin Papers, MH)

MY DEAR NORTON: . . . We shall vote the proposition down flatly this afternoon, come what may.[1] Whenever the stockholders choose to vote the paper down they may, but I shall not help Stearns to bring its destruction about. I care nothing for his "mixed motive." His case is no harder, nor . . . as hard as mine. I have induced my friends to put their money in, and have put my own, and am spending some years of my life over it. . . . G. and S. Ward think we ought not to yield an inch, on the point of editorial independence, and Sam has written a very strong letter on the subject, of which I shall send you a copy. They are both in favour of fighting it out to the last. Come what will, we shall not meet our fate helplessly, and I am determined that we shall make an example of Stearns today.—So don't feel troubled about us. He is simply a cunning and malicious old blackguard, and I think meets with far too much toleration. I will write an account of the meeting tomorrow.

1. Stearns had requested an opportunity at a stockholders' meeting to put to the stockholders his proposal for the formation of a committee of inquiry into the *Nation*'s affairs.

To Charles Eliot Norton

[21 April 1866] (Godkin Papers, MH)

. . . DEAR NORTON: I enclose a more formal letter, that you can show to others. Also one from S. G. Ward. Stearns got awfully mauled, and was beaten horse, foot, and dragoons. George Ward lost temper, and denounced him fiercely to his face for his perfidy. He (Ward) felt mortified by this afterwards, but Stearns richly deserved what he said, and as for me, I let loose the pent up wrath of months, and gave him my full mind, about all his performances though without excitement. It was perfect luxury, and I could not have died comfortably had I not done it. I also exposed several of his worst lies, and the man's condition, had he any moral sense would have been pitiable. . . .

In haste, yours as ever
ELG

To Charles Eliot Norton

April 22, 1866 (Ogden 1:246–47)

. . . I want to state to you, and through you to the Boston stockholders, a little more distinctly than I have ever done my position as regards the *Nation*. If necessary or desirable I will write out what I have to say in a separate letter, as a circular, but perhaps this may suffice.

When the editorship was offered me, I took it on the understanding, which was afterwards reduced to writing, that I was to be completely independent to any extent that an honorable man could be. Of course, I could not call myself an honorable man, if, having been converted to proslaveryism or secession, I failed instantly to resign. But it was never understood or hinted that I was to be inspired by, or was to edit the paper under the supervision of Major Stearns, or of any body else. No man of character or education would accept such a position. Moreover, a part of the inducement offered me was that the hugeness of the capital would insure a full trial of the experiment. The whole $100,000 was to be spent if necessary; but we hoped it would not be necessary. It was not to be a party paper. It was to devote a good deal of attention to the social and political condition of the blacks at the South, not as their organ, *but as one of the great questions* of the day. And it was to discuss this and all other questions in such a tone and style as to secure the attention of a class to which anti-slavery journals have never had access.

I, on my part, undertook not to produce a paper that would be certain to sell well, but to produce a good paper, one that good and intelligent men would say *ought* to sell, and whose influence on those who read it, and on the country papers, would be enlightening, elevating, and refining. Commercial success I never guaranteed. The whole thing was well understood to be an experiment, and it was this very fact that rendered a large capital so necessary.

I accordingly raised upwards of $20,000 amongst my friends here, and put in some money of my own. Some of those who have invested I shall feel bound in honor to reimburse if the thing fails, so that I shall really find myself in that event not only without recompense for my time, but actually out of pocket.

I started the work at short notice, in the hot weather, and under how many difficulties you know perhaps better than any one. I made some mistakes, and of course fell considerably short, as I fall still short, of my own ideal. On the appearance of the third number, Major Stearns got hold of a hasty private note of mine, interpreted it to suit himself, and made it the text of a pair of circulars, in which my character was assailed in the grossest and most insulting terms. I own I was greatly shocked to find that I was associated in any way with a person capable of such an act.

I think, from all I can learn, that I have fulfilled my share of the contract. The *Nation*, I am led to believe, is a good paper. Its influence is, I know, growing, and from this influence I expect pecuniary success ultimately to come. Mr. Stearns I cannot prevent from trying to injure it; but I feel bound in the interest of those who have confided in my honor and ability, to say nothing of higher interests than these, to oppose him by every means in my power.

At the same time I wish it to be clearly understood that I do not desire the *Nation* to be carried on as a personal favor to me. As soon as any sufficient number of the stockholders whom there is no ground for suspecting of personal hostility to me, come to the conclusion that it is of no value, I shall be glad to aid them in getting rid of it. But any such movement ought in decency to have some one else than Major Stearns at its head. . . .

To Charles Eliot Norton

Nation Office   New York, April 26 [1866] (Godkin Papers, MH)

MY DEAR NORTON: . . . You must do as you think best, about my letter touching the *Nation*. I have remained very silent for nine months, and my forbearance does not seem to have in the least "assuaged the malice" of my friend the Major, and the crew who make him do their dirty work. So if there is to be a general blow up, I think I ought to have my say. I do think that after all that has occurred it is rather hard for those who have borne the burden and heat of the day to find such a man as Stearns and his twelve thousand dollars, subjects of such tender consideration. I think we shall come out victorious yet. The *Round Table* will probably last only three or four more numbers. The remaining proprietor offered to sell out to Richards for $5000. He says the circulation is 3000.

In haste, ever yours
ELG

I have mislaid Ropes' address. Please send it to me. Is he competent to review Swinton's *Army of the Potomac?* [1]

1. Military historian John Codman Ropes (1836–99) of Boston.

To Charles Eliot Norton

Nation Office   New York, May 12, 1866 (Godkin Papers, MH)

MY DEAR NORTON: Stearns has been in town, conspiring with Cannon. They discovered or thought they discovered that the omission to call a meeting of the Trustees to confirm the action of the Stockholders was a fatal defect, and rendered us liable to be wound up. I thought not, but Cannon alleged thirty years experience in joint Stock Cos, so we called a meeting of the Trustees to rectify it, and Stearns was supposed to be in the meantime studying Blackstone—and Wheaton. Cannon under Detmold's manipulation, however, separated himself from the Major, and became friendly in his way. I doubt if we can get a quorum for the meeting. I wrote you in the first moments of alarm yesterday asking if you could come on, in case of necessity. I have consulted Judge Slosson this morning however, and he says there is nothing in Cannon's point whatever, so I am not going to trouble my head about it again, and you need not come on (unless you would like to do so!) Write a letter of apology to Detmold.

I have lost two days over this business, and the paper of course suffers. I wonder if Stearns is to be in heaven, and if he will there have stock in newspapers edited by his enemies, or if he will be allowed to run round and lie and intrigue as he does here? What do you think? I should like very much to know before expiring. Get Emerson to discuss this in the *North American!*

Love to all your household. Tell Eliot there is not much laugh left in me today.

ELG

To Charles Eliot Norton

Nation Office   New York, May 17, 1866 (Godkin Papers, MH)

MY DEAR NORTON: Since I wrote to you yesterday, I have had further consultation with Richards, and here is the result. . . .

   1. We are satisfied the enterprize cannot succeed in the hands of a large joint Stock Co. . . . While the publisher and I have been working away here, a portion of the Stockholders have been using the knowledge acquired by them as Stockholders to decry the concern, and spread the belief that it was a failure. . . .

   2. To get a company organized, to see that its machinery works smoothly and legally is in itself work for one man. This has all fallen on me in addition to my regular duties. The anxiety and trouble of it is too much for me. . . .

3. It is as absurd to try to produce a newspaper which forty different men selected at haphazard will like, as to produce a picture, book, or sermon. . . .

4. . . . We propose that the company be wound up; and that all who please withdraw their capital. That those who like the paper leave what remains in our hands or the hands of one or two trustees, who sympathize with us, say Mr. Blodgett, or G. C. Ward, or both, with absolute control. If in this and other ways we can secure $25,000 we will try it for another year—cutting it down to what it ought to have been at the beginning, 16 pages, charging $3 or $4 for it, and reducing all expenses to a minimum. We would both agree to draw only $2500 a year each for salary, until the paper was paying. . . .

Yours ever
ELG

To Charles Eliot Norton

Nation Office   New York, May 18, 1866 (Godkin Papers, MH)

MY DEAR NORTON: Many thanks for your letter. I see you had not got my last when it was written, though your plan and mine nearly coincide. I am willing to try the thing once more, if I can get $25,000 or better still $28,000. I would only draw $2500 as my salary until the paper was on a paying basis. Richards would stay on the same terms, and all things considered, we could not do better than to have him. He is honest, energetic, understands the business, has the connections, and is docile. . . . A sub editor at $1500 or $1200, is all else that would be necessary. Dennett might do, there is fine raw material in him, but he is slow, and it would be a question whether we could wait for him to acquire the necessary practice, and Garrison has done very well, and McKim has been angelic.[1]

But the essential thing would be that the money should be handed over to George Ward and Blodgett, or either, absolutely, and that no contributor should be entitled to interfere, or make enquiries or demand accounts. . . .[2]

I think the Stockholders here will be influenced (except Cannon, who is a bitter narrow bigot) by what you do in Boston. I may say the same thing for Philadelphia. But I doubt if the remnant of the stock will provide the necessary amount after the malcontents have been weeded out. Some further contributions would have to be made, and some money might I think be got here. Blodgett might be got to do a great deal, if asked by your set (you, Lowell and Co.) in Cambridge. It would flatter him immensely, to be made the instrument of carrying out such a scheme here and I suggest your writing to him. . . .

Very cordially yours
ELG

1. John R. Dennett (1838–74), literary editor of the *Nation* from 1868 to 1869 whose letters from the South were a prominent feature in the *Nation* during its first year. Like many of Godkin's writers, Dennett was recruited by Charles Eliot Norton.

2. William F. Blodgett was a rich New York stockholder in the *Nation*.

To Charles Eliot Norton

Nation Office   New York, May 23, 1866 (Godkin Papers, MH)

MY DEAR NORTON: I write in haste to say that S. G. Ward is not satisfied that the burden of deciding whether the money of these Boston gentlemen should be left in the concern, should be thrown on him, as it is by the paper they have sent him. He says truly, that he has not examined its affairs, and has no means of judging, whether it will succeed or not; that he leaves his money in because we are willing to try the experiment, and thinks others ought to do so too. Philbrick has struck his name out, and says he cannot afford to risk anything more. . . .[1]

In great haste, yours as ever
ELG. . . .

1. Edward Philbrick was a Boston stockholder in the *Nation*.

To Charles Eliot Norton

Nation Office   New York, May 28, 1866 (Godkin Papers, MH)

MY DEAR NORTON: . . . I think I see daylight, but the difficulties are great. Blodgett is very zealous, and I am glad you wrote to him. I sent him the letter. Cannon and Stearns want not only to wind the company up, but to prevent the paper going on in any one's hands. S. G. Ward is all right. . . .

ELG

To Charles Eliot Norton

Nation Office   New York, June 20, 1866 (Godkin Papers, MH)

MY DEAR NORTON: I have made one journey myself to Philadelphia and Garrison has made three, and is now there, negotiating the loan. We found them somewhat difficult. Sellers and others wanting a bonus, to be paid out of profits to compensate them for money already sunk. . . .[1] They were desirous of having McKim in, and he seemed to think himself entitled to be in, in virtue of his position of the original proprietor, and fast friend of the paper. I think that you are entitled to be in, on the same grounds, if you desire to be. Do you? I hope so. If so, I suggest, as an arrangement that seems to me just, that the new firm consist of us four; that as I have borne and have to bear nearly all the responsibility have, say one half, and that the other half be divided between you three. . . . If I could choose my employment for the next year, I would settle in the country, read, and write articles for the *North American* and forbid the introduction of newspapers into the house. I wonder if most men who are actively engaged are torn as I am by a longing for retirement. . . .

Ever yours
ELG

1. Manufacturer John Sellers, Jr., a Philadelphia stockholder in the *Nation*.

To Charles Eliot Norton

[6 July 1866] (Ogden 1:250)

. . . If the paper succeeds, I shall always ascribe it to you, as without your support and encouragement I do not think I should have been able to endure to the end. . . .

To Charles Eliot Norton

Nation Office   New York, July 18, 1866 (Godkin Papers, MH)

MY DEAR NORTON: . . . You asked for a history of proceedings since you left. I think I told you of the difficulties with the Philadelphians. The negotiations with them consumed a fortnight. . . . Jessup goes out, I am glad to say—as he never much liked the paper, and is afraid of free trade. ... . Field also declines, partly through inability to afford further risk, and partly through protectionism also. The Baltimore men stay in, and are very cordial. In Boston, Endicott signed, also Ames; [1] but Claflin refused, and was abusive. . . . Every one here signs except Cannon and the Minturn Estate. . . .[2]

When it came to arrange about the proprietorship, I found that McKim was intent on getting one third, and considered himself entitled to it. I wanted to have a third divided between him and you, but finding him so much in earnest, and that you did not much care, I let it go. The paper is now owned, one half by me; one third by McKim, and two sixths [*sic*] by Olmsted. I have complete control. The name of the firm is E. L. Godkin and Co. . . .

Richards remains on till our arrangements are completed. I am every day less and less satisfied with him, but want to part on good terms. After he goes I will either put in Garrison or an admirable man whom I have had my eye on for some time. . . .

Dennett is doing admirably, and is working clear of his diffidence, which was his greatest defect. I have arranged for him to stay on. . . .

Yours ever
ELG

1. Boston stockholder in the *Nation* Oakes Ames (1804–73) is remembered mainly for the notoriety he suffered during the Crédit Mobilier scandal of 1872.
2. The New York merchant and philanthropist, Robert B. Minturn, Sr. (1805–66), was one of the original New York stockholders in the *Nation*. He died soon after its founding.

4. This *Nation* Under Godkin

Godkin set about in the *Nation* to capture the best features of two highbrow English weeklies, the *Saturday Review* and the *Spectator*. In its literary criticism the *Nation* came close to rivaling the Tory *Saturday Review* in its palmy days, and in its pithy editorial leaders it rivaled the Liberal *Spectator* of R. H. Hutton and Meredith Townsend. Matthew Arnold and James Bryce thought the *Nation* the best weekly in the United States and perhaps in the world. For this, Godkin rightly is given credit, but without the volunteer help of Norton and the spartan office labors of Wendell P. Garrison the weekly would not have succeeded.

Contrary to legend, Godkin did not write most of the *Nation*, although he sometimes contributed as many as five pages to an issue. The lead political article was usually his, and with other contributors he wrote editorial paragraphs for "The Week," a topical miscellany, mainly political, at the front of the paper. The literary part of the paper he left to John Dennett and Garrison. The unsentimental Dennett, a talented Nova Scotian with an unfortunate tendency to carp, excited almost as much animosity from readers as Godkin. "They are very thin skinned people at *The Nation*," Thomas Bailey Aldrich irritably told E. C. Stedman, "and though they are fond of being saucy, they can't stand the least roughing themselves." "If six or seven of us younger fellows were to systematically rap Dennet [*sic*] across the knucks whenever we got the opportunity, it wouldn't make him courteous but it might teach him decency."

When it seemed that the olympian *Nation* might perish for lack of readers, Godkin tried without success to lighten its fare. "The cultivated class we have with us," he explained to Norton, "but the class next below do not know quite what to make of us, and are suspicious and hostile."

In his hard-hitting political and social articles Godkin directed his fire at anyone who violated the "laws of trade" and his elevated conception of culture. Toward this end he deplored Irish-American politicians, labor reformers, the "Western type of man," evangelical clergymen, the growing "servant problem," the eight-hour day, the failure of Americans to dress for dinner, "sentiment," ignorant immigrants, and universal manhood suffrage. He denounced "War Horse politicians," popular journalists, inflationists, noisy patriots, reactionaries, and reformers of all hue. An adherent of the "devil theory" of politics, he made many enemies by his resort in the *Nation* to personalities. To someone who remonstrated that political corruption in New York City was traceable not to individuals but to a "system," he characteristically retorted: "This city is badly governed owing to the bad conduct of certain men, and owing to nothing else under heaven."

Underneath Godkin's brusque, often icy, exterior lay a hearty appreciation of the ridiculous in man's affairs. When he was at his best, no one could match the force and humor, as well as common sense, of his editorials. This earned the *Nation* an admiration among nineteenth-century intellectuals unrivaled by any other journal in the United States. "The *Nation* was my first love," testified historian Worthington C. Ford, "and it has served as a weekly inspiration and counsellor for more than thirty years, and the longer I live the more do I hold to the political ideals it has maintained." In like vein historian Frederick Bancroft wrote, "In twenty-five years, I doubt if I have failed to read three numbers of the *Nation*. . . ." Young Woodrow Wilson kept careful notations from Godkin editorials in his notebooks while a student at Princeton University, and in Emporia, Kansas, young William Allen White learned from one of his professors that Godkin's journal was a model of literary and political excellence.

To credit to the influence of the Godkin *Nation* all of the judgments that late nineteenth-century American historians reached on the Gilded Age would be risky, but the *Nation*'s pronouncements carried greater weight with historians than the pronouncements of other journals. James Ford Rhodes, who became a disciple of the *Nation* in his student days at the University of Chicago, probably understated his debt to Godkin when he told Charles Francis Adams, Jr., "It is pleasant to know that your [historical] opinions agree so well with my own. . . . Like you . . . I have been profoundly influenced by the *Nation*." For example, a study of volumes six and seven of Rhodes's widely read history of the United States reveals that they are drawn almost exclusively from the *Nation*.

To Charles Eliot Norton

Hastings, New York, August 23 [1866] (Godkin Papers, MH)

MY DEAR NORTON: We got home on Monday, after a very pleasant trip. . . . But we have both come to the conclusion that travelling in America for pleasure hardly pays. The people with whom one has to *herd*, for herding it is are not pleasant, those whom we met were unusually disagreeable. Then the democratic plan of doing everything *en masse* is the grave of sentiment and often of real enjoyment. If you want to climb a mountain, or visit a scene, you can not either conveniently or cheaply—mostly not at all—get guide or horse or carriage to yourself. You go with a ruck of your "fellow citizens," to whose inane conversation you are compelled to listen, even in the sublimest scenes. . . .

I found everything going on well at the office. Garrison seems so far, worth a dozen Richards! . . .

I am spending the day at home—a very rainy one, and have just finished the last number of the *Revue*. The article on the "Precurseurs Italiens" is very interesting. That is the kind of "narrative article" which I think most valuable for a quarterly—but I think Parton's are better done.

The amount of reading that I find you and Lowell do, always plunges me in despair, after I come back from a visit to you. . . . The capacity for protracted and close application I have lost for ever and must now content myself with browzing [*sic*] along the roadside *chemin faisant*, like the donkies of the itinerant tinkers. . . .

Ever yours
ELG. . . .

To Charles Eliot Norton

Nation office   New York, September 1, 1866
(Godkin Papers, MH)

MY DEAR NORTON: I was going to send you 5 gallons of the Whiskey, as a contribution from me to your health and happiness, and a slight acknowledgment of all the good offices I had received from you. That I have not done so sooner has been due to delay in distributing the contents of the cask which lies at a friend's house here in town. I was, therefore, sorry to receive your check, but its arrival has so far marred my scheme, that I shall not now attempt to carry it out, and will watch for another opportunity. I will send the Whiskey early next week. I know, if it comes up to the sample I have tasted, that it is good.

I feel bound, in spite of your preliminary defence of yourself, to say that I think your "Poetry of the War," too strong.[1] I am satisfied that if some expressions are toned down, it will be more effective, and I shall take the liberty of doing it, reminding you, that I concede to you as editor of the *N. A. R.* the same omniscience that I claim for myself as editor of the *Nation*. I do not think you are as philosophical in literary as you are in political criticism;—you have less patience, and make fewer allowances. . . .

Johnson is shocking. He will come to a bad end. He is really stumping the North for Congress. I wonder why his managers do not make him either hold his tongue, or avoid polemics. The demand for the *Nation* for the last two weeks from the News agents has been greater than we could supply, and we are increasing our impression by 100 copies every issue in consequence. Subscriptions come in at the usual rate, but our expenses are small and I feel that we can meet them, and am happy. Garrison is doing excellently. There is a different atmosphere about the office. Dennett too is turning out very well. He is a little slow, but this is "a fault not unallied to virtue, and even capable of admiration." I have not had as much peace of mind since July 1865, as I have now. The only unsatisfied longing I have is for vengeance on the three rascally Stearns radicals. But in a "law abiding community," I suppose I must yearn for it in vain, and content myself with grinding my teeth, as General Govone, a Piedmontese friend of mine with whom I travelled in the east, used to do, over the annoyances of the road—and say—"Ah—si jamais je suis conquérant!"

I am glad Curtis is going to be penman of the Convention. His articles are excellent.

Your philosophical observations on travelling in the White Mountains are excellent, but not consolatory. On my return here with you "a hundred years hence," the mode of travelling

and the nature of the accomodation offered by the hotels of that
region will, I trust, be a matter of complete indifference to us
both, as we shall be so situated, that they can neither please us,
nor jolt us, nor make us visit the lions, and admire nature in company with batches of pork packers, shoe dealers, stock "operators," and gentlemen in the dry goods line—excellent and worthy
persons, but for whose company you don't care when in a sentimental mood, and whose conversation is neither elevating nor
instructive. We shall fly about through the hills by ourselves, and
flap our wings over the densely packed wagons and stages with
disdain.

Yours ever
ELG

You say nothing of Mrs. Norton. This means that she is very
well? and the baby? Love to her and all.

1. "More Poetry of the War," *Nation*, 6 September 1866, pp. 187–88.

To Charles Eliot Norton

[Fall 1866] (Ogden 1:292–93 [1])

. . . I write in haste to say that the practical men—Dana, for
instance, whom Olmsted or I consulted—are all of the opinion
that there is no chance whatever for Curtis.[2] We find no encouragement from anybody but Nordhoff. Everyone says that if
Greeley got wind of the scheme he would trample it out furiously. And in fact I fear that any further agitation of it might
prove injurious to Curtis hereafter. Greeley is as time-serving and
ambitious and scheming an old fellow as any of them. So I think
we had better drop it for the present, and hope and wish for the
good time coming. As long as the press is what it is, a kind of
moral and intellectual dunghill (excuse the strong language), it
will produce Tiltons and Greeleys—the fungi of our system,
and they will keep all men like Curtis out of the places they
ought to occupy. And we shall not have a better press as long as
the men of strong moral sense, who take to journalism, go off
crazy like most of our reformers. . . .

1. Ogden misdated the letter.

2. Godkin hurriedly wrote this when he learned Norton was starting a campaign to obtain his friend George W. Curtis a seat in the United States Senate. When Curtis ran anyway the *Nation* supported him, but Godkin refused any further support to Curtis's political ambitions, just as he declined to support a Cabinet post for James Russell Lowell, lending credence to the charge that the editor preferred the role of critic to the role of reformer. For Godkin's unfavorable estimate of Curtis's abilities see his letter to Norton on pp. 185–86 herein.

To Charles Eliot Norton

Nation Office   New York, September 21, 1866
(Godkin Papers, MH)

MY DEAR NORTON: I got the whiskey off today *at last;* I owe you many apologies for having delayed it so long. But I was disappointed several days in succession in getting a man to demijohn and box it . . . you had better keep the box for transportation to Cambridge unless indeed your consumption is more rapid than I suppose it to be. . . . I only wish we lived nearer to each other. The prospect of growing old in "New York Society" is often rather dismal to me. . . . If the *Nation* were once firmly established, I would certainly quit the city, and establish myself somewhere in the country. . . .

Your faithful friend
ELG

To Charles Eliot Norton

October 7, 1866 (Ogden 2:34)

. . . A new weekly magazine is about to be started here under the editorship of Mr. Howe and Edmund Kirke. All the New York litterateurs—the funny ones—are to be engaged on it. If the issue of magazines continues much longer at the present rate, I shall want to shake off this mortal coil. They are a fearful phenomenon. I have been thinking seriously for some weeks, now that my existence has become a little more tranquil than it was last year, of bringing out in England next spring, not the edition of my letters to the *Daily News*, which you have so often and so kindly advised, but a sort of "étude" on the struggle from 1860 to March, 1867, when it will probably end; that is, a sort of historical analysis of the political movements which accompanied the war and influenced it, and an examination or rather an account of the ideas which from time to time animated the various parties and sections of parties, and of the character, tone of mind, and so forth, of the leaders. Of course, I could not do this half as accurately or half as well as yourself or hundreds of other Americans, but I think I could do it better for Englishmen than any American has done it, or is likely to do it, because I know the English public better and see things more readily from their point of view. I should be compelled to say many things which would probably expose me to a tempest of abuse here. . . .

To Simon Newcomb

Nation Office   New York, October 27 [1866]
(Newcomb Papers, DLC)

DEAR SIR: Mr. Charles Norton encourages me in hoping that you will favor us with a review of Walker's "Science of Wealth" for the *Nation*. It need not exceed a page in length, and you can treat the book as you see fit.[1]

In any event, please to let me know at your earliest convenience.

Yours respectfully
ELG

Professor Simon Newcomb

1. This letter heralded the debut in the *Nation* of the noted astronomer and amateur political economist, Simon Newcomb (1835–1909). The belligerent Newcomb employed the columns of the *Nation* for thirty-five years to further his and Godkin's allegiance to laissez-faire.

To Charles Eliot Norton

8 West 48th St., New York [4 November 1866]
(Norton Papers, MH)

MY DEAR NORTON: I am annoyed by my absurd over sight about the promissory note. I trust you would not have done anything so foolish, as *not* to return, even if you had not been acting as trustee. I will send it on in proper form tomorrow or Thursday.

As regards the article, one of my chapters will be on "The Majority System," which haunts the minds of Englishmen.[1] I would try to show apropos of some rather foolish writing of Macauley's and of Hare's scheme of representation, that no mechanical contrivance can prevent the majority from ruling in the last resort in any free country. The majority will not respect your contrivance for preventing their tyranny any more than anything else. You have to choose between trusting to their good sense and good feeling, and to the influence on them of argument, and pathos, or else to govern by force. All restraints imposed must be imposed by themselves. Historically considered, the majority in the few cases in which they have possessed power have abused it less than minorities. A majority cannot continue to misgovern without feeling the effects themselves. Moreover the feeling so common that a minority is more apt to be right than a majority is based on a fallacy. It is amongst Englishmen almost a superstition. There is no certainty that either is right. An ass in a minority remains still an ass. Minorities have owed their political success mainly to their superior powers of combination, and their monopoly of knowledge, and education in past ages. The conditions of the experiment are however now totally changed. It is not through elaborate constitutions, and systems of balance of power, and checks, and minority representations, that the more odious forms of tyranny have disappeared, but because the people are wiser and more humane. Witches are no longer burned, or protestants, or quakers hanged, because these ugly old women, and the heretics are "represented," but because the majority are more enlightened. The fear that the poor would, if armed with power, confiscate the property of the rich is based on the supposition that the mediaeval division of society which the face of the Roman Empire left behind it will continue to exist, and does now exist—very wealthy men, and degraded proletarians. The class that confiscates must be a *hopeless* class. Otherwise it is *natural* to love security and peace. All social *instincts* forbid men from robbing their neighbors on a great scale. It has never been done except as *retribution.* The respect for property was never so strong amongst Frenchmen as after the Revolution. . . .

Much love from us both to you all, children included. Please answer at once.

Yours ever

ELG

1. E. L. Godkin, "The Tyranny of the Majority," *North American Review* 104 (January 1867): 205–30.

To Charles Eliot Norton

December 14, 1866 (Ogden 2:37)

. . . I was very glad to hear that you have been able to have the baby christened in a way satisfactory to yourself. You know I have not entirely got rid of the mediaeval faith in forms, and, although I have never been able to muster courage to get my own children christened, I am glad to find any of my friends able to manage it. I trust Lily may find the ceremony really "the outward and visible sign of an inward and spiritual grace," and her father and mother may long retain it as a happy memory. God bless the whole party who were present at it! . . .

To Charles Eliot Norton

[1866] (Ogden 2:72–73)

. . . There is something very charming about Lowell—something of the European flavor which, you will forgive me for saying, makes an American, when he has it, the best style of man in the world. . . .

To Charles Eliot Norton

[ca. 1866] (Ogden 2:51)

. . . Ten years hence, if things go on as they are now, I shall be the most odious man in America. Not that I shall not have plenty of friends, but my enemies will be far more numerous and active. . . .

To Edward Atkinson

Nation Office   New York, January 12, 1867
(Atkinson Papers, MHi)

MY DEAR ATKINSON: I am reminded by the article from the *Boston Advertizer* which you have been good enough to send me how derelict I have been about writing to you. I have on my table some pamphlets on cotton which you sent me some time ago, and which I have been keeping till the Christmas pressure was past to have worked up into something about the crop and its prospects. I read your letter in the *Evening Post* with great interest. It is the first bit of good information I have ever seen about the present manufacturing population of New England, and I don't think there is any piece of humanity in America more interesting, for there is none that is likely to excite a larger influence on the political and social condition of the east at least.

Wells' pamphlet is very good, though in places a little rusty. But how much of it will they pay any attention to? . . .

Yours very truly
ELG

To George P. Marsh

Nation Office   New York, January 20, 1867
(Godkin Papers, MH)

MY DEAR SIR: I enclose you a statement of your account, agreeably to your request, and trust you may find it satisfactory. . . .

Judging from the outrageous and disgraceful attack on Mr. Motley, by Mr. Seward, of which we had the news this morning, I am afraid you will not long be spared, or any other man of character and standing in the service of the government.[1] Johnson and Seward seem to have completely lost their heads, and I doubt if there is now any means of avoiding an impeachment —which I for one—however, it may end, shall look on as a great calamity.

With best regards
Yours very truly
ELG

Honorable G. P. Marsh.

1. A reference to the difficulties between historian John L. Motley (1814–77) and Secretary of State Seward. Shortly afterwards, Motley resigned as United States minister to Austria, but Marsh retained his post as minister to Italy, serving in it until his death in 1882.

To Edward Atkinson

Nation Office   New York, January 30, 1867
(Atkinson Papers, MHi)

MY DEAR ATKINSON: . . . I hope to show you next week, that we are not wrong about what Mr. Sumner said. I think he does not weigh his words very carefully, and when he finds the construction which other people naturally put upon them, he feels wronged. For instance, he denied stoutly the sense which we attached to the "Whitewashing" speech, but when afterwards Johnson turned out to be the very kind of fellow which he then pronounced him, he boasted in Boston, and since in Washington of having used it in the very sense we attributed to it.

I can assure you—and I wish there was any use in assuring him, that nobody here, has the slightest wish to do him injustice, or even find fault with him unnecessarily, or captiously. Nobody has a higher respect for his character and services than I have, but I cannot take the lofty estimate of all his intellectual efforts that he does himself. This may be a misfortune, but if I were to be shot for it, I cannot get over it. If I am not right in what he objects to in the *Nation,* I will make the amplest amends.

Yours very truly
ELG

To Daniel Coit Gilman

Nation Office   New York, January 31, 1867
(Gilman Papers, MdBJ)

MY DEAR SIR: Your article on the schools will appear next week. The statement on the 4th page, where you say that you can name towns in which "the public schools have swallowed up the parochial institute," has startled some people to whom I have repeated it—who say they have never heard of "parochial schools" in this country. Is this your last word on it?

Yours

ELG

To The Reverend Henry W. Bellows

10 West 48th St., New York, February 4 [1867]

(Bellows Papers, MHi)

MY DEAR DR. BELLOWS: I suppose you have been astonished by my apparent inattention to your request with regard to your friend's proposed amendment to the Constitution.[1] My long silence has been due to the fact, that shortly after I received it, the printed copy was utterly defaced by an accident, and in order to replace it, I was obliged to wait on the printer's convenience who has been in his turn, delayed by a strike. I now enclose you two copies of the new edition, with many apologies for the mishap.

I do not publish it because it is not so much the form of an amendment we need, I think, as a public sentiment favorable to the change. That we have not got, but I think it is coming. I think every year is bringing people to the conclusion, that democracy to be successful must rest on intelligence, and that modern republicans must be reading republicans, and that an ignorant citizen is but one degree removed from a traitor or alien enemy.

I remain, dear Sir, very faithfully yours

ELG

Rev. H. W. Bellows D.D.

1. A constitutional convention was meeting in Albany to draw up a new constitution for the State of New York. The voters rejected it.

To Daniel Coit Gilman

Nation Office   New York, March 13, 1867

(Gilman Papers, MdBJ)

MY DEAR SIR: In your last batch of "Notes" which will appear next week, you say the value of the new Bureau of Education will depend very much on the person placed at its head, etc. Since then, as you have seen, Barnard has been appointed.[1] Will you please forward me an expression of opinion about him to go in the note. I hear him well spoken of; but his Life of Colonel Colt —"Armsmear"—reads like the work of a half educated lunatic. If you have never seen it, do get a peep at it. He ascribes all the glories of "Armsmear" to "one seminal pistol-idea!"

Yours very truly
ELG

Professor Gilman

1. Educational reformer Henry Barnard (1811–1900) had been appointed United States Commissioner of Education.

To Charles Eliot Norton

March 18, 1867 (Ogden 1:295)

. . . Goldwin Smith's letter is very interesting, but I think his view of public affairs is colored by his dismal life. It is very sad to think that a man of his aims and powers should be so situated. But the aristocracy and middle classes are not so bad as he thinks they are—that is, they are not so ready for desperate courses, or so impervious to the voice of reason and humanity. If they were, England would never have produced such men as it does produce in every generation. Figs do not grow on thistles, and Brights and Cobdens and Gladstones and Smiths are not produced by such a society as he describes. Still, I think the class feeling in England, and the worship of wealth and rank, do develop and have developed a kind of paganism, and a real brutality, which would long ago have ruined the country, if the *race* had not had so many fine qualities. English flunkeyism, accompanied as it usually is by an almost total absence of sympathy with people of a different class or social position, is one of the most detestable sights in the world.

Did you see poor Sumner's last "bill" and "resolutions"? What a pitiable spectacle! Was there *ever* anything in the man, and if so, what has become of it? I felt so grateful to Fessenden, ungentlemanly though he was, for sticking his pin into the bladder. How long shall we have to treat such people with tenderness and respect! When I think of my dinner at the "Radical Club," with Sumner opposite me smiling like a benign god on his disciples and dispensing wisdom piecemeal, it seems as if I must have dreamed it all.[1] If the *Nation* will only live, and give us all a chance some day to speak out our minds as Agassiz says—"without reticence". . . .

1. A reference to Massachusetts' Senator Charles Sumner and to the Radical Club of Boston, devoted to the philosophical discussion of political and social questions.

To Charles Eliot Norton

April 3, 1867 (Ogden 1:292)

. . . George Curtis dined with us on Sunday, and was as usual very entertaining. His Connecticut experiences were very amusing. Barnum told him the article in the *Nation* was written by the Copperheads in Connecticut and sent on to New York to be published as a matter of form. The Copperheads had it reprinted on a fly-leaf, a broad-sheet, and circulated by the thousand. "Tant mieux," say I, but the politician breed look on this as awful. Barnum was badly "scratched" by the Republicans and ran far behind his ticket even in Bridgeport—showing that a good word, spoken at the right season, even by "an obscure literary paper," as the *Tribune* savagely called it, is not spoken in vain. It has had two attacks on us of this childish, silly kind, exhibiting the newspaper mind in its most degraded condition, and would you believe it, Ripley (aet. 62) thought them "capital!" [1] We surely must all keep at work. . . .

1. A reference to Congressman William H. Barnum (1818–89) of Connecticut and to George Ripley (1802–80), the literary editor of the New York *Tribune*.

To Charles Eliot Norton

[ca. 19 April] 1867 (Ogden 2:44–45)

. . . There is one other subject, which, however, I should like to write [for you] about, because I have got my ideas about it ready, and that is the present aspect of the labor question, *à propos* of the strikes, and general disturbance of the relation of employer and employed all over the world.[1] I think I could show that in this matter the law of supply and demand, by which economists dispose of it, does not cover the case; that the workingman's poverty, ignorance, and social position, prevent his being what the economists assume him to be, a free agent contracting with full knowledge, and yet the ordinary condemnation of strikes, which one hears so often, is based on this assumption. The strike of the English engine-drivers and, in fact, the whole system of combination, I consider a remarkable indication of the general eagerness of men of all classes to get rid of the arbitrary rule of individuals, and get under the government of *law.* A little outline of what I should like to say will appear in the next *Nation.* . . .

1. E. L. Godkin, "The Labor Crisis," *North American Review* 105 (July 1867): 177–213.

To Charles Eliot Norton

April 23, 1867 (Ogden 1:297)

. . . There is a man named Barnard here on the bench of the Supreme Court. Some years ago, in the early part of his career, he kept a gambling saloon in San Francisco, and was a notorious blackleg and *vaurien.* He came then to New York, plunged into the lowest depths of city politics, and emerged Recorder (criminal judge). After two or three years there, he got by the same means to be a judge of the Supreme Court, and married a rich woman. His reputation is now of the very worst. He is unscrupulous, audacious, barefaced, and corrupt to the last degree. He not only takes bribes, but he does not wait for them to be offered him. He sends for suitors, or rather for the counsel, and asks for the money as the price of his judgments. A more unprincipled scoundrel does not breathe. There is no way in which he does not prostitute his office, and in saying this I am giving you the unanimous opinion of the bar and the public. His appearance on the bench I consider literally an awful occurrence.[1]

This man by sheer force of money got a bill passed at the last session of the Legislature, authorizing the Governor to confer on one judge the sole and exclusive right to transact all the Chamber business of the Supreme Court,—that is, to hear all *ex-parte* motions, make all references, grant injunctions, and so forth,—an enormous power which the best man is not fitted to exercise, and which may be grossly abused. He has, I am informed, so effectually bought up the executive council that the bill was signed without difficulty, and he secured Greeley's support with the Governor to get his appointment, the *Tribune* lawyer acting as go-between, and the bestowal of the legal advertizing (which will be in his gift) on the *Tribune*, being part of the consideration. The fact that Barnard has quarrelled with the regular "ring," and fights them in the courts, gives the *Tribune* an excuse for supporting him, and Greeley, I believe, tries to persuade himself that by an alliance with men of this stamp here and with "Miles O'Reilly," he can win over a portion of the dregs of the Democracy to the Republican party. The *Tribune* accordingly came out this morning in Barnard's favor. Besides having the *Tribune* enlisted in this way, he owns part of the *World*; he has bought up the *Herald*, and works on the *Times*, I know not how. I went to see Nordhoff, who has spoken freely against the transactions, but he says he dare not say more. All the facts I have mentioned would be rather difficult to prove; lawyers do not like to come forward, as Barnard might damage their business, and Nordhoff is afraid of libel suits, and feels it to be hopeless. He has written twice to the Governor, warning him against the deep damnation of this thing, but doubts if it will produce any effect. In fact, the press and bar are muzzled, that is what it comes to, and this infamous scoundrel has actually got possession of the highest court in the State, and dares the Christian public to expose his villainy.

If I were satisfied that, if the public knew all this, it would lie down under it, I would hand the *Nation* over to its creditors, and take myself and my children out of the community. I will not believe that yet. I am about to say all I dare say—as yet—in the *Nation* tomorrow. Barnard is capable of ruining us, if he thought it worth his while, and would and could imprison me for con-

tempt, if he took it into his head, and I should have no redress.
You have no idea what a labyrinth of wickedness and chicane
surrounds him. Moreover, I have no desire either for notoriety or
martyrdom, and am in various ways not well fitted to take a
stand against rascality on such a scale as this. Moreover, charges
which cannot be proved in court, there is very little use in making. But this I do think—that it is the duty of every honest man
to do something towards exposing the crew of trading editors
like Greeley, Tilton and Company, who have crawled into fame
and fortune and influence on the negro question and are now
using their power in aid of the schemes of the worst class even
of their political enemies. Greeley's support of Barnard is a coun-
terpart of his Fenianism. He has grown into an intriguer and enjoys it. Barnard has now got possession of the courts, and if he
can silence the press also, where is reform to come from?

The doings of the last Legislature at Albany have been shocking—far worse than appears in the papers, and I fear there is
little hope of reform from the regular politicians. They are all
banded together for plunder, no matter how much difference of
opinion they may effect on the reconstruction question, or "the
equal suffrage" question. If the country is to be saved and puri-
fied, it must be by some force outside their ranks—that is, by
an energetic movement on the part of the best class of men, of
the class who carried the war through. The Union League Club
here shows some signs of an awakened conscience, but how much
it will do I cannot tell. The men who manage it are a very poor
set—I mean mentally. I think some movement in this direction
ought to be set on foot everywhere, having for its object the
hunting down of corrupt politicians, the stoppage of unscrupulous nominations, the exposure of jobs, of the sale of franchises
and votes, and the sharpening of the public conscience on the
whole subject of political purity. If this cannot be done, the
growing wealth will, you may rely on it, kill—not the nation,
but the form of government without which, as you and I believe,
the nation would be of little value to humanity. . . .

1. The object of Godkin's censure, Judge George G. Barnard, was impeached by the New York State Senate five years later and removed from
his post.

To Charles Eliot Norton

10 West 48th St., New York, May 4 [1867]
(Norton Papers, MH)

My dear Norton: Shearman will furnish you the article on the administration of justice in New York. He knows all the ins and outs of it, and though he cannot dress the story up as Parton would, he is a clear forcible writer, and will I think make a readable and telling article, which ought to create a sensation. It is a horrid and repulsive story. Shearman's faults of style are numerous, but he has the greatest of all merits—perspicacity.[1] It will be ready by June 1. and will occupy about 25 pages.

                                        Yours as ever. . . .
                                        ELG

1. Thomas G. Sherman (1834–1900) was a law partner of David Dudley Field in New York. Later Godkin changed his good opinion of him.

To Daniel Coit Gilman

Nation Office   New York, May 4 [1867]
(Gilman Papers, MdBJ)

My dear Sir: I do not know what else you had in your mind, but what you have sent is almost exactly what we want. . . . Everything relating to schools, schoolbooks, teachers, professors, colleges, and or that can be put into detached paragraphs of a reasonable size will come in very well. Anything you can do to expose the humbugs of education—there must be a great many—will be very acceptable also.

You can send me a supply of this sort of thing, as fast as it comes to you for the present, and then regulate the quantity according to the proportion of it you see used, in the paper. . . .

                                        Very truly yours
                                        ELG

To Charles Eliot Norton

May 9, 1867 (Ogden 1:301–2)

. . . Affairs in this State have confessedly never been so low, and we shall see in the manner in which the labors of the Convention are received, how much recuperative power we have got amongst us.[1] Evarts, Curtis says, thinks we are witnessing the decline of public morality which usually presages revolution. But he is somewhat of a croaker, though one of the clearest heads in America—a political *thinker* of the highest order. Barnard is squelched, but he said aloud on the bench "that he had spotted the fellows who opposed him" and as he *ran* Tammany, he "would be even with them." I beg of you to use what influence you have now, not for the promotion any longer of the virtues of pity, humanity, sympathy, generosity, and so forth,—for of these we have an abundance—but for the promotion of the habit of thinking clearly about politics, of looking disagreeable facts sternly in the face, of legislating not as if men were lumps of clay that a Congressional Committee can fashion at its pleasure, but for men as we find them with their passions, prejudices, hates, loves, and defects of all sorts. We are saying this every day to the English about the Irish; ought we not apply the lesson to the work before us? The negro, I think, is safe. I would insist on equality for him at any cost, but do not let us ruin the country in order to set him up in business. At the bottom of all these confiscation schemes, there are rascals you may be sure. . . .

1. A reference to the recently concluded New York State constitutional convention.

To Simon Newcomb

Nation Office   New York, May 22, 1867
(Newcomb Papers, DLC)

DEAR SIR: Although I agree with you generally on politico-economical questions—there is a passage in your notice of Gibbon's book which I am unable to swallow.[1] I enclose you the proof with the passage marked. You will find it difficult I think to persuade me, that if a dollar is taken from me, who am using it in my business, and is devoted to the paying off of a portion of the national debt, or in other words handed over to a bondholder, there is "an increase of one dollar in the productive capital of the country." There is the transfer of a dollar, it seems to me, from one hand to another, but this is all. The legitimate consequence of such a theory, is that a national debt is a national blessing is it not?

> Yours truly
> ELG

Professor Newcomb

1. "The Public Debt," *Nation*, 6 June 1867, pp. 452–53.

To Moses Coit Tyler [1]

Nation Office   New York, May 25, 1867 (Tyler Papers, NIC)

MY DEAR SIR: Lest you should think that our failure to annex your name to your articles, is due to any desire to rob an able man of his due credit and appropriate it to ourselves let me say, that our present plan of the anonymous has been resolved upon, and is adhered to, after mutual consideration, as the only plan, by which a periodical can be kept up to a really high standard. The publication of names, of writers, by shifting the responsibility as to quality from the editor's shoulders makes him careless as to quality, and in part converts his paper into a dumping ground in which "celebrities" shuck their rubbish. Moreover, it makes writers careless, too, because "names," have acquired such a potency, that in the existing state of culture in America, a good many men, are enabled under cover of them to palm off trash on the reader—Witness Everett's balderdash in the *New York Ledger*. Then also, if you publish one man's name, you have to publish all, and publishing all, any week you are not able to get some distinguished body to "scratch off" something for you, people think the number a poor one, though it may contain excellent writing, and the editor's office is reduced to that of a canvasser for articles—or in other words a rag and bone collector. Our motto, therefore, is—"Good Writing—hang names"! . . .

Yours very truly
ELG

1. Historian Moses Coit Tyler (1835–1900) was an occasional contributor to the *Nation*.

To Frederick Law Olmsted

Nation Office   New York, June 24, 1867 (Olmsted Papers, DLC)

Dear Olmsted: Would there be any use or any propriety in my seeing the chair of Political Economy and Jurisprudence—if there will be such a thing in the Cornell Univ? There ought to be such a chair, and my claims to it, are of course, on the surface small. I am a foreigner, and have produced no book, and have neither the faculty nor the habit of making my merits known. But I think I can say without indelicacy or self deception, that as far as my experience goes, there are but few men in the country—few young men certainly, who have given as much attention to these subjects as I have. I am a little rusty in my reading, but this could be speedily remedied.

It has occurred to me that it might be possible to do the work required in this department by simply spending one or two or three months at Ithaca, while residing in New York, and by the time the thing comes into operation, the *Nation* will be dead or a success.

I should of course be glad of pay, but would be gladder still of some good work of this kind, on which my reading and thinking could be brought to bear, and in which I would have a hearing from young men, who have not begun to read the *Tribune*.

If you give an adverse opinion either on what you know of me or what you know of White, of course the matter drops.[1] If you think well of it, I would move further.

Yours ever
ELG

1. A reference to Andrew D. White (1832–1918), the president of the newly founded Cornell University.

To Moses Coit Tyler

Nation Office   New York, June 29, 1867 (Tyler Papers, NIC)

MY DEAR SIR: I am not aware that there was any change made in your articles except to shorten them, so as to get both within the compass of one number, and this was a work of necessity, as we were close on the end of the volume, and had much standing matter. I do not think they were improved in the process, but I do not think they were seriously damaged. I can quite understand your objection even to this, but I can only say in reply, that it is only the editors of quarterlies, or yearlies, if there be such things, who can supply vows that they will never take liberties of this kind with an author's MS. What with the pressure of time, pressure of space, instantaneous action is constantly necessary. An editor has to be independent within the limits of ordinary moral responsibility, or he may as well, retire into civil life. . . .

Yours very truly
ELG

To Andrew D. White

Nation Office   New York, July 15 [1867] (White Papers, NIC)

DEAR SIR: I understand that you, or the Committee of which you are a leading member, are engaged in making appointments to the professorships in the Cornell University. If the Chair of Political Economy, with which I would take the liberty of suggesting, Jurisprudence ought to be combined—be not already filled, I propose to offer myself as a candidate for it. I have made both these subjects my study for many years, and although I have not produced any formal treatise on either of them, I think I can satisfy you of my fitness for the position, if no other arrangements have as yet been made.

I understand the professorship to be a non resident one, and this contributes one of its main attractions for me, as I could not leave New York permanently.

I beg, therefore, on the strength of my slight acquaintance with you to ask you to be good enough to tell me, whether the field be still open, and what should be the nature of the evidence I ought to offer of my fitness. I am very well known to Messrs. F. L. Olmsted, D. C. Gilman, and Chas. E. Norton of Cambridge. The first and last are my most intimate friends, and I am sure would be glad to give you any information you might seek as to my character and qualifications.[1]

Yours respectfully
ELG

1. President White, after considering warm letters in Godkin's behalf from Olmsted, Norton, and George W. Curtis, decided not to hire the editor. Godkin's wish to see Political Economy combined with Jurisprudence arose from the fact that as a youth he studied the two under one professor at Queen's College, Belfast.

To Daniel Coit Gilman

Nation Office   New York, July 20 [1867]
(Gilman Papers, MdBJ)

MY DEAR SIR: The more I have thought of the article you suggested on college degrees, the better I like it. . . . Universities, as at present constructed are approaching a grave crisis in their history. The utilitarian eye of "the age," is being turned on them, as well as on everything else, and it is absolutely necessary to their usefulness, and influence, that they be divested of all sham and humbug. Moreover, if the system of granting degrees as rewards of merit, or as indication, of a certain degree of proficiency, is to be continued, it is a kind of fraud on the public and on the men who have earned them in the regular way, to bestow them arbitrarily, and as mere tokens of the approval and admiration of the Faculty. And, lastly, there is perhaps no country in which so many quacks, charlatans and pretenders in the fields of literature and science are to be met with, as in this. The public, however, has no means of detecting them, and the colleges instead of helping to expose and weed them out, aids them with their diplomas in keeping up the cheat. . . .

Very truly yours
ELG

Professor D. C. Gilman

To Charles Eliot Norton

10 West 48th St., New York, July 24 [1867]
(Norton Papers, MH)

MY DEAR NORTON: Your note reached me last night, and Fanny arrived very prettily from New Haven this morning, so that I am enabled to join her most hearty congratulations to my own, on the birth of your son. That he may be worthy of his father and mother, and delights their eyes and hearts through many happy years, is the earnest prayer of both of us. We—you and I, I mean —have as you say, many causes for joy and rejoicing. I have hardly any greater than the accident which brought us together, and which has made your pleasures and pains so nearly my own. I trust as our children grow up they may take as much comfort in their fathers' friendship as I do.

Give our best love to Mrs. Norton. She knows I am not a poet, and perhaps rejoices in it; but tell her that such prose as I have at command cannot fully express how glad we both are that she is safe, and well, and happy.

Your affectionate friend
ELG

To Charles Eliot Norton

August 1, 1867 (Ogden 1:300–301)

. . . On Saturday Governor Fenton was in town and I went with Nordhoff to see him, taking with me a witness to some of Barnard's rascalities. We stayed an hour with him, and found that the pressure of *rich men* here in favor of Barnard was enormous. They know he has quarrelled with "the ring," and therefore are willing to use him to put it down, on the plan of setting a thief to catch thieves, just as in 1856 they publicly signed a paper re-commending Fernando Wood to the voters for the Mayoralty, well knowing that he was a convicted swindler and forger. They count in this way on protecting their own property for the present, and know that Barnard will not assail them, and for judicial purity, or for the future of the community, apparently care nothing. This is just the same kind of bourgeois selfishness and baseness which led to the *coup d'état* in Paris in 1851. Not one of these men denies the badness of Barnard's character. Fenton heard all we had to say patiently, and seemed alarmed and anxious to do right, and finally said that his difficulty was that everybody refused to put the charges against Barnard in writing. We then got a letter from D. D. Field, offering to prove that B. had forced a client of his to share the amount of a judgment with him, as a condition of deciding in his favor.[1] This settled the matter, I think, I did not see Fenton afterwards, but we heard he would make no appointment and leave the Constitutional Convention to settle the courts. So far, we have succeeded; but the root of the evil—the debauched popular sentiment, the indifference of many "leading citizens" to what is in reality the foundation of political society, judicial purity and independence—remains, and must be attacked in some way. The discoveries I have made on this point during the last two or three weeks are perfectly sickening. I shall thank God when the anti-slavery and negro question is fairly disposed of, and we can get a fair range at the corrupt rascals who grew up under it. The *Tribune*'s and Greeley's share in this matter has been positively shocking. The managing editor, Young, is a friend of Barnard's and Hackett's (another scoundrel), and took a trip to Florida with them this winter, the trip being paid for with some of Hackett's plunder.[2] Greeley supported this nefarious bill with all his might, and Fenton acknowledged to us that Williams, the *Tribune*'s lawyer, was Barnard's chief advocate with him. The consideration was to be "references" for Williams, legal advertizing for the *Tribune*. . . .

1. A reference to the prominent New York legal reformer David Dudley Field (1805–94), in whose offices Godkin read law in 1857.

2. A reference to John Russell Young (1840–99), managing editor of the New York *Tribune*.

To Edward Atkinson

Nation Office   New York, September 19, 1867
(Atkinson Papers, MHi)

DEAR ATKINSON: I have published both your articles in one this week.[1] I thought it better to do so than drag on any longer, but in order to do so, I was obliged to cut it one or two paragraphs. I endeavoured to select ones which did not seem necessary to the thread of the argument, and hope you will agree with me.

I was very glad you took Butler up. He and some of the men of the lower order (normally) of republican politicians, are trying to hit on a popular "cry," and they are hankering after repudiation. These men always underrate popular principle. They ought on this point to get no quarter.

Yours
ELG

1. "Real Nature of Legal Tenders," *Nation*, 19 September 1867, pp. 234–35.

To Charles Eliot Norton

September 22, 1867 (Ogden 1:302–3)

. . . I sent you a scrap of Nordhoff's stuff yesterday. It amazes me to read such immoral trash. An ignorant, unthinking "Red" in charge of an influential newspaper is an unpleasant sight, and I am afraid that is what must be said of it. When he talks of "the people having a right to misgovern," he most probably does not know what he means, and this is perhaps the kindest construction we can put on his balderdash. Godwin has come home with more of his history ready.[1] The "historians" here, however, are considerably embarrassed by "George's departure. They do not know which way to turn when in difficulties.

Macmillan, the London publisher, has turned up here—an excellent plain Scotchman, humorous and a good story-teller. I am sorry you will miss him in Boston, as he is a capital contrast to the dirty and silent Englishmen of whom you have had such a run.[2] . . .

1. A reference to New York journalist Parke Godwin (1816–1904), to whom Godkin tried to sell the *Nation* in 1881.
2. Meanwhile, Alexander Macmillan was telling John Morley that he found Godkin "about the soundest, *sanest* man" he met in New York, although a "little odd." Charles L. Graves, *Life and Letters of Alexander Macmillan* (London 1910), pp. 279–80.

To Professor William D. Whitney

Nation Office   New York, October 11, 1867
(Whitney Papers, CtY)

MY DEAR SIR: . . . I have read your preface carefully, and also our own announcement, and although I endeavor as a matter of conscience to cultivate a proper readiness to "own up," I am bound to say I do not think there is any essential variation from your own explanation in our mention of the book. Will you not read both over again? Mr. Dennett who writes the "Notes" is a very conscientious painstaking man. Still we shall in the next number, give your own statement of the matter, though not of course, as if coming from you.[1]

　　　　　Believe me, in haste, very truly yours
　　　　　ELG

1. A fault of Godkin, acknowledged by his closest admirers, was his reluctance to admit error.

To James M. McKim

10 West 48th St., New York, November 5 [1867?]
(Godkin Papers, MH)

MY DEAR MCKIM: I have had both your letters, and have been going to write every day, but the burden of the *Nation* has fallen rather heavily on me ever since I came home. Your squib about the *Advance* is very amusing, but I hesitate about publishing it.[1] We have [raked?] the tribe up so badly that I am inclined to let them alone, except when their immoralities are too flagrant to be passed over. . . . I doubt if I have ever seen a mixture of humbug and piety.

The "Broad Churchmen" of this and the adjacent dioceses, headed by Washburn of Calvary, Potter of Grace (son of the bishop etc.) are going to get up a monthly paper to advocate their peculiar views. They say they want to do for the religious press, which in its present state sickens them, "what the *Nation* has done for the political press," and they want to issue it exactly the same size, appearance etc. as the *Nation*. A deputa-

tion of them came to me last week, to ask if we would take
charge of the publication of it, so as to save them clerking [,]
publishing, office rent etc., etc., and I have half agreed to do so.
Mr. Garrison thinks, we can work it perfectly well without increasing our staff, and we might make a couple of thousand a
year by it. What do you think of the effect of its issue in the
same style as the *Nation*, and of our selling it over the counter,
on our position and reputation? Of course, we have nothing
whatever to do with the editing. The mere invitation by such
people, is I think a very high compliment to us, and would undoubtedly extend the knowledge of us amongst the heathen.

I hope you are having a good time, and will come back bound-
ing like the roe. The *Nation* is doing better every month, and
the crimes and immoralities of the Phillipians and Butlerites increases; but the Lord has delivered them into our hand. Ben is
elected, but he will avenge himself.[2] I would bet on him. . . .

Yours ever

ELG

1. A reference to a Congregational religious journal published in Chicago.
2. A reference to the Radical supporters of Wendell Phillips and Benjamin F. Butler and the reelection of Butler to Congress.

To Charles Eliot Norton

December 4, 1867 (Ogden 1:303)

. . . I am about, though with some reluctance, to give a letter
of introduction to you to Mr. John Morley, the editor of the
Fortnightly Review, and a Saturday Reviewer of some years'
standing. He is going into political life, and has come out here
for the usual preliminary training. He is a very sensible and
good fellow, though not hilarious; is well dressed and mild man-
nered. I found he was not likely to see anybody in Boston of any
particular value, and as he is to a greater or less extent an influence in England, I thought it desirable he should see you.
You will have the consolation of knowing that nearly all the
statesmen of the new régime in England have passed through
your hands. . . .

To Daniel Coit Gilman

Nation Office   New York, December 26, 1867
(Gilman Papers, MdBJ)

MY DEAR SIR: I have given Mr. McKim, who has a small pecuniary interest in the *Nation*,[1] but is a very warm friend of it on other grounds, a note to you. He is going out west, and wants to start with an expression of opinion about the paper, from persons of weight in the east, which will enable him to recommend it, on *educational grounds*. If you can by your advice, keep him from doing the wrong thing, and direct him into the right one in New Haven, you will do us a favor. He talks more than is quite necessary, but is an excellent man.

Yours ever
ELG. . . .

1. Godkin is not being candid about McKim's role as his partner. For the extent of McKim's financial involvement in the *Nation*, see pages 86 and 180 herein.

To Charles Eliot Norton

[ca. 1867] (Ogden 2:36)

. . . I think the article an admirable statement of your case, and do not think it can do the *Review* any harm even in the eyes of the orthodox; but you ask from the orthodox what you will never get as long as orthodoxy exists. They cannot concede that your rule of life is a religion, without giving up their whole position, for the essence of their system lies in their certainty that they have the truth, and that *their* truth is necessary to salvation. But I do think that if there be anything in the world which needs preaching, and proving, it is the possibility of Christian life outside the church. You are yourself one of the very few men I know who seems or tries to lead it. Most others are pagans to all intents and purposes. . . .

To Samuel G. Ward

10 West 48th St., New York, January 1 [1868]
(Ward Papers, MH)

MY DEAR MR. WARD: No success the *Nation* could achieve would be satisfactory to me personally unless I were satisfied that those who had faith in it, in its early and troublous days, and gave me their kind support in carrying it on, believed that it deserved to succeed and was of some value to the community. I should never be able to look you all calmly in the face, if all I could say for it was, that "it was paying." Such testimony to its value as you offer in your note is therefore, very grateful, and we receive so many of the same sort—though not many from as good judges as yourself, that I suppose I may conclude, without any lack of modesty, that it is really doing good, and is destined to do more.

Let me add that I am very glad indeed to have the opportunity which your note affords me to say, without seeming demonstrative, how very warmly I have always appreciated the sympathy and support the enterprize has had from yourself and your brother. If the busts of its founders are ever set up in its office, yours and his shall occupy the place of honor.

I remain very faithfully yours
ELG

To Harry Foote [1]

10 West 48th St., New York, January 24 [1868]
(Godkin Papers, MH)

MY DEAR HARRY: We are greatly delighted to hear that you are improving. . . . I would have written to you before now, but that I am very hard worked and keep my writing down to the lowest possible point.

I enclose a draft on Paris for 1837.10 francs, Duncan Sherman and Co. on Hottinguer and Co. at sight.-Dated Jan. 24, 1868-to your order being the product of $504. in currency; from

Government coupons	$219
Little Miami less 5 per cent tax	285
	$504

The Wilmington and Manchester, I am sorry to say, is not paying its coupons. . . . I fear this will disappoint you a good deal, but I cannot help hoping, that as business revives in the spring, it will come [out] all right. Everything at the South is now greatly depressed. . . .

Those checks were sent to me from New Haven, but before they came I had got a note from Chas. Elliott, asking me, if Mrs. Foote had sailed to send them back to him. As I knew nothing about them I did so, and have heard no more of them except from you. . . . I think both C. W. and his wife are cracked.[2] From the way I hear of them talking, I can form no other conclusion. He conveyed the Milwaukee St. Pauls stock to *you* and *Rockwell*, leaving me out, so that they would not deliver the certificate to me. I suppose this was done to spite me, or in pursuance of a vow; but I forgive the poor man and took no notice of it. I could wish him a better employment for the latter end of his life.

There is no news. The *Nation* is doing well. Kate and Rockwell are installed and have Mrs. Rockwell down upon them.[3]

Ever yours
ELG

1. Godkin's invalid brother-in-law.

2. "C. W." is Charles Wyllys Elliott (1817–83), the brother of Godkin's mother-in-law Mrs. Samuel E. Foote. With Calvert Vaux, Elliott studied landscape architecture under Andrew Jackson Downing and was one of the founders with Charles Loring Brace of the Children's Aid Society. In 1857 he was one of the commissioners for laying out New York's Central Park.

3. Catherine (Kate) Foote Rockwell, Godkin's sister-in-law, was married to Professor Rockwell, a mining engineer. Godkin did not get along well with the Elliotts and the Rockwells, partly because of his wish to handle the finances of his widowed mother-in-law without interference from the family.

To Charles Francis Adams, Jr.

New York, February 8 [1868] (Adams Family Papers, MHi)

My dear Sir: I am very much obliged for your note and for the pamphlet on "Railroad Legislation" by which it was accompanied. . . .

The plan of paying railroad employees in funds out of profits, has been tried on the Orleans railroad in France. I am not quite sure about the particular line, but certainly it is one of the French ones, and I am informed with great success. I think co-operation, or some modification of it, will yet be resorted to in all employments and occupations, in which *zeal* is of high importance and cannot be secured by constant inspection. On railroads, the effect of dependence of the servants for part of their wages, on net receipts, would undoubtedly diminish waste, promote vigilance, and politeness to passengers. I think the employer's art—the art, that is, of getting the most out of men, of bringing their faculties most effectively into play in industry, is still in the rudest condition in all civilized countries. Fixed wages is one degree better than slavery, which only appeals to one motive of action, and that a low one.

I read all you write in the *N. A. Review* with pleasure, and profit, and wish very much that when you have anything to say, which can be said in smaller space, you would try the *Nation* with it.

I am, dear Sir, very faithfully yours
ELG

To Charles Eliot Norton

[Spring 1868] (Ogden 2:3)

. . . Only for the *Nation*, I should be tempted to pull up my stakes and leave with you, to come back when the principal balderdashes of the present epoch are dead. . . .[1]

1. A reference to Norton's impending voyage to Europe.

To Charles Eliot Norton

10 West 48th St., New York, June 10 [1868]
(Norton Papers, MH)

MY DEAR NORTON: "Circumstances over which I have no control," have I am sorry to say, kept me back with my article.[1] It is all composed, but I am copying it out, and have not got through. I am afraid to delay any longer, and send you on one instalment—about a third of the whole. The remainder you shall have on Friday and Saturday. I think you may without hesitation send it piecemeal to the printer. It will be as good as anything I have done for you, and therefore, if your praises of me be sincere, will not disgrace the *Review*.

Yours in great haste.
ELG

C. E. Norton Esq., Cambridge, Mass.
This is done somewhat too hastily. I hope you will alter, amend, or reject altogether, freely.

1. E. L. Godkin, "Commercial Immorality and Political Corruption," *North American Review* 107 (July 1868): 248–66.

To Frederick Law Olmsted

Nation Office   New York, July 18, 1868
(Olmsted Papers, DLC)

DEAR OLMSTED: I enclose a check for $351.42. The 7/207 have all been out and had to be converted this month into 5/201. The remainder of the interest comprises about $90, fully due I believe in August.[1] I am going away next week, and shall be gone a fortnight. I commend the *Nation* to your remembrance during my absence. I have told Dennett and Garrison to apply to you in difficult or doubtful cases.

Yours ever
ELG

Could you lunch with me today at that shop near here, where we went last time?

1. Godkin handled some of Olmsted's investments and occasionally borrowed money from the older man.

To Moses Coit Tyler

New York, September 2 [1868?] (Tyler Papers, NIC)

MY DEAR SIR: I had not seen the *Birmingham Traveler;* but its failure to give us credit for the article, we shall forgive in the belief that the value of the article will be in no degree diminished thereby. Besides we have grown hardened to this kind of treatment.[1]

                                        Yours very sincerely
                                        ELG
Prof. M. C. Tyler

    1. Plagiarism from the *Nation* was not uncommon.

To Charles Eliot Norton

                        September 7, 1868 (Ogden 1: 290)

    . . . I hardly know where to begin with an account of what has happened since you left. Lowell, as I feared he would, backed out of the Canadian trip when it came to the point, but I went on and spent Sunday with him on my way, and had a most delightful day. He was all and more than all that you have ever represented him. You know, I have never felt that I really saw the man when I met him at your house. He was erudite and bookish, and seemed to feel bound to be instructive. At his own house, however, he was simply a delightful host and companion. We talked so steadily that on Sunday I was before dinner fairly tired out, and had to go off for a solitary walk to get rested. . . .

To Theodore Tilton

                        Nation Office   September 7, 1868
                        (Godkin Miscellaneous Papers, NN)
Private

DEAR SIR: In the interest of good morals as well as good business, I think it well to say in reference to your personal allusion to me in the *Independent* of last week—that it obviously suggests a falsehood. It suggests, what I am sure the writer knew to be untrue, that the circumstance of my having been born in Ireland prevented my taking a rational and just view of the Louisiana School question. . . .

    We have endeavored in the *Nation,* and successfully endeavored, in the interest of reason as well as of decency, to make discussion *impersonal*. If I were to make your birth or education a means of exciting either a prejudice against you personally, or of weakening the effect of your arguments, I should consider myself a very base and malignant person. We have commented often severely on the course of the *Independent*, but no personal allusion to the writers have, I am glad to say ever found its way into our columns. It seems to me that you should be amongst the last to encourage a tendency which is the curse of the press and of the country, and which has made the Pomeroys possible, and which cherishes the coarse and brutalized public opinion to which so many public abuses owe their continuance.

I address you privately, simply because a public controversy over a small "hit" at my person, is something in which, please God, I shall never engage, because I am a great deal more anxious to secure your support for the cause of decent journalism, than enjoy the small triumph of pointing out the pettiness of your mode of assailing *me*, who have never assailed you.

I am, dear Sir, yours truly
ELG

To Theodore Tilton

New Haven, Conn., September 15 [1868]
(Godkin Miscellaneous Papers, NN)

DEAR MR. TILTON: Your kind expression of sympathy with us on our recent loss reached me yesterday, and I would of course be strangely constituted, if I were not touched by it.[1] Only those who have themselves suffered in this way, know I am sure what the trial is, and peculiar circumstances have made it in our case, very severe. Later, it would however, have been harder to bear, and you, who have, I believe, lost older children, have, perhaps, touched lower depths of this great sorrow than we have as yet reached. It requires all one's faith in Infinite Goodness, not [to] see something very hard as well as very mysterious in the fate of these little ones thus hurried from the world, before they have well opened their eyes on it.

Mr. Garrison told me you had called, after I left town to explain that you were ignorant of the paragraph about me in the *Independent*, which drew forth the remonstrance which I addressed to you some days ago. I was delighted to hear it and beg you will consider my note as *non avenu*. Let me say at the same time, that to me a newspaper is simply the expression on paper of certain opinions, and although I am aware that the *Nation* is considered to attack these with harsh bitterness, my earnest desire is that nothing should ever appear in it, which one human being should consider calculated to wound him as a man, as long as he does not offer his person for criticism, by making it part of his claim to honor or reward. The *Nation*, itself, is fair game for all comers. I ask no mercy for it. But *I*, who hope and seek nothing from the public, except a hearing, am entitled to have my poor person left out of sight. I have certain opinions I hold to dearly, and them I fling into the arena.

　　　　　　　　　　　With much regard, I remain very truly yours
　　　　　　　　　　　ELG

　　1. Tilton's letter was occasioned by the death of a two-month-old son of the Godkins.

To Earl Shinn [1]

　　　　　　　　　　Nation Office　New York, September 26, 1868
　　　　　　　　　　　　　　(Friends Historical Library, PSC)

MY DEAR SIR: . . . I should like you by all means to work up your materials for us. We shall pay you as much for them as any body, and publish them with reasonable rapidity. I say this on the supposition that they will be in the style of those you sent us, the first of which, in particular, I thought an admirable piece of writing. But do not put in too much art, or art criticism, except as an accessory. Make them pictures of life and manners, and if possible, each paper complete in itself, and we will number them like Howell's "Italian Journeys"—all the earlier ones of which were published in the *Nation*. I may add, that we desire not only that things should be "lively," but show thought and culture and *finish*. The reason why we don't have more "lively" matter in the *Nation*, is that the article is generally, thin, and weak, as supplied by the bulk of magazine writers.

The sooner you can begin this the better.

> Yours very truly
> ELG

1. Earl B. Shinn (1837–86) was the *Nation's* chief art critic, 1873–81.

To Harry Foote

> 10 West 48th St., New York, October 6 [1868]
> (Godkin Papers, MH)

MY DEAR HARRY: I wrote to you at some length on the 18th of July. . . . In that letter, enclosing the draft I set out my "views" as to what you ought to do, at great length. They were in substance this: that you ought to give up all plans of study, sight seeing or mental or moral improvement and devote yourself steadily to the care of your left lung, as your great object in life —the one thing needful, that, therefore, you ought not to risk yourself on any uncertain climate, you ought not to go to Dresden; that you should seek some dry bracing air, establish yourself there, with a horse, beefsteaks, and whiskey, and stick it out until the lung gets well. I recommended for this purpose *Algiers*, and suggested the possibility of your Aunt going with you. There you would have the *dryest* air in the world; there has not been a case of lung disease in it, since the days of Hannibal; you would have French hotels, French cookery, French doctors, and French society, plenty of horses, and a new life and new people and manners, and the winter I am sure would pass pleasantly. . . . I wept when I heard you had . . . gone to Baden; I knew how it would end. I also weep when I hear of your attempting any sightseeing, or mental or moral improvement. It is all wrong. Open air, beef steaks and whiskey and the saddle, should be your motto. . . . Take a servant with you, and take your passage by the first steamer. There are lots of Arab horses there, and you can scour the desert in the rear and explore Mt. Atlas. . . . We are still here in the house, waiting for the church to be finished in order to sell. Your mother spends the winter with us of course. We see little of New York society, but have a small stream of foreigners and people from the provinces. . . . The *Nation* jogs on. . . . Nothing would I like better than to join you for a few months ramble, but then, with a paper not yet fully established, there is no breathing time. It will be five years yet, I think before I can safely leave it. I went to Canada for a fortnight this summer and enjoyed it greatly, but of course it is only a very pale reflection of a European trip.

Public affairs, will go well I think if Grant is elected. The South will I am sure recover as soon as order is restored, and uncertainty at an end. I hope then your bonds will begin to pay.

To sum up—Go to a good, and *unquestionable* climate (Mentone, is I am told, relaxing); spend your money on good food, good liquor, good quarters and a horse. Keep quiet, and amused; frequent French company, they are very amusing once you know them well; and get at ease in the language, and come home cured next year, and we will laugh once more till our sides ache.[1]

                                        Yours ever
                                        ELG. . . .

1. Young Foote died of tuberculosis a few years later.

To James Russell Lowell

                        10 West 48th St., New York, October 22 [1868]
                                        (Lowell Papers, MH)

MY DEAR LOWELL: I have been laid up by an accident during the last week, or I would have written to you to say how glad we should be to have something from you on the Byron question. . . . If we get this from you, it would as far as we are concerned close the subject, and we should be willing to pledge even the office dictionaries, *Congressional Globe*, and other properties to remunerate you,—not handsomely, that would be impossible; but without positive meanness.

I was also going to tell you, in the projected letter, that the "omniscience" of the *Nation* is a composite quality, and is not to be predicated on any individual in particular, and that, consequently, I am not the man, who has been contending with you on Spanish *asonancia*, but Heilprin, our many sided Jew.[1] I mention this now, so that you may not "tackle" me on Spanish construction or versification when you see me. It is only in my office

wig, and robes, and high heeled shoes that I am really formidable
on any subject. . . .

Yours ever
ELG

1. Michael Heilprin (1823–88), a versatile Pole who fled Hungary and
came to the United States, wrote on many subjects for the *Nation* during
its first twenty years. In a vein of mild reproof Lowell had cautioned Godkin to "beware of omniscience."

To Manton Marble

Nation Office   November 3, 1868
(Marble Papers, DLC)

DEAR MR. MARBLE: I want very much to show "the Unterrified"
in their glory to two English friends tonight, at Tammany Hall,
and write to ask whether you could kindly put me in the way of
getting three tickets to the platform, or other sacred enclosure,
from which the performance could be observed with safety and
comfort.[1]

Very truly yours
ELG

1. Manton Marble (1835–1917) was the proprietor of the New York
World. He did not take kindly to Godkin's request for tickets to the Tammany rally, filing with Godkin's letter a clipping from the *Nation* bearing
penciled exclamation points and other indications of his (Marble's) dissatisfaction with the *Nation*.

To James Russell Lowell

10 West 48th St., New York, November 17 [1868]
(Lowell Papers, MH)

MY DEAR LOWELL: . . . The radical savages, have taken once
more, by way of vengeance for our treatment of Butler, to announcing in the papers that I received and misapplied certain
funds of the Recruiting Committee voted for the establishment of
the *Nation*. A formal and deliberate statement of this kind appeared in the *Commonwealth* last week signed by R. P. Hallowell.[1] They have been making assertions of this kind for three
years, on the strength of Stearns's lying circulars, and I have

suffered a good deal from it in mind, but by the advice of Norton and the Wards, have kept quiet. I feel now that I cannot stand it any longer, and as vindication of myself . . . I have sent one to the *Advertizer*, which will probably appear on Friday or Saturday morning. . . . I have done in it one doubtful thing—that is cited Norton's appreciation in a private letter written to me at the time of the circular of Stearns, on which all these charges against me are based. I did so because he was Stearns's co-trustee, cognizant of all the facts, and would be my principal witness, in case I brought these scamps to justice. I am a little uncertain as to the effect of this on Norton, but still concluded that he says no more than he would be willing to say again, if I now called on him.

I am made all the more sensitive in this matter because the disadvantages of being a stranger are great enough, without having added to them the disadvantages of being denounced as a knave by a parcel of humanitarians. . . .[2]

Very sincerely yours
ELG

1. To help finance the *Nation*, in the expectation that it would become a vehicle of Freedmen's rights, about $16,000 was taken from the funds of the "Recruiting Committee," a fund-raising organization formed in 1863 by George Stearns and others to recruit black soldiers in Massachusetts for the Union Army. Stearns-supporter Richard P. Hallowell was the committee's treasurer, and many of the Boston investors in the *Nation* belonged to it. Hallowell's charges against Godkin were not wholly without foundation.

2. Ogden printed this sentence with the final words, "by a parcel of humanitarians," silently deleted.

To James M. McKim

10 West 48th St., New York, November 22 [1868]
(Godkin Papers, MH)

MY DEAR McKIM: You could not have written a more suitable letter if you had been inspired. . . .

The story is simply—that Harry Lee of Boston exposed in the *Nation* Butler's lying about his opposition to the vote of the recruiting fund. I availed myself of the opportunity thus offered to deny formally that I was instrumental in procuring that vote, or that the *Nation* was started as a "freedmen's paper." I knew this would draw their fire. "Warrington," first assailed me in a blackguard personal letter in the *Tribune*, which I could not notice, representing the *Nation* as having been got up by Stearns, who hired me to edite [*sic*] it, and I grossly deceived him etc., omitting, as they have done all along, all mention of Norton or you.

However, as good luck would have it, R. P. Hallowell appeared on the scene in the *Commonwealth*, charging me, on the strength of Stearns's circular[,] with deceiving the Recruiting Committee, evidently however knowing nothing of the facts, and, as usual, making no mention of you and Norton, but otherwise respectful in tone. This was all I needed: I sounded the charge, and for the first time made a clean breast of it. I shall now sleep comfortably; thanks to you and Norton. For the others Satan is waiting—not anxiously for he knows well he will get them eventually—nor yet eagerly for he, of course, desires the measure of their iniquity to be as full as possible.

Very cordially yours
ELG

To Charles Francis Adams, Jr.

10 West 48th St., New York, November 29 [1868]
(Adams Family Papers, MHi)

MY DEAR SIR: The review of your article, as well as the recent paragraph in the "Week" in the *Nation* were written by a lawyer who had closely followed the Erie Suit and in whose integrity I have the utmost confidence.[1] But I admit that Haskin's relations with Barnard, of which I was not aware till recently— Crane has the reputation of being his go between—are such as to throw doubt on the character of the retainer. I have, as a good means of getting at the truth of the matter, and for other reasons, taken the liberty of showing your letter both to our contributor and to Field. The former writes me—"The $50,000 transmission was one with which neither Field nor Haskin had anything to do, and knew nothing about it, until it was over. It happened thus: John J. Crane, who is Barnard's go-between, promised Gould to get the injunction modified for $50,000, saying (truly no doubt), that Barnard had authorized him to do so. Fisk took him the money, and Crane took the paper to Barnard's house, when the latter seeing Dudley Field's writing refused to sign, fearing that Dudley knew about it, and would expose him. But in fact Dudley knew nothing at all about it, and gave his client the paper he had previously drawn, supposing they were going to apply to some other lawyer."

Mr. Field writes me a letter which I enclose, and which as you may discuss the case further, it is desirable you should see, but you will please not make any allusion to it in print.

Yours very truly
ELG

C. F. Adams, Jr., Esq.

I have shown your letter, under the impression, which I hope is not a mistaken one, that you did not care about the authorship being known.

1. This letter discusses the Erie Scandal, occasioned when Jay Gould and Jim Fisk obtained control of the Erie Railroad and began "watering" its stock. The author of the *Nation* review that Adams questioned was J. B. Hodgskin.

To Charles Eliot Norton

December 15, 1868 (Ogden 1: 303–4)

. . . I am sorry you saw the last number of the *N.A.R.* It was a sad failure, but Gurney at least was conscious of it, and deplored it.[1] He is going to try very hard to keep it up, but I have my doubts whether he will succeed. You were born for that place, and must go back to it. There is only one dark spot in your career, but that is a *very* dark one—your admitting Parton to the *Review.* Not that the articles you accepted from him were not good, but in printing them you displayed an indifference to and a forgetfulness of the *remote* consequences of your acts, which was unworthy of a political philosopher of your standing. You gave him thereby a weight and authority he could not possibly have got otherwise, and the truth is he is now writing, and with great acceptance, the most outrageous nonsense that ever came from the pen of a decently dressed man. His sermon on "Smoking and Drinking" is a real disgrace to the country. It is far more ignorant, foolish, and presumptuous than Holland, but Holland never wrote in the *N.A.R.* John Fiske has written a reply utterly demolishing him, but think of a man like Fiske having to demolish such a creature! It is using siege artillery to quell a riot. For all this you are to blame. Nothing but your getting well quickly and coming home soon will enable you to atone for it. . . .

1. Norton had gone to Europe for a protracted stay, and Professor Ephraim Whitman Gurney (1829–86), the brother-in-law of Henry Adams had taken over the editorship of the *North American Review.* Later, Professor and Mrs. Gurney were among the closest of Godkin's Harvard friends.

To James Russell Lowell

Nation Office   New York, December 16, 1868
(Lowell Papers, MH)

MY DEAR LOWELL: The parcel came yesterday and I have distributed the books as you desired. Even if I did not "care for verses," I should be gratified more than I can express to you, without seeming extravagant, by the use you have made of the copy you are good enough to present to me.[1] But I *do* care for verses, and care in a special manner for yours, and had read this last volume with great enjoyment when it first arrived. . . . I seldom say anything about my enjoyment of poetry, however, mainly because I seldom say much about a certain class of my own feelings at all—but in fact also, because, want of training, and want of practice, in the description or analysis of sentiment— either my own or other peoples', have made my powers of expression in that field very feeble.

I wish I could persuade myself that you do not over estimate the value of the *Nation's* services. . . . You need not fear that I shall have any more encounters with "the brethren". . . . My letter has cleansed my bosom . . . and I shall now calmly and confidently cherish the doctrine of future punishment, which in a rash moment, I had come very near giving up. . . .

Yours very cordially
ELG

1. Apparently Lowell inscribed a copy of the book to Godkin; later he dedicated a small volume of verse to him.

To Andrew D. White

Nation Office   New York, January 16, 1869
(White Papers, NIC)

MY DEAR SIR: I sincerely hope you did not suppose I sent you Rosenblatt's letter because *I* supposed any explanation or defence from you was necessary. I did it because people like him are sure to find vent for their complaints somewhere, and I was desirous, in case the matter was in any way forced on our attention, to be able to say exactly what were the facts of the case. I have refused to publish his letter unless he reduces it to a bare statement of what he considers the facts, and if he consents to this, I shall reply from your letter, and thus settle the matter.

I have not forgotten the engagement to do something on and of the University, of which you kindly remind me, and if next year you have any class you think likely to profit by anything I may be able to supply I shall be very happy to respond to any call you may make on me. Wishing you every success, I remain,

Yours very truly
ELG

You may be sure it is not with me, if anywhere, that any failure to appreciate your work, will ever be found. I never think of the place you fill, in using the rude hope, and energy, and enterprize with which the country so abounds, in aid of culture, without thanking Heaven that anybody was found who could fill it.

To Harry Foote

10 West 48th St., New York, February 10 [1869]
(Godkin Papers, MH)

MY DEAR HARRY: . . . Mr. Read has delivered me three bonds, and gave me at the same time six coupons on your account. Little Miami has paid a dividend, and Milwaukie [*sic*] and St. Paul has declared one, so I think the income will probably be at its best this year. I have filed my accounts for the year ending October 1. with the Judge of Probate. I enclose you the capital account, brought down to *Jan. 1.* by which you will see *all* the changes in investment that have been made. . . . The Norwich and Worcester has got into the hands of speculators, and I think it highly desirable to get out of it. . . . I gave an order to sell, if it reached 110. It has reached 100, but I fear will not get up to my limit. I am rather sick of railroad stock, and believe most people are getting to be so. John I. Foote of Cincinnati came in a month or two ago to get my proxy for Little Miami, in which he has $40,000, and speaks very hopefully of it. . . . I will not touch your bonds except as a last resort. But as long as I do not say anything *you may conclude that all is going on well, and there is money in the chest.* . . . You may be sure your drafts will always be provided for.

We are still in a quandary about the house here. Fanny and I are of course delighted to be in it, but we feel strongly that you all need the income. I have consulted Rockwell, and various real estate men about selling it now, and the general advice is to hold on till our street and neighborhood is more built up. . . .

Davidson is still in New Haven. I warned him against lending the books, and he was mad as a hatter. He pays his rent regularly, but has not paid for the coal. I am satisfied it will be almost impossible to get the right sort of tenant for that house.[1] Only small mean people will take it. The big wigs want to buy always, if they are going to live in the country. We are all going up there in the summer, if nothing happens. . . .

Everything looks well politically. Not that fools do not abound, but somehow, the right side keeps uppermost. With best love from all here.

Affectionately yours
ELG

1. A reference to Windy Knowe, the Foote residence in New Haven that Godkin rented out for his mother-in-law.

To Charles Nordhoff

Nation Office   New York, February 12, 1869
(Godkin Miscellaneous Papers, NN)

DEAR NORDHOFF: I have a warrant out against a conductor, for a great outrage, of which I was the victim, though I am not hurt, and I think you will serve the public as well as me, by inserting the enclosed notice as conspicuously as convenient. I was flung suddenly on my back, into the street, from the platform of a car going seven miles an hour, for simply asking to see the man's badge, before paying my fare, he having been previously misconducting himself. The company has dismissed him, but these things need to be followed up.

> Yours ever
> ELG

I hope this will not be too late for this afternoon's paper.

To James M. McKim

> *Nation* Office　New York, March 19, 1869
> (Godkin Papers, MH)

DEAR SIR: The Social Science Association are desirous of forming a Committee in this City, and have charged me with the task of organizing it.[1] You have, I think, been already requested to serve on it; should you still be willing to do so, you will do me a favor by attending a meeting to be held at my house, 10 West 48th St., on Wednesday evening March 24th at half past eight o'clock.

I should be glad if convenient to be informed whether you will be able to do so.

Annexed is a list of gentlemen to whom similar invitations have been sent.

> Faithfully yours
> ELG

Professor Theodore Dwight	William F. Blodgett
Judge Daly	Dr. E. C. Wines
Judge Arnett	Dr. C. R. Agnew
George Cabot Ward	Charles L. Brace
Howard Potter	George W. Curtis
Frederick Kapp	R. M. Hoe
Frederick Law Olmsted	Joseph Choate
J. M. McKim	R. O. Williams
Henry Holt	

1. The American Social Science Association, to which Godkin, George W. Curtis, Edward Atkinson, David A. Wells, and other genteel eastern reformers belonged, was founded in Boston in 1865 with Henry Villard its general secretary. The association did little except talk.

To James A. Garfield [1]

10 West 48th St., New York, March 26 [1869?]
(Garfield Papers, DLC)

MY DEAR SIR: I have taken the liberty of giving a letter of introduction to you to Count Wierzbicki, a Polish cavalry officer, who
served on General's staff in 1848–9 in Hungary, and com-
manded a Polish regiment in the Turkish service through the
Danube, and Crimean campaigns from 1853 to 1856. He is an old
and valued friend of mine and has married an American lady, and
is now making a short visit to this country in company with his
wife. He will probably be a day or two, in Washington, and as he
speaks no English, but French and German perfectly, I have been
somewhat at a loss to know with whom to put him in relations,
so that he can be aided in seeing a little of the city.

It has occurred to me that even if you are not yourself at home
in French or German, you may be able to put him into the hands
of somebody who is, and who can explain to him a little of what
he sees. He has naturally a soldier's desire to see Grant and Sherman, and if you can put him in the way of doing this, you will
confer an additional favor both on me and him.

I am much obliged for the Census document. I will endeavor
as far as the *Nation* is concerned to have the subject well discussed.

Yours very truly
ELG

Honble James A. Garfield

1. Garfield, a regular subscriber to the *Nation*, was then a member of
Congress.

To Charles Eliot Norton

April 15, 1869 (Ogden 1:304–5)

. . . Grant's appointments, are I think, on the whole, good. He
has necessarily made some mistakes; under the system, it is impossible to avoid them. Motley's appointment is a good one from
the social point of view—bad, I think, in every other way.[1] I do
not think he has the necessary mental furniture for the discussion

of the questions now pending between England and America, and he is a little too ardent. His lectures here have been very disappointing—commonplace rhetoric without any thought. I wish you could have got Switzerland or Belgium; but Massachusetts has been so heavily drawn upon already that I suppose there is no chance for anybody else from the State. Hoar's appointment was perfect. You will have seen Sumner's speech by this time; it is perfectly characteristic. He works his adjectives so hard that if they ever catch him alone, they will murder him. I was greatly amused by his quoting Edge's pamphlet in proof of the extent of the damage done by the *Alabama*.[2] Edge was a weak and seedy fellow, who wandered over here in an aimless vagabond way during the war, and had to and did beg money to keep himself, obtaining contributions from Bellows and others, and he endeavored to repay it when he got home by writing one or two pamphlets on the American side, usually trash. Sumner, Parton-like, treats his statements as "proof". . . .

1. A reference to the appointment of John L. Motley as United States minister to England. Grant removed him the next year.

2. The *Alabama* Controversy arose out of charges by the United States that England had followed an unneutral course during the Civil War by issuing a hasty proclamation at the outset declaring a state of civil war in the United States and then by permitting war vessels to be constructed in the British Isles for the Confederacy, notable among them the *Alabama*. A detailed account of Godkin's editorial role in the long controversy appears in William M. Armstrong, *E. L. Godkin and American Foreign Policy, 1865–1900* (New York: Bookman Associates, 1957) pp. 80–101.

To James Russell Lowell

10 West 48th St., New York, April 26 [1869]
(Lowell Papers, MH)

MY DEAR LOWELL: I submit to a Master's eye, an essay of mine in the *Daily News* on one of the social questions of the day. May I ask you to return it to me—not that I value it particularly but because it may involve me in a controversy and I may, therefore, want to refer to it. . . .

If I have not written to tell you how much I enjoyed my visit to Cambridge, it is because I have been worked nearly to death, and have been reduced by it to a condition of depression which has at times been overpowering, but I am getting better. Summer always makes me gloomy; to a New Yorker it is a hateful season.

I hope you are well and happy, and wish I could join you this morning in "a whiff of [brandy?]."

I took up, while at your house, a history of or letters on the French occupation of Rome (under Napoleon I). There were in it some figures showing the results of the abolition of capital punishment in the Papal States, which, you would oblige me very much by jotting down, at your leisure, and sending them to me. . . .[1]

> Ever yours
> ELG

1. Godkin was a staunch supporter of capital punishment.

To Charles Eliot Norton

> [Early July 1869] (Ogden 2:70)

. . . There was a large and very interesting gathering of about seven hundred. I made a few remarks in the nature of a speech, and was received by the audience with extraordinary and un-looked for cordiality. The thing was in some respects not well managed. Lowell, for instance, not having been called on for his verses till the room had begun to thin. He praised Adams in them, a high and well-merited compliment. I stayed at Shady Hill, I believe in your mother's room. I felt at times as if my visits to you there had been a pleasant dream. . . .[1]

1. Godkin had been invited to speak at the annual Alumni Commencement Dinner at Harvard, and while in Cambridge he stayed at Norton's home, Shady Hill.

To James Russell Lowell

> 10 West 48th St., New York, July 15 [1869]
> (Lowell Papers, MH)

MY DEAR LOWELL: When I went up to New Haven last Sunday, I found a note from you to my wife, which was evidently written with the kind intention of exalting me in her eyes. The most palpable result of it, however, I found to be the exaltation of yourself. I had to listen for thirty-six hours to ejaculations about your kindness, goodness and thoughtfulness, which finally grew almost wearisome to even as enthusiastic admirer of you as I am myself. I came away deeply impressed with the idea that if you long for public life, and the absurd custom about the residence of candidates is ever done away, you would do well to try your fortunes in New Haven. My wife has "local influence," and you would have all the women on your side, which in the world we are going to live in will be no mean advantage for a politician.

I was unfortunately obliged, in order to prevent unscrupulous rivals from getting ahead of me, to send the *Daily News* the copy of your eulogy on Adams, as it stood in the papers. As the edition you were good enough to send was an amended one, I am sorry I did not have it in time, and I would have waited, even at the risk of being outstripped, if I had felt certain you would think it worth your while to send a copy; but you spoke doubtfully when I saw you.

Would there be no chance of your and Mrs. Lowell's spending a few quiet days with us in New Haven, this summer? Pray meditate on it.

I have been spoken *of*, I believe, but not *to*, about the *Times*, but whether by anybody in authority I don't know. They have offered it to Curtis, who has refused, and Bigelow of the *Post*, has it now, under consideration. . . .[1]

I was really surprized and touched by my reception at Harvard, and think it the most valuable compliment the paper has received, or could receive. There could be no gathering of men in the country whose praise would be so grateful. You know I do not believe in "the self made man," not because I have any aristocratic prejudice against [him] but because I believe the Almighty intended the world to be governed by cultivated reason.

I was delighted by your compliment to Adams, and disgusted at your not having been called on before he left the room. Depend upon it, that with all their faults, the tribe to which he belongs, are on the whole the most valuable of the nation's possessions.

Yours ever most cordially
ELG

1. Henry J. Raymond, the editor and proprietor of the *New York Times*, had recently died, and a search had begun for his successor under the direction of *Times* publisher George Jones. Godkin was not given consideration.

To William Dean Howells

Nation Office   New York, September 8, 1869
(Godkin Papers, MH)

My dear Howells: You are one of the last men in the world I would suspect of "a dodge" of any kind, much less an "advertizing dodge," either for your "ancestral paper" or any other periodical, and am sorry you thought it necessary to say one word in explanation. I was very glad to see the *Sentinel* article, as it strengthened me in my impressions, against the weight of a "powerful article," in an agricultural paper, defending farm life, against the base assaults of the malignant sheet which I edite.

I am glad you are going to lecture to Harvard, and, in fact, glad of everything which shows that you are as highly appreciated by others, as by

Your faithful friend
ELG

Why don't you bring out "a theory" of the "Byron Scandal," with some "fresh details from a reliable source?"

To George Jones

October 7, 1869 (*New York Times*, 27 March 1872)

My dear Mr. Jones: Nobody has more interest—as reader, I mean—in the *Times* than I have, and I would do anything in my power to help you. But the fact is, I am hard worked as it is, and whether I work harder is with me entirely a question of money. I might agree to furnish you with two articles a week, if you would allow me to choose my own days of the week, and pecuniarily speaking, make it worth my while and *kept private*. It might prove embarrassing to me in some ways to have my connection with the *Times* made public, on account of the *Nation*. If you will make me an offer I will do my best to accept it, and even if I don't we shall be none the worse friends.[1]

Yours very truly
ELG

1. Godkin accepted Jones's offer and for the next year served as a contributor to the *New York Times*.

To Charles Eliot Norton

October 16, 1869 (Ogden 1:305)

. . . The *Sun*, Dana's paper, has been rivalling the New York *Herald*, in its worst days, in ribaldry, falsehood, indecency, levity, and dishonesty—championing Judge Barnard for instance, and levying blackmail, to the horror of Dana's friends. He is now an object of general execration, I think I have never seen such nearly unanimous condemnation of a rascal, which is a good sign. . . .

To Professor William D. Whitney

Nation Office   New York, October 28, 1869
(Whitney Papers, Cty)

MY DEAR SIR: . . . I am waiting very impatiently to hear your decision about Harvard and confess I am rent by conflicting emotions. For personal reasons I want you to stay in New Haven, but as a friend of science, I think I want you to go to Harvard. Put in this way the struggle seems to be one between my higher and lower nature; it is however something better than that. I am afraid, although I know you can do excellent work in New Haven, the *University* atmosphere, is not or may not be as good at Yale for a long while as at Harvard.[1]

Yours very truly
ELG

1. Whitney, one of the leading scholars of his day, declined Harvard's offer.

To James M. McKim

Nation Office   New York, November 11, 1869
(Godkin Papers, MH)

Better keep all this to yourself for the present.

MY DEAR McKIM: . . . I have been looking into *Nation* matters for the last few days and think it is time for us to come to some definite understanding as to the future. Our subscription list since July has not been gaining as it did. In fact our receipts from that source now, are not as good as they have been. . . .[1]

In the meantime we have reached the bottom of our capital. Nothing is left. I have been working hard for three years at half wages, and today, the paper owes me I find

On acct of salary	$182.72
On acct of loans	613.39
	$796.11

Of course I cannot go on at this pace, and the question comes up for solution, and speedy solution, what had better be done. I would be content to work without salary for a while, ill as I could afford it, if I clearly saw better times ahead; but I do not know what the future has in store, and cannot run heavy risks.

Now are you willing to bear one third of possible losses from now till Jan. 1st. and in fact what do you think or propose?

Yours very truly
ELG

1. The circulation of the *Nation* had fallen below 5,000.

To James Russell Lowell

10 West 48th St., New York, December 5 [1869]
(Lowell Papers, MH)

My dear Lowell: . . . I do not know what complexion the Byron affair will wear after the appearance of Mrs. Stowe's volume. . . . If after it appears you continue to be of the same opinion about the matter, I have no more to say; but I hope you may think differently. Is it not wonderful to see a woman deliberately becoming the author of a book about a charge of incest, of all earthly subjects?

We hope to get more writing out of Dennett in Cambridge than here.[1] In fact it is this hope which reconciles me to his going. I handed over the complete charge of the literary side to him a year ago, and since then he has written very little. He is naturally indolent and desultory, and readily fritters time away in the small details of editorship. His writing is what is most valuable about him; his general editorial judgment is not worth much, I mean on points of policy etc. . . . The *Nation* is doing well. . . .

Yours ever
ELG

1. John R. Dennett had taken a teaching post at Harvard.

To Theodore Dwight Woolsey

Nation Office   New York, December 6, 1869
(Woolsey Papers, Cty)

President Woolsey, My dear Sir: The bearer, Mr. H. D. Lloyd, whom I have great pleasure in introducing to you, is the Assistant Secretary of the Free Trade League.[1] He goes to New Haven to make arrangements for a meeting to be held there before long, and in the hope of inducing you to preside at it. The League has been working vigorously for two or three years, mainly owing to the devotion of three or four gentlemen in this City, who have given to it lavishly both their time and their money. They have now spread their organization over the West, and unless I am greatly mistaken in the signs of the times, free trade will be the great national question of the next three or four years. By giving the movement your public countenance and support, even in so far as presiding at the local meeting, you would greatly help it in all parts of the Country, and I earnestly trust, that you will see fit to do so.

The arrangements here are in excellent hands, and I am sure I may guarantee that they will be in every way satisfactory to you. Mr. Lloyd is a gentleman in whom you may repose the fullest confidence.

I remain, my dear Sir, with great respect,
very faithfully yours
ELG

President Woolsey, Yale College

1. Reformer Henry Demarest Lloyd (1847–1903) was an infrequent literary contributor to the *Nation*.

To Daniel Coit Gilman

Nation Office   New York, December 6, 1869
(Gilman Papers, MdBJ)

MY DEAR GILMAN: Mr. Lloyd, the bearer is Assistant Secretary of the Free Trade League, and goes to New Haven to ask President Woolsey to preside at a meeting, they propose to hold there shortly. *Faute de mieux*, I have given him a note of introduction to the President, but as he ought to be approached cautiously, I recommend Mr. Lloyd to take your advice, as to the best time and manner of doing so. If you can give him any other assistance, I shall be greatly obliged to you, unless you are a protectionist, in which case I pity and forgive you.

Yours very cordially
ELG

Professor D. C. Gilman

5. Ivy *aficionado* and Liberal Republican, 1870–72

Question the stature of Godkin as one will, argued William R. Thayer, "posterity will get at the truth of the chief public affairs in America between 1865 and 1881, in the *Nation* better than in any other contemporary source; time has confirmed most of his verdicts." It was natural for Thayer, who graduated from Harvard in the same class with Godkin's son, to be drawn to Godkin's olympian journal, for it was assertedly read only by "the best men." Thus Harvard awarded its editor an honorary degree, tendered him a professorship, appointed him to its committee of annual Visitors, and on his death inaugurated the annual Godkin Lectures. The *Nation* was enough of an institution at Harvard during the 1870s that class poet George Pellew exhorted his fellow students at an 1880 Hasty Pudding farce to cast aside Godkin's weekly so that they might "Hail Indifference":

> May the Pudding leave their *Nations*
> and neglect their recitations

Godkin earned followers in the intellectual community because he made the *Nation* a repository for the conventional wisdom of the "best people," which is to say that he also made it a repository for their conventional prejudices. His principal objection to Jim Fisk was not the financier's business morals but the fact that he had begun life as a peddler. The kind of awakened conscience that prompted Helen Hunt Jackson in 1881 to issue her indictment of the white man's treatment of the Indian, *A Century of Dishonor*, found no sympathetic vibration in Godkin, who embraced the conventional Anglo-Saxon racial prejudices of his day. Not only are his editorials during the 1870s silent on the moral implications of the "final solution of the Indian problems," they are equally silent toward the anti-Semitism that distorted the vision of many of the intelligentsia of his day. He never overcame the personal prejudice that as a young war correspondent he had shared with readers of the *Daily News*, recounting to them his discomfiture at being refused passage on a British troop transport in the Crimea while accommodations were given to "a German Jew, an adventurer from New York, who was roaming about, probably seeing whom he might devour."

Godkin's letters during this period reflect his prejudices, as well as some of the high-minded qualities that made him admired. As an independent editor he seldom gave unreserved support to any cause, but in 1868 the *Nation* warmly endorsed the presidential bid of Ulysses S. Grant. Four years later Grant's assurance of renomination triggered open revolt in the Republican party. The revolt had been brewing for some months. Godkin, one of the early malcontents, hoped the seceders would nominate Charles Francis Adams, and when the Liberal Republicans, as they styled themselves, instead chose the high-tariff Horace Greeley, the editor was dumbfounded. Declaring to Carl Schurz that he would under no circumstances support this "conceited, ignorant, half cracked, obstinate old creature," he threw the *Nation* during the campaign back behind the President. Grant won reelection easily.

To Charles Eliot Norton

February 17, 1870 (Ogden 1:294)

. . . I was invited to the dinner of the Harvard Club last week, where Eliot made his first appearance before a New York public, and sat next him and enjoyed seeing him very much.[1] He seems to have been born for the place, and has gone into the work with his whole heart and soul, and is winning golden opinions. He made a very favorable impression at the dinner, and a very good speech. Evarts, who has a very keen wit, made one very good hit at him.[2] Eliot in his speech had endeavored to explain the religious position of Harvard: "She was," he said, "reverent yet free"—though what that means I don't exactly know,—and made a tolerably successful effort to give her an unobjectionable look in orthodox eyes. Evarts followed, and after showing that his early associations were all with Harvard, said—with a very quizzical look—that the reason why his father had not sent him there to receive his education was that "at that time the relations of the university to religion were not properly understood." This brought down the house. He (Eliot) and Curtis dined with us the following evening, and I had a good deal more pleasant talk with him. He is shocking orthodox susceptibilities a good deal by some of his appointments, but the general impression on the public mind, I think, is that he is inaugurating a new era in collegiate education in this country, and that under his auspices America is at last going to have a university of the right sort. . . .

1. A reference to the elevation of Charles W. Eliot to the presidency of Harvard College.
2. Political leader William M. Evarts (1818–1901) served as Secretary of State of the United States, 1877–81.

To Theodore Dwight Woolsey

Nation Office   New York, May 19, 1870 (Woolsey Papers CtY)

MY DEAR SIR: Your notice of Bernard would have appeared before now, if it were not for the presence of long standing arrears. I would have acknowledged its receipt and thanked you for it, however, if I had not hoped that its appearance in the *Nation* would before this have advised you of its safe arrival.[1]

Our rule is to pay everybody for everything, but when a master of a subject refuses money, as in the present instance, we do not feel sufficiently favored by fortune to force anything on him except our thanks, which in your case, I assure you are especially hearty.

Yours very truly
ELG

President Woolsey, New Haven

1. "Bernard's British Neutrality," *Nation*, 26 May 1870, pp. 339–40. President Woolsey of Yale College was an occasional contributor to the *Nation*. It was in his home in 1857 that Godkin met his first wife.

To Frederick Law Olmsted

Nation Office   New York, July 25, 1870
(Olmsted Papers, DLC)

MY DEAR OLMSTED: I am heartily glad to hear that you have a son. Fanny who goes to Mt. Desert today, and to whom I have sent your letter, will be so too. The best thing I can wish him, is that he may be in all respects like his father. May his enemies be scattered, their politics confounded, their knavish bricks frustrated, and his hours be exalted for seventy years at least.[1] Give my love to your wife, and let me hear how she gets on.

Yours heartily
ELG

Eliot has offered me the professorship of history at Harvard—at $4000. a year. I am inclined, if I can combine it with the *Nation* to take it. What do you think? Couldn't you lunch with me tomorrow, and talk of it—at one o'clock. Answer.

ELG

1. Frederick Law Olmsted, Jr. He followed in his father's footsteps to become a landscape architect and with his wife lived unpretentiously to an advanced age in California.

To Charles Eliot Norton

July 28, 1870 (Ogden 2:61–62)

MY DEAR NORTON: I am going through mental perplexities, in which I should dearly like to have your advice if it were within reach. Eliot has offered me the professorship of History at Harvard, and I am strongly tempted to accept. I should like the work —it is the optional course of the senior and junior classes; and I want to live at Cambridge,—strange as it may seem to you, who do live there,—partly on Fanny's account and mine, and partly on account of the children, whom I can hardly bear to see growing up in New York. To be near you, and Lowell and Gurney, in the latter end of my life, would be a great pleasure. But then the salary is small to settle down upon—$4000—and doubtless there is less of a certain kind of influence than in the *Nation*. I would not think of going, however, if I did not think that I might safely leave the *Nation* in the hands of Dennett—who would come back to it—and Garrison, and become myself a contributor and general supervisor. At all events my present idea is to try this, though as yet I have decided nothing. The Wards and Olmsted advise me to go, if it can be done without serious detriment to the *Nation*, and treat the offer as a clear "promotion" for me, which I am not at liberty to reject, as a valuable recognition of the work the *Nation* has done. The only thing I fear, or rather what I fear most, is that my leaving may produce an unfavorable impression on the public mind as to its condition.

Apart from the social attractions of the thing, I am tempted by the opportunity and inducement it offers to the cultivation of one subject. You can hardly understand how strong this craving is with me, and could not without passing as many years as I have done writing *de omnibus rebus*. I think it would be an important help to my mental growth, to which, "newspaper man" though I am, I am not altogether indifferent. And then I confess I have a burning longing to help to train up a generation of young men to hate Greeley and Tilton and their ways.

I wish I could get your opinion on all this before the die is cast, and am half tempted to ask you to telegraph it, at my expense, but if you write at once, I shall receive it before all is over. But I am deplorably one-sided myself. My judgment is completely warped by the prospect of living near you all. Fanny's mind is not yet made up, but she feels reluctant to abandon New York yet for many reasons, believing apparently that, as long as we are here, there is a chance of discovering somewhere a pot of gold. . . .

To Frederick Law Olmsted

Boston, August 2, 1870 (Olmsted Papers, DLC)

MY DEAR OLMSTED: I was very sorry indeed, to miss seeing you before I left town, as I wanted very much to talk over this Harvard proposition with you. I have stopped here on my way to Mt. Desert, to see Eliot and Gurney, and talk the matter over with them; and submitted to Eliot the plan you suggested—that is that I should continue to contribute to the *Nation*, and control, its general drift, but rather in the character of proprietor, than editor, while filling the office of professor of history here; but he submitted this to the leading members of the Corporation, and they exact an absolute cessation of all control or direction of the paper on my part.—though making no objection to my contributing as much as I please. To fulfil this condition in good faith, I would have, it seems to me, either to find a man to take my place, of whom I have no trace now, or else surrender all my interest present and future in the paper; in other words, give up all the fruits of my five years labor, except such reputation, as I may have derived from it, and (probably) ensure its death. You are the only man I know, to whom I would be willing to surrender completely all control, and act as a simple contributor for, and I suppose there is no use in talking of you.

On the other hand, I get very little money from the *Nation*, and its future is of course purely speculative, while the professorship offers me a moderate salary ($4000) for life, comparatively light work, long vacations, a cheaper place of residence, the society of agreeable friends, and certainly a better moral and social atmosphere for my children. These are strong temptations; but then, I give up all hope of larger income, and I confess, I don't think my value to the community would be as great, as a professor, as an editor. There is one other consideration which

affects me. A professorship, at Harvard, would do a great deal
to naturalize me—so to speak, that is would give me more of a
settled status as a member of the American community, than I
have now. I am a good deal perplexed in mind, and wish you
would turn the matter over, and give me your opinion. Nobody's
will affect me more, except my wife's, and whom I have not yet
seen. My address till Wednesday week will be *East Eden*, Maine,
and I have promised Eliot an answer by Friday week. If you
mail a letter on Thursday I shall get it on Saturday next, otherwise not till the following Wednesday; but I would sooner have
it on Wednesday than not at all.

My love to your wife, who, I hope is doing well.

Yours ever
ELG

To Samuel G. Ward

Boston, August 2 [1870] Ward Papers, MH

My dear Mr. Ward: I hoped to have got on here, before you
left, but was unable, and am now going on to Mt. Desert for a
few days. I wanted to ask your advice, about an offer of a professorship of history at Harvard Eliot has made me. . . . [It]
would amount, I think, to the death of the *Nation*. The position
at Harvard would be very pleasant, in every way, but the salary
is a very small one to settle down on for a finality, and I confess
I don't think I am of as much value as a professor as a journalist.

What do you think of the matter socially, pecuniarily, and
professionally? . . .

Yours very truly
ELG

To Professor E. Whitman Gurney

East Eden, Maine,   August 4 [1870] (Eliot Papers, MH-Ar)

My dear Gurney: The proposition I have to consider now, is
really whether I shall abandon the *Nation* altogether—dissolving
all connections with it, which I should consider tantamount to

killing it. As this is something more serious than I have hitherto
had in my mind, and indeed as the whole matter is for me, rather
ponderous, I wonder whether Eliot cannot give me a longer time
for consideration.[1] I have to see a great many people, who will
not be accessible for some weeks, and do not see, how I can
avoid, as a measure of safety, saying no absolutely, unless I have a
good deal of time for reflection. Could I have, till Sept 1. do
you suppose?

Yours ever
ELG

1. Professor Gurney was chairman of the history department at Harvard,
but Eliot made decisions about hiring faculty.

To Charles W. Eliot

East Eden, Maine,   August 6, 1870 (Eliot Papers, MH-Ar)

MY DEAR SIR: I think it would be hardly fair to you, to come to
a decision on your proposal, without saying what is passing in
my mind after a good deal of consideration, and taking the opinion of many friends, with regard to the objection you make on
behalf of the Corporation to my retaining my connection with
the *Nation*. It seems to me that allowing me to contribute to a
paper, provided I did not "control" it, would be a distinction
without a difference. A paper is only a collection of articles;
if I wrote many of them on the important questions of the day,
the fact could not be concealed, and my control of it though
not nominal would be real. This would be true whether I wrote
for the *Nation* or any other paper. In fact if by accepting your
offer under the condition proposed, I dissolved my pecuniary
and editorial connection with the paper, I should, I think acknowledge virtually, the right of the Corporation to enquire
into the nature of my work outside the College, and restrain
the expression of my opinions and the use of my pen, even where
they in no way [impair] my efficiency as a professor. They
could always say that I was "compromising" the college by my
contributions just as much as by my editing. I hardly think any
man worthy of the place, would put himself in a position of this
kind.

Moreover, I cannot help saying that the restriction sought to be imposed on me is unusual if not unprecedented. I cannot admit, that a University such as you seek to make Harvard, can be compromised by any action on the part of its professors, which does not betray ignorance, or absurdity, or want of moral principle. The professors of all the leading Universities of the world, publish what opinions they please, as long as they are not in direct opposition to doctrines—theological for instance, which they are paid to teach. Goldwin Smith, while professor of history at Oxford, took a public and prominent part with pen and tongue, in an agitation for objects, which were intensely obnoxious to the University, and the class which supports [it]. I do not believe that the professional propriety of his doing so, was ever questioned. I might multiply these illustrations. One of the great uses of history is to furnish a key to contemporary problems, and a professor of history who was forbidden to apply his knowledge or influence to their solution, as an observer and not as a party politician—no one can suspect me of any tendency in that direction—would be, in a position which I cannot help calling false. You might as well forbid a medical professor to attend a patient, or a chemist to analyze for judicial purposes. If, however, there is in my career anything which seems to the Corporation to call for exceptional *restrictions*, I need hardly say that I can have no hesitation in declining any position they would think of offering me.

Will you pardon me, if as a personal friend I make one more remark, which does not directly concern my case. I find that one great cause of the small account in which a University education, and University men are popularly held, in this country, is the general belief that they have no connection with practical affairs. A professor is looked on as a sort of bookish monk, of whose opinions on the affairs of the world, nobody need take any account. My friends advise m[e] not to accept your offer, because it will be the loss of all my influence, and power, whatever they may be, and relegation to a sort of comfortable obscurity. I cannot help thinking that it is the business of the University to fight this feeling by every means in their power, to show that their history and political economy have a direct relation to the affairs of the day, and that a professor can be something more than a teacher of speculative opinions to boys.

I shall reserve my final answer, till you have considered these objections, etc.

> Very truly yours
> ELG

To Frederick Law Olmsted

East Eden, Maine,   August 8 [1870] (Olmsted Papers, DLC)

MY DEAR OLMSTED: Many thanks for your letters.

Take into account—that the *Nation* is this year barely abreast, with its expenses, that it gains very slowly, that I have for four years drawn only $2000 from it, per annum; that when money is short, for the payment of interest or any office purpose, it is I who suffer,—that it comes out of my pocket; that I positively cannot afford to give my time any more for any such sum, inasmuch as my expenses are increasing, that nobody turns up to take my place, and relieve me from the dead grind for even a month; that I see no prospect ahead of any relaxation, relief, or vacation; that the loss of my health would kill it inevitably, and leave me with slender means, and without a profession,—for journalism unless you can have a paper, and own it, is not a profession—Consider these things as elements in the problem. How much risk to myself and family am I bound to run for the public good? Is there any thoroughly good work of this kind done for the world except by men, whose minds are at ease about the pecuniary future?

I do not mention these things as complete answers to your arguments, which are very powerful, and indeed have strengthened Fanny's mind, and affected my own so powerfully against Harvard, that I doubt if I shall not refuse; but they are things I am bound to consider. Going to Harvard would put me at my ease pecuniarily both as regards my present and future, and indeed take all anxiety on this score completely out of my life. How far is a man of forty bound to disregard a consideration of this kind?

On general principles, even looking at life from its material side, I confess, I think there seems to be folly in working at an enterprize for five years, and when one has got it to the brink of success abandoning it. It is against all the ordinary rules, and I don't like to do it without being very well satisfied in my own mind, that I am making a step onward. I shall be here till next Monday.

Fanny joins me in love to your wife. I wish you were both up here.

Yours ever
ELG

To Charles W. Eliot

Nation Office   New York, August 25, 1870
(Eliot Papers, MH-Ar)

MY DEAR SIR: After mature deliberation I have come to the conclusion that I must decline your offer of the professorship. In doing so, I do great violence to my own personal inclinations, which all urge me to accept, but I do not feel at liberty to run counter to the almost unanimous counsel of my friends, given on public as well as private grounds, not to abandon the *Nation*. I may be differently minded a year hence, but do not feel warranted in asking you to delay your arrangements on this chance.

With the warmest sympathy for your work, and many thanks for the honor you have done me, I remain

Very truly yours
ELG

To Charles Eliot Norton

[September, 1870] (Ogden 1:254)

. . . If it were not for Louis Napoleon's fate . . . I would say that all those cups of the wicked have holes in them. What a splendid 'Special Providence' he now seems! The Lord is evidently not dead yet. . . .[1]

1. His earlier admiration for Louis Napoleon now changed to deep dislike, Godkin supported victorious Prussia during the Franco-Prussian War, just ending.

To Frederick Law Olmsted

10 West 48th St., New York, September 19 [1870]
(Olmsted Papers, DLC)

MY DEAR OLMSTED: I have only got back from New Haven to-day. I am glad to hear what you say about Potter, and very much obliged to him. The Philadelphians have all surrendered their notes, with very handsome expressions of confidence and good will.[1] If the other New Yorkers and Bostonians do the same, it will be a great help to us. I will send you the Philadelphia letters, as soon as I can get them from McKim. It is the more creditable to them, as they are protectionists, and feel that the paper is hostile to them.

Yours ever
ELG

The total amt of notes is about $18000—Potter and Brown abt $400 each. You ought to reply *at once* to the disgraceful obituary notice of Pilot in today's *Tribune*.

1. A reference to Godkin's successful effort to get majority ownership of the *Nation* by persuading the remaining stockholders to donate their interest in the weekly to E. L. Godkin and Company.

To Frederick F. Cook [1]

Nation Office   New York, October 6, 1870 (Ogden 2:69–70)

DEAR SIR: The *Nation* receives from time to time very warm expressions of sympathy and approval from men of all sorts, but I assure you there is none which has half the value in my eyes of testimony such as yours from young men who have been led by it to believe that there are better things in store for the world than can be reached through "the regular ticket," and that democracy will never have half a fair trial till brains and knowledge and good morals have been enlisted into its service, which they never yet have been.

I think we may fairly look forward to building up on the ruins of the Republican party a better party than we have yet had, and I trust that in a year hence we shall see our way to it more clearly than we do now, having for its object Tariff Reform, Civil Service Reform, and Minority Representation, and basing its action on the facts of human nature and the experience of the human race. We shall always have plenty of old hacks and windbags to deal with, but the day will come when they will simply amuse us.

> Very truly yours
> ELG

1. A young reporter on the *Chicago Tribune*.

To George P. Marsh

10 West 48th St., New York, October 6, 1870
(Marsh Papers, VtU)

MY DEAR MR. MARSH: I have duly received your two papers on the Revision of the Scriptures: one is in type and will appear next week; the rest in succession. Many thanks for them. Your amanuensis has left us cause for anxiety as regards the proofs; though it would ill become me to find fault, in my own handwriting, with the legibility of yours.

I am very much flattered and gratified by what you say about the Cambridge professorship. It was of course a compliment, for which I could not but feel grateful, to have the chair offered me, and it was in various ways very tempting to me personally. But I could not see my way to leaving the *Nation*. It would probably have died had I done so, and I received so many strong expressions of the importance of keeping it going at this juncture, that I could not escape the conclusion that I was bound in honor to remain, though I do so at the sacrifice of a good deal of comfort, and at some cost to my children, whom I dislike exceedingly to bring up in New York.

Things political look as badly here, as I have ever known them, and I fear will not improve during the present administration. A conversation yesterday with Secretary Coxe [*sic*], leads me to fear his and Fish's resignation before Christmas, and the Administration then will be literally rudderless. With Morton in London, and God knows who in the State Department there would be material for some serious complications.[1]

Very cordially yours
ELG

Hon. G. P. Marsh.

1. Godkin is referring to Grant's Secretary of State Hamilton Fish (1808–93) and to Secretary of the Interior Jacob Dolson Cox (1828–1900), who served from 1874–90 as military critic of the *Nation*. Cox's forced resignation from Grant's cabinet shortly after this letter was written angered Republican independents and was one of the underlying causes of the Liberal Republican revolt of 1872. In spite of Godkin's fears, Republican leader Oliver P. Morton (1823–77) declined the English mission.

To Daniel Coit Gilman

Nation Office   New York, November 20 [1870]
(Gilman Papers, MdBJ)

MY DEAR GILMAN: Hoyt is badly bruised by your notice of him.[1] I send you by mail his last production, of which I should like to have a brief notice from you, and on which you might perhaps let him down easier.

Yours very truly
ELG

1. *Nation*, 13 October 1870, p. 242. Review of John W. Hoyt, "Report on Education." Vol. 6 of *Reports of the United States Commissioners to the Paris Universal Exposition* (Washington, D.C., 1870). Hoyt (1831–1912) was an early supporter of the National University scheme.

To Moses Coit Tyler

Nation Office   New York, November 30, 1870
(Tyler Papers, NIC)

MY DEAR SIR: I think we shall be glad to have another letter; the present one is very interesting.[1]

I am, of course, very much gratified by the testimony you are pleased to bear to the character and influence of the *Nation;* and particularly by what you say as to the soundness of the judgment we passed on Professor Evans.[2] I was embarassed and somewhat pained by his calling on me, on his way through, and offering to send us contributions from Europe, which I was of course obliged to decline. It was on the whole a pitiable affair. I shall be very glad to see you at Christmas.

Yours very truly
ELG

1. "Affairs at the University of Michigan," *Nation*, 5 December 1870, pp. 383–84.
2. Edward P. Evans (1831–1917) resigned his professorship at the University of Michigan and expatriated himself after a charge of plagiarism was made against him in connection with his textbook, *Abriss der Deutschen Literaturgeschichte*. See *Nation*, 24 February 1870, pp. 123–24.

To Carl Schurz

Nation Office   New York, December 1, 1870
(Schurz Papers, DLC)

MY DEAR SIR: Could you be persuaded to find us a fortnightly letter from Washington during the Session, giving not a recital of events, but the comments on them of a well-informed and intelligent observer?

If you would do this under your own name, I think you would do your reputation no harm, and you would reach as good, and in the long run as influential public as there is in the country, and greatly help the various reforms which you as well as we have at heart.

If on the other hand you would prefer to do it anonymously, we would keep your secret with the greatest ease, and be willing to pay you well.

May I hear from you on the subject in any event at your earliest convenience.[1] Let me remind you, before closing, that the *Nation* is read with a care which is accorded to no other paper in the country, and your letters would not be thrown aside, after one day, as mere "Washington Correspondence."

Yours very truly
ELG

1. Schurz, then United States Senator from Missouri, subsequently agreed to supply the *Nation* with anonymous contributions.

To his wife

10 West 48th St., New York, December 1, 1870
(Godkin Papers, MH)

MY DEAR FANNY: The evening you left, I dined at J. P. Thompsons, old girl named Stetson on one side; old Dr. Buddington of Brooklyn on other. Company—Bryant, odious Dr. Thompson, (Brace's) and Dr. Allen, editor of *British Quarterly Review*, Congregational Minister from London—a conceited blatherskite, whose head is turned by the attentions he is receiving in America. To me who know what an Islington Congregation is, it was amusing to hear his talk about them.

Nov. 4. went to New Haven to attend Civil Service meeting in the College. Stayed at Gilman's; tea party in my honor. Cook, Fisher, Brush, and Porter. Gorgeous—oysters, partridges, and finches. Meeting in college, Woolsey presiding—all the bigwigs there. I was called on to open proceedings with a speech, and made some remarks. A very warm letter to Cox was drawn up and signed. It will do good.[1]

Nov. 5. . . . Went to Century [Club] in the evening, and had a nice time as usual. Mundella was there, we elected Sturgis, after some amusing opposition from Vaux, who hates him, and also Lord Walter Campbell, with whom I had some talk and who is really a good fellow.[2] Got home late.

6th. Quiet morning. Work steady. Jenny here. She and Fred to tea in the evening.[3] She tries to talk up to me, and does it by asking me incessantly silly questions—such as—Do *you* like Dickens?—or Will the Prussians take Paris; a great bore. Lost my evening with them and was awfully glad when they went.

7th. Breakfast at Bolton's—Mundella, Ripley, S. D. Ruggles (awful old bore), Brace, H. M. Field, Julius Bing (!) and one or two others. Mundella and Ripley talked well; the others said little. Left early. Sumner came to dinner in the evening. Went in inadvertently to front parlor in afternoon, and found him and Jenny in a tender position—very embarrassing for all. Sumner's style of speaking very vulgar and trying.[4] Jenny's inadvertent revelations of the way he is trying to educate her very amusing; but she is really improving; the heathen darkness of old times is passing away. . . .

10th. . . . I went to the annual dinner of the Mercantile Library Association at Delmonico's. Large company, 200. Guests, A. T. Stewart, Peter Cooper, Hewitt, Gens McDowell and Webb, Dr. Adams, Potter, and Tiffany, (Rockwell's) S. L. Woodford, (defeated candidate for Governor) common genial blatherskite, who sat near me, and was very attentive, and flattering, two Dodges, etc, etc. I responded for the press, and made the best speech of my ignoble oratorical career. I said some very plain things about the absurdity of abusing the press, while reading and supporting the blackguard papers. . . . It was curious to see the flattery and attention Stewart received; the selfish old hog, was even taken into dinner before old Peter Cooper, who with all his faults is worth ten of him. . . .

11th. . . . Went down town in the p.m. and saw Mannion,— you remember him in Paris—the mellifluous Irishman. He is now the agent of the Rothschilds in New Orleans, and came to see me with an article from a distressed Southern woman one of the Hugers of S.C. a pitiful story; she wants to write, and doesn't know enough, and is wretchedly poor. Dined in the evening at the Schuylers—Georgie, Professor and Mrs. H. B. Smith. Pleasant enough. H. B. is quite entertaining. General Van Alen—gassy —came in the evening. . . . I am looking about for a house; if I see anything tempting I will buy. But the elections have had and will have a very depressing effect on city property. The Ring are again victorious.

12th. . . . Went to the office in the p.m. and while there received a visit from Carl Schurz, the German Senator from Missouri; a tall gaunt man, but very pleasant. Like so many others profuse in his compliments about the *Nation*. . . . Went to the Century in the evening leaving your mother fast asleep. Saw Judge Daly, Mundella, Fred Kingsbury and Curtis, and Robinson. Long talk with Daly and found to my surprise, he was a Prussian sympathizer. Mundella is fairly used up; two dinners a day and never in bed before one a.m.

13th. Sunday. . . . Went to Brevoort House by appointment to see Mundella, and set [*sic*] nearly two hours with him, talking of things here, and listening to a piece of a lecture he is going to deliver tomorrow evening. He is a very nice fellow, and it is curious to see how his Italian blood makes him effervesce. . . .

14th. Went in evening to hear Mundella's lecture—saw and talked with Curtis (G.W.), the Schuylers, Dodge, General Howard, Potter etc. Lecture very good, an account of courts of arbitration in Nottingham very interesting. Went to Century afterwards, met the whole party. Saw Whittredge, who talked of Cincinnati [*sic*] in the older time. Had some bier [*sic*] and came home. Brace there in his foolish mood. Mrs. F[oote] got cold on Sunday by going to hear Osgood in St. Thomas's. The poor idiot (Osgood) is now an Episcopalian. . . . I am very busy and have been out a good deal in the evening. What with the Cox business, and the fight among the Massachusetts radicals, these are great times for the *Nation*. . . .

15th. Went down to Staten Island today with the California Ashburner, to see a house the Olmsteds had discovered. Saw a charming old house in perfect repair—on a hill top between New Brighton and Clifton; 15 minutes from boat; $25,000 for house and four acres, a perfectly enchanting place—The Olmsteds think so too, and would like to take half the house, and are very eager to go there with us. It is very cheap as an investment; but I don't want to be burdened with another big house. If you were here we might consider it. Dined in the evening at the [Free] Trade Club—Sands, Marshall, Robinson, Pell, Minturn, Blake and two others; very pleasant indeed. Robinson told me, that the *Nation* had been ordered for the reading room of the Bar association, although they only take legal periodicals, on the ground that it "discusses legal questions with much acuteness". . . .

16th. Went to dentist, and had teeth overhauled. Advancing years is telling on them. Wheat says that the nerve "is the most wonderful of all things created by the Creator of the Universe." Went to see Sarah Woolsey, who is in town for a day or two [,] after dinner. She is looking very well and hearty. Was greatly shocked at hearing you were gone. Dorsey and his wife were there; wife a perfect stick. Like most New Yorkers she looks greatly puzzled by a joke. . . . I am going to the Gurneys the first week in December.

18th. Rainy day. There being no news of steamer in morning papers, [your mother] was in a terrible state. I remained, however, very calm—even cold; had there been any one here to talk the matter over with, and to sympathize with her, she would have gone into perfect tantrums. The steamer arrived about noon, and we are expecting your letters tomorrow morning. If by any mischance they don't come, I don't know what will happen. I think she would be far more comfortable with Kate, as she would then have some one to talk to. I should not be at all surprised if she started by the next steamer for Nassau. . . .[5]

19th. Your letter arrived this morning. . . . I think she was almost disappointed to find all the news so good; but she fastened with a good deal of tenacity on Harry's having moved up another story, and if there were any one here to talk about it, would, I think, make trouble. I am satisfied, that nothing is so good for her as to have no sympathizer near her. . . . Your letter was a masterpiece. . . . It is quite evident that all your correspondence hitherto has suffered from simple laziness. If you would sit down and take pains you would write as well as any one. . . . Harry must be sure and go on a voyage in the spring. Let there be no shilly–shallying about this. . . .

21th. Hard at work; little or nothing from Dennett, who is one of the most unreliable men, it has pleased God to create. He will never come to anything. The Conference of "revenue reformers," comes off here tomorrow, and is to wind up with a public dinner next week. There is an awful row going on about Cox in the papers. Scurrility fills the air. . . .

22th. Was as usual busy all day. Went in the evening in torrents of rain to the meeting of revenue reformers. There were about forty present. It was very successful, and I was amused by the growing deference with which my opinions are treated. The two Adamses were there. C. F. is growing quite fat and chubby, and looks more comical than ever. All our people are in high spirits. The Lord is delivering the politicians into our hands. Hawley of Hartford takes the President's side against Cox; isn't that characteristic? [6] We broke up late, and Sands slept here. An invitation from Mrs. Barlow to dine there on Friday and meet Mrs. Lowell (sister). Furious storm.

23th. Had to get [up] very early; went down town and did chores till half past 12. Then had lunch with the Adamses, and went about with Henry arranging with booksellers to push *N A Review*. . . .[7] The Adamses say the hold the *Nation* is taking of people in Boston is something unparalleled. Our circulation is increasing *really* very rapidly. Sarah Woolsey sends an article on women in politics—but rather feeble. Wherever Sarah has to reflect she breaks down; but how good she is. . . .

24th. Thanksgiving. Beautiful day. 10 lb. turkey, and dinner ordered at two o'clock at Lawrence's earnest request. . . . After dinner I took Lawrence down to see the newsboys take theirs in Eighteenth St. It was a fearful scene of stuffing, and I called his attention to how "piggy," they ate. George Ward was there, the usual halo round his brow. . . . Invitation today to the great free trade dinner on Monday. I am having so much dining out this winter that I am forced to put myself on a strict regimen. I have stopped smoking, and coffee; I suppose I shall always have to be patching myself up in order to be equal to the ordinary duties of life, till the day comes when I shall be pronounced not worth further repairs.

25th. . . . Dined at the Barlows; nobody but Mrs. Lowell. She is a very interesting person; rather sad, but evidently full of feeling and enthusiasm, and talks very well. Barlow had to go out after dinner, and I spent a couple of hours very pleasantly with the ladies. These Shaw women are not pretty, however, except Mrs. Minturn. The Barlow table looks very nice, especially the China. They are very pleasant, and of our kind and I enjoyed myself.

26th. . . . Found on going down to the office, that Schuyler Colfax had called to pay his respects to me!! Never was more amused in my life. We have bombarded this man and all his breed, seed and generation for five years, and now, he finds that it would be well to be on good terms, so in he walks. Went to Century in the evening—with Sands who called here after dinner —Curtis, (W. E.), Blodgett, Robbins, Robinson, Cyrus Field. Field called me aside and enquired after much hemming and hawing, whether a half of the *Nation* could be purchased. I told him I thought not. It is not for this that I have lived laborious days.

27th. Sunday. . . . Went in the carriage with Sands after dinner to call on Horace White of Chicago at Albemarle. . . . Fred called at tea time, I declining an invitation to meet the Ripleys at tea at the Fields'. Went over there at nine o'clock and found several queer, and a few nice people. The Sands are in their house which looks lovely.[8] The dining room is a gem, particularly as regards the paper and the chandelier. How pleasant it must be to have money!

28th. . . . Went to the Free Trade dinner at Delmonicos in the evening. Large company, Wells made a capital speech, but Minturn presided and was terribly embarrassed, this being his first appearance in public. Sands made a speech, too, and broke down in the middle but not badly. Marshall seeing the fate that had overtaken his two companions, looked very nervous.[9] I having nothing of this kind impending over me, ate a quiet and comfortable dinner, and enjoyed the troubles of the Young Apostles. Walked home with Schlesinger, who used to live next to us in Nineteenth St. He has been subscribing to the *Nation* for some time without knowing that I edited it. . . .

29th. . . . Mr. and Mrs. Stetson have just been in, and sat for a good while. She told us about Charlotte [Varian's?] troubles with old Hoffman her husband. He is drunk as a fiddler most of his time, and she has left him. I was tempted to ask her about the [Tulmans?] but forebore, lest I should laugh. Charley Richards has lost his eye through an accident, but *per contra*, is rector of the principal Episcopal church in Providence. Mrs. Stetson seems very well. . . .

We hear nothing from the Woolseys about the house; several other people have been to see it. I don't like to be here when they come; it always irritates me to have them poking about and making remarks. One fellow asked me if it was not built for a clergyman; the architecture was he said, "Kind o' ecclesiastical," and he said it would make a capital parsonage for the church over the way.

Dennett came on today, looking fat and well. If the wretch had any conscience how delightful it would be.

Your flowers began to die out, and we had to have them removed. I don't know what was the matter with them. I sat next to Blake at the dinner, and he told me about Talboys, whose life he said is now positively scandalous. What a disgusting set those Stebbinses are. . . .

Nov. 30. *I have paid your passage*, and enclose receipt, which you must not give up except in return for a ticket, which they will give you at the office in Nassau or on board. You can arrange it with the purser. They will write out from here, *and have writ-*

ten to Havana to secure you a stateroom. Lawrence is all right again today, and we are all well. And now good bye, my dear love, till I see you on the wharf. I trust you will have smooth weather.

Your affectionate husband
ELG [10]

1. A letter of support to J. D. Cox in his dispute with the Grant Administration. Professor George P. Fisher (1827–1909) was one of Godkin's Yale acquaintances and an occasional contributor on church history to the *Nation*. Professor Noah Porter (1811–92) was soon to be appointed president of Yale, Woolsey having announced his retirement, and George J. Brush (1831–1912) was professor of mineralogy at Yale.

2. Anthony J. Mundella (1825–97) was an English political leader and reformer. Russell Sturgis (1836–1909) served for thirty years as the art and architecture critic of the *Nation*.

3. Mrs. Godkin's cousins, Jeannie [*sic*] and Fred Elliott.

4. The political economist William Graham Sumner of Yale (1840–1910) married Jeannie Elliott. His relations with Godkin were never cordial.

5. Mrs. Godkin was in Nassau, helping her brother Harry seek relief for his tuberculosis. Meanwhile, their mother Mrs. Foote stayed at Godkin's home to care for the two Godkin children, Lawrence and Lizzie (Kittens).

6. Former Governor Joseph R. Hawley (1826–1905) of Connecticut. In 1868 Hawley was permanent chairman of the Republican National Convention.

7. Henry Adams (1838–1918), a friend of Godkin and sometime Washington D.C. correspondent of the *Nation*, had just supplanted Gurney as editor of the *North American Review*.

8. Katharine Buckley Sands would ultimately become Godkin's second wife.

9. A reference to the American Free Trade League founded in 1867. Active in it in New York were revenue reformer David A. Wells, Robert B. Minturn, Mahlon Sands, R. R. Bowker, Charles H. Marshall, and Alfred Pell. Linked to it was the Round Table, a dining club which met at the Knickerbocker Club and whose genteel members made tariff reform the principal cause for which they were "ready to dine." Besides Godkin, its habitués included Marshall, Pell, and New York lawyer E. Randolph Robinson, a transplanted Virginian descended from John Randolph. Later the interests of the club broadened with the addition of painter John LaFarge, geologist Clarence King, psychiatrist S. Weir Mitchell, and New York lawyer James C. Carter. Wells, Minturn, Marshall, Sands, and LaFarge were occasional contributors to the *Nation*.

10. It is interesting to compare the text of this letter with the bowdlerized one in Ogden.

To Jacob Dolson Cox

Nation Office   New York, Dec. 3, 1870 (Cox Papers, OO)

MY DEAR SIR: I don't want to pester you, but as long as this controversy is raging you can hardly call your Civil Service work
done. May I trouble you to read the enclosed from the N. Y.
Times of today, and write me a line on it. It is very amusing to
see the way in which your opponents are now at work. They
are gradually trying to make you into not only no help to Civil
Service Reform, but a hindrance to it, and Boutwell as the great
friend of the movement.[1]

Yours very truly
ELG

1. Cox resigned from Grant's cabinet in October 1870, under fire from
party stalwarts around the President. George S. Boutwell (1818–1905) was
Grant's secretary of the treasury.

To Frederick A. P. Barnard

10 West 48th St., New York [January, 1871?]
(Special Collection, NNC)

MY DEAR SIR: We are to have a meeting of the committee of the
Social Science Association here at my house this evening, to
which I am asking a few other gentlemen interested in the work
of the organization, to hear some explanatory remarks from Dr.
Eliot.[1]

I shall be very much gratified, if you can make it convenient to
be present.

Yours very truly
ELG

1. Frederick A. P. Barnard (1809–89) was the president of Columbia College. Charles W. Eliot had recently become president of the American Social Science Association.

To James A. Garfield

New York, January 11, 1871 (Garfield Papers, DLC)

MY DEAR GENERAL: Could you be persuaded to furnish us a Washington letter once a fortnight or thereabouts? We should be glad to pay you well for it, and if you chose to be anonymous to keep your secret carefully. We want something better than can be got from the ordinary newspaper man and since Henry Adams left Washington [we] are at sea.

Yours very truly
ELG

To George Jones

10 West 48th St., New York, February 17 [1871?]
(*New York Times*, 27 March 1872)

DEAR MR. JONES: I have just received a note from H. F. Raymond and Co. expressing dissatisfaction with the working of the arrangement for my contributions to the *Times*, and proposing to pay me only for what you use.

The difficulty in meeting your wants is, I think, somewhat due to the very delicate way the *Times* handles a great many questions; but, then, this is your affair.

I am willing to consider anything you propose as a substitute, but it would hardly pay me to write chance articles now and then for any compensation you would be likely to offer, or even to hold myself ready to write them, for, of course, I have to regulate my time and engagements, with reference to my liabilities in the way of literary work.

Still, if you will suggest topics, say twice a week, and say what you will pay for each article used, I will say yes or no, if no, of course the arrangements drops.

Yours very truly
ELG

To George Jones

February 19 [1871?] (*New York Times*, 27 March 1872)

. . . [the *Times* ought to] speak out more strongly. . . . My belief is, your policy is to pitch in, and not handle things too gingerly. . . .

To Mrs. Samuel E. Foote

10 West 48th St., New York, March 28 [1871]
(Godkin Papers, MH)

DEAR MRS. FOOTE: . . . I am afraid you will never cease to feel responsible for this house, and to wish it was something else than it is. As long as you do so, we shall never be comfortable in it. My object in taking it off the hands of the estate, and assuming the whole burden of it, was to clear everybody else's mind of all care about it. . . . The house is not what it might be, but there is no better house *for the money*, and I am assured it could not now be built for the same sum; and we are very well satisfied with it. But unless all complaints about it can be given up, I will not stay in it under any circumstances. . . .

About John Woodward [and your other nephews] I think it is highly desirable that you made it clearly understood by all these young men, that if they want capital they must save it, and if they get into straits, they cannot depend on you. . . .

All this will perhaps sound hard, but I think the case calls for hard speech. I have rarely known a case less deserving of commiseration than John Woodward's except Fred Elliott's, and he has three able bodied brothers.[1] Surely such a bunch ought to be able to make their way. . . .

Yours affectly
ELG

We had a short note from Harry which Fanny will send you.

1. Nephews of Godkin's mother-in-law.

To Carl Schurz

Nation Office New York, April 5, 1871 (Schurz Papers, DLC)

My DEAR SIR: Of course you are the best judge of the propriety of your appearing at the revenue reform meeting here; and I confess your arguments against it do seem convincing. I suppose on the whole, it is questionable whether your open connection with the Free Trade League would not lessen your influence in the Senate. At the same time, the revenue reform movement suffers among the people from not having older and better known men openly related to it, if not actively working for it, but they will probably get over this difficulty before long.

I humbly agree with you as to the necessity for breaking down the Administration and its hangers on. It has turned out a deplorable failure, and nothing ought to be left undone to put an end to the prospect of Grant's renomination. But I think the points of attack should be points that are clearly vulnerable and at which success is certain. I did not think Sumner's removal was of this class.[1] Doubtless the interference of the Administration with the legislature is offensive, and injurious, but there is a widespread and not wholly unfounded impression that the encroachments for some years back have been the other way, so that you could get up much popular indignation on this cry. Moreover Sumner's faults of temper, and especially his vanity and annoyance are well known; you cannot, therefore, persuade people that he is altogether in the right in any controversy, in which his self love is wounded, or that it would be possible for anybody to whom he bore a grudge, to transact business with him. It seemed to me, therefore, not possible to make anything out of the Sumner affair, against the Administration; while an unsuccessful attempt to do so, would injure the party at large, and open the way to the Democrats. The St. Domingo affair on the other hand, and his gross misconduct with regard to the Civil Service; his coarse surroundings, his gross ignorance, and the general atmosphere of corruption in which he has enveloped himself afford plenty of opportunity for attacks on him, that will injure *him* only.

My firm belief is that if in the next few years, a strong reform party, led by thoughtful, educated, highminded men—gentlemen in short—does not get possession of the government we shall witness some great catastrophe. I know that the New York view of matters is apt to be gloomy, and with good reason, but I find the same story comes in from all parts of the country.

The first thing to be done, is of course, as you say, to get rid of the officemongering element, composed of the rash politicians and the corrupt schemers whom they serve. But I think, in order to strengthen your forces for the nominating Convention, you cannot be too outspoken, or throw yourself *too* strongly on the reform element in public opinion. There is nothing just now so strong as this. The party, apart from reform, is very weak, and has a very slight hold on the country.

I am sorry not to have the prospect of seeing you here; perhaps I may in Washington before you break up.

Very truly yours
ELG

1. Grant had succeeded through his partisans in the Senate in having Senator Charles Sumner stripped of his post as chairman of the Senate Foreign Relations Committee, principally because of Sumner's opposition to his Santo Domingo annexation scheme.

To Charles Eliot Norton

May 6, 1871 (Ogden 1:307)

. . . Howells has just breakfasted with us, and is gone, as sweet and gentle and winning in all ways as ever. He succeeds to the *Atlantic Monthly* in August, *vice* Fields, who retires into private life. Howells *grows* steadily, I think, and in all ways, for he has become very stout. He talks despondently like everybody else about the condition of morals and manners. Fields and Osgood have had a valuable reinforcement within the last month in the person of Bret Harte, who has come from San Francisco and is our latest literary sensation. I suppose you have read his sketches of California life which appeared in the *Overland Monthly*, and which showed real genius. His poems, too, have been very popular, and the "Heathen Chinee" has become a household word. He is, too, a very sensible fellow, whom all the braying there has been about him has not spoilt, and I think will not. There can be no doubt that the literary men of the country, as a class, improve every year, and so do the newspapers; is not this a good sign? . . .

Eliot has asked me to deliver a course of "University lectures," but I doubt if I shall do so. I am too hard worked and cannot afford to do anything more, without pay, and these lectures are so poorly attended that the pay amounts to nothing. The audiences average ten or twelve persons, mainly women. They would be more successful if delivered in Boston; but also more "popular" than "University." Harvard seems to flourish, and it is curious and amusing to see the new life it has infused into Yale. The healthy influence of competition was never better illustrated. The Yale men have started a post-graduate course in Philology, which it would be hard to beat, having Whitney and Hadley for the principal lecturers.[1] Hadley is an uncommonly able man, of immense learning and thorough in all that he touches, who is kept from being famous by his modesty, which is aggravated by lameness. . . .

1. William D. Whitney and James Hadley (1821–72), the latter a distinguished professor of Greek at Yale and occasional contributor to the *Nation*.

To Edward Atkinson

New York, June 29, 1871 (Atkinson Papers, MHi)

MY DEAR SIR: The note of Godkin, Olmsted and McKim which you hold, falls due July 1. We have applied to all the other holders to allow the notes to lie over for the present, and if possible without payment of the interest, inasmuch as we are unable to meet them, and have the alternative, as you may remember under the agreement, of surrendering the paper. This we have no disposition to do. . . . I have myself given it five years hard and incessant labors and have drawn from it by way of salary about $1300 a year. . . .

I, therefore, during the winter laid the matter before the ex-stockholders, and asked each one to do whatever he thought proper in the matter. All the Philadelphians except one surrendered their notes; all the New Yorkers except two did the same thing, and all the Bostonians except Mr. Endicott and Mr. Ames, to whom owing to his recent failure we did not apply. . . .

I should be very much obliged if you would turn the matter over in your mind, and let me know your decision. Should you feel bound to insist on payment now, we can, I believe arrange for it.

Yours very truly
ELG

To John Seeley Hart

New York, August 26 [1871] (Hart Papers, NIC)

DEAR SIR: . . . In reply to your inquiries, I have to say that I was born in 1831 in Wicklow Co, thirty miles from Dublin (Ireland), my father being at the time of my birth, a candidate for orders in the Episcopal Church, but subsequently becoming a Congregational minister.[1] I was educated at a Grammar School near Wakefield, Yorkshire (England) and at Queen's College Belfast, one of the three colleges of the Queen's University in Ireland. After leaving college, and while preparing myself for the bar, Mr. Knight Hunt, the then editor of the *Daily News*, whose attention had been attracted by some of my contributions to the periodical press, requested me to go to Turkey as the correspondent of that paper, in view of the war then impending between Turkey and Russia.

I accordingly went out in that capacity in the fall of 1853, reaching the Turkish headquarters on the Danube immediately after the action of Oltenitza. I passed the winter in the Turkish camp at Kalafat on the Upper Danube, crossed the river with the main body in the summer of 1854, after witnessing the operations at Silistria, and passed the autumn travelling about in Transylvania, and the Danubian Principalities.

In January 1855, I went to the Crimea, and passed the remainder of the winter at Eupatoria, going to Sebastopol in April, where I witnessed the battles of the Tchernaia, of June 18th and the final assault on the place. After some excursions in Asia Minor, I returned to England, broken down in health, in the following winter.

In the fall of 1856, I came to this country, and passed the months of November, December, and January following in a horse back journey through the Southern, and South Western states, an account of which I communicated to the *Daily News* in a series of letters. On my return to New York I determined to settle here and engage in the practice of the law and entered the office of Mr. D. D. Field by way of preparation, and in 1858, was admitted to the bar. In 1859, my health broke down, and I returned to Europe, passing the years 1861–2 on the continent, mainly in Paris and Switzerland, but doing no work, beyond making occasional editorial contributions to the *Daily News* on American questions. The opening articles, which threw that journal on the northern side, were, perhaps I may mention, written by me.[2] I returned to New York towards the close of 1862, and until the establishment of the *Nation* in 1865, was the correspondent of the *Daily News* here, and a regular editorial contributor to the *New York Times*, as I had been in the years 1858–9, but nothing more. Beyond a few articles in quarterlies on political or economical topics, my literary work has been done wholly for the newspaper press, and my only book, is a small history of Hungary, written in a flash of enthusiasm after I had left college and which I do not care to own, or have recalled. . . .

I am, dear Sir, your obedient Servant
ELG

J. S. Hart Esq. LL. D.
May I request you to acknowledge the receipt of this?

1. Godkin is supplying Hart with biographical information for a literary encyclopedia. See "Edwin L. Godkin," in John Seeley Hart, ed., *A Manual of American Literature* (Philadelphia, 1873), p. 413

2. This statement is false. In a subsequent letter to Hart, Godkin partly corrected the impression that he was responsible for the pro-Union stance of the *Daily News* at the beginning of the war.

To John Seeley Hart

New York, August 28 [1871] (Hart Papers, NIC)

DEAR SIR: It has occurred to me as perhaps proper to mention that my connection with the New York *Times* has never been anything more than a contributor of two articles a week, on topics selected by myself. I never had any closer connection with the paper, seldom went to the office, and had but a slight acquaintance

with the late Mr. Raymond. I say this, inasmuch as I find I am
described in the life of him published soon after his death, as one
of his "assistants," and the impression conveyed that I took some
part in the office work of the paper. It is also untrue as has been
asserted, that I was at one time a foreign correspondent of the
Times.[1] I never had any connection of any sort with the paper
when abroad. . . .

Yours truly
ELG

1. It has also been stated inaccurately that Godkin served as a foreign
correspondent of the New York *Evening Post,* supplying it in 1862 with
"the shrewdest and clearest view of French opinion published in any American Newspaper." (Allan Nevins, *The Evening Post; A Century of Journalism* [New York, 1922] p. 318.) Godkin wrote nothing for the *Evening
Post* in the 1860s. His eagerness in the above letter to minimize his connection with the *New York Times* was probably attributable to the fact that
he was now feuding with that paper.

To John Seeley Hart

New York, August 31, 1871 (Hart Papers, NIC)

DEAR SIR: I was under the impression that you were sufficiently
familiar with the history of the *Nation,* to make it unnecessary
for me to say anything about it. It was established in 1865, by a
joint stock company. I have been from the start editor in chief,
with absolute and exclusive control of it. Owing [to] internal
dissensions—as is not uncommon in such matters—the company
was dissolved in 1866, and the paper sold to myself and two other
persons, Fred. Law Olmsted, and J. M. McKim, who are now
sole proprietors of it. During the first and second years, it lost
money heavily; the third it paid nearly all its expenses, but furnished little or nothing to its conductors. The fourth it got nearly
abreast of all outgoings; last year we had some profit; this year,
we shall have more. Our circulation slowly but steadily increases;
our advertizing returns very rapidly. Our circulation is now
8000, which considering the price and character of the paper, is
I think, not bad. . . .

Yours very truly
ELG. . . .

To Whitelaw Reid

Nation Office   New York, October 17, 1871
(Reid Papers, DLC)

Private

DEAR SIR: Some of Collector Murphy's friends—including his counsel in the case before the Committee of Investigation, have applied to me to examine the evidence taken on the trial, with the view of convincing me that he committed no fraud in his hat contract; spirited away no witnesses and altered no standard, and that Mr. Olcott's case finally broke down. After all we have said about him in the *Nation*, I cannot well refuse to do this, and am to meet them for the purpose some evening this week.[1]

I do not, however, wish to go into the matter without being better informed than I am now of the real strength of the anti-Murphy side of the controversy. I have relied mainly, thus far, on the presentation made by the *Tribune*, but I should like very much to get some detailed statement of it, and know more, if possible, of Murphy's general career, and antecedents. . . .

Yours truly
ELG

1. The *Nation* accused Thomas Murphy, the Collector of the Port of New York, of defrauding the United States government. Confronted with evidence to the contrary by Murphy's lawyer, Godkin withdrew his charges and printed a retraction in the *Nation* the next week. See "Collector Murphy's Case," *Nation*, 26 October 1871, p. 270.

To Daniel Coit Gilman

10 West 48th St., New York, October 30 [1871]
(Gilman Papers, MdBJ)

MY DEAR MR. GILMAN: I received either President White's letter to you, or a copy of it, in his handwriting before I got yours, and had, as you will have seen, said my say on the matter to which it referred, in the *Nation*.

I am, I confess, at a loss to know what he meant by the "slur" in *The Nation*. I know of nothing of the kind. I refrained from doing more than recording the fact that the minority were dissatisfied with his rulings, lest the qualified approval of his course, which was all I could express, might at that juncture give him pain.[1] I had no doubt of his integrity—how could I have?—but I did doubt the wisdom of his giving into that Convention, (situated as he was towards the Administration of the college) in the capacity of presiding officer. The Archangel Gabriel could not under the circumstances have given satisfaction; but the Archangel would have been and could have been indifferent to subsequent clamor. It would be a thousand pities, if such things should drive him out of politics; I sincerely hope the only result will be that, he will not again beg to reconcile the Conkingites and Fentonites, and hold the scales between them. It is not in the power of mortal man to do this.

Ever yours
ELG

1. Andrew D. White presided over the New York State Republican convention, in which capacity he angered the Fentonites—followers of former Governor Reuben E. Fenton—by his rulings and drew editorial criticism from Whitelaw Reid's New York *Tribune*.

To Whitelaw Reid

Nation Office   New York, November 8, 1871
(Reid Papers, DLC)

MY DEAR SIR: I am really pained and astonished by the correspondence you send me, about Mr. A. D. White. The paragraphs in the *Nation* were the result of a long written explanation sent me by him, and which bore every mark of grief and sincerity—though he did not specifically deny the charges made against him.

I have never liked the way he has conducted the University at Cornell. It has always seemed too sensational for a man whose heart was really in his work, But I did not suspect him of "little games," in politics. If he has really been seduced, it is only one proof more of the desirableness of putting somebody in Grant's place, who will surround himself with heavier guns, than he seems to fancy.

Is it, or is it not true that it has been the custom for the State

Committee to frame the Committees of the Convention, and for the Chairman to adopt them [as a matter] of *course?*

Yours very truly
ELG

To The Reverend Joseph P. Thompson [1]

10 West 48th St., New York, November 10, 1871
(Thompson Collection, CtY)

MY DEAR SIR: I was prevented by an attack of rheumatism from calling on you, when your resignation was first announced to tell you how sorry I was to hear of it, particularly as it was due to loss of health, and how deeply I felt in common, I think with everybody who knows you—the extent to which the city, the country at large would suffer by your departure. There has certainly been no good cause, which has not for a great many years been helped greatly by your labor and influence—good government, good morals, and enlightened tolerant Christianity. . . .

Very cordially yours
ELG

Rev. J. P. Thompson, LLD

1. The Rev. Joseph P. Thompson (1819–79) was one of the earliest contributors to the *Nation;* a prolific writer and participant in community concerns, he was pastor of the Broadway Tabernacle Church from 1845 to 1871.

To Daniel Coit Gilman

10 West 48th St., New York, November 27, 1871
(Gilman Papers, MdBJ)

Private

MY DEAR MR. GILMAN: I must say I think Yale College—if Professor Silliman is still in it—ought either to put a stop to his mining operations, or end its connection with him. He has now turned up as the endorser of this Emma Silver Mining Company,

which I am informed on excellent authority, is a new swindle, or
likely to become so, and has brought Schenck to grief in London.[1] It would be a great help to reform in politics, if Yale College would make an example and a public one in a case of this
kind; but anyhow, he ought not to be able to call himself a
College officer.

Yours ever
ELG

1. The noted Yale chemist and mineralogist Benjamin Silliman, Jr. (1816–
85) spent much time advancing mining schemes. With General Robert
Schenck, who had succeeded John L. Motley as United States minister to
England, he suffered embarrassment as a result of their endorsement of the
Emma Mine scheme, in which Britons lost money.

To Daniel Coit Gilman

10 West 48th St., New York, December 20, 1871
(Gilman Papers, MdBJ)

Private

MY DEAR MR. GILMAN: Mr. Reid the managing editor of the
Tribune undertook last night to defend Schenck, in a private conversation with me, and showed me letters from Schenck's secretary, declaring that he had only gone into the enterprize after a
"thorough examination." Now the whole scheme, rests in the
eyes of the English public on Silliman's report, and I found that
Reid knew nothing of Silliman's reputation, did not know how
he stood with scientific men, and that he had been turned out of
the Scientific School, and that his connection with the College was
merely nominal, and therefore that that portion of the prospectus
of the Emma Mine, which eulogized him as a man of high and independent—"Character—, and of reliable judgement," was fraudulent.

He admitted that this put a different complexion on the case. He
informed me too, that within a day or two, he had agreed to print
a letter from Silliman puffing some other mine.

I then told him that I would try to obtain from you or Mr.
Brush an exact statement of the circumstances which led to
Silliman's expulsion from the Scientific School, and of the nature

of his present connection with the college, and of the opinion entertained by scientific men of the value of his judgment on mining enterprizes. If you will send me such a letter, I will promise that no one but Reid shall see it, and that it shall simply inform his judgment. By so doing you will help to put an end to a very gross form of swindling on a great scale.

> Yours very truly
> ELG

To James M. McKim

> *Nation* Office   New York, January 4, 1872
> (Godkin Papers, *Nation* Business Records, MH)

DEAR MR. McKIM: I enclose a draft of a new copartnership agreement, modelled in all essential particulars on the old one. If you approve of it, I propose to have Mr. Garrison, who writes a clear hand make two copies of it, and have it signed at once. It ought to be done as soon as possible. If you object, please write your objections, and come in tomorrow and let us discuss them. I would like to close the matter up this week. You know we are now in an unorganized condition. I will keep any appointment you make tomorrow or Saturday.

> Yours ever
> ELG

To Whitelaw Reid

10 West 48th St., New York, January 8, 1872 (Reid Papers, DLC)
Private

DEAR MR. REID: The enclosed is marked "private," but I told Mr. Gilman I should show you whatever he sent. I will endeavor the next time, he or Professor Brush is in town to bring you together, so that you may hear the story yourself. But of this, I assure you —in the mean time—that Professor Silliman was compelled to withdraw from the Scientific School, by the united remonstrance of the Faculty. They at first refused to assign him any duties; and on his asking for the reason why, gave his connection with fraudulent mining schemes, and this in a formal letter to President Woolsey. He then withdrew. The other claim, as I told you is a mere sham.

Please return me Mr. Gilman's letter.

Yours very truly

ELG

To Daniel Coit Gilman

Nation Office   New York, January 11, 1872

(Gilman Papers, MdBJ)

DEAR MR. GILMAN: Would you have any objection to Reid's repeating what you say [,] to Schenck, *for Schenck's information simply*? Schenck is an old friend of his, and he is confident he has been led into the Emma mine in ignorance of the facts.

Yours ever

ELG

To Whitelaw Reid

10 West 48th St., New York, January 25, 1872

(Reid Papers, DLC)

MY DEAR MR. REID: Professor Gilman is coming to town and will pass the night with me on Wednesday next. Will you do me the favor to come and meet him at a quiet dinner at half past six, when he will unfold the iniquities of the mining world, which may be an agreeable change, after you have supped so full of custom house honors.

Yours very truly

ELG

To E. C. Wines

10 West 48th St., New York, January 27, 1872

(Simon Gratz Autograph Collection, PHi)

DEAR DR. WINES: I was sorry not to be able to attend your meeting last night,—as I was detained at home by another engagement till it was too late.

I see you have put me on the committee. I am not a useful man on committees, as I am tied down so closely by my own work, but I am always willing to serve any good cause, within the limits of my ability.[1]

Yours very truly
ELG

1. Enoch C. Wines (1806–79) was a leading prison reformer who was organizing the first International Penitentiary Congress to be held in London in 1872. Godkin was not interested in prison reform.

To Charles Eliot Norton

March 6, 1872 (Ogden 2:109)

MY DEAR FRIEND: We were shocked and grieved beyond measure this morning by the receipt of your terrible news.[1] I held your letter and Janes's in my hand unopened, while Fanny read aloud a line from Cambridge announcing "the good news," from Dresden; one second more, and the dreadful issue burst upon us. This will reach you, my dear fellow, a month after the blow has fallen, and I don't like to say one word that will bring it up again freshly before you; but if I wrote all day I should not have expressed half the sympathy I feel, or half what I know Fanny feels. I cannot, too, I know, say one word by way of alleviation. The calamity which has befallen you is one which I have over and over again contemplated as possible in my own case and asked myself how I should bear it. I do not know; no man who loves his wife can ever tell beforehand. I know you will bear it as bravely as man can. God bless and comfort you all. I cannot yet realize that we shall never see poor Susan any more, and I think sadly of the merry day ten years ago when I first saw her on the steps at Shady Hill, and began the friendship and intercourse which has ever since been one of the delights of our life, and perhaps the greatest of them all.

I shall write again in a day or two. To-day I am tied to the van.

Your devoted friend
ELG

1. The death of Mrs. Norton in Europe.

To Whitelaw Reid

New York, March 23 [1872] (Reid Papers, DLC)

DEAR MR. REID: I enclose a letter to the *Tribune*, which I shall ask you to do me the favor to publish, and as prominently as you conveniently can. There are two enclosures—letters—which are for your eye only, and which I shall ask you to have the kindness to return.

The *Times* is becoming a public nuisance.[1]

Yours very truly
ELG

1. A reference to the controversy between Godkin and the *New York Times* that began after the *Times* ended his services as a contributor because of disagreements over editorial policy. In the *Nation* Godkin retaliated with editorial criticism of the *Times*, whereupon the *Times* charged that Godkin was a "quarrelsome and somewhat reckless, though able man" who did not hesitate to write in secrecy while he denounced secrecy in others. Among the charges of the *Times* that Godkin denied in the letter he sent to the *Tribune* was that by prearrangement with the *Times* he adopted the pseudonym James Madison and wrote letters to that paper signed "J. M." In controversies in which he was involved, Godkin's veracity was often questioned.

To Whitelaw Reid

Cambridge, Mass., March 31, 1872 (Reid Papers, DLC)
Not for Publication

DEAR MR. REID: I have only seen the New York papers containing my "scrimmage" since coming here, on Friday, and as you were kind enough to back me up with a vigorous blast in the *Tribune*, you will perhaps allow me, to bore you with one or two words of explanation about the last article in the *Times*, to which I cannot reply—both men being clearly blackguards, and "John Thomas" evidently the worse of the two.[1] There is, you know no blackguard like the British blackguard.

1. The story about Raymond is pure fiction. Moreover they printed all articles I ever sent to them except two, and I never wrote a line for them about Grant and the Presidency, the ques-

tion of the nomination not having come up. This is a characteristic and rather cunning invention of Jones's.

2. I stopped writing of my own accord, and wrote to Jones telling him so, in a perfectly friendly way, received from him a warm expression of regret, which he repeated verbally to one of my friends.

3. The attack on my "temper" is funny, considering that I have never seen Jennings, or had any intercourse with him; have only seen Jones once in seven years, and have never seen him for more than five minutes and have never had a word of dispute or disagreement with him on any subject till now.

4. Ask yourself, what would have been my motive in writing notes to them signed "J. M.," when I was according to their own showing corresponding with them on this very business, and receiving checks from them as "E. L. Godkin."

Believe me to remain

Sincerely and gratefully yours

ELG

P. S. I regret to mention that "John Thomas," actually *threatens*, at the close of the article, to publish two notes I wrote to him before sending my letter to you for publication. One of these, points out to him the outrageous impropriety of his conduct, and the other asks him for a formal and public retraction! From this you may judge of the state of morals in that particular kitchen. I am paying the natural and perhaps legitimate penalty of entering into confidential relations with men, possessing neither honor nor sense of decency.

ELG

Do not trouble yourself to answer this. I shall be in New York, by the end of the week, and shall perhaps see you.

---

1. A reference to *New York Times* publisher George Jones (1811–91) and his fiery editor Louis J. Jennings ("John Thomas"). A man of similar temperament to Godkin, Jennings resigned his post a few years later and returned to England where he was elected to Parliament.

To Daniel Coit Gilman

Cambridge, Mass., April 3, 1872 (Gilman Papers, MdBJ)

DEAR MR. GILMAN: I have to thank you for your kind note of the 29th inst. which has been forwarded to me here. I am glad to find that the *Times* article appears to be, what it really is, a tissue of falsehoods and misrepresentations. There is hardly a direct assertion in it which is not [an] awful lie while the inuendoes [*sic*] are most ingenious. As a specimen I mention, that the complaints of my "bad temper" came from two men, whom I hardly know and have never had any difference with till now. Jennings the editor, I have never seen or had any intercourse with, and with Jones I have only spoken once in seven years, and then for five minutes. Moreover, I have never written and offered to the *Times* any article on General Grant and the Presidency. I stopped writing owing to the breakdown of my eyes, and on informing Jones of the fact received from him a strong expression of regret, which he repeated verbally to one of my friends. You will readily see that when one gets into a controversy with men of this sort, the only resource for one who has any sense of decency, or any self respect is silence. All these squabbles are very disgusting to me, as they are to the public. I have always done what I can to avoid them, but they do not seem to become less [evil?]. The new editor of the *Times*, is I am afraid—a sorry addition to the press of New York. The rascal's *threat* to publish two notes I wrote him pointing out the impropriety of his conduct—, and asking him to retract formally, I am afraid, reveals an impudent blackguard.

Yours very cordially
ELG

To Charles Eliot Norton

[Early 1872?] (Ogden 1:293–94)

. . . The letter about Curtis, as you leave it to my judgment, I shall not publish. At this distance ahead, I think, it would only injure him or bring a laugh on him. There is so much nominating of absurd and worthless candidates going on.

In addition to this, much as I like and respect him, I don't think I should like to see him in the Presidency. His political judgment is not strong enough, and he is too easily influenced by the persons around him. Indeed, one sees by his way of dealing with the new questions which are now coming up, that he is not naturally a politician, and only became one by accident, under the heat of his anti-slavery feeling. A month ago I dined with him at Olmsted's, and he insisted that the tariff could not become an issue, and that the badness of the Democrats was capital enough to keep the Republican party going. He is now preaching the opposite of all this in *Harper's*. I might give you half a dozen other instances of the same thing. His mind does not raise political ideas in the open air. They grow under glass, and are feeble when exposed. He is by temperament and training a literary man, and has not, I think, enough combativeness, or rather of the tenacity and distinct consciousness of what he wants, of which combativeness is so often the expression, to put in [a] difficult post. I say all this with the strongest liking and admiration of him, and I would not say it to any one who did not know and like him as well as you do. It will never do for us reformers to put any more men in the forefront of our battle who are not strong men intellectually, and cannot prevent themselves being fooled as Grant has been, for instance, about the navigation laws. . . .

To Carl Schurz

10 West 48th St., New York, May 19, 1872 (Schurz Papers, DLC)
Private

DEAR MR. SCHURZ: Is there no way out of the wretched mess into which these Cincinnati nominations have plunged us? [1] If the matter is left as it stands, it will be impossible for anyone to speak of "reform," during the next fifteen years, without causing shouts of laughter. No man of standing and character can take the stump for Greeley without putting his whole future in peril. His election every man of sobriety and thoughtfulness concedes would be a national calamity of the first magnitude. If it occurs it will be the triumph of [treachery?], charlatanry, and recklessness, over the sober common sense which has thus far saved republican government on this continent. I do not know whether you are aware what a conceited, ignorant, half cracked, obstinate old creature he is; but you must know enough to feel that we did at Cincinnati, a most serious, and dangerous thing. It was a shocking mishap. I assure you this feeling about the matter deepens every day. Can nothing be done to make amends?

Did you read the address to the people of the great state of New York, the other day signed on behalf of the "reformers," by John Cochrane, and Theodore Tilton, the biographer of Wm. Woodhall! Has it really come to this complexion with us?

Yours very cordially
ELG

1. A reference to the selection of Horace Greeley to head the Liberal Republican ticket instead of Charles Francis Adams who was the choice of Godkin, David A. Wells, Atkinson, and other eastern intellectuals who joined the revolt against a second term for Grant in 1872. The diplomatic historian and Godkin admirer, Dexter Perkins, errs in stating that Godkin supported Greeley in the campaign that followed. See Dexter Perkins and Glyndon G. Van Deusen, *The United States of America: A History* (New York: Macmillan, 1962), 2:43.

To Edward Atkinson

Nation Office   New York, May 29, 1872
(Atkinson Papers, MHi)

DEAR ATKINSON: Horace White and I have had a little correspondence about his support of Greeley, which makes it look as if our differences were not reconcilable. However, he says he wishes that all we "who have been conspiring together for the last three years," could meet together once more before we separate, and talk matters over, and he proposes that we should do this in New York immediately after the Philadelphia Convention, and asks me to make the arrangement.

I think it is highly desirable, and write to ask whether you cannot come on. We should have to fix the day and hour to suit the convenience of those who come from the greatest distance, but the place will be my house. I hope Trumbull and Schurz will be present.[1]

Yours truly

ELG

1. Lyman Trumbull (1813–96) was, with Schurz, one of the leaders in the United States Senate of the Liberal Republican revolt of 1872.

To Senator Lyman Trumbull

Nation Office   New York, May 29, 1872

(Trumbull Papers, DLC)

Senator Trumbull,

DEAR SIR: We who have been acting together in opposition for the last two or three years, and are now in danger of being irrevocably divided by Greeley, propose on Horace White's suggestion to have one more meeting here in New York, immediately after the Philadelphia Convention. The place will be my house, and we shall endeavor to make the hour and day suit your and Mr. Schurz's convenience.

May we count on your presence? I think, and we all think, it is highly desirable you should be here.

Yours very truly

ELG

Telegram to Theodore Dwight Woolsey

10 West 48th St., New York, June 6, 1872

(Telegram Woolsey Papers, CtY)

To: President Theodore D. Woolsey

An earnest effort is making to secure nomination of Charles Francis Adams by a conference of notables in this City, not over fifty in all from all parts of the country, summoned by special private invitation. The call will not be published and is signed already by William Cullen Bryant, Carl Schurz, Cox of Ohio, Governor Randolph, Judge Handley, and David A. Wells. Will you sign it also? Let me beg of you to do so. If you wish further explanation I will come to New Haven. Answer if possible to-night.

ELG

To Andrew D. White

10 West 48th St., New York, June 15, 1872 (White Papers, NIC)

President White

MY DEAR SIR: My eyes have been very weak—so much so as to seriously curtail my powers of work during the past year. They are now under medical treatment, and have been somewhat improving, and I hoped that by getting my address printed in large type, I would be able to read it at your Commencement. I find, however, that even with this precaution, it will be a very dangerous attempt, and may throw me back again indefinitely. I have not used them by artificial light, now for over a year. . . .

I am exceedingly sorry that I should not have reached this conclusion, sooner. You will not lose much by my failure, but I am afraid you will be prevented making a satisfactory arrangement for a substitute.[1]

I remain, very sincerely yours
ELG

1. Godkin had agreed to give a commencement address at Cornell University ten days hence on "University Instruction in Political and Social Science."

To Carl Schurz

Lenox, Mass., June 28, 1872 (Schurz Papers, DLC)

MY DEAR SIR: I have carefully considered all you say about Greeley. . . .

But I maturely considered what I could and would do about Greeley when he was first nominated. If any possibility of standing by him, had offered itself, I would, in view of the part I had taken in creating the state of public opinion, which had led to the Convention, have seized upon it eagerly. . . .

If you got the pledges you speak of from Greeley, and [he] broke them, *as I believe he would*, it would be no consolation to me that our opposition would immediately be raised up against him. I have gone through this once, and to go through it again, would utterly destroy what little influence I possess, even if my reason allowed me to entertain the idea. I supported Grant with far better guarantees than Greeley offers, and he made fine promises, and broke them, and good appointments and reversed them, and I have, as [a] consequence, been for three years in opposition. I cannot afford to go through this process again. Greeley would have to change his whole nature, at the age of 62, in order not to deceive and destroy you, and you will not be able to atone for your support of him under present circumstances, by *then* arraying yourself against him. You will simply bring your judgment into discredit, and lay yourself open to the suspicion of having been disappointed by him in some personal way, and politics will be in a far worse condition than they were in the Spring of 1872, because the small band of reformers who then inspired the country with some hope, will have fallen into disrepute and become ridiculous. . . .

I understand perfectly the difference . . . in your position and mine. It is very difficult for you, or any man who is practically engaged in politics to make up his mind to allow himself to be thrown out of the current whatever it be, and thus be rendered, at least temporarily, powerless. But I cannot divest myself of the idea that you are to some extent sacrificing the future to the present in accepting Greeley under any circumstances. The Cincinnati Convention did a great deal for your reputation and influence, but it was through the fact that you were plainly disappointed that you were a party to the wretched folly which nominated Greeley, and that you sought really to elevate politics. In fact it carried you far towards that moral position which when combined with such oratorical gifts as you have, gives a man an unshakable hold on the people, and *forces* him on any party which wishes to succeed. It has given Sumner, donkey as he is, the wonderful weight which he has possessed for 20 years. I am afraid—pardon me as a sincere friend and admirer for saying so —that by taking up "anything to beat Grant," you are going to set yourself back, for the long run. . . . Greeley's Administration will be nothing but a series of wretched intrigues, out of which no new organization can grow. It will make a great difference to you, whether when the foundation of the new party comes to be laid . . . you come to the work with an unquestioned reputation for the highest principle . . . or come as simply as a man so hostile to Grant, that he tried to make [a] "reform president" —out of poor old Greeley, and failed miserably.

What I seek, is not a sham break up of parties, such as the Greeley movement promises, but a real break up. . . . Bowles, White and the rest are to me preaching the very doctrines now, against which we have been all thundering for three years. They are accepting blindly a grossly unfit candidate at the hands of a bellowing Convention and are going to support him solely because he is "available" . . . and they are denouncing as silly and dishonest, all those who having supported the Cincinnati Convention for better things, now refuse to "fall into line," as they call it. If this be not the old "party tyranny," pray, what it is? . . .

Be assured of my continued esteem, and my earnest good wishes. . . . Keep yourself for the great party of the future, if you can and believe me,

Very cordially yours
ELG

To Whitelaw Reid

10 West 48th St., New York, July 20, 1872 (Reid Papers, DLC)

DEAR MR. REID: Mr. A. G. Sedgwick, whom I think you know, and who is the owner of an interest in the *Nation*, and is now one of my assistants, has more time on his hands than we need, and would like to write for some other periodical. He did the political article in the *Atlantic* until it was cut off. He is an excellent writer, and it has occurred to me that if you need any contributions he might suit you very well, as a leader writer. . . .

Yours very truly
ELG

Memorandum to Arthur G. Sedgwick

Nation Office   New York, October 7, 1872
(Godkin Papers, *Nation* Business Records, MH)

DEAR SIR: . . . We are willing to try the experiment of publishing a daily evening edition of the *Nation* . . . on the following conditions,

1. That not less than $75,000 capital be raised, no part of which the present Editor of the *Nation* shall be expected either to raise or contribute.

2. That a third interest in the new enterprize shall be given to E. L. Godkin and Co. in return for the name and good will, and the labor and attention of the editorial staff and of the business management, as well as office expenses.

3. That the whole sole and supreme editorial control shall be placed in the hands of Mr. E. L. Godkin.

None of the present members of the above firm, which includes Mr. Godkin, Mr. Garrison the publisher of the *Nation*, and Mr. Condit its advertizing agent, would expect to derive any salary or remuneration from the new paper, until it was on a paying basis, except that the editor in chief would draw (say) 600 a year to meet additional incidental expenses imposed on him personally by the increase in his work. . . .

To Edward Atkinson

Nation Office   New York, October 31, 1872,
(Atkinson Papers, MHi)

MY DEAR ATKINSON: I had intended to enclose the check which Garrison sent you the other day, myself with a few words of acknowledgment of the support and forbearance which the *Nation* has experienced at your hands. Let me assure you that I at least am very sensible of them. I am very sorry that you have lost money by the enterprize; the best apology I can make to you and others for this is that I have myself given it six of my best years for nearly nothing, and that it is now firmly established.[1]

Yours very truly
ELG

We shall have our revenge for Cincinnati on Tuesday.[2]

1. Godkin had just bought up Atkinson's interest in the *Nation* for less than the Bostonian's original investment.

2. A reference to Election Day and Grant's anticipated victory over Horace Greeley.

To Horace White

10 West 48th St., New York, November 11, 1872
(Schurz Papers, DLC)

MY DEAR MR. WHITE: I have spoken to some of the old set about your proposal to have a meeting in December, and find the general opinion is, and I share it, that while such a gathering might be pleasant socially, it is doubtful whether any good could come out of it politically. I do not see that we could come to any conclusion about the future. The result of the Cincinnati movement has been so unfortunate, that there is at present a slight odor of ridicule hanging around everybody who had anything to do with getting it up. Moreover we do not yet know what the election meant exactly, beyond contempt for Greeley. How far it was an endorsement of Grant has yet to appear. Nor do we know what Grant is going to do, or what is likely to be the drift of public sentiment during the next year. In short the field is still covered with smoke, the dead unburied, and the wounded uncared for.

My idea is that such a meeting would be highly desirable about February. We shall then know the new Cabinet, and a great many other things.

I agree with all you say about reform, and hope we may be found side by side on the old ground.

Yours very truly
ELG

To Carl Schurz

Nation Office   New York, December 16, 1872
(Schurz Papers, DLC)

MY DEAR SIR: . . . Your letter to us was very good and acceptable.[1]

Watterson's "Confession," as I suppose I may call it, has produced a very unpleasant impression both on your friends and enemies.[2] What good purpose he hoped to serve by such a long piece of babbling I cannot imagine, and what can have impelled him to produce it beyond mere garrulousness, I cannot imagine either. If you can induce him to "shut-up," you will render us all a service. His tongue is evidently too long, and I am afraid he is deficient in ballast. Nobody can gain anything now by going over that miserable story. The opposition which sought to bust Grant, can only regain, influence and position now by the honest, and fair and able discussion of public affairs, and the avoidance of extravagance and blatherskite. . . .

> Yours very truly
> ELG

1. "The Undercurrent at Washington," *Nation*, 26 December 1872, p. 424. Schurz was now serving without pay as the Washington, D.C. correspondent of the *Nation*. For his secret contributions see William M. Armstrong, "Additions to the *Nation Index*," *Bulletin of the New York Public Library*, vol. 73, no. 4 (April 1969): 271.

2. Relations between Godkin and the influential editor of the Louisville *Courier-Journal*, Henry Watterson (1840–1921) were characterized by a mutual lack of respect. For a witty reply by Watterson to Godkin's ridicule, see *Nation*, 20 November 1873, p. 338.

6. The "Chromo-Civilization" of the 1870s

In 1874 occurred the Beecher Scandal, arising out of public charges by Theodore Tilton that his wife was having sexual relations with Mrs. Godkin's cousin, the noted clergyman, Henry Ward Beecher. The affair afforded ammunition for a *Nation* editorial in which Godkin, raking the publicity given to the sordid dispute, gave a name to the age—"Chromo-civilization."

During these years Godkin enlarged his circle of friendly acquaintances to include Henry James *père et fils*, Charles W. Eliot, Professor Ephraim Whitman Gurney and his wife, Professor Francis J. Child, Carl Schurz, James A. Garfield, Henry Adams and his wife, Whitelaw Reid, and Henry Cabot Lodge. Although his cordiality with the last six did not endure, his capacity for friendship with persons who could withstand his haughty personality remained undimmed.

During the seventies Godkin made the currency question a leading issue in the *Nation*, stoutly defending the hard-money position of Eastern financial circles against what he termed the "paper money intrigue" of the inflationists. He called for Civil Service Reform; he examined with distaste the labor movement in England, the Granger Movement, the Paris Commune, and the manners and morals of the *nouveau riche*. Critical of Latin, as well as black and Catholic, people, he opposed American expansion into the southern part of the hemisphere, while at home he accepted the return of white supremacy to the South.

In 1875 Fanny Godkin died after a lingering illness. Shattered to the extent of momentarily ruminating on suicide, Godkin dropped some of his editorial duties and, leaving Wendell P. Garrison in charge of the *Nation* office, went to live among his admirers in Cambridge, causing a pundit to aver that the *Nation* was "the best New York newspaper edited in Massachusetts."

When he returned to New York several years later, his ego had been reinflated but the *Nation* was in serious financial trouble and its influence was waning. For the tactics he used to give moral support to Samuel J. Tilden in the disputed Hayes-Tilden election of 1876, Godkin suffered strained relations with his old friends Charles Eliot Norton and Frederick L. Olmsted, and the *Nation* lost several thousand subscribers. It never again paid its expenses. For several years Godkin tried to find a buyer for the weekly but in vain; the great days of the *Nation* were over.

To Carl Schurz

10 West 48th St., New York, January 29, 1873
(Schurz Papers, DLC)

MY DEAR MR. SCHURZ: . . . What a horrible thing this Crédit Mobilier is for all of us! Nobody whose home is on American soil, or whose children are Americans can feel anything about it but shame and sorrow. I was sickened by the Colfax revelations! And all this miserable lying was done for "the great party!" The Lord has plainly delivered these rascals into our hands, as Cromwell said, and we can now slaughter them at our leisure, but no slaughter will do any good, without the break up of the wretched machinery by which such paltry rogues, are raised into the position of "statesmen." I hope you will hold off for the present. You don't need to say a word. Providence has taken charge of the matter.

Yours ever
ELG

To Whitelaw Reid

10 West 48 St., New York, March 10 [1873] (Reid Papers, DLC)

DEAR MR. REID: I am of course very much obliged and flattered by your offer as regards the lectures. Unfortunately I was compelled last week to write to President Porter, that I could not deliver them, owing to a break down in my eyes. . . .[1]

Let me take this opportunity of congratulating you sincerely on the *Tribune*, which is, in my judgment, by long odds, the best newspaper there has ever been here, and I trust you may have the patience to persevere in your present course, and that the Lord will in some manner remove that annoying blackguard in the *Times* office.[2]

Yours very truly
ELG

1. Yale College had invited Godkin to deliver some lectures, and Reid offered to publish them in the *Tribune*. Godkin, who had no organic eye trouble, was apprehensive of the lecture platform.

2. The *Tribune* was feuding editorially with Louis Jennings and the *New York Times*.

To Carl Schurz

10 West 48th St., New York, March 21, 1873
(Schurz Papers, DLC)

DEAR MR. SCHURZ: I am urged by several persons, who are interested in your career, to take the liberty of hoping that you will not under any circumstances accept "the back pay". . . .

Yours ever
ELG

To Carl Schurz

10 West 48th St., New York, March 26, 1873
(Schurz Papers, DLC)

MY DEAR MR. SCHURZ: You have got the idea to perfection—return it without fuss. I think all the donations "at home" are producing a bad effect. There is a slight atmosphere of humbug about them.

Adams (C. F. Jr.) was in here last week, and we talked about our proposed "Conciliabulum." I do not think it will be well to do anything before the Fall. We must let Grant's *new* Administration show itself, and the Civil Service "reform" work itself out a little more, before showing ourselves. But in September or October, I proposed having a little reunion of contributors and friends of the *Nation,* to celebrate our attaining what once seemed the impossible circulation of 10,000. Adams suggests, and I think well, that this should be turned into, or (I think better perhaps), accompanied by some sort of political demonstration. I should not like anything that savored of advertizing the *Nation,* but the men being here, we could do what we pleased. What do you think?

Yours ever
ELG

To Wendell P. Garrison

April 1, 1873 (Godkin Papers, MH)

DEAR MR. GARRISON: My darling little girl is dying, and will probably not survive till night.

I am so unstrung, that I do not believe I shall be able to [do]
any work for a couple of weeks.

                                        Yours ever
                                        ELG

To The Reverend Henry W. Bellows

10 West 48th St., New York, April 2 [1873]
(Bellows Papers, MHi)

MY DEAR MR. BELLOWS: I did not need your kind visit the other
day to feel assured that you will sympathize with us, when you
hear that our poor darling has been dying since yesterday morning, and that we look for the end every minute. . . .[1]

My special object . . . is to ask whether we can count on you
any day this week for a funeral service here at the house. I do
not care how short and simple it may be; I would like a few
words from a feeling heart expressive of what we feel, or ought
to feel as our darling leaves her father's house for the last time. I
wish we only *knew* that she was in the hands of a heavenly father,
under whose eye she would become all that I fondly and rashly
hoped to see her, one day under mine. . . .

                                        Ever truly yours
                                        ELG

1. The child died soon after Godkin wrote this.

To Professor William D. Whitney

Nation Office   New York, May 26, 1873
(Whitney Papers, CtY)

MY DEAR SIR: I enclose a letter which we have received from
Grant White, and I shall, I think publish, though he is a dreadful

bore.[1] But I wish very much you would give us as much editorial reply to it, as you think it calls for. It affords an opportunity of finally shutting him up.

Yours very truly
ELG

Professor Whitney
We shall publish it next week, and would need to have it back by Saturday.

1. Shakespeare scholar Richard Grant White (1821–85).

To Charles W. Eliot

Nation Office   New York, June 18, 1873 (Eliot Papers, MH-Ar)

DEAR SIR: In reply to the enquiries contained in your favor of yesterday I beg to say—

1. That I *was* notified of my appointment on the permanent Committee of the National Educational Association, on the subject of a National University in August 1871, but not of any meeting either to discuss or fill vacancies, in so far as my recollection serves.

2. That I did not serve on the Committee but promptly declined to do so, in a letter addressed to Dr. Hoyt.

3. That I had no hand in the preparation of the bill of which you enclose a copy.

4. That the general object of the bill, did *not* commend itself to my judgment, so that my name could have been properly used in support of the measure. I expressed interest in and approval of the scheme of a National University, if it could be richly endowed, and could be made wholly independent of the Government, but on these conditions alone.[1]

Very truly yours
ELG

1. The Eliot papers in the Harvard University Archives contain much material on the debate over the proposed National University, including the *Nation*'s role in the dispute. President Eliot of Harvard strongly objected to the proposed university.

To Carl Schurz

Nation Office   New York, December 5, 1873
(Schurz Papers, DLC)

MY DEAR MR. SCHURZ: We have no Washington correspondent, and I wish very much you would begin again, not regularly but occasionally. For instance give us a letter *now*, telling how things are looking. I expect to be in Washington after the holidays. I cannot go now. Adams has written to you about our projected demonstration. I believe in it, but I am very much afraid that unless we can make a respectable show of new names, we shall not make much impression. For instance, I will say to you confidentially, that I dread Grosvenor's appearance in the forefront of the battle. He is an able and useful man, but he has no character, or rather a very bad one. Everybody looks on him as a charlatan and adventurer, of those whom we desire to win over and conciliate.

Burn this, and believe me

Ever yours very truly
ELG

Who *does* supply Grant's finance?
Send your letters to my house, if you write—10. W. 48.

To James A. Garfield

Nation Office   New York, December 11, 1873
(Garfield Papers, DLC)

MY DEAR SIR: I have given a letter of introduction to you to Mr. Albert O. Rutson an English friend of mine who is travelling in this country and goes to Washington tommorrow. He is a Fellow of Magdalen College, Oxford, and was for four or five years private secretary of Mr. Bruce when Home Secretary under the Gladstone Ministry. He is a very intelligent man, well versed in English politics, and with a pretty good political career before him, I think. I have no doubt you will be pleased to know him, if it comes in your way to pay him any attentions in Washington, I shall be very much indebted to you.

Very truly yours
ELG

General Garfield, Washington

To Carl Schurz

[Ca. 22 December 1873] (Schurz Papers, DLC)

DEAR MR. SCHURZ: I propose that the meeting (preliminary) be held at my house here, any day after the 5th of Jan'y. I cannot be back in New York, until after that day. Anything you have to say on the subject will reach me during the next ten days, care of Miss Ashburner, Cambridge, Mass.

Yours ever
ELG

To Theodore Dwight Woolsey

Care of E. W. Gurney   Cambridge, Mass. January 2, 1874
(Woolsey Papers, CtY)

DEAR SIR: The recommendations in the President's late message, and the efforts by which they are supported in so many quarters in Washington, make those who are opposed to the extension of government patronage, and especially to such a form of it as a government University, very desirous of keeping before the public the arguments against the scheme put forward by President Eliot in his late report. Some of us have, therefore, spoken to him about having it reprinted and more widely circulated, but he is reluctant to move in the matter, himself, because it was not favorably received by the larger portion, I believe, of the body to which it was addressed, as well as on grounds of personal delicacy.

I think, however, that he would reissue it, if requested to do so by a few men of weight, of whom I venture to hope you might be willing to be one. The other signatures, which it is proposed to get, to the letter which I enclose, are those of Judge Curtis (B. R.) and Dr. Anderson of Rochester—the President of the Baptist College. We should like however, to have you lead off, and I venture to ask you, therefore to sign the enclosed and return it to me here, if it meets with your approbation.

I remain, dear Sir, with much respect

Yours very truly
ELG

To William D. Whitney

Nation Office   New York, January 20, 1874
(Whitney Papers, CtY)

MY DEAR MR. WHITNEY: I saw the terrible news in the paper before leaving home this morning. You have my own and my wife's
deepest and most heartfelt sympathy. I would say more, if I did
not know from fresh and bitter experience, how idle is all that
friends can say, at such a time.

Yours very cordially
ELG

To William D. Whitney

Nation Office   New York, January 24, 1874
(Whitney Papers, CtY)

MY DEAR SIR: I enclose a letter which I have today received from
Professor Silliman and ask your advice and that of such gentlemen of the Scientific School, as you think proper to consult as to
the course to be pursued.[1] We are willing to meet the matter anywhere, and any how, and bear the cost, but I trust we may receive
a fair amount of support, in the way of information, evidence and
advice from those who have been grieved and scandalized by this
Emma Mine and similar enterprizes, in which Mr. Silliman and his
confederates have been engaged.

   This is the first time, to my knowledge, that he has offered "to
face the music."

Yours very truly
ELG

1. A reference to the Sheffield Scientific School of Yale College.

To Professor Benjamin Silliman, Jr.

New York, February 2, 1874 (Unsigned rough draft,
Godkin Papers, *Nation* Business Records, MH)

SIR: In reply to your letter of Jan. 23rd I beg to say that the article in the *Nation* of Dec. 18, entitled "The True History of a

Govt. Mining Enterprize," to which you refer, was, and was stated to be a summary of the contents of a pamphlet, professing to give the history of the "Emma Silver Mining Co.," printed and published in London in August 1873, by Mr. L. T. Pafford a shareholder of the Company, under his own name. For the accuracy of his statements, or for anything except the correctness of our précis, I decline to be held responsible. They have been before the public now for over half a year, and have not so far as I know been challenged by you or anybody else, though circulated freely among the stockholders, and containing the gravest imputations on the character of most of those concerned in getting up the company, and they do not—on most important points —differ from the allegations made by Mr. C. N. Ewing at the second annual meeting of the Company on the 6th of March 1873, at Glasgow, in a speech in which he designated the promoters of the mine as a "set of swindlers." To that speech no answer has I believe been made by the persons whose character he thus seriously assailed. I may add before leaving this point— that the term "The Sir Roderick Murchison of America" to which you object as "a sneer," was quoted by the *Nation*, as the typography showed, and was applied to you in the first instance by the vendors of the mine when they were negotiating its sale in England.

I must, therefore, decline to enter into the arrangement you suggest for satisfying me personally, of the truthfulness of the contradictions you offer to Mr. Pafford's statements. I do so with great regret, both for reasons which mature consideration has only strengthened—*viz*—

1. That I am not in a position to conduct such an investigation in a manner that would either convince me, or enable me to vindicate you. Any evidence you would offer would prove insufficient—, as long as it was not subjected to the test of counter evidence or cross examination, and this test I personally could not possibly furnish, in dealing with a transaction occurring over so wide an area, and so largely technical in its details.

2. Because such an investigation is not, or it seems to me your *obvious* remedy. It is in England that your character has been gravely impeached with regard to the Emma Mine. It is there and in Scotland that the stockholders of the company who con-

ceive themselves to have been deceived to their pecuniary damage by your reports reside, and one at least, and I believe more,
have challenged your pursuits in a court of law. The very first
step in any process of vindication would, therefore, seem to be
either the proffer of an explanation to them, or else the commencement of a suit against them.

3. Because even if no palpable evidence of fraudulent intent in
your report on the Emma Mine were forthcoming—and I do not
allege that any *is* forthcoming—the mistake made by you in es-
timating the value of the mine, has been proved so great by the
results that it raises a presumption of fraud, which can only be
effectively upset by your professional reputation. Therefore to
make your answer in the matter complete you would have to
show that your professional history made it very unlikely that
you would have made such a mistake knowingly. In other words,
the enquiry into your connection with the Emma Mine, would
have to include an enquiry into your connection with various
other enterprizes of a similar character touching which charges of
a grave character have been freely made against you.

I am informed that this connection and also your connection
with the Emma Mine, are about to be made the subject of investigation by the National Academy of Science. This body, or Yale
College, which has the strongest interest in your good name, is
certainly I need hardly say, much better fitted, and much more
plainly called upon, to undertake such a task than a private person like myself. Should you satisfy them, or either of them, that
the imputations so freely cast upon you during the last four or
five years, are unfounded, you may rely upon it that I shall leave
nothing, in my power, undone to spread abroad your vindication, but I must add in closing, that I think, you owe it to the
country, as well as to Science, and to your friends and associates
to insist upon full inquiry at once at the hands of some really
competent tribunal.

                I am, Sir, Your Obedient Servant

To Charles Eliot Norton

Washington, D. C., February 6, 1874 (Ogden 1:310–11)

. . . I came on here for mingled instruction and recreation on Wednesday, and am having a somewhat interesting experience which I wish you were here to share. Phelps, my host, gave a dinner party last night which was comic in some of its aspects, but also very entertaining. It included Richardson of the Treasury. I supposed, of course, he would be unwilling to meet me, but he came with the greatest alacrity and was quite cordial. There were also Sherman—the Senator—Blaine the Speaker, Allison of Iowa, Dawes, Hooper, and Garfield, and the talk was very well worth listening to. They discussed the power of the Senate to make alterations in money bills, in the very best way; gave amusing reminiscences of Congress, a defunct Congressman, —Stevens, for instance,—and finally got upon the press, on which they were also excellent. Blaine made on me the impression of a very strong man indeed—that is, of a man with more power than he needed for his daily work, while most of these men seem to be struggling in a hopeless way with their circumstances. Sherman talked in a very clear, steady way. Dawes seemed a *good* man, with whom life had gone hard, but who tried to do his duty. One gets sick of this class, however.

Phelps asked Sumner to come, but when he heard whom he was to meet he nearly kicked him out of the room. P. did not know of our relations, like many other people who refer to the *Nation* as a good topic on which to hang a conversation with the great statesman and *litterateur;* but they speedily receive a black eye, and have to change the subject.

They tell me that the House is decidedly inflationist, and the Senate is sufficiently tainted to make it probable that the limitation of the currency to $400,000,000 is all that can be accomplished this session. The policy of the sound men in the Senate is now one of delay. They are going to stave off all debate and action on the currency question as long as possible, in the belief that every day sees a favorable change in public opinion, which is hastened by the ease of money in New York and the rising tide of speculation.

Washington seems to be becoming more and more of a resort

for people who want to amuse themselves in the winter in a mild climate, and is greatly changed in all respects. The streets are paved, a great many new houses have gone up, and a general air of smartness and enterprize has come over the place. There is something pathetic in the appearance of the crowd of "plain people" from the country one sees going into the Capitol every morning in their best clothes, and crowding the gallery and looking down at the legislators with mingled awe and admiration. I think what strikes one most about members of the House is the cleanness of their shirts. There is a kind of man, you know, whom clean linen gives an odd Sunday look to, and most of these men belong to it. I think we underrate their honesty, but we overrate their intelligence. Their ignorance is awful, and it is not tempered and restrained as the ignorance of the corresponding class is in Europe by contact with foreign nations. There is a paper here called the *Capitol,* a savage satirist,—a literary Gilray,—which they all read and dread, but speak of with loathing, edited by Don Piatt. One of its last jokes is that there was a rush of Congressmen on a certain day to a bookstore, to ask for "John Smith on the Wealth of the People." The bookseller said he hadn't it, but he had Boorman's "Art of making Money," which they declared "would do just as well."

Rutson is down here, and is still planning trips to all parts of the United States and Canada. He says he will start on Sunday in some direction, but I doubt. He was in here a few minutes ago with Schurz. The latter I like more and more. He has the keenest enjoyment of the fun of political life, and laughs till the tears run down his cheeks over the slips and blunders and oddities of his colleagues. He is a born orator and musician, but it is curious and interesting to see what sinew the German training has given to his mind, and how readily he masters matters for which he has no natural bent. I am going to dine with him this evening and—Jane will be amused to hear—am going there to-morrow evening to a musical party at which a Mrs. Moulton will be the star. There is a great deal of "society" here,—constant dinners and receptions, —and the excitement of the less fortunate Congressmen and their wives over them is curious to witness. We breakfast over at the hotel with two couples of them at the same table. One is a blatant, empty creature named ———. He discharges platitudes of the most fatuous kind at my head as a newspaper editor, at intervals of about two minutes, with a solemn look; *e.g.* "Mr. Godkin, the more I see of Mr. Blaine, the more I am satisfied that he is a very remarkable man, sir." This very slowly in oratorical tones. . . .

To George P. Marsh

Nation Office   New York, February 10, 1874
(Marsh Papers, UVT)

DEAR MR. MARSH: You may possibly remember that five years ago in an article in the *Nation* on the Papal Syllabus, you mentioned the fact, that the present Cardinal Cullen had in an orthodox paper published and edited by him in Rome, maintained that the earth stood still, and the sun went around it. . . .

I have recently alluded to it, in the *Nation*, and the result has been a torrent of abuse from the Catholic press here, who defy us to prove it. . . .

Would it be trespassing on your kindness too much to ask you to send us the name of the Cardinal's paper, and the date on which the article appeared? . . .

I remain, dear Sir, with much regard,

Very truly yours
ELG

To William D. Whitney

Nation Office   New York, February 16, 1874
(Whitney Papers, CtY)

MY DEAR SIR: By all means send [my] letter to Mr. Bowles. I have a letter this morning from Professor Silliman's lawyer, again asking me to go over the evidence with *them*, and agree to apologize and retract, if I am convinced, and threatening a suit, if I refuse. But I do refuse.

Yours very truly
ELG

To Prentice and Mather, Attorneys-at-Law

Nation Office   New York, February 18, 1874
(signed rough draft, Godkin Papers,
Nation Business Records, MH)

Messrs. Prentice and Mather,

GENTLEMEN: In reply to your letter of the 14th inst. I beg to say
that the proposal you make that I should "review the evidence"
with you, in the matter of Professor Silliman's connection with
the Emma Mine, cannot be accepted by me, for reasons given in
full in a letter to Professor Silliman of the 2nd inst. in reply to a
similar suggestion on his part. I am, however, prepared to abide
the result of an examination of this and other charges against
him, which I understood are now pending before the National
Academy of Science, or the result of an investigation by Yale
College, which I think he ought to demand, and in case of his
vindication by either of these bodies, to make every possible effort to spread it abroad. If however, he should, as you threaten,
resort to the more tedious, and much less satisfactory process of a
libel suit, we shall defend ourselves to the best of our ability, and
do what we can to make the trial interesting and instructive for
the investors of all nations.

I am,

Your Obedient Servant
ELG

To William D. Whitney

Nation Office   New York, March 16, 1874
(Whitney Papers, CtY)

MY DEAR SIR: Silas Williams the Superintendent of the Emma
Mine has begun a suit against us. From Silliman we have heard
nothing since we got a letter from his lawyers some weeks ago,
making substantially the same request which he made in his letter
to me. I made substantially the same reply, and repeated my offer
to abide by the result of an investigation by the Academy of
Science, or Yale College. I understand now from a note received

from Professor Fisher last week, that Mr. Silliman is disposed to fall in with this suggestion.

How is the investigation before the Academy going? . . .

Will you kindly send me your brother's address in California. I want to communicate with him, and get his aid in preparing our defence.

> Yours very truly
> ELG

To William D. Whitney

Nation Office   New York, March 21, 1874
(Whitney Papers, CtY)

MY DEAR MR. WHITNEY: I hasten to say that the fact of Silliman's arraignment by your brother before the Academy of Science, was communicated to me last Christmas at Cambridge by President Eliot in the presence of Jeffreys Wyman, and they both talked of it as a matter of public notoriety, without caution or reservation of any kind. My knowledge of it was therefore, in no way "Confidential." What was confidential in my estimation, in my correspondence with you, was the nature and form of the charges. This was all that I learnt from you, and of this I have divulged nothing.

> Yours very truly
> ELG

To James Russell Lowell

10 West 48th St., New York, July 12 [1874]
(Lowell Papers, MH)

MY DEAR LOWELL: I must tell you how glad I am to hear of your being safe home again—how glad indeed we both are—for my wife shares all my emotions about you. She, however, adds, that she does not wish to see you, until she has assurance, that you are not offended by anything which has appeared in the *Nation* during the past two years. This is now a standing enquiry of hers with regard to all authors, poets, artists, and metaphysicians. It was made about you, *à propos* of a plan of the Nortons to have us meet you at Ashfield. I have examined my conscience and my files strictly, and have assured her, that both are void of offence, and that all allusions to you since your departure have been of a respectful character.

Consequently I look forward to seeing you again in the flesh with innocent joy. I have heard of you pretty constantly through one person [or] another, besides reading the accounts of you in the correspondence of my daily paper, from which I judge that your presence was constant consolation to the "downtrodden masses of the Old World." We both join in cordial remembrances to Mrs. Lowell.

Yours ever faithfully
ELG

To his son

10 West 48th St., New York, July 22, 1874
(Godkin Papers, MH)

MY DEAR LAWRENCE: Mama is at Narragansett, and I have sent on your letter to her. She will be back here on Saturday or Monday. I do not think it is best for you to come here on Saturday, and then have to go back over the same road on Monday. Go down the Housatonic line to Hawleyville, and then take the Shepaug Valley line to Litchfield, and come home here on the following Saturday. On Monday week we start for Vermont. I will bring your gun down from New Haven. I want you to practice quick shooting, and shooting on the wing diligently at Ripton, now that you know how to load and hold your gun.

I am very glad to hear that you are so well, and enjoying yourself so much.[1]

I think Harvard would have won, if Yale had not behaved so badly. The Yale stroke is a low blackguard, whom they ought not to have had. When you get to Litchfield, I will send you some money. Let me hear on your arrival.

Your affectionate Father
ELG

1. Godkin's fourteen-year-old son was spending the summer in Connecticut.

To James Russell Lowell

10 West 48th St., New York, July 30, 1874
(Lowell Papers, MH)

MY DEAR LOWELL: After the first glow of pleasure over your letter was past, I began at once to take a business view of it, and said to myself—"Seeing that he is in such a good humor, would there be a possibility of getting something out of him for the *Nation?* He probably has a great deal to say on various topics, and has written no prose for a long time, besides which as a D. C. L. he probably knows more now than he ever did, and will after wandering about so much, [find] the need of occupation this summer. His enthusiasm about his grandson must gradually subside, but can hardly do so without leaving a certain amount of general fervor, which may find vent in work."

I shall wait to see what effect this soliloquy will produce.

We are going into Vermont for a few weeks on Monday, but hope we may pass your way some time this fall. The "Beecher Scandal," is making New York almost uninhabitable just now. What with the nastiness of it, and the newspaper rhetoric on it, it is absolutely sickening.

Yours most affectionately
ELG

To Charles Eliot Norton

October 5, 1874 (Ogden 2:110)

MY DEAR NORTON: I hope you know. . . . if I should survive you, nothing would be more grateful to me than to be the instrument of carrying out your wishes with regard to your property or anything else. I must tell you frankly, however, I think I have even less reason to anticipate a long life than you. The nervous weakness from which I have now suffered for fourteen years makes me fear an early collapse, once I get on the shady side of the hill, and I am entering on it now.

Many thanks for Lowell's sonnet.[1] We shall be glad to pay him for it. . . . You would have to . . . try and make the arrangement with him. He is so skittish and shy about money matters that it is difficult to negotiate with him by letter. . . .

Your devoted friend
ELG

1. Godkin was not a connoisseur of poetry, and Lowell was one of the few poets published in the *Nation* during the Godkin era.

To Henry Cabot Lodge [1]

10 West 48th St., New York, October 21, 1874
(Lodge Papers, MHi)

DEAR SIR: I am sorry to say it will be entirely out of my power to review Froude's *Ireland* for the Jan. *North American*. I have as much work as I can do, and even more than I can do, on hand already. It is a most discreditable performance, and I hope you may get some one to do justice to it.

Yours very truly
ELG

1. The recent Harvard graduate, Henry Cabot Lodge (1850–1924), was helping Henry Adams edit the *North American Review*.

To Professor James M. Hoppin [1]

10 West 48th St., New York, November 4, 1874
(Rare Book Room, CtY)

DEAR MR. HOPPIN: I ought before now to have acknowledged the receipt of your book, which presents a very handsome appearance. I have only had time to look through it, but we shall have a [rest] next week or the week after. I am glad to know you are all well, and flourishing. We are leading somewhat lonely lives owing to Lawrence's having left us for school. I found the city so unsuited to him, that I have put him with Mr. Morris up at Peekskill, where he is doing very well. I hope we may see you down here at Christmas. . . .

Yours very truly
ELG

1. Professor James M. Hoppin (1820–1906) of Yale College had just completed a biography of a distant cousin of Mrs. Godkin, Union naval hero Admiral Andrew H. Foote.

To his son

10 West 48th St., New York, January 9, 1875
(Godkin Papers, MH)

MY DEAR LAWRENCE: I am glad on the whole that Mr. Morris has made up his mind that something must be done with the blackguards. I think, however, it is hardly fair to shut up for a whole month the boys of whose integrity he has no doubt, because the bad characters will not confess. But I am not disposed to blame him very much, because I suppose, if he sends all the rascals away, he will have great difficulty in carrying on the school.

However, if you like, I will write to him on this point, and call his attention to what I think is wrong in his arrangement. Where I think he has been most mistaken is in letting these boys stay so long. He ought not to have asked respectable gentlemanly boys, to associate with liars and cheats. A boy who lies and cheats is not fit company for gentlemen, any more than a man would be.

I have great sympathy with Mr. Morris, and I am glad you have too. He is really a good man, who if he had a good set of boys would be an excellent teacher. Anybody who was tormented every day by a parcel of blackguards would be sure to seem unjust at times.

I wanted to tell you, before you left home, how much we enjoyed your visit, and how much we miss you—you were so pleasant, and good tempered and kind.

God bless you, my dear boy. Take care of your health, and try and be an honorable, truthful, manly fellow, even if you do have rascals about you. Never be afraid of any man enough to lie or deceive. Tell me if you would like me to write to Mr. Morris.

Your affectionate Father
ELG

To Edmund Clarence Stedman

10 West 48th St., New York, January 14, 1875
(Stedman Papers, NNC)

DEAR MR. STEDMAN: You are entirely mistaken in supposing that there is, as far as I am concerned, the slightest feeling of coolness between us. . . .

The omission of your name in the notice of *Scribners*, was I believe merely accidental. Mr. Dennett had looked after the magazines for many years. His illness and death obliged us to make other provision for the December Nos, and the person we employed for the purpose did the work so unsatisfactorily that it had to be done over again in the office at the last moment, and the result was a sort of hash from which I believe many believe many things were left out.[1] As regards my manner, it has seemed to me when I have met you at the Club that you were a little "uppish," and I supposed you were perhaps troubled by something that had appeared in the *Nation*. I have however, had so many experiences of this kind among literary men, that I have now ceased to enquire into the causes of this sort of thing, and indeed to trouble my head about it, and have made a practice of letting people who did not like the *Nation's* treatment of them give vent to their feelings in their own way, remaining myself perfectly ready to be friendly in any degree they pleased. You will see the necessity of this when I tell you that last summer I was followed into the country, by an abusive and insulting letter from a novel writer whose name I barely knew, on account of a notice in the *Nation*—and a very moderate one—which I had never seen, of a book of which I had never heard. He was under the impression that I was watching his career with vindictive eyes, and seizing every opportunity I could get to stab him.

I am very sorry if I have in any degree misunderstood you. When men do not meet often these misconceptions are of course liable to occur; but I beg you will dismiss from your mind the notion that I or anybody connected with the paper, bear you any grudge, or seek to do you anything but justice.

Believe me

Very truly yours
ELG

1. The final illness and death of John R. Dennett was a severe blow to the *Nation* (see Godkin's tribute to him, *Nation*, 3 December 1874, pp. 362–63). "You know we have in all these years accumulated a stock of established judgments about certain people which we cannot suddenly throw overboard," Godkin told Norton, explaining why he was dissatisfied with George P. Lathrop (1851–98), who had been hired to notice the magazines in Dennett's place. Few denied Dennett's talent, although his captiousness as a critic angered many.

To Whitelaw Reid

Nation Office   New York, March 1, 1875
(Reid Papers, DLC)

DEAR MR. REID: I do not think much importance need be attached to what Woodman says about Lyon. They are undoubtedly a bad lot those mining men, but they all blackguard each other in a general way. In their dealings with each other, they regard each other, and rightly as thieves, and liars. But this does not, in my opinion shake the substantial accuracy of Lyon's statement.

I have received the proof, and am going to go over it with McFarland, with reference to its safety. My private opinion is that the statement cannot be shaken. I will drop you a line again in a few days.

I would have returned the enclosed sooner, but my wife's illness has prevented my looking into it until two days ago.[1]

Very truly yours
ELG

1. Godkin's wife never recovered from the death of their favorite child followed the same year by that of her invalid brother, and she was now in a physical decline.

To Wendell P. Garrison

New York [mid March 1875?] (Godkin Papers, MH)

DEAR MR. GARRISON: Mrs. Godkin is rather better today, but had a very bad day yesterday. She is now, however, leaving off the milk, so with ever so many thanks for your kindness, you need not keep up the supply any longer.[1]

Yours ever
ELG

1. On 11 April 1875 Mrs. Godkin died.

To Wendell P. Garrison

New York [1 May 1875]
(Godkin Papers, *Nation* Business Records, MH)

I, Edwin L. Godkin of the City of New York do hereby constitute and appoint Wendell P. Garrison my true and lawful attorney, to endorse checks, and money orders, and to sign such other papers as may be necessary in the transaction of my private business, or the business of the firm of E. L. Godkin & Company with my name and on my behalf, for the space of one year from the date hereof.[1]

Witness my hand this first day of May in the year Eighteen hundred and Seventy-five.

ELG

Witness
C. E. Norton

1. Distraught at the death of his wife, Godkin was preparing to put Garrison in charge of the *Nation* and move to Cambridge.

To Wendell P. Garrison

Cambridge, Mass., May 5, 1875 (Godkin Papers, MH)

DEAR MR. GARRISON: . . . I have bought a house here from Richardson of the Treasury, and shall go on on Monday week to move my furniture. . . .[1]

Remember me affectionately to your wife. I do not yet know how things are going with me. My responsibilities to other people are all that keep me in motion. You may guess I am not in very hearty condition when I say that the one pleasant thought that has come to me in the last three weeks is that of a speedy end to my troubles.

Yours ever

ELG

I am going to make my will, and would like to know your feelings and Sedgwick's and Condit's—about the disposition of my interest—supposing the paper to go on after my death.

---

1. The home of former Secretary of the Treasury William A. Richardson at 59 Kirkland St., near the Harvard Yard.

To Wendell P. Garrison

Cambridge, Mass., May 6, 1875 (Godkin Papers, MH)

DEAR MR. GARRISON: I made the explanation to Blodgett, which I made to everyone else, when we broke up the old arrangement, and he told me in reply "he would do whatever I pleased" about the note. I did not *ask* him directly to surrender. . . .[1]

He spoke to me about his not having had any interest, in a semi jocose way, two or three months ago, but I was then troubled a good deal about weightier matters, and I forgot to say anything to you about it.

However, we have thus far followed the course of paying those who refused to surrender. We cannot well make an exception of him, and any dispute with him on such a debt would ill become us.

In other words—as he insists we must pay—that is you and I—Sedgwick and Condit are not, and ought not to be liable.[2] I propose therefore, that we pay him now the arrears of interest, and offer to extinguish the note within two years. . . .

Yours ever

ELG

---

1. A reference to Godkin's efforts to get all of the original stockholders in the *Nation* to donate their interests to E. L. Godkin and Company.

2. The death during the previous year of Garrison's father-in-law, James M. McKim, who held a one-third interest in E. L. Godkin and Company, left Garrison partly responsible for the original debts of the company. God-

kin held seven-twelfths of the stock, and Sedgwick and advertizing agent Condit one twelfth each, apparently acquired when Olmsted quit the concern.

To Wendell P. Garrison

Cambridge, Mass., May 8, 1875 (Godkin Papers, MH)

DEAR MR. GARRISON: I am going to leave my interest in the paper in trust to Charles Norton. He will have both its interest and mine equally at heart, and will, I think, try to make them harmonize, if the occasion should arise. I do not anticipate that it will, but I now feel very uncertain about everything in the future. I dare say I shall before long be in better working order than I am now. I have pretty well decided to stay here now with frequent visits to New York until Lawrence has graduated—say seven years. But I shall then be over fifty, and have had twenty years of uninterrupted labor behind me, and I think all concerned, without saying anything about it to outsiders, had better make up their minds that I shall then retire. . . .

I shall now say nothing in reply to the more purely personal part of your letter. . . . You will have your reward somewhere and somehow, I am sure.

As regards Blodgett, I am likely to be very much pressed for money during the coming year, and would rather not settle up now. As you wish to do so, I propose that you should pay your share . . . and I will . . . assume the balance. . . .

Yours ever
ELG

To Daniel Coit Gilman

Cambridge, Mass., August 11, 1875
(Gilman Papers, MdBJ)

MY DEAR GILMAN: I hope the enclosed may not reach you too late. You will find Bryce a very thoughtful man, full of original ideas, and very familiar with the weak as well as the strong points of the English university system.[1] He lectures at the Lowell Institute this winter on Cathedral Building.

I hope your trip is proving profitable.

Yours ever

ELG

1. Godkin was just beginning his long friendship with James Bryce (1838–1922).

To Frederick Law Olmsted

Cambridge, Mass., November 16, 1875 (Olmsted Papers, DLC)

MY DEAR OLMSTED: I have a letter from Sedgwick, written under your inspiration asking whether I would take a place on Tilden's Municipal Government Commission. . . . The things in its favor are, that it is a kind of work I would like to do, and which perhaps, having criticized so much, I am in a measure bound to do if I get a chance, and in so far as it relieved me of the reputation of being simply a critic, might help the *Nation.*

On the other hand, Tilden is an active and prominent politician, and a possible candidate for the Presidency, and it is a question whether accepting an appointment from him, which even if unpaid, is a compliment would not seem, in the public eye, to compromise my editorial independence and impartiality. . . . The composition of the Commission is the essential point, however. . . . If they are mere politicians or fellows in search of political capital, or blatherskite intuitionists of the Jeffersonian School, I could do no good on the Commission, and would be sure to get hurt, and to hurt my paper.

In short, I will say privately, that I will serve if the other members are persons with whom I can work satisfactorily.[1]

Yours ever

ELG

1. Godkin accepted the invitation to serve on Governor Tilden's Municipal Government Commission, charged with the task of studying the "decay of municipal government" and of devising a plan of municipal government for New York City. The Commission's report, issued in 1877, failed to win attention from the Legislature. One of its proposed changes was that propertyless nontaxpayers be disenfranchised in New York City.

To Wendell P. Garrison

Cambridge, Mass., November 18, 1875
(Godkin Papers, *Nation* Business Records, MH)

DEAR MR. GARRISON: . . . I can throw no light on the question of the pressure on our space; we have [admittedly] diminished our size as far as readers are concerned during the past year, but we must have some money, and they must bear with it for the moment. I have written stopping Pearson absolutely. I do not see how we can cut down Laugel or Sellar.[1] They are a valuable variety—we must do the best we can for the present and trust to Providence for deliverance.

As regards Mr. Powers, an increase of our salaries, if only payable at the end of the year, would simply amount to commuting our share of the profits for a fixed sum.[2] My position in this matter is a trifle delicate, owing to my holding the control, and you may remember I anticipated this, and provided for it in my agreement with Mr. McKim. I have always felt that whenever the shareholders were receiving 7% on a capital of $60,000, I would ask for an increase of my salary, say to $6,000 . . . and I was going to suggest that your salary should be established on a permanent basis, of half of mine. . . . it does not indicate any low estimate of the value of your services, I simply say that I think the proper proportion in view of all the circumstances should be 3 to 6 instead of 3 to 5, and I am as entirely frank in the matter with you, as I used to be with Mr. McKim. . . . This I think ought to be treated as something distinct from the arrangement with Powers. . . .

I propose this: that if on the basis of the memorandum as to profits of 1874 and 5 made last Spring, it should appear that the profits of this year are 7% . . . my salary in 1876 shall be $6,000, and I shall leave the arrangement with Powers to the vote of the shareholders. . . .[3]

Yours ever
ELG

---

1. Alexander C. Sellar (1835–90) was the British correspondent of the *Nation*, and the prominent French journalist August Laugel (1830–1914) was the *Nation*'s Paris correspondent.

2. J. E. Powers succeeded Garrison, who was now managing editor, as publisher of the *Nation*.

3. Powers was employed on a commission basis, and Godkin now proposed to Garrison, Sedgwick, and Condit, that, effective 1 January 1876, Power's commission be 25 percent of the *Nation*'s profits until his annual commission reached $4,000, any additional commission above that being 10 percent of profits.

To F. E. Abbot [1]

Cambridge, Mass., November 20, 1875 (Abbot Papers, MH-Ar)
Personal

DEAR SIR: Every now and then a copy of the *Index* is sent me containing an attack on me by Mr. R. P. Hallowell with regard to the circumstances attending the establishment of the *Nation*. Nearly everything that has been said against me on that score rests on the statements of the late Mr. Geo. Stearns. When last I had occasion to reply to these attacks about six years ago, I was obliged to produce evidence showing this gentleman to have been a reckless and confirmed liar. . . .

Mr. C. E. Norton who was in Europe when I last touched on this matter is now here. He was with Mr. Stearns, Mr. McKim, and myself the founder of the *Nation*. If I return to the subject I shall have what I had not then, his testimony in full, and in using it I shall consider my own interests and good name only. This letter is not for publication, and is not to form the text of any public discussion, but you are at liberty to show it to Mr. Hallowell.

Your obedient servant
ELG

1. The clergyman and philosopher, Francis E. Abbot (1836–1903), was editor of the *Index*, a journal of religious and philosophical free thought to which Hallowell contributed.

To Richard P. Hallowell

Cambridge, Mass., November 27, 1875
(Printed letter, Abbot Papers, MH-Ar)

Sɪʀ: If it were not for the tediousness, and in some respects incon-
clusiveness of legal proceedings, I should long ago have sued you
for your published statements reflecting on my character. I now
desire, however, to attain the same object in a shorter and more
effective way, by proposing that we request Mr. James B. Thayer,
of Cambridge, to select two other impartial persons, to form with
him a tribunal, before which you will bring whatever charges you
have to make, or have been making, against me in connection with
the establishment of the *Nation*. . . .

Yours, etc.
ELG

To F. E. Abbot

Cambridge, Mass., November 28, 1875 (Abbot Papers, MH-Ar)

Dᴇᴀʀ Sɪʀ: I have called on Mr. Hallowell to bring his charges and
proofs before a tribunal selected by ourselves, and either make
them good, or be condemned to silence as a slanderer. Should he
refuse I shall ask for the publication of my offer in the *Index*, and
shall take other means of making the public acquainted with his
bad character, and with the burlesque of his parading himself as a
"religious philosopher." You are at liberty to show him this letter,
and I remain with thanks for your note,

Yours truly
ELG

To Richard P. Hallowell

Nation Office   New York, December 2, 1875
(Printed letter, Abbot Papers, MH-Ar)

Sɪʀ: I knew you to be untruthful and malignant. I now pronounce
you grossly impudent. You are mistaken in supposing that I will

carry on a controversy with you in your paper. You are no longer worth controverting. I shall now confine myself to exposing you thoroughly as a most cowardly and unprincipled slanderer.

ELG

To F. E. Abbot

Nation Office   New York, December [3?], 1875
(Abbot Papers, MH-Ar)

DEAR SIR: Your editorial contributor Mr. R. P. Hallowell has refused my challenge to carry his charges before a tribunal, after having slandered me for ten years. I have never encountered the like of this in the way of effrontery except in the distinctly criminal class of society. It will now be my duty to expose him as an unprincipled and cowardly libeller, and I mean to do it effectively, and thus if I cannot make him ashamed, at least diminish his powers of mischief. For this purpose I am about to have my correspondence with him set up in type, together with some observations of my own on him, and the class to which he belongs, and I shall begin my work by calling on you to publish it in full in your next issue, if I can get it to you in time. My [communication?] is not to be taken as the opening of a controversy with him, however. He is no longer a person with whom an honorable man can have any discussion.

Truly yours
ELG

I expect to have the copy in your hands by Monday morning.

To Richard P. Hallowell

New York, December 6, 1875
(Printed letter, Abbot Papers, MH-Ar)

SIR: . . . Your objection to the examination of Mr. C. E. Norton as a witness, he being actually one of the two persons who obtained the money from the Recruiting Committee on which you have based your charges against me and one of the four founders of the *Nation*, must be either made humorously, or is one of the shifts of a knave brought to bay by his victim. Your objection also to the strength of my language comes strangely from you after your ten years of mendacious assaults on my character. Let me add in conclusion . . . that I have never refused any man's challenge to go before a Court of any kind, and that your refusal shows a degree of moral insensibility and social indecency of which even I did not believe you would be guilty.

ELG

To F. E. Abbot

Nation Office   New York, December 6, 1875
(Abbot Papers, MH-Ar)

Personal

DEAR SIR: I enclose my letter. I shall expect for it all the prominence as to type and position given to Mr. Hallowell's attacks on me, and rely on its being printed verbatim, heading and all.

Please send me the 100 copies of the paper to this office, with the bill, and oblige.

Yours truly
ELG

To F. E. Abbot

Cambridge, Mass., December 10, 1875 (Abbot Papers, MH-Ar)

SIR: . . . I express to you my regrets in the most unqualified way for whatever has offended you in my letter, and will erase anything you object to on that score. Indeed I have already done so, and if you will forward me the copy will put it in a shape which I think will leave you no cause of complaint. . . . I am sensible that I had no right to involve you in the matter.

Truly yours
ELG

To F. E. Abbot

Cambridge, Mass., December 11, 1875 (Abbot Papers, MH-Ar)

DEAR SIR: I again enclose my letter. I removed every word which seemed to me capable of giving you any cause of complaint, either on your own account or that of the *Index*. I shall look for it in your next number. . . .

Yours very truly
ELG

To F. E. Abbot

Cambridge. Mass., December 17, 1875 (Abbot Papers, MH-Ar)

DEAR SIR: . . . I cannot consent to carry on a controversy in print with a person so irrational and untruthful as Hallowell. Nor could I reply to him in any way without impugning his character. There is only one defense to a slander. What I sought through your paper was permission to make known to your subscribers that I was endeavoring to bring him to justice. I am still doing so. I have now challenged him to meet me before the Recruiting Committee. Should he refuse, as I have little doubt he will, I shall probably bring him before the Courts, and shall have I fear, to include you and the proprietor of the *Index* in the proceeding, much as I shall regret it. . . .

Yours truly
ELG

To Frederick Law Olmsted

Cambridge, Mass., December 17 [1875] (Olmsted Papers, DCL)

MY DEAR OLMSTED: I had expected to be in New Haven and New York about the 27th or 28th to settle Harry Foote's estate, and attend to your business, but learnt as I came through New Haven yesterday, that owing to the necessity of advertizing, we cannot do the New Haven business before the early part of

January, when I shall have to go on and bring Mrs. Foote up to
New Haven probably. As I hope then to go on to Washington
also and be gone two or three weeks, I am desirous of not making another journey in the interval, particularly as it is holiday
time, and I am rather used up, and have today been put on bro-
mide of potassium. . . .

I propose to settle up my own account with you in full at the
same time. I think it will . . . amount to about $1500, on Jan
1st. . . . Do you expect more than 7% on the balance since July
last?

I also think it will be as well, and more convenient for you to
let me put $10,000 of Mrs. O's money in the mortgage, as it is an
even and neat sum, and you do something else with the balance
coming to you, but just as you like.

I was in New York on Wednesday to attend the opening
meeting of the Commission, but was sick in the cars going in,
and got back last night in a low state. . . . I feel today as if the
end of the world, or the Second Coming of Satan was at hand,
but hope a night's sleep may make things look brighter.

I saw Bishop Niles in the cars and found him very entertaining.

Yours ever
ELG

Find out positively, whether those men, wish to *assign the mort-
gage*, or to give a *satisfaction piece*.

To F. E. Abbot

Cambridge, Mass., December 19, 1875 (Abbot Papers, MH-Ar)

DEAR SIR: My invitation to Mr. Hallowell to go before Mr.
Thayer and others is likely to be made very unimportant by
what may happen in this matter hereafter. . . .

Let me add that I am at this moment unwell, which may delay
my further action for some days. But I am going to procure a
meeting of the Recruiting Committee, before which he declines
to appear with me, and their resolution will probably end the
matter, as far as the public is concerned. . . .

Let me hope in conclusion that nothing in my treatment of the matter has caused you any permanent dissatisfaction.

Truly yours
ELG

This letter is purely personal and I keep no copy of it.

To F. E. Abbot

Cambridge, Mass., December 25, 1875 (Abbot Papers, MH-Ar)
Personal

DEAR SIR: I am obliged to you for the copies of the *Index* containing Mr. Hallowell's card and your reply. There is certainly nothing in the latter of which I can complain. . . .

I have put the whole matter, as far as I am concerned, into the hands of my lawyer, with instructions to do everything in his power to obtain a full investigation either by the Recruiting Committee, or some other tribunal, before which everything and all kinds of evidence can be brought, before resorting to a court of law. But the matter will now be pushed to an end of some kind. I will no longer permit my character to be made the subject of "trial by newspaper," or of amateur essay writing in religious or philosophical journals.

Whenever arrangements for an investigation are made, you will do me a favor by being present, and I shall ask to have the judgment whatever it may be, printed in your columns.

If you can attend I am sure you will as an honorable and intelligent man, be amazed by the evidence, in which two or three persons have for ten years been assailing my reputation.

Truly yours
ELG

To F. E. Abbot

Cambridge, Mass., December 30, 1875 (Abbot Papers, MH-Ar)

DEAR SIR: I would not willingly do Mr. Hallowell wrong, and do not know him personally, but I am unable to acquit him of the charge of dishonesty without getting up a new code of morality for his benefit. . . .

I look upon the practice of claiming a presumption of honesty for persons of his description, on the ground of his strong phil-anthropic feeling and active service in some humane cause, as in no respect different from the practice of claiming a similar pre-sumption for "church members," of which the public is now heartily tired. For Mr. Hallowell's account of "his heart" I care nothing, and I am under no obligation that I know of to construe his falsehoods, and evasions and dishonest omissions in a sense favorable to him. He must like other men, stand or fall by his *conduct* judged by the old standards. I may not succeed in per-suading other people of this, but I shall never knowingly con-nive at the setting up of an extra standard of morality for the benefit of a particular set of social philosophers.[1]

Yours very truly
ELG

This needs no answer.

1. At this point the matter was dropped, possibly in deference to the wishes of Norton, who could scarcely risk being Godkin's scapegoat in an inquiry. There is little doubt that Godkin dissimulated with Stearns in his 1865 interview with him in the presence of Wendell Phillips for the post of editor-in-chief of the *Nation*. But it was Norton who proposed God-kin for the post, knowing Godkin's views toward the freedmen clashed with those of the *Nation*'s leading sponsor, and it was Norton who helped Godkin persuade Stearns to hand over part of the Negro funds (the "Recruiting Fund") to the *Nation*.

To Wendell P. Garrison

Cambridge, Mass., February 8, 1876
(Godkin Papers, Nation Business Records, MH)

DEAR MR. GARRISON: I had some talk with Mr. Powers on Fri-day p.m. in which he revealed that he was much dissatisfied with the agreement, of Jan. 1, 1876, as it seemed to fail in proper recognition of his work during the year, and thinks the commis-sion to him ought to rise instead of diminishing in the ratio of the rise of the profits, or at all events ought not to diminish. I did not discuss it much, but told him to put on paper what he had to say. He accordingly sends me a note which I enclose asking for 25% throughout, after an increase of my salary. He seems exceedingly confident about the future. Please debate it with Sedgwick and Condit. I would suggest an offer of 20%. I do not quite like his growing restive so soon, but I think he has done extremely well.

As regards my salary, I did not press the point of increase last Dec. because it was still uncertain how we should come out, but the paper seems to be now on a good dividend paying basis, and I do not think I am unreasonable in asking for $6000 now right along, beginning—say Feb. 1. This amounts to diminishing the profits of this year by $1000, but they will hardly fail to be 7% or $4200, in any case.

As I have said before I do not wish to settle this question by my own powers, and indeed am bound not to do so, and take it for granted, that you will all treat it as a business matter and utter freely any objections you have to it. In which case I would leave it on all the facts to any man of "approved sagacity" except H. C. Bowen.[1] I think *between ourselves,* there will need to be discretion used to prevent Powers imagining that he is carrying on the *Nation.* There is that tendency in all such cases. When had I better begin to take my fortnight holiday? I am solidly tired. I have been working now since the summer of 1874, or at all events have had no relaxation.

I agree to the declaration of dividend.

Yours ever
ELG

Tell Sedgwick Powers values the paper now at $100,000, which makes a rise of over $3000 on his share.[2]

1. The proprietor of the *Independent.*
2. Five years later Godkin sold the *Nation,* which heretofore he valued at $60,000, for $40,000.

To Daniel Coit Gilman

Cambridge, Mass., February 11, 1876 (Gilman Papers MdBJ)

DEAR MR. GILMAN: I am not sure yet whether I can go but I will try and let you know early next week.

I am giving a letter of introduction to you at his request, to Mr. Heilprin, a Hungarian Jew, but one of the most worthy and modest men I ever knew. He is an old contributor of ours, and is now assistant editor of *Appleton's Encyclopaedia*. He is a mine of *facts*—particularly historical, and of great learning in certain philological fields. He tells me he is going to try to get your professorship of History.[1] Candidly, I must say I do not think him fit for any such position. He is not a man with any great hold of principles or any great power of expression and is too shy for a teacher. But he is an excellent fellow, and you must not indicate in any way that I have thrown cold water on his aspirations.[2]

Yours sincerely
ELG

1. Gilman was now president of the newly-established Johns Hopkins University.

2. Heilprin was not hired.

To Richard Henry Dana [1]

Cambridge, Mass., March 7, 1876 (Dana Papers, MHi)

DEAR MR. DANA: I take the liberty of urging you most earnestly to accept the proferred English mission. Your prompt appearance in London, will go far to stem the flood of disgrace which that rascal Schenck has brought on the American name, and though the period for which the position can be assured to you is short, the need of the country is so pressing that I earnestly hope you will not decline.

Yours very sincerely
ELG

1. The noted author and legal authority, Richard Henry Dana (1815–82), was an occasional contributor to the *Nation*.

To Frederick Law Olmsted

Albermarle Hotel   New York, March 15, 1876
(Olmsted Papers, DLC)

MY DEAR OLMSTED: I enclose my check for $1214.88 in full set-
tlement of your account, including the coupons on Mrs. F[oote]'s
bonds due Jan. 1. on which and on the balance of $760.97 I have
calculated the interest at 7%. Please send me an acknowledgment of the settlement to date. Considering the uncertainty of
life too, I hope you have those other mortgages on the house
discharged of record.

I have not had a minute's time to go see you since I came to
town until today, and today I am not well and very tired. I am
sick at heart of the fraud business; the "Week" in the *Nation* this
week will be entirely and legitimately, devoted to fraud and
adultery.

I will come round to dinner tomorrow evening if you say so.

Yours ever
ELG

To Charles Eliot Norton

Washington, D. C., March 22, 1876 (Ogden 2:309)

. . . There seems to be no doubt that they have caught
Robeson in two impeachable offences at least—of which the il-
legality is clear, and the corruption probable.[1] Whether he will
be impeached or not is another question; but the effect on the
public will be the same. One of the offences—a large loan of
public money to Jay Cooke on the security of old iron—is a
wonderful illustration of the pitch to which the lawlessness of the
the Administration had grown.

I heard ——— examined in the committee yesterday. He lied
like clockwork, and a very curious scene is expected today on
cross-examination; but the committee, except Hewitt and Faulkner
of Virginia, are very ordinary men. . . .[2] What a shameful state
of mind, on the part of the Senate, the treatment of Dana reveals! [3]

Blaine I have watched in the House, and he cuts a very poor

figure, shows a feminine waspishness, and screams over every trifle that comes up. Hewitt says the inflationists gain ground sensibly. The one satisfactory and hopeful sight in Washington is the Supreme Court. I am going to see Bristow today. . . .[4]

1. Godkin was in Washington, D.C., witnessing the deliberations of a House Committee formed to investigate newspaper charges that Secretary of the Navy George M. Robeson (1829–97) was guilty of gross favoritism and extravagance. Godkin had opposed Robeson's appointment in the *Nation* in 1869.

2. Abram S. Hewitt (1822–1903) and Charles J. Faulkner (1806–84), Democratic Representatives from New York and West Virginia, respectively. Faulkner, a former Confederate, served only one term in Congress.

3. A reference to the refusal of the United States Senate to confirm R. H. Dana as Robert Schenck's successor as American minister to England.

4. As secretary of the Treasury under Grant, Benjamin H. Bristow (1832–96) vigorously prosecuted the Whisky Ring, resigning from the cabinet after differences with the President in June 1876.

To Richard Henry Dana

Cambridge, Mass., March 31 [1876] (Dana Papers, MHi)

DEAR MR. DANA: I was on the point of writing to you to ask you, how you became aware that the Senate Committee had asked the President to withdraw your name, and whether you were aware of it, in any certain way before you write your letter to Boutwell, when your note of yesterday and Mr. Russell's pamphlet reached me. . . .

I ask these questions because I am going to write at greater length on the case next week than I have yet done, and want to be sure of some of the later incidents. . . .

In explanation of the paragraph [in the *Nation*] to which you take exception, I ought to say that in New York, from which I have just returned I was constantly met by Judge Clifford's decision, the language of which is strong and sweeping, and it was useless in any *short* comment on the case for us to set up our own denial of *any* violation of the Copyright—against the opinion of the Court.[1] My use of the word "carelessness" was due to my recollection of a correspondence on the subject with your brother in 1866. . . .

I have only to say that as regards your own fame, you could

not have desired anything better than your rejection and the controversy it has [raised]; but as regards the future of the country I think the course of the Senate is an alarming phenomenon.

Yours very truly
ELG

1. A reference to the successful suit of William Beach Lawrence against Dana for copyright infringement.

To William D. Whitney

Nation Office   New York, April 1, 1876 (Whitney Papers, CtY)

MY DEAR MR. WHITNEY: I am wholly responsible for the erasures in your letter, which you complain of to Mr. Garrison. . . . Moreover I ought to say frankly that I disliked the tone of Mr. Van Name's article, and had not my absence in Washington prevented my seeing it before it went in, I would have asked him to make some modifications in it, that is to say, I thought it written in such a way as to make the *Nation* seem a *party* to the controversy rather than a judicial reviewer of it, which is the position we aim at, and which our public expects us to take.[1] The same thing occurred in our recent notice of Tyndall, which I regretted much and had determined to avoid in future. . . .

You are entirely mistaken, let me add, as to our having any consideration for the *Academy*. . . . If as you say "you cannot help contrasting the support we give you, with that the *Academy* gives Müller," and find that the "*Academy* is content to be his organ," I am sure your conclusion must be to our advantage, as we avoid being or seeming anybody's "organ," and I am sure you will on calmer consideration of your past relations to the *Nation*, which have certainly been marked by great kindness on your part, regret your charge of injustice.

Very sincerely yours
ELG

P. S. I have shown the printed letter and my erasures to two or three of my friends here, who agree that they are manifestly to your advantage, that the letter in the *Nation* contains a sufficient statement of your case against the *Academy*. . . . You will pardon me for saying in conclusion, that in spite of the constant and loyal support we have given you all through this controversy I have found that if it lasted long, we should reach a point at which we should fail to satisfy you, because a long experience of quarrels, both my own and other people's, has shown me, that when they become protracted, the combatants are apt to lose their sense of proportion and unduly magnify the importance of their own reputation.

ELG

1. "Müller's Chips from a German Workshop," *Nation*, 23 March 1876, pp. 195–97. Godkin's letter concerns the protracted controversy between the noted philologist F. Max Müller and William D. Whitney. One of their points of disagreement was that Whitney regarded language as innate, whereas Müller saw it as a product of experience. Addison Van Name, the librarian of Yale College who was a student of oriental languages, came to Whitney's defense in the *Nation* after the London *Academy* took Müller's side in the dispute.

To Daniel Coit Gilman

Cambridge, Mass., April 12, 1876 (Gilman Papers MdBJ)

MY DEAR GILMAN: There is a very excellent man, in New York, who wants a professorship of Greek or Latin, of whom I think you ought to know, and to whom I beg your serious attention if not for your chief chair, for something subordinate—Chas. D. Morris now professor in—Crosby's New York University. He was formerly Fellow of Oriel (Oxford) and settled in this country in consequence of his marriage, which was unfortunate, his wife being an opium eater. He was for five or six years master of Trinity School, but they did not pay him enough, and he then set up for himself near Peekskill, and had a school to which I sent my boy for a year. He was broken down there by the goodness of his reputation; that is to say he had achieved so much fame as a manager of boys, that before he knew it, his school was filled with reprobates and dunces, who had been sent away from other places, and they fairly ruined him, as he is entirely unfit for dealing with such cases. But he is I believe in the estimation of the best judges, one of the best Latin and Greek scholars on either side of the Atlantic, the author of remarkable grammars, and a wonderful teacher of *good* boys, or of boys old enough, as college students would be, to wish *to learn*. Pray enquire about him.[1]

Yours very truly
ELG

1. Charles D'Urban Morris (1827–86) published several elementary Latin grammars and a brief *Introduction to the Greek Language.* Gilman hired him, but he did not bear out Godkin's estimate of him as a scholar.

To Wendell P. Garrison

Cambridge, Mass., June 22, 1876
(Godkin Papers, *Nation* Business Records, MH)

DEAR MR. GARRISON: . . . I cannot help considering the money matter as described in your note a serious state of things. . . . I must remind you that the accounts showed over $6000 *on the table,* on April 1st. What has become of it? Why is none of it available for the payment of salaries?

I want to have now, at as early a day as possible, a list of the accounts *due* April 1st., that is names of the firms, and the amounts, with the sums since collected, and *the reasons why the balance has not been collected*. This is all the more trying to me, because I am this year more pressed for money than I think I have ever been in my life, having taken a quantity of real estate in N. H. and borrowed money to discharge the legacies on it. . . .

Yours ever
ELG

To Wendell P. Garrison

Cambridge, Mass., July 4, 1876
(Godkin Papers, *Nation* Business Records, MH)

DEAR MR. G: . . . I must . . . call your attention to the fact that as things now go, carrying on the paper with "capital" means carrying it on at a loss. If the current receipts *from quarter to quarter* do not pay the current expenses, having "capital" will not save us. Our receipts this year up to May, have shown a steady aggregate gain over last year, *so that the trouble must lie in the outgo.* In other words, there is a leak somewhere, which must be stopped. Is Powers' machinery—(Miss Gleason, etc.) not to (*sic*) ponderous and expensive for the result? . . .

As regards myself, I have done everything I can to reduce my salary for mere editing to the lowest possible figure, by as nearly as possible furnishing contributions for all I receive. I write about 4½ to 5 pages, which at the rate we pay leading contributors, has nearly equalled the whole amount of my salary, and this has now gone on for eleven years. I am no longer a young man and have very little left in this world to look forward to. Lawrence will soon be connected, and be independent of me, and there is no earthly ambition which tempts me. But I would like—and it is almost the only thing I desire strongly—that the *Nation* could somehow be got and kept in a condition in which we should have in the figures some basis even for prudence, and should be exempted from these periodical storms. I cannot help feeling now that I shall have to return to New York, and live much more inexpensively than I am doing . . . and with my present feeling about a solitary life in New York, I should look on this almost as if it were my death warrant. This will account for any warmth in my language about our affairs, and it is not, my dear friend, due to any fault found with you, or to any diminution of the esteem and admiration bred by so many years of faithful and valuable devotion to the paper on your part.

I agree with what you say about the payments of contributors. . . . You might by looking over your accounts strike a reasonable average amount, which would give us a saving say of $1000, or $1500, a year. . . .

Yours ever
ELG

To Daniel Coit Gilman

Cambridge, Mass., July 5, 1876
(Gilman Papers, MdBJ)

DEAR GILMAN: Have ten fellowships been founded in connection with the Johns Hopkins Un. obtainable by writing essays on subjects selected by the candidates themselves, competition open to all the world—and have they been awarded last month, and has one *Henry C. Adams* been one of the successful candidates—, his subject being American literature, and are the duties of these fellowships, the care of their own department respectively, of literature in the library?[1]

If you will be kind enough to answer these questions you will either deliver me from an impostor, or save a worthy man from suspicion. . . .

Yours very truly
ELG

1. Henry C. Adams (1851–1921) was awarded a fellowship at Johns Hopkins in 1876, taking his doctorate there in 1878 before beginning his brilliant career as an economist.

To Charles Eliot Norton

U. S. Hotel, Saratoga, N. Y., July 14, 1876 (Ogden 2:112)

MY DEAR NORTON: . . . Tilden and Hendricks are both here, and I have had a good deal of talk with both of them, and also with various other shrewd and intelligent men from various parts of the country—you know what a rendezvous this is for people of a political turn. Hendricks makes a very unpleasant impression on me, though this may be in large part because I do not like the Western type of man.[1] He has a good head, and well-cut features, but has a loose, shifty expression of face, and one which gives you the impression of a thorough politician in the bad sense of the word. In talking to him you feel you are getting only very little idea of what he is thinking, though what he is after is very plain. Tilden told me he had been laboring with him all day yesterday about finance, and had, he thought, satisfied him that he must "scramble up on the platform." One of the arguments he used was a caricature in Harper's, I think, representing them both pulling different ways.

Tilden, I find, is absolutely confident of his election, and it was curious as well as interesting to hear him last night on the piazza giving Evarts, W. A. Butler, and myself an explanation of the data on which he bases his judgments and predictions about elections. He is exceedingly shrewd. He acknowledged to me that the insertion of the denunciation of the Resumption Act in the platform was a mistake.

I find it to be a widespread and growing opinion that the Republican party cannot stand the present performances of the chiefs, to say nothing of the President's. Just think of a Civil Service reform party making Zack Chandler chairman of the National Committee, and A. B. Cornell of New York chairman of the Executive Committee. It is impossible for the public to avoid the conclusion that these fellows regard the Civil Service part of the Hayes letter as mere bunkum, and intend, after it has produced its proper effect in the popular mind, to play the game over again in the old way, as they did with Grant.

I have had a very warm letter about Hayes from Schurz, who is fully satisfied with him after several prolonged interviews, and I suppose we must support him in the *Nation*, but I confess I do it with great misgivings. Moreover, I am doing, in it, something which runs against all my convictions and traditions as regards party government—that is, acceding to the doctrine that a party is not to be held responsible for its chiefs, and that after they have all been found out in theft and jobbery and been cashiered, it is allowable for the party to turn around and say—"Don't put us out of office. True, Tom, Dick, and Harry, our best men have been found out, but here is Bill, who is an honest fellow, and has stolen nothing; try us under him." Isn't there a savor of the nursery about this?

Evarts is very cranky and skittish.[2] I should not be greatly surprised to see him go for Tilden before the canvas is over. Think of Stoughton in the forefront of the Republican ratification meeting in New York! He, too, is here. He is said to have refused the English mission, fearing exposure. . . .

1. Thomas A. Hendricks (1819–85) was Tilden's running mate in the election of 1876. In 1884 he was elected Vice-President of the United States.

2. After Hayes was declared the victor over Tilden in the disputed election on 1876, he appointed William M. Evarts his Secretary of State.

To Wendell P. Garrison

Cambridge, Mass., August 2, 1876
(Godkin Papers, *Nation* Business Records, MH)

DEAR MR. GARRISON: There is nothing or very little to be tried under such circumstances, except "retrench."

1. Cancel the balance of salary due me on the books.

2. Cut down my salary from Aug. 1. to $5000—the old figure.

3. I have written to Powers, telling him I thought Miss Gleason should go. *In fact she must go.*

4. Say, whether all the additions made to salaries last year, ought not, in view of the situation be struck off?

5. Reduce all the contributors to a *maximum* of $15 remorselessly.

6. You and I must do as much work as possible. Look into Powers' expenses. The machinery is, I am sure not producing results to pay for the heavy consumption of fuel.

7. Sound Carter about *settling* Williams' suit.[1] We have no complete defense to that.

I go to Cambridge tomorrow, and feel pretty blue.

Yours ever
ELG. . . .

1. Silas Williams was the superintendent of the Emma Mine. The prominent New York lawyer James C. Carter was one of Godkin's attorneys and supporters.

To William Dean Howells

September 1 [1876] (Godkin Papers, MH)

MY DEAR HOWELLS: I have long ago given up apologizing to anybody for anything that appears in the *Nation;* but there was a mention of your fiction in the notice of the *Atlantic,* in the last number, which hurts me sufficiently to make me fear it may hurt you and forces me to take the yoke on me again. I am sure the writer had no depreciatory intention in his mind, for I know how highly he rates you, and I know too that your position is in no way affected by anything that any critic can say of you. But this passage did not catch my eye until it was published, and I saw with a pang that it was capable of being construed as meaning that the *Nation* (which is to the benevolent minded always E. L. G.) meant to give you a "little dig."

I want, therefore, to assure you that as it stands it is the result of careless editing, and that I would sooner rob a church than knowingly allow you to receive "a dig," in my sheet, or any sheet, over which I had control. I make this declaration for the good of my own soul, as well as to assure you how truly and sincerely I remain

Yours
ELG

To J. E. Powers

Cambridge, Mass., October 9, 1876
(copy, Godkin Papers, Nation Business Records, MH)

DEAR SIR: As the time for the renewal of our contract with you approaches, I have been thinking over the terms on which it should be done. . . . Our margin of profit during the past two years, in spite of the development of the advertising under your management, has been so small as to convince me that the expenses of the publishing department must and may be considerably reduced.

I should, therefore, hardly be willing again to give you a percentage on the profits until we had actually *pocketed* 7% on the assumed capital of $60,000, and would consider $2,500 a large salary in case you had paid assistance.

I think it but right to lay these considerations before you at this early date.

Truly yours,
ELG

To Manning F. Force [1]

October 17, 1876 (Fragment, Godkin Papers, MH)

. . . The only difference between the *Nation* now, and the *Nation* two or four years ago, is that it happens at this moment to be in your eyes injurious to a cause you have very much at heart. . . .

1. Manning F. Force (1824–99) was a United States Superior Court Judge in Cincinnati, Ohio.

To Wendell P. Garrison

Nation Office   New York, November 2, 1876
(Godkin Papers, *Nation* Business Records, MH)

Private.

DEAR MR. GARRISON: . . . The only remark I have to make about your relation to the finances in the editorial management is this, that I do not think money ever is or was made in a newspaper unless there is someone in the office, to whom money is a leading consideration, who is sensitive on that side, and gives that side the benefit of all doubts. In literary matters I think you lean to excellence above all things, which is very noble, but then as the man said—"I have a family to support."

In the publishing department, we have no such person either. Powers is sanguinary, speculative, and indifferent to small economies. The result is that do what we may to increase returns, the outlay keeps up behind, and year by year goes by, and profits still fly before us. Now I want a man in the publishing office, who will (be) *close, careful,* and economical, and not too hopeful, and for this reason I want Powers to go. This system does not work and eats its own head up, and I want to give St. John a chance. . . .

So please encourage Powers' going, and remember (1) that our May dividend has vanished; (2) *that we are in debt;* (3) that we have an expensive law suit pending, (4) and that with a circulation of 10,000, we are apparently not better off than when we had five.

Yours ever
ELG

To J. E. Powers

Nation Office   New York, November 2, 1876
(Copy, Godkin Papers, Nation Business Records, MH)

DEAR MR. POWERS: It is but fair to tell you, that we have been considering a reorganization of the whole publishing department with a view to greater economy of management, and that among the things we have decided on is that we should not be willing to renew your contract on the same terms, if at all, or to pay you anything more than $2500, salary, without any share in the profits and without assistance. . . .[1]

Truly yours
ELG

1. Powers bowed to Godkin's wishes and withdrew from the *Nation*, and St. John took over his duties in the publishing department.

To Frederick Law Olmsted

Cambridge, Mass., December 30, 1876 (Olmsted Papers, DLC)

MY DEAR OLMSTED: The flight of Otis D. Swan, and the general condition of morals in the Republican party leads me to say that I have uncollected coupons on your Five twenty, and Arkansas Branch bonds. I forgot when going on last to New York to take the key of the safe with me or I would have collected them then. If you are pressed for money, I can send you a check from here for the bulk of it, and adjust the gold premium afterwards; if not I shall be in New York about Jan. 15th. and will then collect the coupons.

I often think of your condition sorrowfully. That a man should have reached your age without having any principles of government, and should be prepared for "anarchy" in order to prevent occasional assaults and assassinations in a semi-barbaric country, is what the Rev. Joseph Cooke calls a "Cesspool circumstance." [1]

I hope, however, the perplexity you are now going through will be overruled for your good. If there be any efficacy in the prayers of so great a sinner as myself, it will be.

I wish you all a happy New Year!

Ever yours
ELG

1. A reference to the ill feeling between Olmsted and Godkin that arose out of their differing attitudes toward the disputed Hayes-Tilden election of 1876. Godkin opposed Hayes' being declared the winner and, toward this objective, editorially proposed that a Massachusetts Republican elector, by inference James Russell Lowell, defect from Hayes and cast his ballot for a third candidate, a proposal that caused Lowell to exclaim, "Godkin seems to have lost his head." The *Nation*'s course cost it many subscribers and the temporary good will of Olmstead and Charles Eliot Norton, a blow from which it never recovered.

To James A. Garfield

New York, January 9, 1877 (Garfield Papers, DLC)

DEAR GENERAL GARFIELD: The bearer, Mr. Arthur G. Sedgwick, whom I beg to introduce to you, has gone to Washington as a "visiting statesman," in behalf of the *Nation,* to "witness the count." [1] Any assistance you can give him in obtaining access to "the pure milk of the word," will be taken as a personal favor by

Yours very sincerely
ELG

1. A reference to the counting of the electoral votes in the disputed presidential election. The Republican Garfield's appreciation of the *Nation* was now cooling.

To Whitelaw Reid

New York, March 15, 1877 (Cortissoz 1:397)

. . . How well Hayes is doing. What will Tilden now do with the Green Seal Johannisberger? . . .[1]

1. This fragment of a letter is in response to a request by Reid for some *Tribune* editorials from Godkin on the report of the Municipal Commission, which Godkin agreed to write. To this letter Reid affably responded: "I cannot answer your conundrum as to what Mr. Tilden will do now with his green seal; but the malicious gossips here . . . say he will drink it."

To Charles Eliot Norton

[Spring? 1877] (Ogden 1:290–91)

. . . Being asked about Lowell, I replied decidedly not, because he would not accept; because not fit physically and otherwise for executive drudgery, and because even an offer to him would give the enterprise a slightly fancy or literary air, that would be injurious. Was this proper? . . .[1]

1. Despite Godkin's lukewarm support of Hayes in 1876 and his apostasy during the dispute that followed the election, his opinion was sought by one of the Hayes people, apparently Carl Schurz, in regard to Hayes's political appointments. The above letter refers to a proposal that James Russell Lowell be offered a cabinet post.

To Whitelaw Reid

Cambridge, Mass., May 8, 1877 (Reid Papers, DLC)

MY DEAR MR. REID: Thanks for the check. I think the scheme has taken hold pretty well of the mind of everybody who is likely to be touched by argument.

I often think of things I would like to write for you about, but the flesh is weak. Perhaps I may now and then manage it.

I have been much amused by Gail Hamilton's letters.[1] Their interest is however rather gynaecological than political. I hope she feels better.

Yours very truly
ELG

1. Gail Hamilton was the pen name of the popular author Mary Abby Dodge (1833–96). Godkin is referring to her series of letters in the *New York Tribune* on civil service reform.

To Rowland Connor [1]

Cambridge, Mass., June 12, 1877
(Copy, Godkin Papers, *Nation* Business Records, MH)

MY DEAR MR. CONNOR: You may feel perfectly sure that I shall do nothing with regard to you that any fair-minded and impartial person will consider inconsiderate or unjust. But I must, especially with your note of June 10 to Mr. Garrison lying before me, remind you that the success of the *Nation*, and in fact its existence, depends on our keeping the standard up *all the time.* We . . . have no place in which we can stow away what is inferior or only slightly unsuitable. . . .

I think it is not "monstrous" but kind for me, considering the nature of your present illness, and the probability that fatigue or worry may hereafter produce a recurrence of such attacks, to ask you whether it is judicious to embark your strength and your money in an enterprise in which your strength will be greatly taxed, and in an office where there is not a man to spare. . . .

Yours very truly
ELG

1. Rowland Connor had recently been added to the editorial staff of the *Nation.*

To Josiah D. Whitney

Cambridge, Mass., July 3 [1877] (Whitney Papers, CtY)

DEAR PROFESSOR: I send you herewith King's address on "Catastrophism." I believe he thinks it an important theory. Could you not say what you think of it in a note—say a column long, in the *Nation*, and if so, could you not let me have it by the end of the week.[1]

Truly yours
ELG

1. Geologists Josiah D. Whitney (1819–96) and Clarence King (1842–1901) were acquaintances of Godkin.

To Carl Schurz

Nation Office   New York, July 15, 1877 (Schurz Papers, DLC)

MY DEAR MR. SCHURZ: Is it really true that the President has excepted members of the National Committee from his late order, and allowed them to hold over on the ground that they will have no "work" to do for three years? This report is making a most unpleasant impression and helping to diffuse the notion that we shall see the Wages reform slowly melt away by dint of exception, and modifications like that of the tormented Grant. I am holding on as well as I can but I really need stimulants. I was sorry I was away from Cambridge unavoidably when you were there.

Ever yours
ELG

To Charles Eliot Norton

Cambridge, Mass., July 25, 1877 (Godkin Papers, MH)

MY DEAR NORTON: I have picked out from my papers *in re Nation*, a few, which will refresh your memory with regard to my relations with Stearns, and the "pledge" to the Philadelphia Stockholders. The "Pledge" you may remember was written at your house and under your advice, and I have a copy of it in New York which I will send when I get there; also the contract with Richards to show that I had no control over expenditures except for literary work; and the prospectus which you may remember was drawn off under the supervision of you three projectors.

The letter to the Philadelphians is in itself conclusive. I incautiously used the word "pledge," but what I really meant was that I had said it would not be a free trade organ, which was a pledge to myself, as any settled plan is to the person who makes it. I will forward from the archives in N. Y. whatever else seems pertinent. I think it best to send you back the letters you forwarded me last winter. Let me direct your attention to the Richards letter, saying in what terms he would come into the paper and this before I had been heard of—(Ap. 1865.)

Going back to those old days has been a sad morning's work; they then seemed to me so full of care and worry, but when I compare them with these!

I go to Newport tonight, and then to Va. Good bye. The archives bring back vividly all your kindness in those old wars.

Yours faithfully
ELG

I send the parcel by express. If there is any point in which you need material please let me know, Newport, care of F. Sheldon till Monday.

To Rowland Connor

Sweet Springs, W. Virginia, August 9, 1877
(Copy, Godkin Papers, *Nation* Business Records, MH)

DEAR MR. CONNOR: On reflection, I am satisfied that a continuance of your connection with the *Nation* is inadvisable, and that the sooner I make you aware of the fact the better for all parties. . . .

As you have once referred to your paragraphing in the *Index* as a means by which I might have made myself acquainted with your powers, I ought to say that I never read them with any attention, or consecutively, because, judging from those I did read, I presumed you were not doing your best, or aiming at anything more than obliging Mr. Abbott. I saw plainly enough that such work would never do for the *Nation*.

Truly yours,
ELG

To Rowland Connor

Sweet Springs, W. Virginia, August 29, 1877
(Copy, Godkin Papers, *Nation* Business Records, MH)

DEAR MR. CONNOR: My note to you was not intended to place you in a "painful position." What I said about our having to engage others to do work properly belonging to you was said by way of an explanation. . . . You surely know that if you were right, you would be doing the work that White and Sedgwick are doing—or part of it at least.[1] I am sorry that it is necessary to put all this before you in this plain bold way.

You have now for the second time made me acquainted with the fact that you do not agree with me as to your qualifications —which is quite natural and reasonable; but you surely must perceive on reflection that the *essential* fact is that *I* am dissatisfied, whether justly or not, and that for business purposes nobody else's opinion, however sound, is of any value whatever.

I trust this will close the controversy.[2]

Very truly yours
ELG

1. Godkin, Horace White, and Arthur Sedgwick were writing most of the domestic political and financial articles for the *Nation*.

2. Connor's anger at being fired was heightened by the fact that he had taken a $5,000 share in the *Nation*.

To Charles Eliot Norton

Sweet Springs, West Va., September 3, 1877 (Ogden 2:114)

MY DEAR NORTON: I am starting for home to-day, though going to spend a day or two at a plantation on the Rapidan on my way. I do not know yet what the result of the baths on my ailment will be, but am somewhat hopeful. The scenery and climate are wonderfully attractive, and ought to be better known at the North, and I cannot help thinking will be. I have seen a great many southerners, some well-known ones such as Wade Hampton and Bradley Johnson, and have talked much with men of various classes and conditions, but my notes are too bulky to put in a letter, and I shall reserve them for talk. My general conclusion is that the condition of the South is all that a Northern *politician* could desire or hope for, though I do not think it by any means satisfactory to a pessimist. I do not see, in short, how the negro is ever to be worked into a system of government for which you and I would have much respect.

I told you last spring, I think, that I had it somewhat in mind to leave Cambridge for New York again. I have not yet absolutely decided to do so, but it is probable I will when I return. If I could rent my house I should decide at once. Inability to do so may make me hang on a little longer from motives of economy. If you know of a tenant with a small familly I would let him have it (furnished) very low.

I may add to you, as an old friend, that although nothing can well be more trying to me than beginning life again in New York, at my age, in a city in which I really never took root, without a home or family ties of any kind, yet Cambridge promises more solitude and sadness than I can well bear. I do not expect hereafter to see much of Lawrence; Jane's death broke one of the few remaining ties that connected me with my old life. Both she and Grace, as you know, were very close and dear to Fanny and me, and became more so than ever in the last winter of Fanny's life, when we were both oppressed already with the shadow of the tremendous misfortune that was in store for me.

I wish it were possible to tell you how much all this that I am saying means to me, and above all how little trust and hope I have with regard to the future, and how sincerely and gratefully, come what may, I shall remain to the end,

Your affectionate friend
ELG

I shall be in Cambridge by Sunday the 9th

To Charles Eliot Norton

Cambridge, Mass., September 12, 1877 (Ogden 2:115)

MY DEAR NORTON: I got your letter the day I got home, but have been so busy for the *Nation* that I have delayed thanking you for it, and saying how much it gratified me. But even as matters stand I think your suggestion that I should pass the winter in New York a sound one, and had intended to do so, and I am accordingly trying to let my house until May, if not for a year. Lawrence would like to have me remain, and as far as physical comfort goes the arguments are weightiest on that side. But I foresee a winter of considerable solitude with surroundings which would be more or less sad and depressing, and I am inclined to think that my sciatica, which is not gone, has more or less connection with the mental conditions of the last two years, and that I had better seek distraction and escape from the inevitable brooding over my situation which comes with a solitary life. I shall, as you suggest, treat my departure as only temporary, as it may prove so, but at present I look forward to nothing even faintly pleasant in the way of change, and shall not look forward to coming back. To have at forty-five, in a country which in many essential things, in spite of all the happiness I have had in it, is a foreign one, neither home nor family after twenty years' residence, I feel as an almost fatal blow. All the circumstances of my life in the past help to make it so, and no outward success to one of my temperament does much to mitigate it.

I shall not attempt to tell you how much you and your sisters have been to me. I fancy you know it.

I am here alone at present. Lawrence has gone up to spend a week with his aunt in the White Mountains, but as I am pretty busy and have my horse, I get along tolerably well. I see a good deal of Miss Grace.[1] I expect to be here when you come back, unless some unexpected tenant turns up for the house. I am at present in pursuit of Professor Bradley. You may hear of some one. I would rent it really low to any one who would take good care of it.

The weather here is warm and pleasant, the country looking delightful, but I am always struck now more or less by the remorselessness and indifference of nature. . . .

1. A reference to Grace Ashburner.

To Frederick Law Olmsted

Cambridge, Mass., October 14, 1877 (Olmsted Papers, DLC)

DEAR OLMSTED: We wish, in order to make shares more readily transferable, to convert the *Nation* into a joint stock company; but it is necessary that a majority of the trustees should be citizens of New York. McKim—Garrison's brother-in-law—or Garrison himself will probably be one.[1] Will you let me assign you a share in trust for me, so that you may serve too? It will involve no liability. Garrison is a citizen of N.J. and for the moment of Massachusetts, which makes the work of organization inconvenient.

Yours ever
ELG

1. By this time all but one of the forty original stockholders in the *Nation* were gone, many of them having acceded to Godkin's suggestion that they make gifts of their stock to the company in recognition of the financial distress of the weekly and of his labors in getting it established. By 1877, with the *Nation* less than one-half its original size and its circulation under 7,000, Godkin controlled most of the stock and was utilizing new expedients to keep the weekly alive without putting money of his own into it. In the end, all connected with the financing of the *Nation* except Godkin lost money.

To Alexander C. Sellar

January 7, 1878 (Olmsted Papers, DLC)

MY DEAR MR. SELLAR: Let me introduce my friend Mr. Frederick Law Olmsted, who is doubtless already known to you by reputation as the author of the best books on the social and economical condition of the Southern States before the war, that have ever been written. During the last twenty years he has been the designer and Architect of our Central Park here, and has had more or less to do with most works of a similar character in other parts of the Union. He is going to Europe somewhat impaired in health by overwork, but is desirous while there of seeing more or less landscape gardening, and there are one or two places in Scotland which he wishes to visit, and about which you can very likely render him some aid.

He is one of my oldest and most intimate friends, and one of the most valued and valuable men in America, and anything you can do to make his stay in England pleasant and profitable I shall take as a personal favor.

Very truly yours
ELG

To Daniel Coit Gilman

New York, February 6, 1878 (Gilman Papers, MdBJ)

MY DEAR MR. GILMAN: I am not in Washington; I wish I were.
Your kind note of the *3rd* inst. has been forwarded to me here.
Mrs. Adams had asked me to Washington for this week, and I
hoped to go, but found myself unable to get away.[1] I shall I trust
be there before the end of the month, however, or very early in
March, and will certainly not pass you by without stopping and
seeing you both, and it will be a great pleasure to do so. With
best remembrances to Mrs. Gilman.

Yours very sincerely

ELG

1. A reference to an invitation from the Henry Adamses. Godkin's friendship with the grandson of the sixth President later cooled.

To I. Wayne MacVeagh [1]

Nation Office   New York, April 20, 1878
(MacVeagh Papers, PHi)

MY DEAR MACVEAGH: I am very glad you liked the Schurz
article, and glad, too, that the President saw it and liked it. The
hatred of Schurz among the politicians is the best possible illustration of the badness of their own condition, and considering
how much he has done both for the party and the public, I am
often provoked by the small amount of support he gets from decent people. The Germans are not worth their salt politically or
they would make much of him.

Keep Hayes supplied with the pure milk of the word. I was
glad to hear you wrote to Norton about him the other day;
Norton was absolutely crazy about him during the Canvas. He
thought one of the greatest statesmen of ancient or modern
times had lain concealed in Ohio up to the age of 55.

Yours ever

ELG

1. Wayne MacVeagh (1833–1917), a subscriber to the *Nation*, was one
of the political leaders admired by the circle of Independents to which

Godkin belonged. A Pennsylvania jurist, he was known for his opposition to machine politics in that state.

To George Edward Woodberry

Nation Office   New York, May 22, 1878
(Woodberry Letters, MH)

DEAR MR. WOODBERRY: [1] We are in need of additional permanent assistance on the editorial staff of the *Nation*, that is, of some one who would write a couple of pages a week, such as literary notes, book reviews, paragraphs in the Week, and occasionally a political article; and keep the run of the news of the day in all fields, by reading or looking over the papers both political and literary, one, in short, who would make himself "generally useful," and feel interest enough in the work to throw himself into it heartily and identify himself with the paper. Would you feel disposed to try it? I would offer you $2000 for the first year as an experiment, and afterwards, if we were both satisfied, it might go as high as three thousand ($3000).

If you accept we should need you promptly. You know enough of the paper, to get an idea of the work required without more minute explanations from me; but the first year would have to be experimental.

Yours very truly
ELG

1. Poet George Edward Woodberry (1855–1930) accepted Godkin's terms, including the requirement (since 1877) that each new employee buy stock in the weekly.

To George Edward Woodberry

New York, May 31, 1878 (Woodberry Letters, MH)

DEAR MR. WOODBERRY: . . . The phrase "generally useful," means this: the permanent office force has consisted of myself, Mr. Garrison and one other person, I mean in the editorial department. Mr. Garrison is what is called "the Managing editor."

He is there every day and all day; sees visitors, conducts the ordinary correspondence, gives out books for review, reads the *MSS.* sent in before submitting them to me, so as to sift them, and attends to the actual make up of the paper before going to press. He also collects and makes the "Notes" in literary and other matters.

You would have to be prepared to take a hand at all this in case of his illness or absence—he is never ill and not often absent—and in addition you would have to contribute your share to the general editorial omniscience by keeping yourself *au courant* of the literary periodicals, and literary news generally, and by looking after politics sufficiently to qualify yourself to write on a political topic now and then, and to contribute some paragraphs every week to the Week. . . . It would not be necessary that you should keep any regular office hours, or write at the office, but it would be desirable that you should put in an appearance at some hour of every day. . . .

Yours very truly
ELG

To Thomas Wentworth Higginson [1]

Cambridge, Mass., July 12, 1878 (Godkin Papers, MH)

MY DEAR HIGGINSON: My excuse for having forgotten to send you the enclosed note sooner is that soon after you left I was immersed in much troublesome business by the death of my mother-in-law, an old lady who since my wife's death has been much dependent on me in various ways. I have only just extricated myself and got back here into my own house for a little quiet and private correspondence, of which I have huge arrears.

I got your letter, for which many thanks, and you will perhaps have seen, used it in a paragraph in the Week about Colonel Wolseley. You must have had a rich treat in watching the progress of the Turkish drama on the spot. Disraeli's performance strikes me here as a wonderful piece of charlatanry the acceptance of which degrades both the Tories and the whole English people. There is a great deal of future trouble stored up in that Turkish alliance.

We are jogging along in the *Nation* as usual, wonderfully well for the times, which however, I think improve a little.

Very truly yours
ELG

1. The former Abolitionist and Civil War leader of black troops, Thomas Wentworth Higginson (1823–1911), was the poetry critic of the *Nation* from 1881 to 1903. After the reorganization of E. L. Godkin and Company into a joint stock company he became a small stockholder in the concern. He held views more liberal than Godkin's and did not write on political or social topics for the *Nation*.

To Wendell P. Garrison

Nation Office   New York, September 20, 1878
(Woodberry Letters, MH)

DEAR MR. G.: . . . As regards the *Proteus and Amadeus* article, I do not think the statement of the case for positivism sufficiently clear or strong, or definite. I have underlined a sentence which begs the question and interrogated one which many if not most people will deny. Moreover I object *in toto* to the order of the motives, *e.g.* placing botany and conchology before family affection. All this part would have to be rewritten to make the article usable. I do not care to have the *Nation* come out as a maintainer of the sufficiency of positivism, and if we describe the Positivist position, we ought to do so very carefully. The obvious deduction from the letters seems to be that Proteus was a weak and silly fellow, one of the many who are constantly hammering about from one extreme to another; but one does not need to [preach] Positivism in order to show this.

Please hand this to Mr. Woodberry.

Ever yours
ELG

I forgot to say anything to him about more care in avoiding newspaper English. I notice in the Week (I am not sure whose it is) "rowdy element and *their* respectable leaders" . . . Senator Barnum, being "on hand," (for present.)

To George Edward Woodberry

Nation Office   New York, September 20, 1878
(Woodberry Letters, MH)

I do not care to make the *Nation* a preacher of Positivism, as regards the belief in a future life. Any man who has it, I think does well to hold it if he can; any man who has it not, and acquires it, does well too; but if one has it not, he is not to blame, and there is nobody competent to call him to account. In fact, I think our best course is to let it alone.

ELG

To George Edward Woodberry

November 14 [1878] (Woodbury Letters, MH)

DEAR MR. WOODBERRY: I find I cannot go down [to the office] today, but will take my chance of finding you tomorrow about the same time.

I wanted simply to ask how you find the work. I notice that you seem to do less and attempt to suggest less, as the months go on, which makes me fear that your interest in it declines and if this is true, I think it would be best for yourself as well as for us to recognize the fact as soon as possible.

Yours very truly
ELG

I shall discuss the matter with you tomorrow.

To Charles Eliot Norton

November 28, 1878 (Ogden 1:309–10)

. . . I *was* very much amused by the notes of the two "Divines," and especially by the lofty origin they ascribe to their differences with the *Nation*. The falling out was due in both cases to small fibbing about matters of fact, which they were too weak and foolish to atone for when detected. What a queer breed they are, and how difficult to describe to a foreigner. . . .

To George Edward Woodberry

December 13, 1878 (Woodberry Letters, MH)

DEAR MR. WOODBERRY: I learn from your conversation with Mr. Garrison, as well as from the previous one with myself, that you are not in sympathy with the *Nation* on various points—so much so in political matters as to prevent your writing in that field. When I proposed your coming on I assumed that you were quite familiar with the tone, temper, methods and opinions of the paper, and knew whether you could accommodate yourself to them or not. Otherwise I should not have thought of offering you the place. There is nothing new, let me add, since your arrival[,] in its management on any of these points.

I need not point out to you the inconvenience and detriment of having your place occupied by a person who is not in entire sympathy with us, and I would therefore put it to you, whether under the circumstances you would consider it worth while trying our year's experiment to the end. Is not the matter already substantially settled in your own mind? [1]

> Truly yours
> ELG

1. The somewhat contentious Woodberry, a minor protégé of Charles Eliot Norton, disliked Godkin and had little respect for Wendell P. Garrison. He did not take the hint that he resign, whereupon Godkin relieved him of his full-time position on the staff. The successor to his two shares of *Nation* stock (valued at $2,000) was Thomas Wentworth Higginson. After 1884 Woodberry sometimes substituted for Garrison during Garrison's infrequent absences from the *Nation*. A partial bibliography of Woodberry's writings for the *Nation* appears in Armstrong, "Additions to the *Nation Index*," pp. 271–74.

To Edmund Clarence Stedman

Nation Office   New York, January 15, 1879
(Stedman Papers, NNC)

DEAR MR. STEDMAN: I had a correspondence with you a few years ago, in which I set forth some of the queer and amusing social troubles of the editor of a critical paper. Of course no editor can keep the run of the possible personal allusions and bearings of all the articles and book notices, and I do not attempt it. When I see an author or artist or poet looking savagely at me, or cutting me, if I have any curiosity as to the cause I usually have to enquire at the *Nation* office, and get it hunted up by one of the boys.

I am just now reminded of my letter to you by finding Mr. Stoddard looking "gloomy and peculiar," on Saturday night at the Century; in fact he cut me, which amused me very much, as I knew at once he was suffering from the usual literary colic.[1] So I made inquiries today as to the origin of his complaint and found it was a deadly allusion in a review of Shelley to his "Anecdote-Biography," a work which to my shame I have never seen and did not know he had written, but which I suppose is very dear to him. I thought this illustration of editorial troubles might entertain you.

Yours very truly
ELG

1. A reference to an encounter between author R. H. Stoddard (1825–1903) and Godkin at the Century Club, the exclusive New York guild of "authors, artists, and amateurs of letters and the fine arts" to which Godkin was elected with the sponsorship of Frederick Law Olmsted in 1863.

To Edmund Clarence Stedman

January 17, 1879 (Stedman Papers, NNC)

DEAR MR. STEDMAN: I remember perfectly well, that if any one was to *blame* for our former correspondence, it was I. I only referred to it as having brought up the subject of which the Stoddard incident is an illustration. There are about fifty men of various kinds writing criticism in the columns of the *Nation*, and it is no longer vexatious but very amusing to me to find myself held personally responsible for all the unkind, or uncomplimentary or depreciatory things they may say of authors and artists. So that you will understand that I really do not feel at all hurt by Stoddard's performance, and I would not have you allude to it to him, if it is at all likely to renew his grief.

Nobody has probably undergone more criticism than I have myself—a good deal of it—blackguardly [*sic*] personal as the newspaper fashion is—so that when I say that it is foolish for a man to be much troubled by it—I am not *inexpertus* etc.

Yours very truly
ELG

To Matilda Lieber [1]

Nation Office   New York, February 3, 1879 (CSmH)

DEAR MADAM: We will insert your request about Dr. Lieber's letters among our "Notes" which will make it more conspicuous and effective than any advertizement would be.

I am sorry to say I have no letters of his. My intercourse with him was all personal, beyond occasional short notes, as we were near neighbors during the period of my acquaintance with him.

Very sincerely yours
ELG

1. This letter is to the daughter of Francis Lieber (1800–72), the pioneer in the codification of international law.

To George Edward Woodberry

Nation Office   New York, February 3, 1879
(Copy, Godkin Papers, *Nation* Business Records, MH)

DEAR MR. WOODBERRY: During the first half-year of your engagement with us, or rather down to the date of your departure at Christmas, I find you only furnished an average of one page of matter per week. . . .[1] I . . . find that you have furnished since Jan. 1 only *two pages in all*, while drawing at the rate of $2000 a year up to Jan. 22.

You will not be surprised if I say that it will be impossible under these circumstances to continue the proposed rate of payment. If for any reason you are unable to keep up the contract had we not better abrogate it?

Yours very truly,
ELG

1. Godkin reached this calculation on the basis of that portion of Woodberry's writings for the *Nation* that he chose to print, as Woodberry was quick to point out.

To George Edward Woodberry

Nation Office   New York, February 7, 1879
(Copy, Godkin Papers, *Nation* Business Records, MH)

DEAR MR. WOODBERRY: . . . As to the amount of your matter printed, that is of course our affair. It rests with you to furnish the required amount.

I made no complaint about the amount of salary up to Jan. 21; my remarks related to the amount of copy received—only two pages and a half to Feb. 1. . . .

Truly yours,
ELG

To Edmund Clarence Stedman

Nation Office   New York, May 3, 1879 (Stedman Papers, NNC)

DEAR MR. STEDMAN: I like Mr. Brownell personally—as far as one can see him in one interview—and I like his writing and think of offering him an engagement.[1]

But, I do not feel that I know enough about him on the moral side. Can you enlighten me? You know the *Nation* is more easily damaged than the daily press by any suspicion of having purchasable or indiscreet persons about it, and is always a much relished subject of scandal and gossip to the correspondents, so we have to be a little careful. Is he all right about money matters?

Excuse my troubling you, and believe me

Very truly yours
ELG

1. Literary essayist and critic William C. Brownell (1851–1928). Godkin hired him to replace Woodberry, and he remained a staff member of the *Nation* for two years, writing mostly magazine and novel criticism.

To Whitelaw Reid

May 17 [1879] (Reid Papers, DLC)

MY DEAR MR. REID: I am excessively sorry that I am engaged on Wednesday. A dinner of our Round Table Club occurs on that day, which I would give up for the pleasure of dining with you and meeting Colonel and Mrs. Hay, if it were not that it is an extra meeting which has been got up at my request and instigation, and from which I have, therefore, not the audacity to absent myself.[1]

I will, however, do myself the pleasure of calling before then.

Yours very truly

ELG

1. John Hay (1838–1905), author and subsequently United States secretary of state, was then assisting Reid in editing the *Tribune*. Although an intimate of Henry Adams and his circle of Independents, Hay did not have a high regard for Godkin and the *Nation*.

To Whitelaw Reid

Cambridge, Mass., June 21 [1879] (Reid Papers, DLC)

DEAR MR. REID: I want to thank you for your mention of the *Nation* in your late address, very sincerely. . . . Subscription to a paper like the *Nation*, which is not a necessity, is somewhat of a fashion, and I fancy many people would drop it, on finding the circulation had by our own confession fallen off. So that in this case honesty has not been altogether the best policy. At the same time from all I can hear, I do not think we have suffered as much in circulation as most papers (weekly) which at all resemble us— or supply our place—such as the religious papers. I liked the address much, though in many things I don't agree. I think of discussing it next week.

This is of course all for your private ear.

I remain, with best wishes yours very sincerely

ELG

To Secretary of the Interior Carl Schurz

Cambridge, Mass., July 7, 1879 (Schurz Papers, DLC)

DEAR MR. SCHURZ: There is a very good fellow here, named George A. Cole, who formerly served during the war in the 38th Mass. Reg. and was a letter carrier on my beat when you were staying with me three years ago. He was an excellent carrier, but resigned and became a peddlar with a cargo wagon, hoping to better his condition. He has had to give this up, as the jolting over stony roads brings back diarrhea from which he was long a sufferer after the war.

He now wants to get back into a carriership, and says there is a vacancy here which a word from you to Mr. Key would probably procure for him.[1]

He is an excellent fellow who has the respect and good will of everybody on his old beat, and if it comes in your way to say the word I shall be much obliged.

Yours very truly
ELG

1. David McK. Key was then United States postmaster general.

To Secretary of the Interior Carl Schurz

Nation Office   New York, November 18, 1879
(Schurz Papers, DLC)

MY DEAR MR. SCHURZ: I am much obliged to you for your letter and the enclosures. I have, I confess regretted the discussion about the Pension Office, which arose out of Mr. Bentley's address, during the week, when I was moving to the city from Cambridge, and was unable to keep the run of things in my office.[1] But I am going to verify for myself the facts of any notations he disputes, and if we cannot hold our ground, or so far as we cannot, I can assure you we will make all needful amends.

Very truly yours
ELG

1. Schurz, now Secretary of Interior under Hayes, had asked Godkin for an explanation of the *Nation*'s criticism of John A. Bentley, United States Commissioner of Pensions. The *Nation* accused Bentley of "prej-

udice against lawyers" when, in a speech to veterans, Bentley upheld the rule that a lawyer could charge a veteran no more than ten dollars to draw up his pension application. Since most pensions were less than nine dollars a month, Bentley had a strong case, but the *Nation*—in spite of Godkin's assurances to Schurz—held its ground.

To Secretary of the Interior Carl Schurz

Nation Office   New York, November 27, 1879
(Schurz Papers, DLC)

DEAR MR. SCHURZ: I enclose herewith the answer of the writer of the comments in the *Nation* on Mr. Bentley's letter. I sent him your letter to me, and Mr. Bentley's report to you, and the copy of your letter to the Vice-president.

I may say that I heartily concur with his remarks as to the tone of Mr. Bentley's letter to me, and report to you. A man who launches forth charges of palpable falsehood and wilful blundering, and "wilful falsifying" and misrepresentation, usually puts himself out of the field of rational discussion.

I have gone over both our contributor's letter and Mr. Bentley's, and I think the former has fairly acknowledged any mistakes he has made, and has also met most of Mr. Bentley's objections pretty conclusively. I am willing should you or he desire it to make myself a further summing up of the controversy in the *Nation.*

Let me add that our contributor is a man of high character, and what is perhaps of importance in this matter,—a man of considerable fortune, so that the insinuation that he is a baffled and greedy "claim agent," is ridiculous.

Very truly yours
ELG

To Charles A. Dana

Nation Office   New York, December 29, 1879
(Mitchell Papers, NHi)

Personal

DEAR SIR: You published in March of this year (?) a list of the offices held in the Federal service by persons who had helped to count in President Hayes in Florida and Louisiana. We have been challenged to give proof of this, and I should feel much obliged if you would tell me whether you obtained your list from any official source, and if so whether it is now accessible.

Truly yours
ELG

The Editor of the *Sun*

To James Russell Lowell

The Grosvenor, 37 5th Ave., New York, February 1, 1880
(Lowell Papers, MH)

MY DEAR LOWELL: . . . I have never relinquished the intention of satisfying you that I hardly ever give a letter of introduction to anyone, and never to anyone whom I do not know—as you assumed, I fear, that I had done in this instance. Smith asked me for the letter to you and, as he was one of three persons to whom the Spanish Government gave the concession of the cable between Cuba, and the United States, I imagined he was going to Spain on that business. . . .[1]

Yours affectionately
ELG

1. Lowell was serving as United States minister to Spain, and Godkin had given General William F. Smith a letter of introduction to him in Madrid.

To Henry James, Sr.[1]

The Grosvenor, 37 5th Ave., New York [ca. 1 February 1880]
(James Family Papers, MH)

DEAR MR. JAMES: I was on the point of writing to you, and in fact have been on it for some days, to express the very great pleasure I have had myself in reading Harry's *Hawthorne*. I believe it to be the best piece of work of the kind we have by an American and I know of no American living or dead who could have done it, not excepting even the boy's father; a more finished masterly piece of criticism I do not know of in this generation.

I consider its appearance indeed, so important an event in the history of American literature, that I put it on the same level of *National* importance with the *Declaration of Independence*.

The writer of the notice in the *Nation* is Mr. Brownell, whom we have had in our regular employ since last July. He may be seen every day in the office producing notices of similar quality, by subscribers to the paper or their friends on the presentation of their cards. He is a graduate of Amherst, aged 30 married but no children, he is a blond, about 5 ft 7 inches in height.

Give my best remembrance and congratulations to Mrs. James and Miss Alice—But you must bring Harry home for a year or two. He is in danger of having the country slip from under his feet, which would be a misfortune for him in all ways—

Yrs. sincerely
ELG

1. Godkin is addressing the Swedenborgian thinker, Henry James Sr. (1811–82), to compliment him on the publication of Henry Jr.'s study of Nathaniel Hawthorne.

To I. Wayne MacVeagh

Nation Office   New York, February 12, 1880
(MacVeagh Papers, PHi)

DEAR MR. MACVEAGH: I have received this morning from Mr. Lea the circular of the "National Republican League."

I would like much to have a line or two from you, not for publication, but for my own information, with your views of what this movement amounts to, or can accomplish. I am disposed, from our experience in this state to be a little hopeless. There are so many men, who "squeal" but won't "bolt," that is who make a little fuss, and then submit, through fear of the Democrats, and the Solid South and so on. Here the Machine men count on this with absolute confidence. They were somewhat frightened by the operations of the Scratchers at the last election, but the Scratchers protested so vehemently that their action was not intended to affect the Presidential Contest, that they have taken heart again, and rely on carrying out their programme. They were never more audacious at Albany than they are today.

Yours very truly
ELG

To George J. Holyoake [1]

The Grosvenor, 37 5th Ave., New York, March 23, 1880
(Holyoake Papers, Holyoake House, Manchester, England)

DEAR MR. HOLYOAKE: Your kind note of the 6th inst. reminds me that I ought long ago [to] have expressed to you the genuine pleasure it gave me to see and hear you at the breakfast here, and the great regret I felt at having to leave without an opportunity of talking with you. It so happened, unfortunately, that the day of the breakfast was the busiest day of my week, when an editor feels that the world will come to an end if he is not at his post. I consequently had to rush off as soon as your speech was over.

I was unfortunate also in being away from New York during most of your visit here, and in being unable to meet you at a lunch, I think, at which Colonel Higginson proposed to bring us together in Cambridge.

But I have frequently expressed since the great satisfaction it gave me to hear you, as one whose career I have long admired, and whose labors have been so honourable and fruitful. I shall hope before long to see you in London.

I am very sorry to hear from various quarters that the Liberal prospects in England are not so good as I have been trying to believe, but it will probably be decided before this reaches you. The worst thing about the Tory success is not, to my mind, the triumph of such political principles as they have, so much as the illustration it seems to furnish of the possibilities which are open in our day to personal charlatanry even in England.

Very sincerely yours
ELG

1. English reformer George J. Holyoake (1817–1906).

To Henry C. Lea [1]

Nation Office   New York, August 7, 1880 (Lea Papers, PU)

DEAR MR. LEA: I return General Garfield's letter for which I am much obliged. As you say, it does not amount to much, and I am still somewhat anxious about his position on this question. I thought his announcement that he would take the advice of Congressmen about appointments, in his letter of acceptance, entirely unnecessary, on any view, and liable to serious misconstruction. But as he says he is very much committed by his speeches and writings to the view *we* hold, and I cannot help hoping that, unlike Hayes, he will be better than his letter. He probably feels that to be of any use to Civil Service reform, he has got to be elected, and is willing to be a little ambiguous for this purpose.

I have been greatly bothered by his Crédit Mobilier and De Golyer affairs, which are very unpleasant, and a great burden. I am not in a position to write to him, and have had no communication from him; but I do feel that he is one of these impressionable men, who are much influenced by their immediate surroundings, and that, therefore, it would be a great mistake for the Independents to now drop out of sight into the party ranks.[2] He ought to be reminded frequently by letter or otherwise of their existence and of their expectations.

Yours very truly
ELG

1. Historian Henry C. Lea was an ardent Philadelphia crusader for cleaner government and a regular reviewer for the *Nation* when not immersed in the books and documents of his splendid library. An active supporter of civil service reform, international arbitration, and international copyright, he disagreed with Godkin on the tariff and other questions and did not write on politics for the *Nation*. For some of his heretofore unidentified *Nation* reviews, see Armstrong, "Additions to the *Nation Index*," pp. 269–70.

2. Garfield, whose cordiality with Godkin cooled after the disputed Hayes-Tilden election of 1876, had just become the Republican nominee for president.

To Daniel Coit Gilman

Cambridge, Mass., August 19, 1880 (Gilman Papers, Md BJ)

MY DEAR MR. GILMAN: I have told the "hospitality committee" of the American Association that I would receive one or two of the visitors to the meeting next week, having them to send me whom they pleased, as I knew of no friend who was coming. Now that I learn that you are to attend it, I wish very much, if Cambridge will not be inconvenient for you that you and Mrs. Gilman would come to me. Part of the proccedings, you know are to be out here, and there are cars close by into Boston every seven minutes, in fact every two minutes. I am all alone, have hot and cold water in every room, fine fruit and shade trees, and a cool easterly breeze every afternoon punctually at three o'clock.

Yours very truly

ELG

To William Dean Howells

Cambridge, Mass., September 12, 1880 (Godkin Papers, MH)

MY DEAR HOWELLS: When you asked me for the paper I was going to read on Libel before the Social Science Assoc. I noticed that you had just been taking some champagne. I will not, therefore, hold you to your request, unless you now repeat it in the calm, and quiet of your own home. The Social Science Assoc. is not a cheerful body, and it may very well be that an article composed for its edification may not suit the *Atlantic*. If you care for it, however, I will send it to you, and if you should decline it, as "though excellent in itself, unsuited to your columns," I "know how it is myself," sufficiently well, not to be at all surprized.[1]

Yours cordially

ELG

1. E. L. Godkin, "Libel and its Legal Remedy" [paper read before the annual convention of the American Social Science Association, Saratoga, New York, 9 September 1880], *Atlantic Monthly* 46 (December 1880): 729–38.

To Henry C. Lea

Nation Office   New York, November 8, 1880 (Lea Papers, PU)

DEAR MR. LEA: I think there *is* something in Barnum's threat. They are furious at finding that they were not dependent on Indiana after all, and that New York, which they had good reason for counting on and probably would have had if Boss Kelly had behaved better, would have done the business for them. They are running about now, collecting "evidence" and getting up "protests." But I do not think the matter will go beyond threats. I hear nothing but reprobation of the scheme from all decent Democrats whom I see.[1]

There is no use in crying over spilt milk, but I must declare that I foresaw in the Republican mode of getting the Presidency in 1876, the introduction of a deplorable precedent. I believe on my conscience, that if Hayes had come out and declared that he would not under such conditions take the place, he would have rendered politics an inestimable service, and have saved the country from a great danger. The Republican operations with the Returning Board in Louisiana, *let the devil loose.*

Yours very truly
ELG

1. Garfield had just defeated the Democratic challenger for the presidency, Winfield S. Hancock, by a narrow margin, and Congressman Barnum and other Democrats were threatening to emulate the Republican strategy of 1876 by challenging the returns in New York State, a challenge which, if successful, would overturn Garfield's victory.

To Secretary of the Interior Carl Schurz

Nation Office   New York, November 24, 1880
(Schurz Papers, DLC)

MY DEAR MR. SCHURZ: Mr. Nathaniel Niles who was through you made a Government director of the C. P. R. R. to fill C. F. Adams Jr's place I think, and to whom I gave a letter of introduction to you, was ousted at the end of six months to make room for General Fitzpatrick, who was unquestionably "on the make," and must have been grievously disappointed. Niles tells me there is now another vacancy, and he would like to get back, and I have promised him I would write to you about it. He is an excellent fellow, whose integrity in railroad matters we have had occasion to see tested here very remarkably some years ago. I feel sure he has no object at all personal in the matter, beyond the professional influence the position might give him. If you can help him I think you will do the public a service.

When are you coming out here? I would greatly like a talk with you.

Yours ever
ELG

7. The *Evening Post* and "Too Many Mules in the Same Pasture"

In 1881 the German-immigrant journalist who was now a promoter, Henry Villard, wanting a newspaper to serve his fledgling financial empire, bought the *Evening Post,* the venerable New York daily made famous under the long editorship of William Cullen Bryant. To keep the transaction a secret from his business rivals, Villard contrived an announcement to the press that the buyers were Carl Schurz, Horace White, and Godkin. To get Godkin, Villard consented to buy the struggling *Nation* and make it a weekly magazine of the *Evening Post.* Schurz, by understanding, became editor-in-chief, and Godkin and White assumed the roles of associate editors. One commentator praised the arrangement as an "editorship of all the talents," but veteran journalist W. H. Huntington more presciently volunteered to John Bigelow the opinion that "if that tricephalic combination don't kill the *Post* within three years, I'll sign the 34 Articles."

The chief obstacle to the success of the venture was that the aggressive Godkin wanted his own daily paper. Two years of bickering with Schurz—who also possessed a disputatious streak —over *Post* policy followed; thereupon Godkin demanded that Villard hand over the editorial reins to him. If not, Godkin threatened, he would withdraw from the *Evening Post* and take the *Nation* with him. Villard gave in, and Schurz resigned from the paper late in 1883 in high dudgeon, intimating that the *Evening Post* was becoming a corporation organ.

Thereafter, Godkin and White officially shared equal editorial authority, but the mild-mannered White did not oppose Godkin's publicly calling himself editor-in-chief. In that way was avoided a repetition of what the *New York Tribune*'s Isaac Bromley had called the outcome of "too many mules in the same pasture."

To witness his new status, Godkin requested Villard to withdraw an invitation to White and instead take him on Villard's six-week western outing to mark the opening of the main line of his Northern Pacific Railroad. During the outing Godkin triumphantly climbed a mountain and made friends with several of the foreign dignitaries that Villard imported for the tour. Two of them, Liberal M.P. Sir Charles Russell and Tory M.P. Albert Pell, remained life-long acquaintances.

To Frederick Law Olmsted

Nation Office   New York, April 21, 1881
(Olmsted Papers, DLC)

MY DEAR OLMSTED: The *Evening Post* (Godwin-Bryant controlling interest) has been bought by Villard and Horace White.[1] *This is strictly confidential.* Schurz is to be the new editor in chief—possession 21st. of May. They are trying to, and will probably succeed, in buying out Henderson also, so as to have the whole concern.

They ask me to join, on the same terms pecuniarily as Schurz, but as "Associate-editor," offer to buy out the *Nation* if I choose, and annex it to the *Post* as a weekly edition like *Pall Mall Budget.* The alternative is to sell it to some one else. I *am* tempted to accept

(1). Because the *Nation* is very dependent on me personally for its success and even existence, and in case of illness, or incapacity would be worthless, and therefore a good opportunity of retiring from it creditably before my natural force is abated, ought not to be lightly let pass.

(2.) Because in the *Post* I would enjoy more liberty: that is be able to take longer holidays, and the work generally would be less exerting.

(3.) Because some of the stock is offered me on terms, which would probably in five or seven years realize something handsome—for an editor.

On the other hand, after sixteen years of absolute power I shall have to work with and defer to another man; I shall exchange the position of a sort of philosophical and literary editor for that of a hammer and tongs ordinary editor, and I shall give up the thing I have created, have spent the best years of my life over, and am most known by.

I should most like your opinion on the whole matter from my point of view. Especially—as I am bound now that I am nearing the end of my career, to take care of such little reputation as I have—do you think my going with the *Post* under such circumstances would be regarded as a loss of prestige, position or reputation? . . .

Yours ever
ELG

1. Horace White (1834–1916), former editor of the *Chicago Tribune* and frequent contributor to the *Nation,* was now on Villard's payroll. During the 1870s Godkin tried to sell the *Nation* to White to whom he owed money. For several years both men had been participating in Villard's speculative schemes, schemes Villard's brother-in-law Wendell P. Garrison declined to join on the grounds they were shady. But now Garrison agreed to buy shares in the *Evening Post* and to serve as treasurer of the new company as well as titular editor of the *Nation.*

To Henry Cabot Lodge

Nation Office   New York, June 9, 1881 (Lodge Papers, MHi)

MY DEAR MR. LODGE: I have sold my interest in the *Nation* and have included your share, to the *Evening Post,* as the weekly edition of which it will hereafter be issued, but unchanged in appearance, and I hope in character, except that a majority of the articles will have previously appeared in the *Post.* I, and Garrison, and in fact the whole *Nation* establishment go over to the *Post,* with it. I have taken a heavy interest (for me) in the *Post* pecuniarily, and think very highly of its prospects. The change in the *Nation* occurs July 1st. The price for the *Nation* is $666.67 a share, but I shall feel bound to reimburse you the full amount you invested, as you did so at my request, and without enquiry. This is somewhat less too than I might have received from other bidders, but it suited my purpose better than anything else.[1] I will send you the money in due course, unless you should wish to add $4000 to it, and take one share (or more if you like) in the *Evening Post.* I wish very much you would do this as I want to have as much of the stock as possible held by my friends. Both the Adamses are going in, and D. A. Wells, and others of your school. The price paid for the *Post* has been $900,000, and in the reorganization, stock will be paid for $1,000,000—$60,000 of which will however be in the Treasury for contingencies. It is paying now $85,000 per annum *net,* with most wretched management in all departments. We expect to make it pay 100,000 very soon.

Will you please treat all this as confidential till July 1st. If you think of taking any stock I should be glad to know soon. It will cost as I have said $5000 a share.

Yours very truly

ELG

1. Godkin lacked candor. The *Nation* was approaching bankruptcy, and, despite Godkin's intensive efforts to sell it in the spring of 1881, Villard's offer of $40,000—two thirds of the capitalized valuation of the weekly—was the best he received.

To Charles Eliot Norton

June 9, 1881 (Ogden 2:121)

MY DEAR NORTON: I sold the *Nation* yesterday, after much deliberation and perplexity, to the *Evening Post*, as the weekly edition of which it will appear after July 1st. It will not be changed in appearance, and I hope not in quality, but most of the articles will have previously appeared in the *Post*. Garrison goes over with me, and will continue in special charge of the *Nation*, and our publisher becomes publisher of the *Post*.

The whole affair has given me a good deal of anxiety during the past fortnight, and I have not the resort of "prayer for guidance," which so many people have; but now that it is decided I am satisfied, and I hope it will seem a wise conclusion to you. I had other offers for the *Nation*, but felt sure in every case that the paper would, if transferred, die in a couple of years. . . .

To Thomas Wentworth Higginson

Nation Office   New York, June 9, 1881 (Godkin Papers, MH)

DEAR COLONEL HIGGINSON: I sold my interest in the *Nation*, and yours, if you approve yesterday to the *Evening Post*, for $40,000 for the whole, or at that rate for a part. This is a much better offer than Godwin made. . . .

The value of your two shares under this sale will be roughly $1332, plus your 1/10 interest in two other shares, or $1465 in all.[1]

The *Evening Post* under the new organization will have $1,000,000 capital in stock—the shares being nominally $1000 each but costing $5000. . . . [It] is now, after years of bad management, paying over 7%—that is $75,000 a year *net*. We hope very soon to make it pay 10%. I would suggest therefore your making the amount from your *Nation* shares up to $5000, and taking one *Post* share. . . .

Very truly yours
ELG

1. Higginson, along with author Brander Matthews, Henry Cabot Lodge and others who purchased stock in the *Nation* after Godkin reorganized the company in 1877, lost one-third of his investment.

To Thomas Bailey Aldrich [1]

Nation Office   New York, July 14, 1881 (Aldrich Papers, MH)

Mr. T. B. Aldrich

DEAR SIR: You flatter me very much, but I am afraid unduly, in thinking that I can say "the right word" about the Grotian attempt, in the *Atlantic*. I doubt greatly whether I can say anything that will be new, or if new, at all valuable. . . .[2]

Yours sincerely
ELG

1. Author Thomas Bailey Aldrich (1836–1907) edited the *Atlantic Monthly*. He disliked Godkin and never wrote for the *Nation*.
2. E. L. Godkin, "The Attempt on the President's Life," *Atlantic Monthly* 48 (September 1881):395–401. At Aldrich's request, in this article Godkin discusses the wounding of President Garfield by Charles Guiteau, an unbalanced office seeker. Garfield died several months later and Guiteau was executed for the crime, a penalty clamorously demanded by the *Nation*.

To Carl Schurz

August 12, 1881 (Schurz Papers, DLC)

DEAR SCHURZ: In a talk with Villard today, he repeated a criticism which I have lately more than once heard from others—that we run some topics into the ground in the *Post*—that for instance there were too many articles on Conkling,[1] and on Civil Service reform. I think there is some ground for this, and that we ought to beware of harping too much on one key.

Yours ever
ELG

1. Roscoe Conkling (1829–88), Republican Stalwart leader in the United States Senate whom Godkin and the Independents opposed.

To Professor Francis James Child

115 East 25th St., New York, September 16 [1881?]
(Child Papers, MH)

MY DEAR CHILD: I did not expect Fitz to live very long, and therefore was not surprised to hear that the poor old fellow was gone, but it did give me a pang nevertheless.[1] You don't know in how many little pictures of happy days, which still linger in my brain, he was a leading figure. I see him now many a time following the two children in single file through the grass at New Haven and Lenox, and see them still gathered over him in delight when I took him out of the basket in which I brought him from New York, and put him on the floor, on a summer evening now so long ago. I have been so very glad during these late years when I have been knocking about so much, that he had such a nice and happy home with your children, and I am glad too, to remember that when I was last in Cambridge he came over to Grace Norton's, and found me on the piazza, and barked round me in most joyful welcome, which was, it seems, also the poor fellow's goodby. I won't write more about him because at fifty, I know it is absurd to have one's eyes grow dim as mine are doing over a dog. Thank you all most sincerely for all your kindness to him.

I enclose a photograph of him taken in 1875. It is not very good, but the children may like to have it.

Yours ever affectionately
ELG

1. When Godkin returned to New York to live in 1879, he left behind his dog with the family of Professor Francis J. "Stubby" Child of Harvard

(1825–96). Although Godkin detested sentimentalism in others, he sometimes succumbed to it himself.

To Thomas Wentworth Higginson

New York, September 17, 1881 (Godkin Papers, MH)

DEAR COLONEL HIGGINSON: It will, it is found, be impossible to issue fractional shares [in the *Evening Post*]. So you will be paid off in cash.

I am very sorry that your venture in the *Nation* has not been more successful, but as far as I am concerned, everything permitted to me by Providence has been done to make it successful. My own return in money for sixteen years hard work is pitiful enough.

With much regard, yours very sincerely
ELG

To Mrs. Frederick Law Olmsted

115 East 25th St., New York, November 24 [1881]
(Olmsted Papers, DLC)

DEAR MRS. OLMSTED: I did not hear until today that your anxiety about Owen was at an end, and that your sorrow had begun.[1] I cannot help telling you how deeply I feel for you both, and how well I know all that it means in bereavement and disappointment. This can hardly be unwelcome from an old friend.

Yours very sincerely
ELG

1. The death of one of the Olmsted children. Godkin was still handling some of Olmsted's investments but was seeing little of him and his family socially.

To Whitelaw Reid

115 East 25th St., New York, February 14, 1882
(Reid Papers, DLC)

My DEAR MR. REID: We had nothing against him whatever.[1] We did not care to carry on the Fresh Air Fund. It was a troublesome business, involving great possible responsibility in case of a railroad accident or anything of that kind, and really no part of a newspaper's function. . . .

Very sincerely yours
ELG

1. A response to a letter from the proprietor of the New York *Tribune* asking for information about the Rev. Parsons, a former *Evening Post* writer who conducted the Fresh Air Fund for children.

To James Bryce

115 East 25th St., New York, February 28, 1882
(Bryce Papers, Oxford University)

My DEAR BRYCE: . . . Blaine, of whose character as a politician you cannot have too low an opinion, and who is utterly distrusted not only by all the educated men, but by all the business men, had I think a good card in the [Panama] Canal business, if he had managed it properly. That is public opinion was quite prepared to support him in an assertion of the American right to control the Canal, but his way of conducting the controversy has utterly disgusted people, he has allowed himself to be so completely unhorsed by Granville. . . .[1] Nothing could have helped him out of his difficulties so much as any sign that he had roused the British lion, but happily this was wanting. Whenever an American politician gets up a row of this kind nothing so completely takes the wind out of his sails as English indifference. I wish you could impress on the London Foreign Office the wisdom in these American crises of not seeming to care. . . . I am rather at [sea?] about your politics and am waiting for your letter. It seems to me Ireland is improving, but I do not understand Gladstone's position in the Bradlaugh affair—or for that matter, Northcote's either. Can it be that they claim the right to expel a man from the House because they don't like his morals?

Freeman turned up soon after you went.[2] His lectures here were (in New York), I am sorry to say, quite a failure. It is not a good lecturing field, and he was too didactic, and his theme —the community of England and America in all sorts of things— is now rather trite. His manners too have annoyed people, and I am afraid his visit cannot be called a success. I could not get very much out of him in talk. I was in Boston a fortnight ago and heard nothing but enthusiastic eulogy about *your* lectures. In fact you are so ready on your legs, that there is a widespread belief that you are really of American origin. . . .

We both enjoyed your visit greatly. I lost some of the plea- sure of it through being somewhat out of sorts, physically; otherwise I should have pumped you a great deal more. Ever since you left, I have been extremely well. Harry James was with me for some weeks as you know. . . . I was very glad to have you both so soon after coming back here. I have been away from New York for several years and returning was rather a dismal business, which I think I should hardly have undertaken but that Lawrence has to live and make his career here. . . .

Remember [me] to Dicey, and encourage him to write. He is the best "Contributor" in the world.[3]

Ever most faithfully yours
ELG

1. As Garfield's Secretary of State, James G. Blaine carried on a vigorous exchange with British Foreign Secretary Lord Granville over the right of the United States to construct a transoceanic canal in Central America. Godkin, although he hated Blaine, concurred in the objective of an American-controlled canal; but Granville pointed out that this was pro- hibited by the Clayton-Bulwer Treaty of 1850. Contrary to Godkin's al- legation, Blaine already knew of this treaty. A detailed exposition of God- kin's views on Blaine diplomacy appears in Armstrong, *Godkin and Ameri- can Foreign Policy*, especially the chapter "Blaine and 'Spirited' Diplomacy."

2. The English historian Edward A. Freeman (1823–92).

3. The English legal scholar Albert V. Dicey (1835–1922). A writer for the *Nation* for more than thirty years, Dicey was one of the few con- tributors that Godkin permitted to disagree with him.

To Whitelaw Reid

115 East 25th St., New York, March 29 [1882]
(Reid Papers, DLC)

MY DEAR REID: Thanks were not needed. Justice, as the jurist says, consists in constantly trying to give everyone his due. People fail in these endeavors often, but now and then, as in your case, we succeed.[1]

Yours very truly
ELG

1. Godkin is accepting Reid's thanks for a friendly paragraph he wrote about the *Tribune* editor in the 24 March *Evening Post*. Relations between the two New York editors, once outwardly cordial, were beginning to cool, and when Godkin turned his editorial guns against Blaine in 1884 in support of Grover Cleveland, the *Tribune* thereafter waged relentless war on Godkin and the Mugwumps.

To James Russell Lowell

115 East 25th St., New York, April 24, 1882
(Lowell Papers, MH)

MY DEAR LOWELL: I have ventured to give a line of introduction to you to Mr. Joseph P. Rockwell a brother of my brother-in-law, and a modest[,] excellent, retiring young fellow who is making, I think, his first visit to England, and desires simply to be known at the Legation during his stay in London as a respectable citizen. He is a man of some fortune, though not a drone, but I wish, and he wishes that you will not consider my letter a draft on your attention. . . .[1]

I have sympathized with you deeply in what you must have been going through in these Irish troubles. They have made but little impression on the public mind here, but the politicians are always more sensitive, and if Blaine had stayed in I fancy he would have carried the flag high. But I confess I think the English ground that alien suspects are not entitled *to a trial*, simply because the subjects are not, is untenable. I enclose an article which I have written on this point today which I think contains the view most current on this point here, among people whose opinion is worth anything and as such may be worth your reading.[2]

> With best wishes most sincerely yours
> ELG

1. Lowell was now United States minister to England.
2. "Aliens and Natives under the Irish Coercion Act," *Evening Post*, 24 April 1882. Between 1881 and 1884 the State Department of the United States was vexed by the British imprisonment without trial of American citizens of Irish origin charged with complicity in Irish disorders. Godkin for the moment did not accept Lowell's view that the men's citizenship had nothing to do with their rights under British law.

To Daniel Coit Gilman

> 115 East 25th St., New York, June 1, 1882
> (Gilman Papers, MdBJ)

DEAR MR. GILMAN: To answer intelligently about Mr. Ely I would have to refresh my memory by looking at his contributions again, and in Garrison's absence, who is in Boston till Monday, I do not know where to find them. As soon as he returns I will write more fully.

I fear I don't know any good young man for an Associate. They are very scarce. . . .[1]

> Very sincerely yours
> ELG

1. The economist Richard T. Ely (1854–1943) won the Johns Hopkins position, only to leave it a decade later under fire from the *Nation* and others for his liberal views. President Gilman mistakenly thought Ely was a writer on political economy for the *Nation*, as did Joseph Dorfman, suggesting a half-century later in *The American Historical Review* that Godkin allowed contributors to express viewpoints on economics opposed to his own. (Dorfman's claim that Ely was a contributor on economics to the *Nation* rests solely on letters of complaint that Ely addressed to that weekly.) *American Historical Review* 59, no. 2 (January 1954): 455. *The Nation; Indexes of Titles and Contributors*, compiled by Daniel C. Haskell (New York: New York Public Library, 1953) 2:145.

To James Bryce

115 East 25th St., New York, June 7, 1882
(Bryce Papers, Oxford University)

MY DEAR BRYCE: I am going to trespass hugely on your good nature in sending you by the next mail after this an article of mine
on the Irish question, and asking you to offer it either to the
Nineteenth Century or the *Fortnightly*. . . .[1]

You will perhaps wonder on reading it why I wrote it: I do
not think it has much merit in the way of originality, but it contains the result of a change in my own way of looking at the
matter which I am conceited enough to think has a certain significance. I am an Irishman of English ancestry, bred in strong attach-
ment to the English government, educated at an English School
and Queen's College Belfast. I have lived in Ireland only four
years continuously since I was thirteen. Here I have lived for
twenty five years among Americans almost exclusively. The Irish
agitators and their ways are altogether destestable to me, and yet
I find myself slowly and steadily becoming at the age of fifty a
Home Ruler, and feeling a certain exasperation towards the British
Government on Irish account, although if Ireland were independent tomorrow, it is about the last place in Europe in which I
should care to take up my abode. . . .

I have been too long absent from England to suppose that I
know much about English opinion. . . . You are, therefore, at
full liberty to edite it in any manner you please, by excision or
modification. . . .

Yours very sincerely
ELG

P. S. Put my name or a *nom de plume* to it as you think best.

---

1. E. L. Godkin, "An American View of Ireland," *Nineteenth Century* 12
(August 1882): 175–92.

To James Bryce

115 East 25th St., New York, June 10 [1882]
(Bryce Papers, Oxford University)

MY DEAR BRYCE: . . . Your letters to the *Nation* are a great light in very thick darkness. The news of the Bourke and other murders yesterday was very disheartening.[1] What is more disheartening still to me is the trouble you are taking in the House to pass that Repression Bill, when you must know that there is not the least reason for supposing that it will be effective. . . . What is the reason the murderers of Mountmorris . . . of Mrs. Smythe, of Burke, and Cavendish, and of Bourke and many others during the past winter and spring have not been brought to justice? [2] Is it because juries would not agree?

These Coercion Bills seem to me to be passed simply to satisfy English pride, and have about as much political value as a review of the fleet.

In haste, yours most truly
ELG

1. The murder of W. M. Bourke, a landlord in Galway, Ireland.
2. A reference to the Phoenix Park murders and other political slayings in Ireland. Lord Frederick Cavendish, who had just taken the oath of office as chief secretary for Ireland, was stabbed to death, together with under secretary Thomas H. Burke, while they were strolling in Dublin's Phoenix Park. Subsequent confessions by an informer established that Burke, not Cavendish, was the intended victim. Later, the informer was murdered on orders of the Irish republicans, and his assailant was executed for the crime.

To Daniel Coit Gilman

115 East 25th St., New York, June 17, 1882
(Gilman Papers, MdBJ)

MY DEAR MR. GILMAN: I find that Mr. Ely has only written one thing for the *Nation*, an account of the Municipal Government of Berlin, and though this was careful and well done, it was simply descriptive, and did not furnish materials for an opinion of any value as to his general equipment as an economist.

Yours very truly
ELG. . . .

To Henry Villard

Evening Post Editorial Rooms   New York, June 23 [1882]
(Villard Papers, MH)

DEAR MR. VILLARD: A very good friend of mine Mr. Nathaniel Niles, the Vice president of the Tradesmen's National Bank, wishes to make your acquaintance, in part, I fancy for business purposes in connection with his bank of which he is the Active Manager. He is an excellent man and first became known to me ten years ago in exposing a railroad swindle in New Jersey through the *Nation,* for which he was unsuccessfully sued for libel. If you can serve him in any way, I shall be very glad, but in any case I shall be obliged if you will let me give him a note of introduction to you. If so, when could you see him?

Yours very truly
ELG

To James Bryce

115 East 25th St., New York, July 12 [1882]
(Bryce Papers, Oxford University)

MY DEAR BRYCE: Many thanks for all your trouble about the article. The more changes you make in it the more obliged I shall be. . . .

I am now afraid that even if it appears, it will come after the Irish question has ceased to be interesting. The Egyptian affair must give another turn to the public thoughts. I am very glad of the bombardment. The position both of the fleet and the Ministry had become ridiculous towards Arabi.[1] I am inclined to think this will help Gladstone—will it not? . . .

Things are going quietly here—there is an *embarras de richesses* in every direction; too much revenue, enormous crops, strikes that are taken simply as signs that the tide is rising, and now your European rows are giving us the *suave mari magno.*

Yours ever
ELG. . . .

1. Egyptian nationalist leader Ahmed-El-Arabi (*c.* 1841–1911). Appointed Egyptian minister of war, Arabi in 1882 armed the Egyptian forts at

Alexandria as a symbolic gesture that his government was independent of European control. The British government proclaimed him a rebel, and the Royal Navy bombarded the forts on July 11. Captured several months later by the British, Arabi was tried for rebellion and banished to Ceylon.

To Carl Schurz

115 East 25th St., New York, September 12 [1882]
(Schurz Papers, DLC)

MY DEAR SCHURZ: I only sent you the extract because I thought you had better see it, not in the least because I thought you ought to notice it. It would be great folly to do so.[1]

As to the Sullivan reception, I at once declined to allow my name to be used, and I advise you to do so too.[2] Not because I do not think Sullivan a good and able fellow, but because I consider the Land League of this city a very disreputable crowd, with whom I should not want to be associated in anything, and even still less to appear to be associated. They will have him in charge.

Things go on smoothly here. . . . Stay away as long as you gain by it.

Yours ever
ELG

1. Schurz was on holiday from his post as editor-in-chief of the *Evening Post*, and Godkin had taken charge of the editorial office and was making changes.

2. A reference to the New York visit of Irish journalist and orator Alexander Martin Sullivan (1830–84), during which he lectured at the Cooper Union. The former proprietor of the *Nation* of Dublin, Sullivan stood for constitutional solutions of Irish grievances.

To James Bryce

September 15, 1882 (Bryce Papers, Oxford University)

MY DEAR BRYCE: . . . I have . . . written a line of explanatory reply to the *Spectator*. . . .[1] I thought I had acknowledged fully that a man's being Irish was no bar whatever to his success in England, and what I meant to say was that this success—no matter how numerous the cases of it—did nothing for the credit of Ireland, as a political community, which is one, I hold, of the palpable and [remediable?] Irish grievances: that is, no matter how many Wolseleys, Robartes, Leckys, Willses, or Burkes Ireland produces, it does not make Englishmen think or speak more hopefully or respectfully about Irish capacity *or Irish*. All these men are appropriated by England and thought of by the English mind as English products. They do nothing to raise the Irish reputation. they do not make men like Goldwin Smith a whit less ready at a time of great trouble and irritation, to come home and engage in elaborate public depreciation and denunciation of Irish character and capacity. . . . Dicey has some good remarks . . . in the June *Contemporary*. . . .

His argument against partition or Federation is I think conclusive and I share your feeling about Ulster. I do not think I am personally prepared for more than the relegation of Irish affairs more completely to Irish members, and the Hibernicizing of the Administration in Ireland. "The Castle" ought to be abolished. It is simply a foreign stronghold. The offices should be given to *popular* Irishmen, and the police should be converted into a National force, and the Irish in the army treated to something in the way of National distinction. In other words means ought to be provided by which the success of Irishmen as Administrators, legislators, soldiers and so on would visibly, palpably redound to the Irish credit, so that every peasant would feel proud of it. . . . but I have little hope that Englishmen will see this, and act on it, until it is too late. Everything has to be extorted from them, and in Ireland the process of extortion, has in spite of Goldwin Smith's "taffy," been, and is very brutalizing. For this the Irish are themselves, I admit partly to blame. They are unable to agitate in the way that moves Englishmen. Their rhetoric is too wild and extravagant. But query—Was any people ever able to agitate peacefully in a way to persuade another *people* holding the power? The Americans[,] though so English, tried it and failed. All the successful powerful agitators have succeeded with their own countrymen, not with foreigners. The foreigner, if he has the power, is always disgusted with the . . . clamor of the discontented. . . .

We have just had from Dicey for the *Nation*, what I think an excellent analysis of the causes of the hatred of Gladstone felt by

Society in England. He is not, in all justice, entirely just to him, as when he says he (Gladstone) might have sailed out of the harbor of Alexandria and therefore was not entitled to use danger to the fleet as an excuse for the bombardment. But on the whole it is a very excellent piece of Dicey's peculiar work. How admirably Wolseley has done his part.[2] It has produced a deep impression here, in spite of a strong tendency to sympathize with Arabi, as a "Nationalist." But I believe there is now in this country a growing, indeed rapidly growing disposition among the native American stock to sympathize with England, and even be a little proud of her exploits. I have observed it for some time, and it is both curious and interesting.

There is absolutely nothing interesting in our politics here just at present. This is "the off year," which we fill up with personalities and "charges"—

Believe me ever

Most sincerely yours
ELG

1. A reference to a reply by the *Spectator* of London to Godkin's *Nineteenth Century* article, "An American View of Ireland," which marked the beginning of a protracted dispute between Godkin and Goldwin Smith.

2. General Garnet Joseph Wolseley (1833–1913). Godkin, who took the imperialist side in the debate over the bombardment of Alexandria, is here rejoicing over Wolseley's capture of Arabi, for which the general received the thanks of Parliament and elevation to the peerage.

To Jonas M. Libbey [1]

115 East 25th St., New York, October 23 [1882]
(Godkin Miscellaneous Papers, NN)

DEAR SIR: Thank you for your invitation to the pages of your *Review*, which is certainly now the best arena for serious discussion in the country. But I do not care to reply to Mr. Goldwin Smith. I have promised the editor of the *Nineteenth Century* to say something more on the Irish question in his magazine sometime this winter, and besides this, I doubt greatly the utility of discussing it in this country, where so few know or care anything and none can *do* anything about it.

If I answered Mr. Smith, too, I fear I should have in many cases to go over the same ground again which is wearisome. . . . I think some ideas about "race" are at the bottom of the position he has taken up on this subject, and my experience is that one argues vainly with anyone who has taken up race as a solution of political problems, though it undoubtedly has weight, and needs to be considered. He alludes to me once or twice as a champion of "my race," I suppose meaning the Celtic race, which is a role I must disclaim. I am an Irishman but I am as English in blood as he is. Pardon me for so much explanation and believe me

Yours very truly
ELG

1. Jonas M. Libbey (1857–1922) the youthful editor of the *Princeton Review*. When Goldwin Smith read Godkin's "An American View of Ireland," followed by a Godkin letter to the *Spectator* that criticized Smith's stand on the Irish question, Smith labelled Godkin "an Irish Nationalist" in the *Spectator* and sent off an article on the Irish question to the *Princeton Review* to which Libbey offered Godkin an opportunity to reply.

To James Bryce

New York, October 27 [1882]
(Bryce Papers, Oxford University)

MY DEAR BRYCE: . . . You may have seen in the *Spectator* that Goldwin Smith played me what I considered a very shabby trick by calling me an "Irish Nationalist who showed the usual hostility of *his* party to Great Britain etc." This was I thought simply a short mode of getting rid of a disagreeable critic by appealing to English prejudice through an epithet, and considering how familiar he is with my antecedents and opinions, quite unpardonable. I was never more surprized than when it was telegraphed here.

Yours ever
ELG

To James Bryce

115 East 25th St., New York, November 17, 1882
(Bryce Papers, Oxford University)

MY DEAR BRYCE: I was very glad to get your opinion as to the general effect of my letter [to the *Spectator* about Goldwin Smith]. . . . His answer to my private letter was funnier than appears, for instead of acknowledging what he said in the *Spectator*, he gave me, I suppose by way of sop, a very complimentary extract from the then forthcoming article in *The Princeton Review*. He has not only been a constant reader of the *Nation*, but a frequent contributor and has republished several of his articles from it, and, moreover, for a year or two published a sort of imitation of it in Montreal. He has had so many newspaper rows there that I am afraid he has learnt some of the tricks of the trade and especially that of disposing of troublesome antagonists with an epithet. He is an able man, but there is some little screw loose in his brain. . . . I thought your article was excellent. Some of your conclusions have been well justified by our late election, which was a splendid triumph. Some of the results of the upheaval have been odd, and need explanation—Butler's success in Massachusetts for instance.[1] He has, however, little or no power, and has already begun, in that thoroughly American way, to act the role of a "dignified Chief Magistrate," and I have no doubt will act it to the end by way of showing how much he has been belied and misunderstood. I think his success is due partly to the fact that it was the worse thing the voters could do to the clique who have long governed the state, and partly to a tendency I have long noticed on the part of American constituencies to rush at something against which they have been solemnly warned as highly dangerous and indecent. They seem occasionally to take pleasure in showing "to pessimists" that in this favored land nothing is dangerous. I really believe the Silver legislation for instance, was somewhat stimulated by the pictures drawn of the awful consequences that it would draw after it. . . .

Yours ever
ELG

1. Godkin, who was now arrayed in opposition to Garfield's successor, Chester A. Arthur, is referring to the November 1882, elections in which

the Democrats captured control of the House of Representatives by nearly one hundred seats, forecasting the Democratic take-over of the Presidency two years later. Benjamin F. Butler was elected governor of Massachusetts. Godkin especially disliked Butler for his support of soft money and other populist schemes.

To Silas W. Burt

December 1, 1882 (Burt Papers, NHi)

DEAR COLONEL BURT: I am writing on Civil Serv. Ref. for the American edition of the *Encycl. Britannica*, and want to be sure on two points.[1]

The examinations etc. under Grant's order were wholly dropped, or not? When restored by Hayes, was the Grant order simply revived, or was a new system started?

If you can answer these questions with the dates before 1. p.m. today, your will greatly oblige me.

Very truly yours
ELG

1. Silas W. Burt (1830–1912), an authority on civil service reform, was the Naval Officer for the Port of New York. From 1895 to 1900 he was civil service commissioner for the State of New York.

To Joseph M. Stoddart

115 East 25th St., New York, December 2, 1882
(Clifton Waller Barrett Collection, ViU)

MY DEAR SIR: I enclose the article on Civil Service Reform, which is, I hope, the kind of thing you wanted.[1] I might have discussed the subject at greater length, but it seemed to me that when the question was in its present very transitory state, it was not desirable to say too much about it in a permanent work of reference like an Encyclopaedia.

Yours very truly
ELG

1. "Civil Service Reform," *Stoddart's Encyclopedia Americana* (American supplement to the ninth edition of the *Encyclopedia Britannica*), 4 vols. (New York, 1883–89), 2:260–62.

To Alice James [1]

115 East 25th St., New York, December 16 [1882]
(James Family Papers, MH)

DEAR MISS ALICE: I have only heard within a few days how grave your father's condition was, and I hope you will not think it too much of an intrusion on you if I ask you to give him a message of heartfelt sympathy and farewell from me who have admired him and enjoyed him so much, and to whom he is associated with so many happy days. I never shall see his like again.

I am not writing to praise him however, but to say how sorry I am both for him and for you, though to him I suppose the prospect of rest is very welcome.

Your affectionate friend
ELG

1. The sister of Henry and William James, Alice James spent her later life as an invalid in London.

To James Bryce

[Between January and April 1883]
(Bryce Papers, Oxford University)

MY DEAR BRYCE: . . . I was just going to write to you when your note came about another and very different matter—the visit of the Lord Chief Justice to this country. He has been invited by "the State Bar Association," that is the State of New York. This sounds very fine, but you or he or somebody ought to know that this is a body of no standing in the profession, that the leading members of the profession either do not belong to it, or have little to do with it. The persons who have acted for it in inviting the Lord Chief Justice, and particularly the most prominent, *Elliot F. Shephard* [sic] have a good deal of the charlatan about them.[1] Shephard in particular if he has any practice, has but little, and that of a shady sort, and enjoys nobody's respect or confidence. The Bar Association which ought to have invited him and whose invitation he could safely accept, is that of New York City, which contains the leading members of the profession.

Several members of the bar have spoken to me about the affair, with a sort of shudder at what is impending, but like all Americans they are very timid in such matters, and will do nothing. In fact I do not know what they can do now. But if the Lord Chief Justice comes over here to be managed by Shephard and Co., it will be a real shame and scandal, worse than Dean Stanley's experiences with Field.[2]

My object in writing to you about it is to see whether you cannot by some means, make the Chief Justice aware of the state of things, and in some way put him on his guard, so that when he comes here he may be in the hands of men of undoubted standing in the profession and socially, and may owe nothing to the State Bar Association, but his dinner. Anyhow he ought to avoid having Shephard as a cicerone or Amphitryon. Dean Stanley's mistake shows how careful Englishmen of high position ought to be in these matters here, because the indications they are accustomed to rely on for guidance in England are wanting here. I of course do not wish to appear as the authority for all this, and am glad to think that I shall be out of the country when the visit comes off, because I retain my boyish feeling about the Lord Chief Justice, and cannot bear to see him dragged about this City and State by a man with whom neither I nor any of my friends would care to associate.

Irish affairs look dreadfully, but do not flatter yourselves that either the United States or this state will do anything against dynamite. Get what comfort you can out of the newspaper denunciations for you will get none from the Courts. I think any attempt to prosecute would be a wretched failure, and ruin those who make it politically, for remember that even those who most detest the Fenians, laugh at your calamity, and are not sorry to see you panic stricken or scared.[3]

Yours ever
ELG

1. A reference to New York lawyer Elliott F. Shepard. Lord Chief Justice Coleridge (1820–94) visited the United States late in the summer of 1883.
2. Arthur P. (Dean) Stanley (1815–81) was the leading liberal theologian of his day in England. He was greatly impressed by his tour of the United States and later published a volume of his American addresses and sermons.
3. A reference to a wave of dynamitings by Irish nationalists allegedly

supplied and financed in the United States. After an unsuccessful attempt in February 1884 to dynamite Victoria Station in London, the *Times* of that city accused the United States government of "conniving" at the outrages. For Godkin's fluctuating attitudes toward American responsibility for the dynamitings, see Armstrong, *Godkin and American Foreign Policy*, pp. 151–58.

To Horace White

115 East 25th Street, New York, May 21 [1883]
(White Papers, IHi)

DEAR WHITE: I have pretty much decided, under the circumstances[,] not to go over this summer, as I had proposed. I should not be easy leaving the *Post* and *Nation*, with the force there would be, or is likely to be[,] in the office. The *Post* suffers, seriously I am satisfied[,] from heaviness and monotony, from which people are too ready to seek relief in the cheap light evening papers. The result of our two years experiment from this point of view troubles me a good deal. We are not gaining circulation, and I can't say I think we deserve it. Half our editorial matter every day is dull reading on uninteresting subjects. I certainly should never think of reading it if I could help it, and I know the same is the case with the average New Yorker.

If you were to be here I should go with any easy mind, but I could not otherwise, and will therefore wait. I found Garrison yesterday in despair at the prospect as regards the *Nation.*[1]

Yours ever
ELG

1. This letter was the opening gun in Godkin's campaign to supplant Schurz as editor-in-chief.

To James Bryce

115 East 25th St., New York, June 9, 1883
(Bryce Papers, Oxford University)

MY DEAR BRYCE: I find that it will be impossible for me to go over this summer, to my very great disappointment. Horace White was . . . to remain here this summer, during my absence, but his wife's health is in such a condition that he has to go abroad with her. . . . Lawrence, however, is going alone and will sail next week, probably Saturday the 16th. He will stay at Henry James's rooms, 3. Bolton St. Picadilly while he is in London which will probably not be very long, as he will only have two months to do everything in.

It really grieves me to ask a man of so many cares and labor as you to take any trouble about anything, but everything in England will be absolutely strange to him, and if you would aid him in seeing such things as the House of Commons and the Law Courts, I should be very much indebted to you. . . .

I enjoyed your article much. The only thing in it, which I considered at all defective, was your presentation of the English charge of want of sense of political responsibility in Irishmen without sufficiently—as I thought—urging the Irish answer, that no such sense has ever shown itself anywhere, without some practice in self government. But it is on the whole an admirable statement of the whole case, and I have distributed many copies of it as such.

Yours very sincerely

ELG

I hope to get over in the autumn, when White returns.

To Whitelaw Reid

Evening Post Editorial Rooms   New York, June 12 [1883]

(Reid Papers, DLC)

DEAR MR. REID: I want very much for a review article I am writing to get hold of the amount of the *foreign vote* at the last Presidential, or any late election in this city, as shown by the registry. I sent up to the Police Headquarters for it, and learnt there that they had no separate record of the foreign vote, but that one [had] been made up within a few years for the *Tribune*. If this is true, would you oblige me with the result?

Yours very truly

ELG

To Carl Schurz

115 East 25th St., New York, June 18, 1883
(Schurz Papers, DLC)

My dear Schurz: I did not see White before he went away after his interview with you. He wrote me a short note giving the results in general terms, and I have been hoping to receive some further communications from you about it.[1] Not hearing from you, and not knowing what he actually said to you, I think it desirable that I should repeat the substance of what I said to him. I do so in the friendliest spirit towards you personally, and with the strong hope that you will take it as simple business as far as I am concerned.

It was that I considered after two year's observations, that the *Evening Post* experiment, as at present managed, was a failure. . . . In brief, though you and I agree on most public questions we differ greatly in opinion as to the *quality* of writing, and I am unwilling longer to father a great deal of writing that appears in the *Post*. I further said to White that if he and Villard did not agree with me as to the need of a change, I was willing to buy the *Nation* back and retire from the Syndicate. I found, however, that they did agree with me in general terms, and White informed me that you were willing to turn the control over to me whenever you went on your vacation.

I should be glad to know now when that will be. . . .

As far as I am concerned I am desirous that all this should cause you as little inconvenience . . . as possible, and do not care how little change there may be externally. I am acting, as I say simply from business motives which at my time of life, I cannot afford to overlook. And if I seem to think you wanting in the special newspaper faculty, you are well aware how much talent of a far higher order I believe you to possess.

If you will kindly let me know what your plans are I will adapt mine to them. I thought of going off for a fortnight myself now or soon, but will not fix a date till I know when you propose to go.

Yours very sincerely
ELG

Godkin's Library

The Evening Post.
NEW YORK.
EDITORIAL ROOMS.

May 31/95

Senator Hoar.

Dear Sir;

As we would like to
comment on your interesting
address yesterday, with intelligence,
will you kindly inform me what
the book is, or who the "poet" by
whom you begin in the following
passage. We are unable to
identify the work in question
through your description.

Truly yours

E. L. Godkin.

One of our own best beloved men of
letters gives his woeful picture of the
degradation of American politics and
then dedicates his book to the most
unscrupulous liar connected with the
American press.

Godkin Letter to Senator George F. Hoar

This irony-filled letter, with a clipping pasted on it of a quotation from a speech by the senator from Massachusetts, began an acrimonious exchange between the two men. To it Hoar replied: "I meant Mr. Lowell by the phrase 'one of our best beloved men of letters.' By 'the most unscrupulous liar connected with the American Press,' I meant you."

THE WORLD: SATURDAY, AUGUST 4, 1900.

CHORUS OF INNOCENTS.

"NOW I WONDER WHOM GODKIN MEANT."

New York World Cartoon

Godkin in 1863

Godkin in 1889

E. L. Godkin.

Godkin as Drawn in 1894

Godkin's Home from 1890 to 1901

Charles Loring Brace in 1855

James Bryce in the 1890s

William James in the 1890s

Frederick Law Olmsted in the 1860s

Shady Hill, the Home of
Charles Eliot Norton

Lawrence Godkin, c. 1890

The Evening Post *Building*
at Broadway and Fulton Street
in 1890

1. A reference to an interview between Horace White and Schurz over Godkin's demand to supplant Schurz as editor-in-chief of the *Evening Post*.

To Carl Schurz

115 East 25th St., New York [July 1883] (Schurz Papers, DLC)

DEAR SCHURZ: Apropos of Adams's address, it must be remembered that the interest in this discussion is very limited, and at this season of the year smaller than usual among our public. People will read a little about such things but only a little in a daily paper in hot weather. And our business is to make the *Post*, readable and attractive and raise our circulation and increase our dividends, and not to publish long essays on the Comparative Merits of Classical and Modern Literature, although it would be gratifying to oblige Adams.[1]

I think the only passage in that address which it would *pay* us to print would be the passage relating to the experience of the Adams family. The rest is simple rehash.

Yours sincerely
ELG

1. A reference to the Phi Beta Kappa address of Charles Francis Adams, Jr., which, contrary to Godkin's prediction, was widely read and launched a movement in the United States for the broadening of the college curriculum. When Godkin discovered his error, he directed Garrison to print the address in the *Nation*.

To Carl Schurz

Lenox Club, Lenox, Mass. [24 July 1883]
(Schurz Papers, DLC)

MY DEAR SCHURZ: The basis of my position is that the telegraphers have a duty to the public, and if they have, then choosing the time when they can inflict most damage on the public to strike, aggravates their offence.[1] It does not differ in the least in principle from the abandonment of their engines by the Massachusetts engineers. They, too, might have said that they did this as the best mode of bringing their employers to terms, in the absence of legal protection. . . .

I think in general, it is wise policy for the *Post*—the very wisest from all points of view, to be the paper which in times of excitement, when the others are running amuck, and talking wild nonsense as the *Herald* and *Times* are now, holds on to law and common sense. We shall gain not lose subscribers in this way and attacks by other papers are simply advertizements. . . .

Very truly yours
ELG. . . .

1. The growing unpleasantness between Schurz and Godkin was heightened in July 1883, when they disagreed over editorial policy toward a nationwide telegraphers' strike. Schurz, who was still editor-in-chief, meant for the *Post* to be neutral, whereas Godkin set about independently through Garrison in the *Nation* to condemn the strikers. A bitter quarrel ensued in which Schurz severed his connection with the paper. For details of the dispute see William M. Armstrong, "The Godkin-Schurz Feud, 1881–83, over Policy Control of the *Evening Post*," The *New-York Historical Society Quarterly* 48, no. 1 (January 1964): 5–29.

To Wendell P. Garrison

Lenox Club, Lenox, Mass., July 24, 1883
(Godkin Papers, MH)

DEAR MR. GARRISON: . . . The way [Schurz'] courage oozes out towards the end of an article, and makes him put in a shilly shally qualifying paragraph is very comic. My notion is, you know, that the *Post* ought to make a specialty of being the paper to which sober minded people would look at crises of this kind, instead of hollering and bellering, and talking platitudes like the *Herald* and *Times*. I was sorry and ashamed to see the excusing paragraph in answer to the *Herald* yesterday.

Yours ever
ELG

I hope you are well. If anything goes wrong with you I will retire into a monastery. You are the one steady and constant man I have ever had to do with.

To Henry Villard

115 East 25th St., New York, August 9, 1883
(Villard Papers, MH)

DEAR MR. VILLARD: I have been carrying 800 shares of O. T. Stock for some time, on a 20% margin, having bought at 85.[1] The late fall has brought the margin down to 6%, and as I have no other resources available, the situation is causing me a good deal of anxiety. Could you, therefore, in case I need it, help me over this emergency? I presume there must be a turn in the tide after the road is open.

I hate to bother you about the matter, but my need is great.

Very truly yours
ELG

1. Godkin is referring to his holdings in Villard's railroad enterprises. Villard, who was also hard pressed by the financial crisis, consented to lend Godkin $16,000 of Mrs. Villard's funds, repayment of which she obtained from Godkin only with difficulty. The last sentence of the letter refers to the Northern Pacific Railroad scheduled shortly to open its main line.

To Carl Schurz

[10 August 1883] (Unsent, Godkin Papers, MH)

MY DEAR SCHURZ: I am very sorry you do not like the article in yesterday's *Post*.[1] I was equally touched by those of yours on the same subject, as on many others during the past two years. But I do not see that any good would result from our discussing the matter. . . . I informed Horace White before he left that I would under no circumstances remain connected with the *Post* under your editorship—for reasons in no way diminishing my respect for your character—and I conveyed the same information to Mr. Villard, the[y] being the persons who had invited me to join the paper. They agreed, thereupon, that I should assume the editorship and responsibility of the paper, and you have assented to my doing so. This of course means the appearance in it[,] in all such questions as the strike[,] of my opinions, which are of as long standing, and I think are as well known as yours, and I am not afraid of being thought the organ of a corporation. This is really *all* I can say in the matter. . . .

Yours truly

ELG

The view taken of the strike and corporation Management has been produced in the *Nation* times without number.

1. "The Telegraph Strike," *Evening Post*, 8 August 1883. In this editorial Godkin flayed the telegraph strikers, proposing that they be "governed on the same principles as an army." Schurz, who had not yet severed his connection with the paper, countered in a private letter to Godkin that it was "monstrous" to declare a strike analogous to "desertion from the army." Instead of laws questioning the right to strike, there should be laws, Schurz insisted, for the arbitration of labor disputes.

To Daniel Coit Gilman

115 East 25th St., New York, October 2 [1883]

(Gilman Papers, MdBJ)

MY DEAR GILMAN: I have given a letter of introduction to you to Mr. Albert Grey, the grandson of the great Earl Grey of Macauley's Warren Hastings essay, and the heir to the present earl, his uncle. He is M. P. for Northumberland, and a very bright interesting man. He will probably be accompanied by his brother in law, Lieutenant Holford of the Life Guards, a nice young fellow.

Grey is very desirous of seeing anything worth seeing in Baltimore, and particularly the University, and anything you can do to help him will confer a favor on me. He is just back from the Northern Pacific trip, on which I found him a delightful companion. . . .[1]

Yours very sincerely

ELG

1. To celebrate the opening of the main line of the Northern Pacific Railway, Villard at great expense imported a party of European dignitaries for a six-week western outing.

To Katharine Sands [1]

[New York, October 1883] (Ogden 2:139)

. . . Yes, I climbed a ten thousand feet mountain, Mt. Mc-Donald, and laughed in going up it over the remembrance of your challenge to me, and wondered what men you had climbed with to get your idea of men's climbing powers. We started in, a party of fifty of various nations, and only eleven, of whom nine, including myself under that term, were English, and two Germans reached the top. Three thousand feet were the hardest kind of work ever seen, except on ice, hands and knees over sloping rocks and up couloirs, or chimneys, with incessant exposure to falling stones. No food or drink from six a.m. to nine p.m.; awful thirst. My glory in the matter, alas, came from my age. I was the oldest man of those who crowned the crest, and for this reason was received with cheers, having left a good many youths behind. I started on the trip with some hesitation, as I had no idea what condition I was in, not having walked much for years, or climbed anything serious since 1862, and having been shut up in the train for nearly three weeks. The Yellowstone valley on the way home was real hardship, intense cold at night, fiery heat in the day, great fatigue and beds on the ground in open tents for four nights. But it was altogether a delightful experience full of wonders and pleasures, not the least of the latter being the company of delightful Englishmen.

1. Katharine Sands was soon to become the second Mrs. Godkin.

To Percy W. Bunting

115 East 25th St., New York, November 12, 1883
(Bunting Papers, ICU)

MY DEAR SIR: The *Contemporary* containing my article, reached me today.[1] The proofreading seems to have been very well done indeed, but there is a mistake in my name for which I am probably myself to blame, owing to my bad writing, but which it is, nevertheless, not in human nature to contemplate with equanimity.

I am made E. D. Godkin, when I am really E. L. Godkin. I am not able to say that any serious consequences either to the world at large or to myself will flow from the error, but if there be any human remedy for it, I trust you will apply it.

Very truly yours
ELG

1. E. L. Godkin, "The Southern States since the War," *Contemporary Review* (London) 44 (November 1883): 681–700. Percy W. Bunting was the editor of the *Contemporary Review*.

To Charles Eliot Norton

November 13, 1883 (Ogden 1:310)

. . . I suppose you have seen a good deal of Arnold.[1] I only got one glimpse of him. The fact is that the way Englishmen of distinction have fallen into of delivering themselves over on their arrival here to obscure, illiterate, and disreputable people, makes it difficult to see anything of them at all. . . .

1. Matthew Arnold (1822–88) was visiting in the United States. He had often expressed admiration for the *Nation*.

To Carl Schurz

115 East 25th St., New York, December 7, 1883
(Unsigned rough draft, Godkin Papers, MH)

MY DEAR SCHURZ: I think I ought to say,—apropos of your reserving to yourself the right to make public explanation of the reasons of your leaving the *Post* besides what appears in the *Post* itself—that this might and very probably would impose on me the duty of publishing my reasons for wishing to sever my connection with the *Post* in May last. . . .

It would of course be disagreeable to lay all this before the public, and would probably cover us both with ridicule, but I shall not shrink from it on that account if it should seem necessary. . . .

I am desirous in every way of making your retirement as easy and agreeable to you as possible but I do not think it ought to be accompanied or explained by anything from you, which would make further explanations from me necessary, or mislead the public as to its causes or effects.

To Carl Schurz

December 10, 1883 (Godkin Papers, MH)

DEAR MR. SCHURZ: I received your letter of this morning and have since seen two reporters who told me what you said, to which I made no objection, and added, what was very well should be known, that we had differed about the telegrapher's strike, and that I had written the articles on the subject. . . .

I am sorry that you should have thought it necessary to assert that you had been the object of underhanded dealing on my part.[1] Because, as you are doubtless aware, this very offensive terminology, that will prevent any friendly intercourse between us until it is remitted, as long as it stands, is a name called. . . .

Yours truly
ELG

1. That the controversy had done harm to Godkin's reputation was suggested by the editorial comment of Charles A. Dana's *Sun* that Godkin gained the post of editor-in-chief of the *Evening Post* "by a series of maneuvers of which an honest man would have no special reason to be proud."

8. Cleveland Backer and Mugwump Editor in the 1880s

Tradition has it that Charles A. Dana had Godkin in mind when he affixed the name "Mugwump" to the eastern intellectuals and politicians who deserted the Republican party during the 1880s to become Independents in politics.

In 1884 Godkin temporarily set aside his differences with Schurz while they joined Horace White and other Independents in supporting the Democratic presidential aspirations of Grover Cleveland. Principle declaredly shaped their decision; the candidacy of Republican James G. Blaine, Godkin assured James Bryce, "is really a conspiracy of jobbers to seize the Treasury, under the lead of a most unprincipled adventurer." (Privately, the *New York Tribune*'s Whitelaw Reid remonstrated with White about the *Evening Post*'s charges against Blaine, pointing out that he knew all about White's whisky speculations while serving in an official capacity during the Civil War.) Cleveland narrowly won the election, but, in editorially supporting him, Godkin contracted a serious libel suit for falsely accusing one of Blaine's clergyman backers of moral turpitude, and a grateful Cleveland paid half his court costs and afterwards entertained the editor and his wife at the White House.

Returning in the early 1880s to New York to live, Godkin set about cultivating friendly relations with influential tycoons in the business world, among them Andrew Carnegie, William C. Whitney, and J. P. Morgan. Frequenting the leading clubs, he spent many hours at the fashionable Century Club. He seldom saw his old patrons Olmsted, Brace, and Norton now, and the bitterness surrounding the election of 1884 put an end to his friendly relations with Whitelaw Reid and Henry Cabot Lodge.

In 1884, now fifty-three, Godkin married thirty-eight-year-old

Katharine B. Sands of the wealthy and socially prominent Sands family of New York and London. A woman of opposite appearance and mien from the statuesque and sociable Fanny Godkin, Katharine Godkin nonetheless made the marriage a successful one. There were no additional children. Lawrence Godkin, a recent graduate of Harvard who lived a bachelor's life at home most of his life, was the only survivor of three children of the editor's first marriage. That fall the Board of Overseers of Harvard, who earlier had assented to the granting to Godkin of an honorary Master of Arts and to his appointment as a Visitor to the College, further honored him by approving his selection as "Lecturer in Free Trade for the year 1884–85."

In the 1880s Godkin began a long friendship with James Bryce. Bryce, a contributor to the *Nation*, was writing his book, *The American Commonwealth* (London: Macmillan, 1888), into which he incorporated many of the views of the *Nation* though not always in the outspoken form in which they originally appeared. When Bryce wrote the acknowledgments to the first edition, he omitted Godkin's name, fearing that it would compromise the book's acceptance in the United States. When Godkin justifiably protested, Bryce promised to acknowledge his friend's help in the second edition. "Indeed," he soothed Godkin, "I may say that I meditated dedicating the book to you."

To Henry Adams

[1 February 1884] (Adams Family Papers, MH)
What shall I say to this? [1]

ELG

1. The terseness of Godkin's question obscures the humor that underlay it. A topic of drawing room speculation during the Gilded Age was the authorship of two brash, anonymous novels satirizing politics and manners, *Democracy* and *The Breadwinners*. Detecting similar crudities of style in them, Charles F. Adams, Jr. one day wrote Godkin to propose that the *Nation* publish his finding that the novels were by the same author. Godkin, who, unknown to Adams, was in on part of the secret of the authorship, at once forwarded the Bostonian's letter to Charles's brother, with the above query scrawled on it. Reading Charles's description of the "coarse, half educated" execution of the novels sent Henry—who with his wife Marian and their bosom friend John Hay had fabricated the literary hoax—into paroxysms of laughter. What Henry, in his glee at having hoodwinked his older brother, did not know was that Godkin relished being on both sides of an intrigue and had long been keeping secret from Henry that it was Charles who wrote the critical review in the *Nation* of Henry's *Albert Gallatin*. But Henry had now come to regard Godkin as a meddlesome and unsafe confidant, and their friendship had cooled.

To Henry C. Lea

New York, February 24 [1884] (Lea Papers, PU)

My dear Mr. Lea: . . . It is not for an old pessimist like myself to gainsay the dismal view you take of the attitude of both the existing parties towards the [civil service] reform. . . . The great difficulty we have to contend with in the Association here is the hopefulness of the members about this person and that.[1]

But the movement does move. The public is getting familiar with the idea as a serious one, and politicians begin to think it is coming. This is a great deal—little as it is.

Yours very truly
ELG

1. A reference to the Civil Service Reform Association of New York, founded in 1880. Among its charter members along with Godkin were George William Curtis, Dorman Eaton, Alexander Mackay-Smith, Silas W. Burt, E. Randolph Robinson, and Everett P. Wheeler. Godkin was chairman of the publication committee.

To Charles Eliot Norton

115 East 25th St., New York, March 13 [1884]
(Norton Papers, MH)

MY DEAR NORTON: I did not answer your letter about the Athletic question, because, to tell the truth, I had not followed the discussion and knew but little about the matter. I turned your letter and the report over to Arthur who had occupied himself with it. . . .[1] From all the talk I have heard among the young men, your task must have been a very difficult one. I saw in one of the papers a story that you had been here at the last Convention on the matter, but I suppose this was not true. . . .

I have again some small expectation of going to England this spring, but as so often before it gets smaller and smaller as the time draws near. I was very glad to hear from Theodora that she and Sally are going over for the summer.[2] Sally will enjoy it immensely.

We are all occupied here with the latest attempt to purify the City Government by giving the Mayor more power. I have been advocating it warmly, but it is about the twenty fifth radical cure for City misgovernment which I have advocated since I came to the United States, and am consequently not much excited about it.

I remain, however, my dear Norton however the City may be governed, the world may go.

Always most faithfully yours
ELG

1. Godkin is referring to the issue of intercollegiate sports at Harvard. See "The Regulation of College Sports," *Nation*, 28 February 1884, pp. 182–83. The author of the piece, Arthur Sedgwick, wrote with ease and clarity; had he put his legal and journalistic talents to better use he would have enjoyed greater prestige. Nonetheless, with Norton and Wendell P. Garrison, he deserves a large share of credit for the success of the *Nation*. In 1909 he gave the Godkin Lectures at Harvard, which when published under the title, *The Democratic Mistake*, encountered criticism from progressives.
2. Sedgwick's unmarried sister, Theodora, and Norton's unmarried daughter, Sally. Norton's deceased wife was a sister of Arthur and Theodora Sedgwick.

To Whitelaw Reid

115 East 25th St., New York [18 May 1884] (Reid Papers, DLC)

MY DEAR MR. REID: . . . You are certainly very generous about your space, I am really ashamed to ask for so much of it for such a purpose, particularly as it will probably draw a terrible blast from Goldwin. . . .[1]

Yours truly
ELG

1. Godkin, who, despite his denials, relished personal combat, was still feuding with Goldwin Smith. See New York *Tribune*, 31 May 1884.

To Charles W. Eliot

115 East 25th St., New York, May 20, 1884 (Eliot Papers, MH)

MY DEAR PRESIDENT ELIOT: If the time were towards the end of October, I think I would undertake the lectures. I understand, however, that they are not to be properly so called controversial, that is, will not have the character of answer to the man on the Protectionist side. . . .[1]

Yours very truly
ELG

1. This letter is in reply to one from President Eliot asking Godkin to deliver some lectures at Harvard on Free Trade. At its September 1884 meeting the Board of Overseers formally approved Eliot's decision to "appoint Edwin L. Godkin Lecturer in Free Trade for the year 1884–85 and Robert E. Thompson Lecturer in Protective Tariffs for the year 1884–85," but the writer has found no evidence that Godkin gave any lectures.

To the Reverend Parsons

115 East 25th St., New York, May 21, 1884 (Hayes Papers, OFH)

MY DEAR PARSONS: I received my copy in due course. Another came to the office today. We will do the right thing by the book for the sake of the church[,] the world, for your sake, and for the sake of "auld lang syne." I was very sorry to have missed you when you were here.

I have been very busy or I would have written sooner.

Yours most sincerely

ELG

To James Bryce

115 East 25th St., New York, June 1, 1884
(Bryce Papers, Oxford University)

MY DEAR BRYCE: I have had hopes, though I confess not strong ones, all the spring that I would see you in London, but again things have not shaped themselves to that end. Villard's break up, introduced some new complications into the affairs of the *Post*, which coupled with Schurz's withdrawal made it necessary I should stick to my post, in more senses than one. . . .[1]

In addition to all these reasons for staying here, is the fact that I am going to be married in a fortnight to Miss Katharine Sands, whom I think you met here one evening—a sister of Mahlon's, who lives in London. . . .

Goldwin Smith has continued to attack me in [a] most discreditable way in his Toronto *Week*. I have again remonstrated with him privately without effect. So I have opened a battery on him in the *Tribune*, where I could write with a better grace over my own name than in the *Post*. I enclose you the first discharge, which I hope you will not consider too savage.

I am much concerned about these dynamite outrages on every ground, but I confess I do not know what the remedy is on this side of the water at least. A prosecution here, under any existing Legislation would not only be futile, but unfortunate for more reasons than I can enumerate and of additional legislation there is no chance that I can see.

The Gladstone Ministry seems at this distance to be laboring in a heavy sea. The Gordon trouble seems to me, to consist chiefly in the fact that they very imprudently sent out a half cracked man to do a very difficult piece of work, and he has suddenly become a martyr on their hands.[2]

The winter has been uneventful politically with us. The condition of business has absorbed most of the public attention. Grant's latest performance has made a terrible sensation, and people are really so much shocked and ashamed that even the newspapers do not like to talk about it.[3] But in my opinion he has been a corrupt man ever since he got the Presidency, and his being found out was only a question of time. Nothing has ever brought home to my mind the evils of war, more forcibly than the fact that it makes a hero of a man like Grant. . . .

Ever faithfully yours
ELG

1. Villard was suffering from a nervous breakdown, and Godkin was trying to get financial control of the *Evening Post*.

2. As this letter was written, General C. G. Gordon (1833–85) with a small Egyptian force was beseiged at Khartoum by the followers of the insurrectionary Mahdi. Public clamor for his rescue prompted a British relief expedition which, after interminable delays, reached Khartoum in January 1885, two days after the fall of the city and its intrepid commander's death. "Chinese" Gordon, contrary to Godkin, seems to have been a man of integrity and purpose.

3. In 1884 the New York banking house to which Ulysses S. Grant had lent his name and his funds went bankrupt under circumstances of fraud with which the too-trusting Grant had no connection. The scandal occurred just as the former president was beginning to suffer from the throat cancer from which he would die in a year. Faced with the alternative of leaving his family virtually penniless, Grant, in a heroic battle with pain, quickly wrote his memoirs, completing them four days before his death.

To Richard Watson Gilder [1]

115 East 25th St., New York, June 9 [1884] (Gilder Papers, NN)

MY DEAR MR. GILDER: I think things are looking as well as possible. If the Democrats nominate Cleveland—as I am in hopes they will, I believe Blaine will be buried under as great a majority in this state as Folger was, and the effect on politics for the next fifty years will be of priceless value.

The Independents are moving for a conference, looking to the calling of a convention immediately after the Democratic nominations. A call for this purpose is now in circulation which it is very desirable you should sign if you have not already done so.

Please send word to R. R. Bowker at *Harper*'s, that you would like your name put to it, if you [are] thus minded.[2]

Do not in your talk or writing give any countenance to Bayard's nomination.[3] Bayard came out for Secession in 1861. It was the error of a young man. but if he were nominated Blaine would pounce on it, and ring charges and very effective ones—on it through the whole campaign. You remember how he answered the Little Rock and Northern Pacific charges in 1876 by calling the Committee "rebel brigadiers."

Yours sincerely
ELG

1. Richard Watson Gilder (1844–1909), the editor of *Century Magazine*. A fellow Mugwump, Gilder was privately critical of Godkin.

2. Publisher Richard R. Bowker (1848–1933) was one of the original Mugwumps.

3. Thomas F. Bayard (1828–98) of Delaware was prominently mentioned for the Democratic nomination in 1884. When Cleveland was elected he made Bayard, against criticism, Secretary of State.

To Charles Eliot Norton

Evening Post Editorial Rooms   New York, August 2, 1884
(Norton Papers, MH)

MY DEAR NORTON: I can truly say that no letter congratulating me on my marriage gave me as much pleasure as yours, because during the last twenty years there has been no one whose friendship in times of trial and suffering has brought me so much comfort, and has left such tender and never to be forgotten associations—and all this in spite of separation or misunderstanding, or anything else that can be called a cloud. . . .

Your old and attached friend.
ELG

To James Bryce

Evening Post Editoral Rooms   New York, October 17 1884
(Godkin Papers, MH)

MY DEAR BRYCE: I have never heard the usefulness of a Second Chamber even discussed here by any one. There seems to be no difference of opinion on the subject. As a matter of fact every state in the Union, the new ones as well as the old thirteen, divides its legislature into two branches. . . .

The value of the Second Chamber in practice, which I think everyone recognizes, lies mainly in the chance it gives for reconsideration, and for bringing public opinion to bear on any particular measure. To appreciate this you must remember that in American legislatures there is very little debating, and most of the work is done in Committee, and excites but little public attention at first. It is consequently comparatively easy to "rush a bill through," the lower and larger house, without attracting observation. By the time it gets to the Senate, however, it is pretty sure to have come to the notice of people interested in it. . . . In fact there is so much, not exactly secrecy, but privacy about American legislation, that all delay is considered useful, particularly when it comes in the form of submission to a new body— even if that body be composed of no better material than the other. As I have said before, I have never heard the matter discussed, but I am satisfied, from the kind of criticism one hears on legislatures in general, that property holders would regard a proposal to legislate by one Chamber with genuine alarm, which would only be allayed by a great increase in the veto power of the governor. . . .

We are in the midst of a bitter and dirty canvas, but I think we shall best the rascals in the bout. The Blaine movement is really a conspiracy of jobbers to seize on the Treasury, under the lead of a most unprincipled adventurer. The majority in Ohio—only 10,000 about, means I think his defeat in New York and Indiana,, and this will be fatal.

Yours ever
ELG

Goldwin Smith has been quiet ever since.

What I say about the similarity in quality of the members of the

two houses, does not apply to the U.S. Senate. There the members of [*sic*] are generally men of mature age and of marked distinction *of some kind in their states.*

To Andrew Carnegie

Evening Post Editorial Rooms   New York, November 7 [1884]
(Carnegie Autograph Collection, NN)

Dear Mr. Carnegie: I am very sorry the result of the election
is not likely to be to your liking, so that I might congratulate
you.[1] But I am sure it is for the good of the country which includes your good as one of its best citizens, so I rejoice over it.

All the more because you may remember you owe me a hat.
I am going to take it in the form of a crush hat which I happen to
need, so you will have the satisfaction of knowing that you are
ministering to my necessities. To save you trouble I will get it,
and send you the bill.

Very sincerely yours
ELG

1. A Blaine supporter, Carnegie disagreed with Cleveland and his supporters on the tariff and other issues.

To James Bryce

115 East 25th St., New York, November 23, 1884
(Bryce Papers, Oxford University)

My dear Bryce: I suppose you take more or less interest in the fight
which has just ended here, and which I think closes the war period
in American politics. It has been a very hard and bitter one, and
was won with great difficulty, and wholly owing, I think to the
Independents and Republican revolters. The nomination of Blaine
was really the final sign that the corrupt element in the party had
got control of the organization, and they had to be resisted just
as you would resist a bunch of thieves. We exposed a great deal
of Blaine's jobbery and corruption, but not *one quarter* of what
came to our knowledge, simply because the proof could not be
presented in a compact readable shape. I do not think you, or any
Englishman could form an idea of the brass with which the fel-

low met the exposures, or of the smallness of the impression they made on the rank and file of the party. A good deal of this was due to the traditional dread of the Democrats left behind by the War—a perfectly unreasoning dread which can only be removed by actual experiment.

We were most troubled by Cleveland's having had an illegitimate child years ago, and the stories based on this, of his continued profligacy. This drew off a great many of the religious people, who, curiously enough, seem to make chastity the greatest of virtues. It has altogether been a very interesting canvas. A great many of the Irish, for the first time I think, left the Democratic party and voted for Blaine, in the belief that he would be more likely to get up a rumpus with England than Cleveland.

Cleveland from all I hear is an excellent man for the crisis. If he turns out well, I think it will break up both the old parties, and I do not think, with a free play of party government—that is with two parties competing on fairly equal terms for popular support either would venture to make such a nomination as Blaine's. But it has been a very narrow escape. We pounded Blaine personally so hard in the *Post* that failure would have put us in a very awkward position.[1]

I see that Abraham Hume of Liverpool is just dead. Had you any relations with him? He was my first Schoolmaster at the Belfast Academy—about 1839–4[0], and was an object of more awe to me that any other human being has ever been. There is a story afloat that Matt. Arnold is going to abandon England, and settle here. Is there any foundation for it? It would be an awful blunder. . . . I read your article on the Second Chamber with much interest. It was excellent, but it rather surprised me that it should be needed. Is there any considerable party that expects to get along with one?

What an awful family scandal this Coleridge affair is! [2]

Yours ever sincerely
ELG

1. Among other accusations, Godkin editorially alleged during the campaign that a clergyman who backed Blaine had been charged with moral turpitude. It was a case of mistaken identity; the clergyman sued Godkin for libel, and Cleveland paid half of the editor's legal fees.

2. A reference to a libel suit against a son of the Lord Chief Justice.

To F. L. Stetson [1]

Evening Post Editorial Rooms   New York, December 16, 1884
(Cleveland Papers, DLC)

MY DEAR MR. STETSON: I think the proposed letter which you showed me, and which I took the liberty of communicating to Mr. White too, is excellent both in matter and manner. The only suggestion I would venture to make is the omission of the apparent recognition of Independent "Claims". . . . I do not believe there are any independents who claim anything or who ask anything from a Democratic administration but good government through Democratic hands. . . .

Therefore I would like to see this letter, as far as may be, and in form at all events, an address of a Democrat to Democrats, and see it deal only with Democratic hopes or fears.

Of the wisdom of a public explanation at this time, nobody of intelligence not an old spoilsman, will, I think, have a doubt. The sooner it comes the more effective it will be. The hopes and illusions of the office holders are rising every day, and so are *the doubts* of Governor Cleveland's well wishers, as to whether he will have the courage and strength to meet them. The time to check these two tendencies is now. . . .

Therefore I wish with all my heart that Mr. Cleveland may see fit to sign the letter and publish it. It will stir the country has [*sic*] it has not been stirred since the war ended.

Yours very truly
ELG

1. Corporation lawyer Francis L. Stetson (1846–1920), the personal counsel of J. Pierpont Morgan, was one of Cleveland's principal advisers, using his influence to persuade the President to support the Trusts and a hard money policy.

To Silas W. Burt

115 East 25th St., New York, February 16, 1885
(Burt Papers, NHi)

MY DEAR COLONEL BURT: White showed me a letter to you this afternoon from him which in most ways expresses my view about

Mr. Manning's going into the Treasury.[1] I do not know him personally, and have never even seen him, and am consequently much in the position of the great body of the public about him. They, I think would not recognize him as one of the chiefs of the Democratic party. . . . They would be apt to say, in fact, that as far as politics was concerned, Mr. Cleveland in giving him a Cabinet position was recognizing his services in the late campaign as an able manager.

Nor is he, associated in the popular mind with finance. I did not know myself until the other day that he was President of a large bank. . . . What helps a Democrat as a political financier in the public eye just now, is, I think, his having some time during the past twenty years having been on the side of sound finance, when his party was rightly or wrongly suspected of unsoundness. McDonald of Indiana, for instance, may have various points of weakness, as far as I know, but his standing up for a good currency against inflation, when his Republican colleague, Morton was gone clean daft about it, would commend him strongly to the public. . . .

Ever truly yours
ELG

1. Cleveland's appointment of Daniel Manning (1831–87), one of his campaign managers, to be Secretary of the Treasury surprised and irritated the Mugwumps. A hard working, unassuming man, Manning was appointed to the cabinet at the behest of Samuel J. Tilden.

To Henry James, Jr.

115 East 25th St., New York, February 17, 1885
(James Family Papers, MH)

MY DEAR JAMES: It may seem strange to you, but it is literally true that I first read the *Nation's* criticism of your father's "Literary Remains" two or three weeks ago, on receiving a remonstrance somewhat like yours, from your brother William. I must confess, too that I read it both with pain and mortification and consequently do not need to report to any of the defences you suggest, such as the detachment of the critic from all such things as "friendliness." I have never recognized this rule, if it exists. Many a time when I could not find a critic to say a good word for a friend's book, I have saved myself by saying nothing at all.

Although as a general rule I read the proofs of the *Nation* carefully, I seldom now take any part in selecting reviewers—leaving it to Garrison except in rare cases. Occasionally the literary side of a whole number escapes me, if I happen to be very busy. During the past month I have been more than usually occupied and in somewhat vexatious way, having taken an office which compels me to supervise the introduction of competitive examinations into the municipal service here.[1] Hence I did not happen to see the review of your father's book, and indeed had not heard of the book, till I got your brother's letter. The tone of the review is as disagreeable to me as you could wish. I am very sorry for it. Among the now long roll of my dead friends, there is hardly one to whose memory it would be more disagreeable to me to be thought wanting in tender respect than his.

I must, however, say this for Garrison, that he gave the book to a man who has done much good work for us, and whom he had every reason to suppose in all ways competent, and that he was not well informed as to my relations with your father. I must also add that when your father wrote his book, I, with the view of securing friendly appreciation, took the task of searching for a reviewer into my own hands, and did it most faithfully, but without success. Nobody possessing the smallest claim to competency would undertake it. Your father's religious philosophy, was, as you know, very subtle and recondite. Few, who could handle it respectfully, liked to handle it at all.

I hope, I do not need to add my dear fellow, that few things in the world could grieve me more than to give you pain and especially pain of this kind. I have followed the trade of a critic for a great many years it is true, but I still have bowels, my friends are still dear to me, dearer than either politics, or literature, or art, and you are one of the best beloved.

Ever affectionately yours
ELG

1. Mayor Grace named Godkin to the civil service advisory commission of New York City, set up to help implement the city's newly-devised civil service rules.

To President-Elect Grover Cleveland

115 East 25th St., New York, February 26, 1885
(Cleveland Papers, DLC)

MY DEAR SIR: I presume the arrangements for putting Mr. Manning in the Treasury are already made, and I should, therefore, not trouble you again with my views about it, if I were not in receipt of communications from Independents in various parts of the country which make it clear that your supporters in the Independent press at least will have some difficulty in putting a good face on the appointment.

In order not to trespass too much on your time I will sum up these communications by saying that I fear it will be insisted on that you have made the appointment partly as a reward for political services in the late canvas, and partly as the beginning of a movement for your reelection. Unfortunately the things for which Mr. Manning is best known will strengthen this impression. His reputation outside the immediate circle of his friends is that of an able political manager simply. One of my correspondents,— a prominent Mugwump, calls him *"The Machine incarnate."*

I do not myself doubt that Mr. Manning's administration will eventually dissipate these fears, but it will take two or three years to do it, and in the meantime a sort of Republican revival may spring up based on them, and we independents may have to go into the Canvas of 1888, seriously, if not fatally discredited.

You will, I am sure, forgive my frankness. It comes from one of your sincerest well wishers. We shall certainly not treat the appointment in the *Evening Post* as a fatal mistake. But I know of no argument which will justify it in the minds of our constituency, and prevent its being a heavy burden for us during a considerable part of your administration. I do not write, I repeat, in the expectation of accomplishing anything more than making you aware beforehand of the difficulty in which the appointment will place some of those who have worked hardest for your election.

In the meantime, however, and always I remain

Most faithfully yours
ELG

To Secretary of the Navy William C. Whitney [1]

115 East 25th St., New York, March 11, 1885
(Whitney Papers, DLC)

MY DEAR WHITNEY: Many thanks for your letter of yesterday. We have no difficulty in standing by the Administration, and shall not have I think. But we got a shower of protests against Manning, which have to be dealt tenderly with. The Mugwumps, you know[,] are a suspicious body. I sincerely trust now all will go on well enough to enable the Democrats to carry this state in the fall, and it can't be done, in my opinion[,] without the shifting vote. So for Heaven's sake don't make any mistakes.

I am glad to hear there will be no trouble about [Morrey] of Miss. I am alarmed, however, at what I hear about W. H. Hurlbert going to Rome. How much there is in it I do not, of course, know, but depend upon it, if anything of the sort is done, it will be a scandal of the first order. . . .[2] He is immensely amusing, but has not a vestige of a character or moral sense, and has not had, to my knowledge, for twenty eight years. It would be an insult to send a man with such a standing at home to any friendly foreign Court. He has during the past two years bilked all the tradespeople near a house he took of the Duke of Sutherland in Scotland. . . . He borrowed money of And. Ripon, about which he (Ripon) wrote to Jones of the *Times*, who answered that to his knowledge Hurlbert never repaid a loan. In fact his going abroad would be a national disgrace, and we, as well as the *Times*, would be compelled very reluctantly to show him up as what he is—an old hardened scamp. For God's sake save us from this.

With best wishes,

Yours most truly
ELG

1. William C. Whitney (1841–1904), a corporate speculator and political manipulator, was, like Manning and Bayard, opposed by reformers when Cleveland made him Secretary of the Navy although he knew virtually nothing about ships. Godkin was cultivating Whitney's friendship for financial reasons.

2. The journalist, William H. Hurlbert, also Hurlbut (1827–95), had incurred the dislike of Godkin as editor of the *New York World*. An able though erratic one-time clergyman, he changed his name from Hurlbut to Hurlbert when an engraver mispelled it on a calling card.

To Daniel S. Lamont [1]

115 East 25th St., New York, March 12, 1885
(Cleveland Papers, DLC)

DEAR COLONEL LAMONT: There are rumours here of a very persistent kind that William Henry Hurlbert formerly of the *World,* is likely to get the mission to Rome. . . . If . . . anything of the kind is contemplated, it will[,] let me say, frankly, constitute a veritable scandal, and would place the *Evening Post* under the very disagreeable necessity of giving reasons for thinking that it would be almost offensive to Italy, and certainly most discreditable to the United States to send a man abroad with such a reputation as Hurlbert has at home. This city swarms with his angry creditors, and I believe they begin to swarm aboard.

I address this to you, not knowing how far the thing may have gone. But if there is anything in it I propose to ask the President and Mr. Bayard most respectfully to allow me to give the reasons why such an appointment is not fit to be made.

Yours very truly
ELG

1. The astute political and financial manager, Daniel S. Lamont (1851–1905), became private secretary to Grover Cleveland during Cleveland's first term and Secretary of War during his second.

To Secretary of State Thomas F. Bayard

[13 March 1885] (Tarsill, p. xxi)

. . . I have known Mr. Hurlbert for twenty-seven years . . . and have never heard anyone . . . who knew him, speak of him without acknowledging his character to be bad. I know of no one who would take his bond on a matter of any importance, or lend him money with the expectation of being repaid. The city swarms with his angry creditors. . . . In short, I do not hesitate to say that the appointment of such a man would be as insulting to the country to which he was sent as it would be discreditable to his own. . . .

To Daniel S. Lamont

March 20, 1885 (Cleveland Papers, DLC)

Confidential

DEAR COLONEL LAMONT: A son of Edwards Pierpont of this city is Secretary of Legation, I think, at Rome.[1] He is a silly dude who was put in the place on his father's account. I hear he now wishes dreadfully to stay, and he and the father are for that purpose "talking Cleveland" up vigorously.

I wish to say to you now for the President's information, that the most indecent and insulting speech about Mr. Cleveland in the canvas was delivered by this same Edwards Pierpont to an audience of Columbia College Republican students. It was so gross in fact, that even they hissed him. To keep any of his kith or kin in office therefore would be to put a premium on blackguardism even if the son were not a born fool.

Truly Yours
ELG

1. Edwards Pierrepont, also Pierpont (1817–92), served as Attorney General of the United States as a Grant Democrat in 1875 and as minister to England 1876–77.

To Everett P. Wheeler

115 East 25th St., New York, March 29, 1885
(James W. Brown Collection, NHi)

DEAR MR. WHEELER: (1.) The proposal to give Mr. Pendleton a dinner commends itself to me.[1]

(2.) I think the dinner should be offered by a Committee of Citizens.

Truly Yours
ELG

1. United States Senator George H. Pendleton (1825–89) introduced the act of 1883 for reforming the civil service that bears his name. The recipient of this letter, New York lawyer Everett P. Wheeler (1840–1925), joined the Civil Service Reform Association of New York in 1880 at Godkin's

request, and four years later he drafted the civil service rules for New York City and was named chairman of the city civil service commission, on which he and Godkin served until Tammany Hall regained power in 1889.

To President Grover Cleveland

Evening Post Editorial Rooms   New York, April 11, 1885
(Cleveland Papers, DLC)

To the President of the United States

DEAR SIR: Allow me to introduce you to my friend Mr. W. J. Stillman, sometime American Consul in Crete, and well known on both sides of the water as an artist and writer.[1] He is seeking redress, preparatory to returning to Europe, for injury done him by the late Administration, in the matter of a dispute with the Turkish government in which the right was I believe wholly on his side. He can prove all this, I believe to your satisfaction by documentary evidence.

I shall be much indebted to you if you can give him a hearing, and a patient consideration of the business he has in hand.

I remain, with great respect,

Very cordially yours
ELG

1. The painter and journalist, William J. Stillman (1828–1901), had been a leading contributor to the *Nation* since 1866, writing mainly on art and archaeology.

To Charles S. Fairchild [1]

Evening Post Editorial Rooms   New York [May 1885]
(Fairchild Papers, NHi)

MY DEAR MR. FAIRCHILD: The enclosed comes to us from a respectable source. Would it be trespassing too much on your kindness and your time to ask you to read it and tell me whether this [has] anything in it, and if so, how much. I do not want the *Post* to be made the vehicle of carping, or untrustworthy criticism,

JUNE 9, 1885

and yet, we can hardly afford to say nothing about things which are really departures from the straight and narrow way.

Very truly yours
ELG

1. Charles S. Fairchild (1842–1924), was at this time assistant U.S. Secretary of the Treasury, succeeding Daniel Manning two years later as Secretary.

To C. A. Spofford [1]

Evening Post Editorial Rooms   New York, June 9, 1885
(Villard Papers, MH)

DEAR MR. SPOFFORD: The state of the case is that I am looking to some money from real estate in New Haven, under the settlement of an estate, which would enable me to pay the note in full, but it drags along as such things are apt to do, and I am unable to name any date about it. . . .[2]

Yours very truly
ELG

1. C. A. Spofford served as assistant to Godkin's employer, Henry Villard, in which capacity he found it his onerous duty to send Godkin—who criticized others for not meeting their obligations—frequent reminders that he was delinquent on his note to Mrs. Villard.

2. Godkin is referring here to the settlement of the Foote estate, through which he expected to come into money through decedent relatives of his first wife.

To Moncure D. Conway [1]

Evening Post Editorial Rooms   New York, July 8, 1885
(James W. Brown Collection, NHi)

MY DEAR MR. CONWAY: I was very sorry to have missed your visit to Bon Repos, as there are many things I should wish to talk to you about.[2] But I hope you will make *us* a visit before long in our hotel.

We are very full of matter such as it is here in the *Post*, so that I could, at present at least, say nothing about permanent and regular contributions from you, but I think if you are open to irregular calls, you may be of great occasional use to us. I shall bear it in mind.

Horace White is here, having just returned from his sad trip to the West.[3] He is well, and sends his remembrances, and desires me to say that he wrote to you some days ago, I think to Philadelphia.

Very sincerely yours

ELG

Rev. M. D. Conway

1. Moncure Conway had recently returned to the United States from a twenty-year pastorate in England.

2. Bon Repos was an antique summer hotel at Premium Point on Long Island Sound that Henry Holt leased to the Godkins between 1884 and 1890 for them to use as a residence when they were not in their New York City apartment.

3. White's wife had died.

To James Russell Lowell

New Rochelle, N. Y., July 8, 1885 (Autograph File, MH)

MY DEAR LOWELL: I was very glad indeed to see your handwriting again, and gladder still to find that there was a chance of seeing you in New York, and saying welcome home, as I was not able to go on to Cambridge to Commencement, as I had hoped.[1]

We are living for the second summer, in what once was a hotel out here on the very edge of the water, with lots of room, if little use, an hour from town. . . .

We are expecting the Gurneys soon, It would be indeed delightful if we could get you both here together.

If you come direct to New York by night boat, as you may, I am at the *Evening Post* office till 1:30 p.m., when I come out here, and you might come with me.

I should enjoy a talk with you "awfully," and want to make you acquainted with my wife.

Yours ever,

Yours ever,
ELG

1. Lowell had returned to the United States after eight years abroad in diplomatic posts. The close of his English stay was saddened by the death of his wife.

To I. Wayne MacVeagh

Evening Post Editorial Rooms   New York, July 30, 1885
(MacVeagh Papers, PHi)

Confidential

My dear MacVeagh: Lawrence has been offered a (favorable) chance of going into the U. S. District Attorney's office under Dorsheimer. I would like him to take it. . . .[1]

The reasons against his taking it, and which he considers strong, are, that it would be called by the newspapers payment to me for my support of the Administration. . . .

In looking about for a candid and well informed friend to advise us in this juncture, you will be sorry to hear that I have fixed on you. Will you kindly tell me what you think of the matter from all points of view. . . .

Yours very cordially
ELG

1. A reference to the editor's son, Lawrence Godkin (1860–1929). Instead, young Godkin joined the New York law firm headed by his father's acquaintance, Everett P. Wheeler.

To C. A. Spofford

Evening Post Editorial Rooms   New York, August 6, 1885
(Villard Papers, MH)

Dear Sir: I am very sorry to say I must again ask for a postponement in the matter of Mrs. Villard's Claim. The transaction to which I referred before is not completed owing to things useless to mention, and I must ask a still further margin of a few weeks. I hope not over two.

Yours truly
ELG

To Professor Francis J. Child

New Rochelle, N. Y., October 6 [1885] (Child Papers, MH)

MY DEAR CHILD: I got a letter from you early in the summer which was almost pathetic in its friendliness and yet which I have never answered. I do not know what you have thought of this. But the truth was, my dear fellow, that it [peeved?] me to think that you thought it necessary to excuse yourself for not having been more demonstrative in proving to me how kindly you felt towards me. . . .

With best remembrances to Mrs. Child and the young people to whom I hope, I am still something of a memory, believe me now [and] always

Your affectionate friend
ELG

To James Bryce

115 East 25th St., New York, November 2, 1885
(Bryce Papers, Oxford University)

MY DEAR BRYCE: . . . I have been several times during the summer on the point of writing to you, if for no other reason, in order to find out whether you held to your earlier impression about Stead of the *Pall Mall*, and his "revelations." To me, from the very beginning the *Spectator*'s ground as to the enormous mischief the thing would do . . . has seemed to me the true one. . . . You have, however, been used a good deal here against the *Nation*'s view, and I shall be glad to hear whether you have held out in thinking Stead a philanthropist.[1]

Our politics though interesting enough to the observer on the spot are so much less stirring than yours, that I shall say nothing about them, except that I think all signs point to a split of some kind in the Democratic party owing to Cleveland's steadiness in his adhesion to his Civil Service policy. Our election tomorrow will be a bad blow to him, if his party wins, and yet he has to appear to desire its success.[2]

I suppose the pace in England does not seem so swift to people on the spot. From this distance, you seem to be going into democracy at full gallop. What is "the true inwardness" of the Dilke affair? How does the British public deal with the chastity question in public life.[3]

As to myself personally, I am jogging on in the old way. . . . Schurz, I am sorry to say, is going to try another newspaper venture, by the purchase of the Boston *Post*, a moribund Democratic sheet, which he thinks he can resuscitate, but in which I am quite sure he will make another failure. His strength lies in his oratory, but he has no money and consequently cannot stick to this in a dignified way.

Lawrence, I am glad to say, has been lifted out of that dreadful slough of despond, a young lawyer's "waiting for business," by a very advantageous offer of a partnership, from one of the leading firms here, Wheeler and Cortis. . . .[4] So if it comes in your way to know any one who wants any legal matters attended to on this side of the water, I should be glad if you would mention the firm.

When are you coming again? How goes *Justinian?* Remember me to any of the Northern Pacifiers you see—particularly Pell, and Grey, and Davey, and the good Rathbone.[5]

Yours as ever most faithfully
ELG

1. William T. Stead (1849-1912), the nonconformist editor of the *Pall Mall Gazette*, had entered on a crusade against the luring into prostitution of young girls in England. Although his lurid articles helped hasten the passage of protective legislation, they did not meet with widespread approval, and Stead eventually served a related three-month prison term. L. T. Brown, a female acquaintance of Mrs. Godkin, protested Godkin's editorial posture toward Stead and expressed to Godkin the hope that the *Evening Post* would push for a society in which men would be "shamed into the same standard of morality that they require of women." (L. T. Brown to Godkin, 26 Nov 1885, Godkin Papers.) Stead, who later made

a sensation in the United States with his muckraking book, *If Christ Came to Chicago*, died in the *Titanic* disaster.

2. A reference to the New York mayoralty election, won by the anti-Tammany candidate William R. Grace.

3. The prominent Liberal M.P., Sir Charles Dilke (1843–1911), found his career nearly destroyed when he was named correspondent in a lurid divorce action. Godkin, a moralist in public affairs, did not attach major importance to sexual chastity. With all his faults, concluded William Dean Howells, he was "no prig."

4. As junior partner in Wheeler, Cortis, and Godkin, the younger Godkin handled legal affairs of the *Evening Post*. Later he formed his own firm, Godkin and Chadbourne.

5. A reference to four members of Parliament whom Godkin met on the 1883 Northern Pacific trip: Albert Pell (1820–1907), Horace (subsequently Lord) Davey 1833–1907), Albert (subsequently 4th Earl) Grey (1851–1917), and William Rathbone (1819–1902). Godkin remained on warm terms with Pell throughout his lifetime.

To Daniel S. Lamont

115 East 25th St., New York, November 7, 1885
(Cleveland Papers, DLC)

DEAR COLONEL LAMONT: Will you kindly tell me when Mr. Trenholm is coming in here, and what his address is now? [1] I want much to have him dine with me on his arrival, and meet some of the Civil Service brethren. We have very good news from the custom house this morning about the result of the examination. At the head of the list stands a disabled soldier, Mr. O'Brien, who has already served in the Treasury, and here as an inspector and assistant weigher. He is also a Catholic, and served in the 69th Regt. A better man to stop the mouths of carpers could not have been created, if Providence had got one up for the occasion, and I believe the Statute makes his appointment compulsory.

Yours very truly
ELG

1. William L. Trenholm (1836–1901), a South Carolina business man, had just been appointed United States Civil Service Commissioner by Cleveland.

To President Grover Cleveland

New York, November 10, 1885 (Cleveland Papers, DLC)

His Excellency, Grover Cleveland,
President of the United States

MY DEAR SIR: I use a type-writer in addressing you to save you trouble as my handwriting is apt to be somewhat puzzling.

Colonel Burt has shown me your letter of the 8th inst. in which there are two or three allusions to me, as well as to the Civil Service Reformers with whom I am connected in this part of the country, which I think warrant me in troubling you with a few words of explanation with regard to Mr. Dorman B. Eaton. . . .[1]

You express great astonishment at the opinion of Mr. Eaton communicated by Colonel Burt and myself to Mr. Lamont at our late interview. I think this not unnatural. But let me now say that I have for years regarded Mr. Eaton as a very impracticable [sic] and wrong-headed person who was singularly unfit to represent the cause of Civil Service Reform either to the government or the country. . . . I knew well that he was afflicted to a remarkable degree with the conceit of being a very practical man engaged in the arduous work of making the theories of some visionary persons acceptable to politicians. This led him constantly to represent to us that he was doing wonders in Washington in keeping the President from jumping over the traces. This was harmless enough. What was not harmless however, was his frequently making and even suggesting relaxations, remissions, and compliances in the application of the rules, either by way of ingratiating himself personally with the powers that be—which is what the uncharitable say—or, as I think, with the mistaken notion that he would thereby strengthen the reform in the eyes of practical politicians. I am satisfied that he had in this way done a good deal of mischief. We knew this was going on all along, but we had no remedy. I am sure you will see on reflection how illadvised [sic] it would have been for us to come out and denounce one of our most prominent men.

You refer to my bringing him with me as a representative of Civil Service Reform when I called on you to urge Mr. Pearson's re-appointment.[2] I brought him to bear witness, as one acquainted with the details, to the kind of work Mr. Pearson had been doing in the New York Post Office through the competitive exams. . . .

As regards the sending in of the whole eligible list in the weighership case or in any other case, I can assure you that nothing can be farther from our thoughts than treating any difference of opinion with you on it as a sign of want of sincerity on your part. . . .

But I must take leave most respectfully, to represent to you that although you may not think it advisable to press the competitive feature of the Civil Service examination on public attention . . . it is in my mind and in that of all my friends here, of the very essence of reform. . . . If you now sanction the submission of the whole eligible list to the appointing officer in a few prominent cases like weighership, on the ground that the necessary qualifications cannot be ascertained by competition, it will not only be received by all the enemies of reform as a complete justification of their opposition, but will furnish Congress with a basis of an attack on it which would probably result in the restoration of the old system. . . .

I am the more strenuous in dwelling on this because much as the reform now owes to you and will doubtless continue to owe, its permanence does not depend on your support alone. If your successor should be unfriendly, or a hostile majority in Congress should find suitable precedents or arguments in your administration of it, for treating competition as unnecessary or mischievous, it would be swept away completely at once. The contempt and ridicule with which Mr. Beattie, the Surveyor here, is openly talking about it shows how bold its opponents have already become, and how confidently they are counting on its near overthrow.

Pardon the freedom and length of these remarks. They come, let me assure you, from one of your sincerest friends and admirers.

I remain, with great respect,

Your faithful Servant
ELG

1. The widely known authority on civil service rules, Dorman B. Eaton (1823–99), drafted the first Federal civil service law in the United States,

the Pendleton Act. Cleveland found the objections of Godkin and Burt to his reappointment to the United States Civil Service Commission quixotic.

2. Godkin was successful in his plea to Cleveland to reappoint Republican Henry G. Pearson postmaster of New York City. When Pearson, who succeeded the reforming Conkling appointee, Thomas L. James, died, Godkin served as one of his pallbearers and delivered his memorial address. See E. L. Godkin, "Henry G. Pearson," a Memorial Address Delivered in New York, 21 June 1894 (privately printed for the Civil Service Commission of New York), 21 pp.

To Silas W. Burt

Evening Post Editorial Rooms   New York, November 13 [1885]
(Burt Papers, NHi)

MY DEAR BURT: I do not feel so gloomy as you. . . . Moreover White has had a letter from Trenholm, in which he says distinctly this thing "will never be repeated." The President was entrapped into it, I think by Eaton, and is sorry. Eaton thought it was a fine stroke of work to give up competition for the sake of an examination, not seeing that it would be far better for us to have no examination at all than one which could be treated, or would be considered by the public, a sham. We must get him out of office, and get rid of him in his representative capacity.

Look in today, if you have time.

Yours
ELG

To James Russell Lowell

115 East 25th St., New York, November 18, 1885
(Lowell Papers, MH)

MY DEAR LOWELL: I have been asked by a Mrs. R. Thurber here to endorse her in some undertaking, of a public kind, not necessary to describe here. I never knew her, or indeed heard of her, until yesterday. But she says, she is an intimate friend of yours; that she stayed with you when she went to London, and that you advise her confidentially in times of doubt or hesitation in her work, and always come to see her when you pass through here. Her forte is music in which she is much interested and to the cultivation of which, she, being rich, contributes freely.

May I trouble you to tell me what you know about her, and how much confidence you place in her statements. I ask because some of them seem to me to need justification.

> Yours as ever
> ELG

Telegram to Henry C. Lea

> *Evening Post*   New York, November 19, 1885
> (Telegram, Lea Papers, PU)

What is feeling among your reformers about Huidekoper's removal? [1] Answer promptly if possible.

> ELG

1. The businessman and National Guard general, Henry S. Huidekoper (1839–1918), was postmaster of Philadelphia from 1880 until 1885 when Cleveland removed him to make way for a Democrat. Lea wired back to Godkin: "We regard it as a lamentable exhibition of weakness and an unjustifiable blow at reform."

To President Grover Cleveland

> 115 East 25th St., New York, November 21, 1885
> (Cleveland Papers, DLC)

MY DEAR SIR: I enclose you a letter which has been lying on my table since the beginning of Summer, and which will probably please and most certainly amuse you. It was from a lady of high position in Rhode Island.[1]

With great respect—

> Yours faithfully
> ELG

His Excellency, The President

1. The letter was from Anna Pell of Rhode Island asking Godkin to urge President Cleveland, for his well-being and that of the country, to do something about his weight.

To Francis Parkman [1]

December 14, 1885 (Ogden 2:131–32)

MY DEAR PARKMAN: I have just finished your "Wolfe and Montcalm," and I cannot help doing what I have never done before,—write to tell the author with what delight I read it. I do not think I have been so much enchained by a historical book, although I was passionately fond of history in my boyhood. Wolfe, too, was one of my earliest heroes, and although I have been familiar for over forty years with his story, I became almost tremulous with anxiety about the result of the night attack when reading your account of the final preparations, a few evenings ago.

What became of Montcalm's family? Has he any descendants now? What a pathetic tale his is!

Also, considering the fearful memories that war must have left in the colonies, and the horror of the French it must have inspired, was not the alliance with and liking of them twenty years—only twenty—later most extraordinary?

Thank you most sincerely for a great pleasure.

Yours very sincerely
ELG

1. Francis Parkman (1823–93) sometimes contributed to the *Nation*. Godkin became acquainted with the historian at Norton's home in 1863.

To Mr. Olin

Evening Post Editorial Rooms New York, January 2, 1886
(Copy, Reid Papers, DLC)

MY DEAR SIR: Mr. Higgins seems to be under a misapprehension about the controversy of the *Evening Post* with Mr. Allen Thorndike Rice. . . .[1] The *Post* has never said that *no* Republicans were disfranchised by the tax laws of Delaware, or that these tax laws were not badly, or injudiciously administered. . . .

What we controverted was Mr. Rice's assertion that the taxes in Delaware were collected in such a way as "to disqualify Republicans in general," and "that a *very large part of the citizens of Delaware* belonging to one of the great political parties, are as *thoroughly disfranchised* by legal chicanery as any community of negroes *ever were* disfranchised by physical intimidation". . . .

I return the MSS herewith, and hope it will appear in Delaware and do good.

Yours very truly
ELG

1. Allan Thorndike Rice (1853–89) since 1876 had been editor and proprietor of the *North American Review*.

To Anthony Higgins

Evening Post Editorial Rooms   New York, January 12 [1886]
(Reid Papers, DLC)

DEAR SIR: I cannot print your letter, and definitely refuse to do so, for the reasons assigned in my note to Mr. Olin.

I will now add that your second letter addressed to me shows that you still do not understand what the controversy of the *Evening Post* with Mr. Rice was about. I repeat to you that the *Post* never said, directly or indirectly that no Republicans were disfranchised in Delaware by the tax laws.

"The point of our comparison" . . . was . . . but to show *that Mr. Rice had been guilty of gross exaggeration at least, and probably of wholesale falsehood.* . . .

We said nothing about fraud I again tell you. We simply said the effect of a fraud could not have been what Rice said it was, or the census returns showed. This makes your observations on "Modern Ethics" etc. at least irrelevant. I might use a stronger term, but I forebear. . . .

Yours truly
ELG

To James Bryce

Lenox, Mass., February 16 [1886]
(Bryce Papers, Oxford University)

MY DEAR BRYCE: Your last letter . . . . found me on the point of answering the former one, in which you ask for sources of information about the Tweed Ring. The best I can do for you is to send you five pamphlets herewith, taken from our archives, and now very scarce. May I ask you to return them without fail, as we could not easily replace them? . . . When do you expect your American book to appear? [1]

As to the correspondence. I knew of course when I saw your appointment, on which I most heartily congratulate both you and Gladstone—that you could not keep it up. It so happened that just that day I received an application for something of the kind from Hill, late of the *D. N.* . . .[2] I know he is a good writer. . . . I have never seen him though his wife is an old friend of mine, so that I have only a very vague notion of his personality. If you think well of him, and have no one else to suggest, I should accept him. . . .

I am very glad you liked my article.[3] I was greatly disappointed in Maine's book. I have enjoyed all his others so much. The amount of loose thinking and talking in it is very remarkable. . . . it is so hard to get the English mind to take in, and *keep in* all the conditions of the Irish problem. I hear Goldwin Smith is starting for England, in a regular Hibernophobic fury. I fear he and Froude and Tyndall will break out into Civil War, before Parliament has time to act. . . . The talk of . . . more coercion has become amusing. . . . I was particularly diverted by seeing that Old Earl Grey views the state of Ireland "with considerable alarm."

What you say about the teachableness of American voters is a large subject. All I meant to say was that they are not teachable by stump orators and candidates for office, or by any one in the political arena. . . . Let me remind you, too, that the Mugwumps owed their strength, not to their superior wisdom or morality, but to that close division of the parties which in some important states enabled a few to turn the scale. On the *mass* of the Republican party our exposures of Blaine made not the slightest impression.

I am glad to see that Russell and Davey are in. I am sorry for, but hopeful about Morley.[4] I see from the collection of his Irish articles lately published that he knows about Thomas Drummond, the Irish Secretary in 1835, a model man for the place, whose early death was one of the greatest of the Irish misfortunes since the Union. . . .

With regard to your most kind expression of friendly feeling to me, let me just say, my dear fellow, that I have considered you, ever since I first set eyes on you, one of the most delightful of friends and companions, separation from whom by the ocean I consider one of the misfortunes of my life. You cannot say anything expressive of regard that I do not reciprocate twice over. I first knew and admired you through the *Holy Roman Empire*—what an introduction! [5]

> Yours ever
> ELG

1. *The American Commonwealth.*

2. Gladstone had appointed Bryce undersecretary of foreign affairs, necessitating his resignation as London correspondent of the *Nation*. Thereupon a former London correspondent of the *Nation*, Frank H. Hill (1830–1910), the recently ousted editor of the *Daily News*, returned to the post. During Godkin's early Belfast days he was friendly with Mrs. Hill, who was then unmarried.

3. E. L. Godkin, "An American View of Popular Government." *Nineteenth Century* 19 (February 1886): 177–90. An acquaintance of Godkin later to be a Liberal cabinet minister, Lord Carrington, also read Godkin's critique of Sir Henry Maine's *Popular Government* and pronounced it to Godkin "the most interesting" paper he had seen on the subject. Carrington to Godkin, 28 March 1886, Godkin Papers.

4. When the Liberals returned to power briefly under Gladstone in February 1886, Sir Charles Russell (1832–1900) became Attorney General; Horace Davey, Solicitor General; and John Morley (1838–1923) got the unenviable post of Irish Secretary. Russell was with Davey on Villard's 1883 Northern Pacific expedition, and there formed an acquaintanceship with Godkin that continued throughout their lives. Godkin first met Morley in New York during the 1860s.

5. Bryce, best known to Americans for his book, *The American Commonwealth*, first attracted attention as an historian in 1864 with his *Holy Roman Empire*.

To Daniel S. Lamont

Evening Post Editorial Rooms   New York, April 3, 1886
(Cleveland Papers, DLC)

DEAR COLONEL LAMONT: Will you kindly call the President's attention to the inclosed Pamphlet. I believe the facts and arguments it contains are unanswerable.

Yours truly
ELG

To William C. Whitney

April 18, 1886 (Whitney Papers, DLC)

MY DEAR WHITNEY: Has it ever come in your way to speak to Mr. Payne again about the matter of the stock? The chance of getting full hold of the paper is a good one which may pass away, and which is very important to me, and any help I could get on it from a good quarter would be very welcome.[1] When shall you be in town again?

Yours very sincerely
ELG

1. While Godkin was vainly trying to persuade Whitney, whom privately he found "a bad fellow," to help him get control of the *Evening Post*, his relations with his employer were deteriorating as he procrastinated in making payments on his overdue note to Mrs. Villard. To try to make sure Godkin would make his payments in the future, a new note was drawn up and given to the treasurer of the *Evening Post* Company, Wendell P. Garrison, to hold.

To James Bryce

Bon Repos, New Rochelle, N. Y., May 28, 1886
(Bryce Papers, Oxford University)

MY DEAR BRYCE: I have just been reading what seems to be a verbatim report of your speech in the *Times*, and I want, without delay to offer you my heartiest Congratulations on it. . . .

It is a great historic fight, and you are playing your part in it splendidly.[1]

I have never known anything short of a great war, watched with as much eagerness here, as this struggle is. People's sympathies as far as my observation goes, are overwhelmingly with Gladstone. Even those who do not like the Irish are amazed by his pluck and vigor. But you must remember also, that the crisis is of immense interest to Americans, because the reconciliation of the Irish with England, will have a marked influence on American politics. It will certainly for instance, make it impossible for Blaine to get the Irish vote in 1888. That the Irish here, except the small criminal faction, will be completely satisfied and pacified by the bill, you may rest assured. . . .

I have written an article in the *XIX Century*, which you will perhaps have seen before this reaches you, on American experience in the matter of home rule. . . .[2]

You have got one of our greatest bores over there in the person of Dr. Holmes.[3] Keep him long I beg. . . .

With best wishes for yourself, and unlimited admiration for the G. O. M.[4] believe me, my dear fellow, to remain

Ever affectionately yours
ELG

1. The "great historic fight" was the struggle for Home Rule for Ireland that the Gladstone government was waging in Parliament.

2. E. L. Godkin, "American Home Rule," *Nineteenth Century* 19 (June 1886): 793–806; reprinted in part in 1887 as the lead article in the *Handbook of Home Rule*, ed. James Bryce (London, 1887).

3. The aging Oliver Wendell Holmes (1809–94) was making a triumphal journey through the British Isles. Holmes had long disliked Godkin and the *Nation*.

4. The initials G. O. M. stood for the "Grand Old Man," Gladstone.

To Theodora Sedgwick

Bon Repos, New Rochelle, N. Y., July 4, 1886
(Godkin Papers, MH)

MY DEAR THEODORA: It was very kind of you to write me about poor Mr. Gurney. We have heard a few times about him from

Mrs. Gurney. . . .[1] I would have run in to see him, but was afraid it would only be an additional tax on them both, and we hope to look in on them at Beverly later.

Many thanks from both of us for your kind reminder of "the room that is always ready". . . . We are planning the Adirondacks with a glimpse of Lenox in August, and intend to take the Gurneys for a day or two on our way home, and if you are either at Ashfield or on the sea shore will look you up also. . . . I am troubled all the time by the feeling that I am dropping out of the memory of my Cambridge friends, and you know what a place among them your household has always occupied. Give my warmest remembrances to your Aunts Anne and Grace.[2] They are both among my best memories of *Auld lang syne*.

I do not know that I have any news of myself worth relating. In the life of what is called "a hardworking journalist," *les jours se suivent et resemblent* [*sic*].I am enjoying this summer home, and the early escape it gives from New York, and the quiet nights enormously.

I have been following Gladstone's fortunes with almost as much anxiety as if they were my own, not so much because I think there is any doubt about the way the home rule struggle will end, or because I cannot bear to see him beaten after so gallant a fight, and end his days in defeat. Not never a better man ever figured in the political arena. All the others are, as somebody said of the best of Louis XIV's generals—"la monnaie de Turenne."

> Ever affectionately yours
> ELG

1. Professor Gurney, unknown to his physician and family, was dying of pernicious anemia.

2. During the Gilded Age, the maiden sisters Anne and Grace Ashburner were popular hostesses to gatherings in their home adjacent to that of Professor Child on Kirkland Street near the Harvard Yard. Along with Child's, Lowell's, Longfellow's, and Norton's. "Miss Ashburner's" (for the dominant sister, Anne) was, in the unpublished testimony of William Dean Howells, where one expected to meet "whoever was most interesting or distinguished in Cambridge society." Godkin spent much time there in the 1870s.

To Silas W. Burt

Evening Post Editorial Rooms   New York, July 8 [1886]
(Burt Papers, NHi)

DEAR BURT, I want to see you about a letter I have had from Vilas, making a proposal which it will be difficult for me to decline.[1] Can you call tomorrow about 12. m.?

Yours ever
ELG

1. William F. Vilas (1840–1908) was Cleveland's Postmaster General. He had written Godkin to answer criticisms of his department by the *Evening Post* and to invite Godkin to come to Washington and see the "facts" for himself.

To Postmaster General William F. Vilas

New York, July 15, 1886 (Vilas Papers, WHi)

Hon. William F. Vilas

MY DEAR SIR: I have been seriously considering the plan of going to Washington, in compliance with your very frank and obliging invitation, to examine the papers relating to the various dismissals which have taken place among the clerks in the Railway Mail Service. . . .

But I do not feel as if I ought to put you to this trouble without going a little more fully into the charges made in the article in the *Evening Post* of which you complain. . . .

As to the removals I do not doubt that they have been made, as you say, in every case, or nearly every case, for "offensive partisanship." . . . But in everything I have ever said or written on this subject I am sure I have, either impliedly or expressly, assumed that in removing a man even for offensive partisanship care would be taken that the service should not suffer in the process; that is, that the offensive partisan, if an efficient officer in other respects, would be retained until a proper substitute for him was found. . . . the *Evening Post* has not complained, or certainly has not intended to complain, of any removals *per se* in the Railway Mail Department or any other branch of the service. If you will kindly look at the article again you will see that the chief complaint made in it is that the "politicians were allowed to get in the mail cars," or in other words that the public had been suffering, not because certain clerks had been dismissed, but because unfit persons had been put in their places.

During the past year we have been in receipt of a greatly increased number of complaints from our subscribers at distant points, of irregularities in the delivery of their paper. . . . due to some mistake or shortcoming in the railway mail service. . . . I learnt on testimony, that thus far I find no reason to doubt, that the filling of vacancies in the railway service has in this State at least, been divided among democratic [sic] Congressmen, and in republican [sic] districts given to Mr. Samuel J. Tilden, Jr. I cannot discover that in making the recommendations for appointment any of these gentlemen have, as a rule, paid any regard whatever to the fitness of the nominees. I have heard of one case in which a man was put to distribute the newspaper sacks on the various stations on the Hudson River Railroad who had . . . previously been employed with a wheelbarrow in the works of the new Groton Aqueduct, and was unable to read correctly the tags on the sacks. . . . Many such appointments I am told have been the work of Mr. Stallknecht; others that of Mr. Tilden, Jr.

. . . If you should be willing to offer me any evidence in refutation of my position with regard to the manner of the appointments I shall be very much indebted to you, and will gladly go to Washington to receive it.

Let me add that I was much surprised by your doubts as to feasibility of placing the railway mail service under the Civil Service rules. . . . Had there been an examination such persons as a wheelbarrow man of whom I have spoken would never have been allowed to engage in the duty of delivering mail parcels in rapid trains.

I do not need to assure you that I would not venture to speak with so much freedom were I not a warm friend of the Administration, most sincerely anxious for its success and engaged almost daily in praising or defending it.

I remain, dear Sir, very sincerely yours

ELG

To Postmaster General William F. Vilas

Nation Office   New York, July 29, 1886 (Vilas Papers, WHi)

My DEAR SIR: I have to acknowledge with many thanks, your letter of the 18th inst. I will endeavor on my return from my holiday, on which I am just starting, to give you the facts of the cause of incompetency in the Railway Mail Service in this State, which I mentioned in a former communication. What you say with regard to Mr. Stallknecher's [*sic*] and Mr. Tilden's appointments certainly seem an answer to the information I had received in that regard.

But let me say most respectfully, that it is to me incomprehensible that, considering what the customs and traditions of political life have been for the last fifty years, you should expect any Member of Congress, ever to look on an invitation to fill an office with a nominee, as anything but an invitation to use the place for his own benefit politically. As this is the very practice against which the friends of Civil Service reform have all along been fighting, its maintenance in full vigor by the Administration in one most important branch of the public service is, of course a heavy blow and great discouragement.

I have consulted several experts here as to the difficulties, if any, in the way of creating eligible lists for the Railway Mail Service, and an answer I have received from Colonel Burt of the Custom House seems to me so important, that I submit it for your consideration, with the request that you will kindly return it.

Let me add that I am taking the liberty of showing your letters in a private way, to some of our friends here, as an illustration of the spirit in which you are doing your work, and they certainly cause us all the greatest gratification. I am very sure that, however we may differ about some details, you are striving in the right direction.

Yours very sincerely
ELG

To the Earl Spencer [1]

Bon Repos, New Rochelle, N.Y., September 5, 1886
(Godkin Papers, MH)

MY LORD: I send you with great pleasure, by this mail a copy of the reports of the select committee of Congress appointed in 1872 to inquire into the condition of the Southern States.

It is the only trustworthy and really detailed account I know of, of the state of things brought about by the "Carpet-Bag" governments. . . .

There is also a very interesting account of the condition of South Carolina under the negro rule, written about the same period by a Mr. Pike, which I find is out of print. But I think I can purchase a copy, and if so will send it to you. . . .

I am very glad indeed to hear that my suggestion that Irish disorders are rather a product of human nature in general working under certain conditions, than of Irish nature, seemed to you worthy of consideration. . . .

Mr. Goldwin Smith set this forth very cleverly a few years ago in his excellent little book, "Irish History and Irish Character" which judging from his recent tirades, he seems to have forgotten all about.

It would in my judgment too have been far better for Irish character from the political point of view, to have kept the Irish absolutely disenfranchised than to have given them the vote and representation without power. . . . As soon as the sense of responsibility comes through the accumulation of property they do very well. The Mayors of both New York and Boston just now are Irish Catholics and are the best that either city had for years. In fact Mayor Grace is the best in forty years, or since universal suffrage was introduced.[2]

I had not intended when I began to trespass on you with so long a letter, but the subject is so very interesting and tempting that I trust you will forgive me. I shall gladly furnish you any further information you may desire, and am

faithfully yours
ELG

1. The Earl Spencer (1835–1910) was Lord President of the Council. Later he was mentioned as a successor to Gladstone.

2. A reference to millionaire shipping magnate William R. Grace (1832–1904). The founder of Grace Lines, he was dubbed the "pirate of Peru" because of his stranglehold over the economy of that South American country.

To Frederick Sheldon

New Rochelle, N. Y., September 19, 1886 (Godkin Papers, MH)

MY DEAR SHELDON: Thanks for the C. B. and Q. cheque just received. . . .[1]

I am waiting Villard's arrival in a week or two to push on the affair I spoke to you of. Negotiation by letter was too difficult. I will advise you when anything more happens. Pierpont Morgan seems at present disposed to behave handsomely, *but this is strictly confidential.* The greatest difficulty with him is the fear of having it known. He thinks it might bother him in financial circles.[2]

We had a month in the Adirondacks, where I saw Cleveland and Madame twice and got a very pleasant impression of her.[3] She is unquestionably working the Second term on "the good American" track, refusing to admit that anything—even women's clothes—are better in Paris than in Buffalo. As the parson in Lenox said, in his sermon on his return from his first European trip—"Europe is all very well, but it is nothing to the Kingdom of Heaven."

On getting home, I found the Sedgwick scandal, which as a tragi-comedy beats all my experience. I am afraid it has foundation, but must have been grossly exaggerated. It has however, ruined him as a diplomatist. It was a chance, which like other chances, he has thrown away. Bayard made a fool of himself in sending him. It was not necessary, and mortally offended the Minister and Consul in Mexico. He is due—Sedgwick I mean—in New York this week; but how he will face Father in law Tuckerman, I don't know.[4]

When do you come to town?

Yours sincerely
ELG

1. Frederick Sheldon was a Providence, Rhode Island, patron of Godkin who, at Godkin's behest, took shares in the *Evening Post* in 1881; evidently Sheldon and Godkin held some stock in the Chicago, Burlington, and Quincy Railroad.

2. Godkin, who already had more than $15,000 outstanding in loans from J. P. Morgan, was trying to persuade him to buy the *Evening Post* from Villard. When Villard learned of his editor-in-chief's negotiations with the controversial financier he suggested that Godkin had adjourned his principles. On Godkin's death Morgan helped endow the Godkin Lectures at Harvard University.

3. The Godkins called to pay their respects to the President and his bride of two months at their retreat at the Saranac Inn, Upper Saranac Lake, New York. Afterwards, Cleveland sent his regrets to Horace White that he had not asked the Godkins to stay with them a few days.

4. Cleveland's secretary of state sent Arthur Sedgwick to Mexico as a special agent of the Department of State to inquire into the vexatious Cutting Case. There Sedgwick became the center of a scandal based on charges that he got drunk in a whorehouse and let male Mexican companions insult him and his country. Although the evidence was against him, the charges seemed to be politically inspired, and Cleveland declined to recall Sedgwick.

To President Grover Cleveland

Evening Post Editorial Rooms   New York, September 24, 1886
(Cleveland Papers, DLC)

DEAR MR. PRESIDENT: Mr. Samuel R. Honey who will present this, is a leading lawyer of Newport, R. I. and has been, and is now, most active and influential in that place in the cause of sound politics.[1] His labors in support of your election in 1884, were most valuable, and were especially grateful to us Mugwumps.

He is now prominently engaged in what is undoubtedly a most important movement in the direction of reform in Rhode Island, with reference to some of the difficulties in the way of this he wishes to see you, and I ask for him your kind attention and consideration, assuring you that you can place the utmost confidence in his statements, and in his discretion.

I remain, with great respect

Faithfully yours
ELG

1. Samuel R. Honey (1842–1927), a fellow stockholder with Godkin and Sheldon in the C. B. and Q., was running for lieutenant governor of Rhode Island.

To Secretary of the Navy William C. Whitney

Box 794, New York, October 18, 1886 (Whitney Papers, DLC)

MY DEAR WHITNEY: The time has come now when if Mr. Payne can or will do *anything*, in that matter, it would be very welcome.[1] Would he be willing to take $100,000 or even $50,000 of [*Evening Post*] stock at a price that would pay 10%? If you could give me definite answer within the coming week, I should be greatly indebted to you.

Yours sincerely
ELG

1. A further reference to Godkin's unsuccessful effort to gain control of the *Evening Post*.

To his wife

Cambridge, Mass., November 7, 1886 (Ogden 2:193–94)

. . . I had a very comfortable journey but arrived in torrents of rain. As I had telegraphed to the stable here to meet me with a cab, I got out, however, very dry and had a cordial welcome.

Lowell and his daughter, Mrs. Burnett, arrived soon after me and are staying here. L. and I and Theodora went up to dinner at the Nortons at seven. We found the Creightons, G. W. Curtis, Howells, and the two semi-Italian Miss Timminses there. I took one of them into dinner; Sallie looked charmingly and the dinner was very pleasant. Curtis is older now and seems to have lost the hang of society, but Lowell and Creighton talked a good deal.[1] I am most comfortable here. Theodora, who looks tired, is full of attentions. It was, however, rather ghostly last night at Shady Hill. The people who sat round that table when I first knew it had all vanished except Norton and myself, and many strange thoughts about life ran through my head as I looked around. . . .

1. The dinner table was set for six men and six women: Godkin, James Russell Lowell, the Timmins Sisters, Charles Eliot Norton, Lowell's daughter Mabel Burnett, Howells, Norton's daughter Sally, George W. Curtis, Theodora Sedgwick, and Bishop and Mrs. Mandell Creighton. Creighton was the editor of the *English Historical Review*.

To Theodora Sedgwick

> 115 East 25th St., New York, November 28, 1886
> (Godkin Papers, MH)

My dear Theodora: I am very sorry to give you so much trouble about my small debts. The last bill I had from Pike was for $2.50, but I presume the one you enclose is all right. I had forgotten the events of 1885. I enclose a cheque for $5, and I shall be much obliged if you will have it paid. The remaining quarter of a dollar you can give to some great cause, but not of education of young men for the Ministry. . . .

With best remembrances to your Aunts, I remain always affectionately yours,

ELG

To Professor Francis J. Child

> 115 East 25th St., New York, December 10, 1886
> (Child Papers, MH)

My dear Child: Lawrence, thank you, is recovering but very slowly. . . .[1]

I hope you are all well, and prosperous. I was very sorry my glimpse of Cambridge was so brief, but I was very uneasy. I had left things at home in such wild confusion. I was delighted to see how gently time deals with you all in Kirkland St. and, especially with you. You seem to me to grow younger as you grow more illustrious.

Good bye, my dear fellow. Remember us both to Mrs. Child, and believe me always affectionately yours,

ELG

1. The editor's son had contracted typhoid fever.

To Postmaster General William F. Vilas

115 East 25th St., New York, January 12, 1887
(Vilas Papers, WHi)

MY DEAR SIR: I have sent you by express today the papers in the case of Gardner the Providence postmaster, which you were good enough to send me, and ask my opinion about. I owe you many apologies for having so long delayed answering about them. . . .

I have spoken to several Rhode Island friends about Gardner, and they all confirm Mr. Honey's charges that he has been in times past the head and front of the Republican ring in that state, and that he controlled the *Providence Journal* during the campaign of 1884. But they agree in saying that they think the business of the office is well conducted now. . . .

In short there is so much uncertainty about the matter, that as I have no direct knowledge of it, I do not feel that I ought to express any opinion about it that might in any way influence your course. In Mr. Honey I have the utmost confidence . . . but all I know is hearsay. . . .

I am the less disposed to put myself on record as having expressed a positive opinion about it, because the President has lately made several appointments and dismissals which do not accord with our Mugwump ideas of fitness. I do not say this by way of criticism, but as a reason why I fear my attempt to influence any appointment or dismissal might be less clearly understood by my own friends here than I would wish. . . .

Yours very sincerely
ELG

To Secretary of the Navy William C. Whitney

115 East 25th St., New York [7 February 1887]
(Whitney Papers, DLC)

MY DEAR MR. WHITNEY: Mr. Godkin asks me to tell you that to his great regret he cannot go to you in Washington just now, as he had hoped to do.

He is laid up with cold and results of colds. . . .

Will you therefore kindly allow him to telegraph you when he is well again and use entire frankness with him if the time then mentioned would not be entirely convenient to you.

With very kind regards to Mrs. Whitney and yourself.

> Very sincerely yours
> Katharine Godkin

To James Russell Lowell

> 115 East 25th St., New York, March 26, 1887
> (Lowell Papers, MH)

MY DEAR LOWELL: Very many thanks for your letter, which I am really sorry you felt it necessary to write in the midst of your lecturer toils.

You say you are to be here early in April. If so, will [you] dine with us on the 4th—Monday week—? The Lanciani's are coming on that day, and if you have not already seen too much of them, we shall be very glad if you will join us. . . .[1]

> Yours affectionately
> ELG

1. Rodolfo A. Lanciani (1847–1929) was an Italian acquaintance of Godkin and an occasional *Nation* contributor.

To President Grover Cleveland

> 115 East 25th St., New York, March 30, 1887
> (Cleveland Papers, DLC)

DEAR MR. PRESIDENT: Allow me to introduce to you my friend Mr. Henry Villard, doubtless already well known to you by reputation. He is paying a short visit to Washington and desires to pay his respects to you before leaving. Mr. Villard holds a large interest in the *Evening Post* as a stockholder,[1] and I believe cordially sympathizes in the attitude of the paper towards your administration, which will, I trust, in addition to his personal qualities, commend him to your kind attention.

I remain,

> Very respectfully and sincerely yours
> ELG

1. Godkin was sensitive about the fact that Villard was the proprietor of the *Evening Post*. Occasionally he dropped hints that he (Godkin) controlled the paper.

To James Bryce

> *Evening Post* Editorial Rooms   New York, March 31, 1887
> (Godkin Papers, MH)

MY DEAR BRYCE: The Coercion Bill, as reported, is I am afraid, going to let loose the devil here. . . . The bill seems to be framed so as to be as insulting and exasperating as possible to everybody with Irish blood in his veins. . . . And then its production, while acknowledging that a scheme of remedy and conciliation was in preparation, brings out the worst and most unbearable side of the English character,—the brutal arrogance, the contempt for physical weakness, the unwillingness to please anybody who cannot lick you. . . .

> Yours ever
> ELG

To Richard Watson Gilder

> *Evening Post* Editorial Rooms   New York, April 11, 1887
> (*Century Magazine* Correspondence, NN)

DEAR MR. GILDER: Here is an article which my friend Mr. J. T. Brooks the counsel of the Penn. R. R. at Pittsburg asks me to get printed in some magazine preferring the *Century*. So I send it to you first, believing it to be timely and interesting, and it comes, from a man who knows what he is talking about. . . .[1]

> Yours very sincerely
> ELG

R. W. Gilder Esq.

1. Gilder, in turn, forwarded the article to the *Forum*.

To Grace Ashburner

115 East 25th St., New York, April 27 [1887]
(Ashburner Papers, MStoc)

MY DEAR MISS GRACE: The stockings came last evening. They are a perfect fit and I am going to wear them to a dinner party tonight with very low shoes. Even if they were not as rich and handsome as they are, they would be more to me than if they had been woven on one of the looms of Cashmere. . . . I owe you a great many pleasant hours, and you are associated with many of the pleasantest years of my life, and [I] can assure you that one of the greatest drawbacks in it now is that your house is so far away.

Lawrence and I are proposing to go over to Europe in June—he certainly, I most probably, and I shall of course get to Cambridge before then, and say not only goodbye, but many other things. I wish I could be there when Arthur is with you.[1] How it would bring back old times!

Give my cordial remembrances to Miss Ashburner and Theodora.[2] I congratulate you on the coming of the summer. It *is* hard for Sir Anthony to be so near the pension period, but we are all near it, without any pension in prospect, which is harder.

Affectionately yours
ELG

1. Arthur Sedgwick was Grace Ashburner's nephew.
2. Anne Ashburner and her unmarried niece, Theodora Sedgwick, Arthur's sister.

To Henry Holt

May 7, 1887 (Ogden 2:128–29)

DEAR HOLT: The "charge" I proposed to take of that piece of ground was simply to keep it mown and free from dirt and débris,—that is, to keep it up as a lawn, which was what I supposed it was going to be, unless built on, when I took the house.

It is very difficult to discuss these things or argue about them, they are so much matters of taste. If you see them, you see them; if you don't, you don't, and there's an end to it.

But I have never had any doubt that we could agree about them whenever we understood each other, and we have clearly not done so in this case as appears from your speaking of "resuming possession." I do not propose to take "possession" of anything. Bacon said to a lady in answer to an inquiry about the ownership of the Temple Gardens, "They are ours, madame, as you are ours, to look upon, but nothing more." [1]

I enclose a check which was due some weeks ago, but I would have been ashamed to offer money to a man in your situation.

Yours ever
ELG

1. Godkin is discussing with Holt, his landlord, their differences over the care of the grounds of Bon Repos.

To Charles L. Brace

May 17, 1887 (Ogden 2:191)

MY DEAR BRACE: The reviewer of Miss Mason's *Georgics* was Gildersleeve of Johns Hopkins, a Grecian of renown, as you know.[1]

The writer of the notice of Beecher was Chadwick, Reverend John, Unitarian minister of Brooklyn. I thought it, and am glad to find you did, an excellent piece of work.

We shall certainly try and arrange a meeting either at New Rochelle or Dobbs Ferry, before you break up for the summer. We have just got settled, but the process is fatiguing, and our horses are hardly fit yet for long drives.

I am afraid "Teddy" Roosevelt has not got his father's level head.

Poor George Ward. I saw you in the distance at his funeral. How the ranks thin as we march on!

Yours ever
ELG

1. Basil L. Gildersleeve (1831–1924) was professor of classics at Johns Hopkins University and a freqeunt reviewer for the *Nation*.

To James B. Thayer

Evening Post Editorial Rooms   New York, June 10, 1887
(Godkin Papers, MH)

MY DEAR MR. THAYER: If I could get now in a detailed shape, the information I asked you for last year, touching the opinions of Harvard Professors and Instructors on Irish Home Rule . . . I would be very grateful. I dislike extremely to trouble you at this busy season, and, therefore, suggest that if you would employ one of the young men to poll the Faculty, with your certificate of propriety and good faith, on the Question—"how they would vote on Irish Home Rule, if they were Englishmen," I would be glad to pay him for his trouble.

I want the information for an article which I am at last about to write on American opinion on the Irish question for the *19th Century Review*. . . .[1]

Always sincerely yours
ELG

1. E. L. Godkin, "American Opinion on the Irish Question," *Nineteenth Century* 22 (August 1887): 285–92. The prominent legal scholar, James B. Thayer (1831–1902), was professor of law at Harvard and an occasional contributor to the *Nation*. He employed a student for Godkin at a cost of $10 to poll the faculty, the poll showing it to be in favor of Irish Home Rule.

To Mrs. William F. Smith [1]

[June 1887?] (Ogden 2:20)

. . . Your asking me to write you a "friendly note" is really too pathetic, as if I were so capable of harboring malice that you needed to be reassured. We are dreadfully sorry that you cannot see your way to coming to us; it is a great disappointment considering what the world is, how rapidly . . . we all drop off after the *mezzo cammin' di nostra vita* is reached. Constantly I consider that after forty every man, and after thirty every woman, is bound to visit his or her friends whenever invited, except in cases of overwhelming necessity. Appearances, as I must frankly say, are against you in this case. I am very glad you enjoyed your trip so much. Your account of Southern California would have made my teeth water if it were possible for anything west of the Alleghenies to make any impression on me, but no scenery or climate I had to share with the Western people would charm me. This is strictly confidential, as I am, in my editorial character, supposed to feel equally affectionate towards the whole American people; but I long ago decided, like the lazy young man whom his friends urged to go "West," that the "highest civilization was not a bit too good for me." We are settled here comfortably and enjoying the place more than ever, but, alas, I have to go to Richfield Springs in July for my infernal rheumatism. This is a bitter pill. There are so many things that would be pleasanter, and I detest the hotel life so cordially—the number of commonplace people who fill them in summer is something appalling. . . .

1. This letter is to Sarah Smith, the youngish wife of General William F. "Baldy" Smith (1824–1903) who became an object for later controversy when he was relieved of his corps command by General Burnside after the Union disaster at Fredericksburg in 1862. The second Mrs. Godkin, a slight, waspish woman who was very attached to her husband, was antagonistic toward some of his female friends but not, it would appear, toward Mrs. Smith.

To Theodora Sedgwick

Saratoga, N. Y., September 6, 1887 (Godkin Papers, MH)

My dear Theodora: Your note came this morning and I must answer it to say, that we calculated . . . on going to the hotel during our stay, which I am sorry to say will only be for two days at best.

. . . If you will kindly take rooms for us, we shall be very much obliged. Will you also kindly ask about the accommodation for horses. We are driving with a pair whose health and comfort is important to us. So if you will drop me a line here to say whether I can get stabling at the hotel, and whether our man who follows us about in the train can be lodged at the hotel in such wise that we shall not have his company at meals, I shall be most indebted to you. The scarcity in the country inns of good hostlers makes him very useful in places where we stay more than a night.

. . . Katharine joins me in best remembrances to your Aunts, whom it will give us great pleasure to see again.

Affectionately yours
ELG

To James Bryce

New Rochelle, N.Y., October 17, 1887
(Bryce Papers, Oxford University)

MY DEAR BRYCE: . . . Barry O'Brien sent me a proof of the article in which I made a few trifling corrections, and sent it back at once, but from what I see in the cable despatches I infer that the book or pamphlet will be out before it reaches London. . . .[1]

I am looking eagerly for the American book, and am sorry to hear it has become such a burden to you.[2] By all means send me the proof of the parts on which you would like my opinion. I shall be delighted to read them, and make any suggestions or criticisms that occur to me, without any delay. I have two men in mind for your chapter on the Tweed Ring, or New York City government. One is Monroe Smith, a professor in the Political Science Department of Columbia College, who would be excellent as regards research and literary workmanship. The other is Ivins, some time a lawyer, but lately and now a partner of ex Mayor Grace in the South American trade, and has been City Chamberlain. . . . I must inquire a little before approaching either of them, but will decide and let you know the result by the end of this week. . . .

I am expecting now and really confidently to go over about the beginning of February for a month only, and the ice being broken, will hope to repeat the visit soon for a longer period. Of course London will be most interesting to me, and I do want to get a glimpse of Gladstone. I had a call on Friday from Lord Herschell, who says he knows you well. I was much taken with him. . . .

I have had a most muddled apology and explanation from Arnold. He really seems to have no political ideas at all.[3] Dicey's letters in the *Spectator*, to tell the truth, have amused me much, by the thought they suggest, that a man who makes so many gloomy prophecies weekly must suffer frightfully from the dumps. How much of all his talk, too, about Ireland is simple naked unadulterated prophecy of things which have never happened anywhere else in the order . . . in which he looks for them there. Charles Norton and I used at one time to have such gloomy talks over the future of modern society late at night in his library that the story got about Cambridge that the dogs used to howl in sympathy with us, but we were I think never as gloomy as Dicey, and we saw the fun of it at intervals, which I am afraid he does not. The *Spectator* too, is delightful in its reverential attitude towards Joe Chamberlain. By the way, is he not a charlatan of the American type? He reminds me much of Blaine. *Between ourselves,* it is a great mistake sending him here on fishery business. The Republican majority in the Senate does not want any settlement at all. They want to embarrass the Administration by pushing it into a warlike attitude, well knowing however, that the country will not stand a war about a small quantity of cod and haddock. They will, therefore, seize hold of any excuse for disapproving of any agreement that may be arrived at, and Chamberlain's blatant Toryism, and abuse of the Irish will furnish a good reason for discrediting anything he has a hand in. They will please the Irish and serve their own ends by sending him home empty handed.

We do not say anything of this publicly in the *Post* or *Nation,* because we hope the negotiations will succeed and do not want to embarrass Bayard but it is a great blunder. I suppose it came about through giving credence to the silly rubbish retailed by Goldwin Smith and Arnold, about American want of sympathy with the Irish. The Commissioner ought to have been a Liberal or a Gladstonian. It sounds extravagant, but I verily believe that no living American, has as much hold as Gladstone on the American imagination today.

Yours ever
ELG

1. A reference to Bryce's *Handbook of Home Rule.* Prepared by Bryce and Barry O'Brien, it was part of the propaganda effort of the Liberal party for home rule for Ireland; Godkin is probably referring to the article, "American Home Rule," that he submitted to it.

2. *The American Commonwealth.*

3. Matthew Arnold and Albert Dicey—Dicey had recently written a book opposing Home Rule—took opposite sides from Godkin and the liberal Nonconformists on national sovereignty versus local sovereignty.

To Charles W. Eliot

Evening Post Editorial Rooms   New York, October 29, 1887
(Eliot Papers, MH-Ar)

MY DEAR PRESIDENT ELIOT: Some time ago while you were in Europe you wrote to me deprecating some criticisms in the *Nation* of Mathews the late Consul at Tangier. . . .[1]

All we said was that the Consul had under his "protection," a considerable number of Levantine Jews and Greeks, whose claims against natives he presented before the Moroccan Courts, and had the debtors thrown into Moorish prisons for indefinite periods, during which they were treated with great cruelty. He did not deny this. He simply disputed the number of the protégés and pleaded that if the Moorish prisons were places of torture it was no fault of his. I quote his own letter for his extraordinary defence.

We asked the State Department to abolish this "Claim agency," to withdraw American protection from these Levantines, and to refuse to prosecute any claims of private creditors the assertion of which involved the imprisonment of the debtors in Moorish prisons. Mr. Bayard did so, but in the doing of it, removed Mathews. Against his general character and qualifications, the *Nation* said nothing.

Yours very sincerely
ELG

1. "A Great Scandal," *Nation*, 30 December 1886. Godkin wrote the editorial that Eliot complained about, basing his charges against Consul Mathews on the complaint of Jon Perdicaris, a Tangiers resident of doubtful American nationality whom Mathews had imprisoned, allegedly for complaining that Mathews was helping foreign merchants to prey on the natives.

To William James

115 East 25th St., New York, November 25 [1887]
(James Family Papers, MH)

MY DEAR JAMES: Many thanks for your letter about poor Ellen Gurney.[1] I went on to the funeral, as you may have heard, and if

I could have spent any time in Cambridge would have gone to see you. But I had to return by the afternoon train. Witnessing the final extinction of that delightful home was one of the saddest experiences I have ever had. What made it worse was my belief that if someone sufficiently near to be entitled to do it, could have taken hold of her last November when I last saw her, and removed her from the scene of her sorrow and saved her from her lonely brooding, in those two empty houses, she might have been saved. But as Omer Khayam says—

> "He that tossed you down into [the] field—
> He knows about it all, He knows, He knows!"

Yours ever most sincerely
ELG

1. Godkin became close to Professor and Mrs. E. Whitman Gurney during his stay in Cambridge in the 1870s. Mrs. Gurney became disoriented soon after her husband's death and committed suicide by wandering in front of a train. Her death followed by two years that of her sister, Mrs. Henry Adams, also a suicide. The tragedies, both occurring when the principals were in the process of occupying new homes, contributed to giving Henry Adams his only superstition—never occupy a new house.

To Postmaster General William F. Vilas

Evening Post Editorial Rooms   November 26, 1887
(Vilas Papers, WHi)

DEAR MR. VILAS: Some expressions in the paragraph of which you complain were undoubtedly too strong, and would have been modified by me, but for a temporary absence from the office. But the main position I cannot help thinking correct. . . .

Very faithfully yours
ELG

To James Bryce

115 East 25th St., New York, November 26 [1887]
(Bryce Papers, Oxford University)

MY DEAR BRYCE: I have read the proofs with the greatest interest and pleasure, and return them herewith. I have made [one] or two marginal annotations of very little value, but they are really all I could attempt by way of criticism.[1] I know of nothing about the United States nearly as acute and accurate and lucid as your talk in these chapters I have read. As Lawrence remarked, I do not see how you came to know the country and people so well, considering that you have visited rather than lived here. The book will be a really valuable addition to everybody's political philosophy. I am sorry not to see what you say about the bar, for that is a tough subject to manage. I think it has much degenerated since Tocqueville's day. Goodnow—not "Good-man" [—] tells me he is working away vigorously and will be ready in good time. . . .[2]

I have met Chamberlain twice, and on both occasions we had warm discussions on home rule. He made a very disagreeable impression on me, or rather confirmed the one I had already. I found him most evasive, disingenious, shifty and in talking with Americans where he has everything his own way, downright mendacious. He has held his tongue in public about the Irish, but at dinner tables he is very voluble. If he is the kind of politician who is to rule the Radical England of the future, the prospect is pretty gloomy. It would amuse you if I had time or space to relate the way he escaped from some of the "corners" I made for him. But he has been most courteous to me personally. The bitterness of talk about Gladstone to Americans I thought most unbecoming, and sometimes positively silly. I still think the outlook for his fishery negotiations very poor.[3] The Republicans in the Senate are so intent on upsetting them. They will not let the Administration settle this question if they can help it. I am bound to say England and Canada have all the rights on their side. The American contention is absolutely childish. . . .

Ever most sincerely yours
ELG

1. Bryce had asked Godkin to read the proofs of some of the chapters of *The American Commonwealth*.

2. The Columbia political scientist, Frank J. Goodnow (1859–1939), was writing the chapter on the Tweed Ring for *The American Commonwealth*. This chapter became the subject of a law suit, and it was not used in succeeding editions of the book.

3. Joseph Chamberlain was the leader of a British commission sent to

Washington in 1887 to negotiate an end to the Canadian fisheries dispute. A *modus vivendi* was reached, even though the Senate refused to ratify the proposed treaty, and Chamberlain's mission was regarded as a success in promoting good relations between England and the United States, the more so when his impending marriage to the daughter of Cleveland's Secretary of War was announced.

To Francis Parkman

November 27, 1887 (Ogden 2:132–33)

MY DEAR PARKMAN: Thank you very much for the engraving of Wolfe! It is very interesting and I am very glad to have it. Thanks to photography no man as famous as he will in our day be as little known in the flesh to his admirers as Wolfe was. I, too, am sorry enough not to get to Boston oftener than I do, but since getting into the editorial harness of a daily paper, escape even for a day is very difficult.

I got a glimpse of your sister at Cambridge on Tuesday. She said a few kindly words which were very grateful at a very sad moment, for I have had few more dismal experiences in my life than witnessing the extinction of the Gurney household in which for so many years I was so welcome and enjoyed myself so much. They were both, husband and wife, very dear friends whose places could not be filled even if I were younger than I am. I hope you are well and busy. No one else does nearly as much for American literature. This is "gospel truth."

Remember me most kindly to Miss Parkman, and believe me,

Ever faithfully yours
ELG

To Charles L. Brace

December 20, 1887 (Ogden 2:191–92)

MY DEAR BRACE: . . . I am very glad indeed that you all think so highly of my home rule efforts. I hope before I die to see some endorsement of my views, by the course of events. But of course it is, at best, a good way off. The agitation is bringing out both the best and the worst side of the English character. I wish you all a Merry Christmas, Happy New Year; my wife joins me in doing so, but the ranks are getting very thin as each successive season comes round. The disappearance of the Gurney household has been a sad blow to me. . . .

Yours ever
ELG

To James Meins

Evening Post Editorial Rooms   New York, December 23, 1887
(Edes Papers, MHi)

James Meins Esq., Secretary
Dear Sir: I regret extremely that my arrangements here will prevent my acceptance of the kind invitation of the Massachusetts Tariff Reform League to their dinner on the 29th inst. all the more because the prospects of tariff reform have, at last, thanks to President Cleveland, become really bright and for the first time since the war. The dinner of such a body will have the air of a triumphal feast.

    With best wishes for the success of the occasion, I am,

Yours sincerely
ELG

To Mrs. William F. Smith

[December 1887?] (Ogden 2:18)

My dear Mrs. Smith: When I tell you that I had been trying for weeks to remember to buy myself some such pencil as you sent me, you may guess what a delightful mixture of the *utile* and the *dolce* yours was. It is evidently the invention of a master mind, and has been "consecrated to my use" by your most kindly hand. May the New Year have many choice gifts in store for you and yours is the earnest prayer of a not very prayerful man, but your attached friend,

ELG

To Mrs. William F. Smith

January 15, 1888 (Ogden 2:18–19)

. . . The rumors of your coming to pay us a visit have again been revived, this time with a certain air of probability.

In deciding how long you will stay, remember the number of years which have elapsed since we have been able to secure a single night or since we have had you without expecting that an overwhelming combination of circumstances would force you to leave us at three A.M. in a howling storm. The hall bedroom, I admit, is not luxurious, but such as it is do not occupy it, I beg, except as a free woman; to know that you slept there in chains would wring my heart. These, let me add, are the utterances of despair as well as friendship; but, come what will, *liberavi* [sic] *animam meam,* as the psalmist says. . . .

To Mrs. William F. Smith

January 22, 1888 (Ogden 2:19)

. . . I knew it, I knew it! I said all along I will not believe it until I see her in her room. . . . I shall say no more on this painful topic now. In all these things my great reliance is Time, the Healer, the Consoler. Perhaps in some remote hereafter the announcement that "Mrs. Smith is coming" will rouse expectation in my aged breast and bring a little fire into my fading eyes; but for the moment I must live in simple darkness, hoping nothing. . . . Katharine, I ought to say, continues to look for you, but she is much younger than I. . . .

To Woodrow Wilson

New York, March 5, 1888 (Wilson 5:707)

DEAR SIR: I enclose a letter sent me to be mailed to you, by James Bryce of London.[1] As I have undertaken to find someone to take your place, in case you are unable to comply with his request, will you kindly let me know what your answer to him is, so as to save time, and thus greatly oblige.

Yours very truly
ELG

1. Bryce wrote the then Princeton professor, Woodrow Wilson, to request him to write a chapter for the *American Commonwealth* on woman suffrage in the United States, but Wilson declined on grounds of inadequate knowledge. Wilson was an avid reader of Godkin and the *Nation*.

To Professor Francis J. Child

115 East 25th St., New York, April 11, 1888
(Child Papers, MH)

MY DEAR CHILD: . . . I get news of you every now and then from Arthur Sedgwick but it is of course meagre and disjointed. I hope the world goes fairly well with you. My thoughts seldom go to Cambridge now without haunting the [Gurney] ruin in Fayerweather St., and it is a relief to think that there is something of *Auld lang syne* still left in Kirkland St. . . .

Yours ever affectionately
ELG

Cleveland is treating us badly.

To Theodora Sedgwick

115 East 25th St., New York, April 18, 1888
(Godkin Papers, MH)

MY DEAR THEODORA: . . . I hope you are all well. My best remembrances to your Aunts. Katharine is at Lakewood taking a little holiday before moving to New Rochelle. Arthur who is also, bereft, dined with Lawrence and me here this evening.[1] He seems in good case. What a terribly sudden taking off poor Arnold's was! [2] I do trust nothing will induce me to jump fences at sixty six.

Ever affectionately yours
ELG

1. Arthur Sedgwick's wife, like Godkin's wife, was away on holiday, and Godkin's son, Lawrence, was a bachelor living at home.

2. Matthew Arnold had suffered a fatal heart attack three days before.

To Theodora Sedgwick

New Rochelle, N. Y., May 16, 1888 (Godkin Papers, MH)

MY DEAR THEODORA: Mahlon Sands's death was a sad affair, and a very great blow to Katharine, as well as to his mother whom it quite prostrated. He leaves a rather helpless wife, and three children of her, two quite young, besides Mabel of the first marriage, who was greatly attached to him and dependent on him for affection and sympathy, and who will until she marries, be very much alone in the world. And he was a really good fellow, most simple and genuine and loyal, who would have made a career if he had had no money. . . .[1] Mrs. Sands is coming to stay for a while before going to Northeast Harbor, where she has taken a house, and Katharine asks me to say, with her love, that we shall look for you early in July. . . .

Affectionately yours
ELG. . . .

1. Mrs. Godkin's New York and London socialite brother, Mahlon D. Sands (1842–88). His widow was a niece of Vice-President Levi P. Morton. Two years later, in an aura of semi-scandal, Mabel Sands, against the opposition of her mother and the Godkins married the son of an English nobleman. Both died soon afterwards.

To Theodora Sedgwick

New Rochelle, N.Y., July 25, 1888 (Godkin Papers, MH)

MY DEAR THEODORA: . . . I think the best observers in England believe now that an election today would give Gladstone 150 majority in the H.C. The notion that he is shelved is, in fact, in my eyes, a little preposterous. I am not at all sure, however, that even with such a majority, he would be able to produce a scheme of Home Rule that he could put through—there would be great fighting over details in spite of the advance the principle has made in England—largely owing to Tory blunders—since 1886. . . .[1]

1. Godkin was right; in 1892 Gladstone returned to power at the age of 83. His second Home Rule bill passed the House of Commons but was thrown out by the House of Lords.

Affectionately yours
ELG

Telegram to Silas W. Burt

New York, August 18, 1888 (Telegram, Burt Papers, NHi)

Am sorry and mortified beyond measure to say that the questions have been lost or taken from my table. . . .

ELG

To Silas W. Burt

New York, August 19 [1888] (Burt Papers, NHi)

MY DEAR COLONEL BURT: . . . I cannot criticize intelligently, of course, without the papers before me, but what I was going to say was (in general terms) that I thought some of the questions as to the abuses of patronage, were repeated in different language or nearly so, and that this gave an air of hostile cross examination to them, such as lawyers employ to an unwilling and evasive witness. But this was all.

I trust you have other copies. Do reassure me on this point.

I remain, yours very truly and sorrowfully
ELG

To Frederick Sheldon

New Rochelle, N.Y., September 2, 1888 (Godkin Papers, MH)

DEAR SHELDON: I got your note about the C. B. and Q. Stock. . . . I . . . am quite prepared to agree to whatever you and Honey think best. I suppose the immediate prospects of the stock are gloomy at best, and, as a general conclusion, that any stock capable of moving down suddenly as it has done is not a proper one for a trust. So, go ahead.

I have no news of any kind. We spent three weeks at Northeast Harbor, with occasional trips to Bar Harbor, which is now to me, one of the least attractive villages on the continent. The cottager is ruining the hotels, but the excursionist continues to come *for the day*, and makes a hellish condition of things. He is taking possession of the world. I am told you often see 200 Cook's tourists among the ruins of Thebes on donkeys and yelling like fury.

Kindly remembrances to Mrs. Sheldon.

Yours ever
ELG

To Frederick Sheldon

Evening Post Editorial Rooms   New York, September 10, 1888
(Godkin Papers, MH)

DEAR SHELDON: I have no objection to the proposed investment in Kansas Pacifics.

The private opinion in this office is that Cleveland will carry this State, and be elected, in spite of the probable nomination of Hill for the Governorship, which is undoubtedly a drawback. On the other hand, if not nominated his machine would probably have "knifed" the Presidential ticket—which leaves the situation about as it was.

According to my best judgment and that of those whom I see, the Republican canvas, in so far as it is not affected by money or intimidation of working men by employers, has been going to pieces since Blaine came back. His blunders have been a terrible disappointment. The press is making no fight. But of course the power of vested interests, when attacked is very great, and I do not [care?]. The Maine election tomorrow will throw some light on it. If it drops—that is the Republican majority there—to 8, or 10,000 or thereabouts, it will undoubtedly mean Republican defeat in November.

Yours ever
ELG

To his wife

New Rochelle, N.Y., October 1, 1888 (Ogden 2:194)

. . . Your talk of the deserted farms touches my imagination. I have seen so many that I would have liked to buy and fit up if I were a man of leisure. Complete retirement seems so attractive to me that I feel I must be growing old. But on "Ben" this afternoon I felt very young; he was and is delightful, such good company. His snort delights me.

I have just finished Vereschagin's "Diary on Turkey and Turkestan," a wonderfully vivid book. He was on Skobeleff's staff in those terrible days on the Danube in 1877, and much of the fighting was on the ground I traversed on that famous ride of mine in the winter of 1853.[1]

All goes well in the house. But the summer is gone, and each summer now is such a loss! and the number which remain dwindles so rapidly. Come back and cheer us up. "Fugit ero citius Tempus edax rerum". . . .

---

1. Godkin is referring to his early career as a Crimean War correspondent. Learning that the Russians were preparing an attack on a Turkish force at Kalafat, Rumania, he and several British officers in December 1853 rode day and night from the Turkish army headquarters at Shumla, Bulgaria, to reach the scene. The expected attack did not come.

To Secretary of the Treasury
Charles S. Fairchild

Evening Post Editorial Rooms   New York, October 10, 1888
(Fairchild Papers, NHi)

Private

MY DEAR MR. FAIRCHILD: May I ask, if the question be not improper or indiscreet—if it is, you will of course not answer it—whether you mean to accept and act on the Frye report, in selecting the Bowling Green site for the new U.S. public buildings in this city?

Let me explain . . . that . . . the valuation of a lot near bye [*sic*] on which I am asked to make a small loan as trustee, has been put up in consequence of the expectation that this Bowling Green site would be selected, and before closing I am naturally desirous of knowing whether it has any reasonable foundation.

I hope the criticisms of some things which have appeared in the *Evening Post*, will not make this request seem an intrusion, or have been neutralized in your mind by this time by the remembrance of the steady respect and support which your career generally has always received from me.[1]

In any event I shall of course consider your answer confidential.

Very truly yours
ELG

Honble Charles S. Fairchild

1. Cleveland's new Secretary of the Treasury had undergone slashing criticism in the *Evening Post*.

To William James

Evening Post Editorial Rooms   New York, October 10, 1888
(James Family Papers, MH)

MY DEAR JAMES: I have given your cousin the second best advice I could give. The best advice—not to think of journalism as a calling—I withheld, as not called for by the terms of your letter. It made me sad to see so young a fellow hoping to enter [a] calling, which when taken up young, I consider destructive both to mind and character. I would nearly as soon see a son of mine opening a faro bank or an assignation house. All the influences of a newspaper office on a young man are extremely demoralizing.

I am glad to hear you are well; we are all "middleaged and omnibus horses," so there is no more use in lamenting over that than over death. Some day I hope again to see something of you, for *auld compagnie* is very dear to me. Give my kindest remembrances to your wife, and believe me

Always yours cordially
ELG

To Silas W. Burt

Evening Post Editorial Rooms   New York, December 10 [1888]
(Burt Papers, NHi)

DEAR BURT: Since sending you the article, I have doubted the
wisdom of forwarding it to the President. There are reserves and
qualifications in it, which in his present irritable condition might
annoy him still further.[1] If it has not already gone, therefore, I
would suggest your simply saying that, we had been defending
him against Lea in the *Post* during the canvas and that I had sent
him Lea's recent letter, without the remotest thought of anything
but informing him of what his critics and enemies were still saying, and what I thought it would be very desirable he should
know before he said his farewell word on this subject.

I note Edgerton.[2] Such things make us sick.

Yours
ELG

1. Cleveland had just been defeated for reelection by Benjamin Harrison.
2. When Alfred P. Edgerton, an aged Democratic politician whom
Cleveland named to succeed Dorman Eaton as president of the United
States Civil Service Commission, gave offense to administration supporters
of civil service reform, Cleveland removed him early in 1889, Edgerton
replying with the charge that the President was a "Mugwump of Mugwumps." In 1885 Godkin had endorsed the little-known Edgerton's appointment in the *Nation*.

To Grace Ashburner

115 East 25th St., New York, December 16, 1888
(Ashburner Papers, MStoc)

MY DEAR MISS GRACE: I have been asking Mrs. Arthur [Sedg-
wick] today what chance there was of seeing you here this winter. . . . I have been on the point of writing several times since
hearing you had not been well, to remind you what good friends
we have been and are, and what pleasant and tender memories I
have of old Cambridge days. . . . Your house has been one of
the pleasantest spots in my life. . . .

As you may guess the election was a severe blow, to me, and
even a greater one to Lawrence, who had taken the stump during

the last month and done himself credit on it. But nobody should have anything to do with politics who is not prepared to see all improvements postponed till after his death.

Give our warmest regards to Miss Anne, and Theodora. We hope to see you soon.

Yours affectionately
ELG

To an unnamed correspondent

[1888] (Ogden 2:1)

. . . When I woke, I was in great grief over Mrs. Gurney's death, of which I thought I had just heard the news. This dream about Mrs. Gurney has frightened me a little. I have had some very striking dreams, and am always impressed by a vivid one. . . .

To Frederick Sheldon

115 East 25th St., New York, January 7, 1889
(Godkin Papers, MH)

DEAR SHELDON: Your note unhappily confirms my own judgment as to Bryce's course. What I have done about it I did on the impulse of the first moment of surprise and annoyance—that is to write to him to say that I could not admit that the mention of my name among the persons to whom he was indebted would injure the sale or influence of the book; that "the men I had been fighting all these years," would never read it, and their judgment would have nothing to do with fixing its place as a philosophical book.[1]

I did not like to go further and say what you say, and what I felt, that I did not see how under heaven an honorable man could feel such obligations to any one, and fail to express them, when he expressed obligations to others. If he had made no acknowledgment to any one, it would have been more excusable. I refrained because I did not want to break an old friendship on a question of self love. But the affair has vexed and disappointed me a good deal, not because he has failed to advertize me, but because he

could bring himself [to] make such a suppression, considering
the relations in which we have lived for twenty years.

Yours ever
ELG

1. When Bryce's *The American Commonwealth* appeared, Godkin found
he had been omitted from the acknowledgments, and he wrote Bryce to
inquire about it. Sheldon rightly thought Bryce's omission of Godkin was
"shabby," and he asked Godkin, "What are you going to do about it?"
This letter is in reply to Sheldon.

To Richard Watson Gilder

Evening Post Editorial Rooms   New York, January 8, 1889
(Gilder Papers, NN)

Dear Mr. Gilder: Chamberlain, on his own admission, was a participant in the frauds and corruption of the Carpetbag ring in
South Carolina. Tommy Shearman was Fisk and Gould's lawyer
during the Tweed period, and was the legal promotor of their
schemes, and got from Barnard the orders and judgments for
which he was afterwards impeached. Their appearance on the
ticket of a "Reform" Club is a great scandal, and will give the
enemy materials for many a sneer.[1]

Yours truly
ELG

1. Godkin is complaining about two New York municipal office-seekers
who had won the endorsement of the Reform Club of New York, of which
he was a member. One of them, attorney Thomas G. Shearman, was a
former contributor to the *Nation* who had participated with Godkin in
tariff reform activities. Daniel H. Chamberlain served briefly as a Reconstruction governor of South Carolina.

To Henry Holt

115 East 25th St., New York, [ca. 14 January 1889]
(Godkin Papers, MH)

My dear Holt: I could not say to you last night, that if you have
not told ——— you would ask me to put him up at the Century,

I should rather not do so. The reason is simply that I have for twenty years, been making a stand against the loss of its distinctive character by the Club, owing to the large introduction of men having no connection of any sort with art, literature, or science. I made a stand against it in the Committee on Admissions in the case of Randolph, of Randolph and Skidmore about 1870. Since then every objection of the kind has been swept away. There are I think more brokers and bankers and merchants in it who merely open a book than any other class—excellent and agreeable men, whom I am glad enough to meet, but not properly Centurions, and I have never had anything to do with the admission of *one* of them, and much as I like ——— I would rather not break my record for him, unless you have told him you were going to ask me, in which case I would not think of hurting his feelings, by refusing.

Yours sincerely
ELG

I send this off early lest you should see ——— before you get it.[1]

1. The name of the man Godkin is opposing has been effaced from the original.

To Rodolfo Lanciani

New York, January 14, 1889 (Ogden 2:133)

MY DEAR MR. LANCIANI: I have just finished reading your volume, and it has so completely renewed the pleasure I had in listening to the lectures, that I cannot help sitting down to thank you most warmly.[1] Your lectures here were, I think I can say, the greatest treat of the kind I have ever had, and I have closed the book with a sigh of regret that there is not another volume of it. It would be hard, I think, to conceive of pleasanter work for a man of your tastes than that you are engaged in, and it must surely heighten the joy of it to be able to tell the rest of the world so much about it in such graceful English.

That you may live long to dig and delve, that your "finds" may be numerous, and your pen ready, is my earnest wish, and that of a large number of admirers here.

I am glad to know that your health is again restored. My wife joins me in kindest remembrances to you and Madame Lanciani, and I remain, with sincere gratitude,

                                        Yours very truly
                                        ELG

1. Rodolfo A. Lanciani, *Ancient Rome in the Light of Recent Discoveries* (Boston and New York, 1888). Signor Lanciani visited the United States in 1887 and lectured in New York, he and his wife seeing much of the Godkins socially.

To Carl Schurz

Evening Post Editorial Rooms   New York, January 30, 1889
                                        (Schurz Papers, DLC)

DEAR SCHURZ: White tells me you want some more information about the Lombard Investment Co. I sent you some time ago, a communication I had from them about you.

My direct knowledge of them ended five years ago. For twelve years previous to that I was trustee of a fund invested through them in farm mortgages—$20000. Their management of it was excellent. We never lost a cent of principle [*sic*] or interest. The trust was closed in 1883, and since then I have only known of them by hearsay but all that I hear is good. I enclose a list of their references. One of their juniors, who is in the office here, at *150 Broadway* would be glad to call on you if you desired it—William L. Lombard, but if you contemplated serious business, I would recommend your seeing the head of the concern James L. Lombard who is now in Kansas.

                                        Truly yours
                                        ELG

To Silas W. Burt

Evening Post Editorial Rooms   New York, February 6, 1889
                                        (Burt Papers, NHi)

MY DEAR BURT: I did hear that Byrne had tried to sell his report to the press here, but only in a general way, and not to any paper in particular. . . . It was your information about the *Times*, I confess, which made me feel warranted in printing it, as a fact, but I did not feel that I was violating any confidence as long as I mentioned no names. . . .[1]

I am very sorry if this is an indiscretion and troubles you.

Yours truly

ELG

1. T. Aubrey Byrne, appointed by the Treasury to investigate the Sugar Division of the Appraisal Department of the New York Custom House, found improper influence being exerted on the Department by sugar brokers, particularly by Colonel James Burt. In the *Evening Post* Godkin, partly on the basis of a remark made to him by Colonel Silas W. Burt, charged that Byrne was an unprincipled adventurer who had tried to sell the report of his investigation to a New York newspaper. Burt viewed Godkin's course as a violation of a confidence.

To James Bryce

115 East 25th St., New York, March 24, 1889
(Bryce Papers, Oxford University)

MY DEAR BRYCE: I got your letter from Bombay in due course, and you must not suppose for a moment that I have had any feeling about the book matter except that you had been unnecessarily cautious. That you had to exercise *some* caution I understood perfectly, but you over-estimated I thought what the Whitelaw Reid type could do or say to damage a book like yours.

I do not know what the sales have been, but if I may judge from what I hear, the success has been extraordinarily great in all other ways. I have not heard or read in any quarter one word of adverse criticism except as to its size, and everybody, male or female, either reads it, or pretends to have done so. It is furnishing too, abundant illustrations to orators and leader writers. In fact, I can only compare its success in a popular sense to that of *Robert Elsmere*.[1]

The Pigott affair was a wonderfully dramatic thing and a very gratifying one to me who had always maintained that the reluctance of the *Times* to give the history of the letters threw doubts of the worst kind on their authenticity.[2] The affair is a very discreditable one to English fairness and good sense both. But what use is it in the face of the Septennial Act?

I sent nothing about Hurlbert because I saw he would not be called. . . . I . . . should like to have exposed Hurlbert as an unprincipled scamp, whom nobody who knows him would believe on his oath, or trust with five dollars. His career in London is one of the comicalities of Anglo American intercourse. . . .

Yours ever
ELG

1. The novel *Robert Elsmere* by Mrs. Humphry Ward (1851–1920) was then at the height of its popularity.

2. The Pigott affair arose when the *Times* of London published a letter that it declared to be the work of the Irish nationalist leader Charles Parnell, excusing the Phoenix park murders, but which its producer Pigott now admitted was a forgery.

To William D. Foulke [1]

115 East 25th St., New York, April 5, 1889
(Foulke Papers, DLC)

DEAR MR. FOULKE: It is difficult to give you an idea of the astonishment and indignation here over the appointment of Van Cott to the post office. It is the surrender after fifteen years of excellent business administration, of the chief government office to a political business of the lowest order. It would have been bad to displace Pearson for a respectable business man, but Van Cott is one of the very bad "Boys," whom we have been fighting for years. And I confess when I remember that the gentleman who inflicts this on us is a loudly professing Christian it makes it very difficult to express myself about it in moderate terms.[2] This is the worst appointment made in this city since 1870. We have tried hard to take a charitable and hopeful view of General Harrison's doings thus far, but this is too bad for poor human nature.

I write to you because I was much impressed by the way you spoke of him at Baltimore.

With much regard and condolence. I remain

Yours very truly
ELG

1. William D. Foulke (1848–1935) was then heading a special committee of the National Civil Reform Association investigating the Federal civil service. The committee's findings were unfavorable to the Harrison administration.

2. Godkin is referring to President Harrison's replacement of Henry G. Pearson as postmaster of New York with State Senator Cornelius Van Cott.

To Isidor Straus

Evening Post Editorial Rooms   New York, April 9, 1889
(Oscar S. Straus Papers, DLC)

Isidor Straus Esq.[1]

DEAR SIR: It seems to me the most effective thing to do in the matter of the *Mail's* attack on your brother is to write a letter to the *Mail*, which we will copy afterwards. In this way it will reach the people who saw the original attack, which it will not do if it appears only in the *Post*.

Very truly yours
ELG

1. Godkin had become slightly acquainted with Isidor Strauss (1845–1912) in the Free Trade Club. Evidently an attack had been made on the New York merchant's brother, Oscar, whom Cleveland had made United States minister to Turkey.

9. Godkin Discovers England

For Godkin the most gratifying event of his later years was his rediscovery of England. During the 1880s he wrote a few pieces for British journals, several of them in support of home rule for Ireland, but he had not been in England for many years. In 1888 James Bryce invited him to contribute to the *Handbook of Home Rule*, produced by the Liberal party to advance Prime Minister Gladstone's bill for Irish home rule.

The next summer Godkin revisited England for the first time in a quarter of a century. To his intense satisfaction, Bryce arranged for him to meet with Gladstone, and a glittering assortment of peers and upper middle-class tastemakers showered him with attentions. To his wife in New York—who had begged off from the trip because she was prone to sea sickness—Godkin exulted from London: "The people here are so polite, and there are so many well dressed, educated men, and life is so well ordered, I am thinking I am not worth a cent as a 'good American.'" Afterwards, except for two years, Godkin spent some part of each year abroad, staying part of the time with the Bryces or with his friend Henry James in London.

From 1889 onward, Godkin's Anglophilism was a favorite topic of banter from his friends as well as reprobation from his enemies. One evening at the Century Club when Godkin missed a billiard shot, Clarence King wittily explained to onlookers that it was a typical Godkin shot, "too much English on the side."

To Sir Charles Russell

115 East 25th St., New York, April 15, 1889
(Godkin Papers, MH)

MY DEAR SIR CHARLES RUSSELL: My congratulations on your great triumph will come rather late, and probably when you have been surfeited with praise, but nobody's will be heartier or more sincere.[1] No one has followed your efforts before the Commission with more interest or admiration than I have. If the cause of Home Rule now triumphs, it will certainly be due to you more than any other man in my opinion, for it is through you it has received moral vindication. Whether it comes or not, however, you have made a great contribution to the fame of the unfortunate country we both love so well, which has produced so many great men, and has benefitted [*sic*] so little by their talents and their labors. It has been a very great pleasure to me to see an Irishman of your power and in your place, at so great a bar, pleading so splendidly for the unhappy Irish people.

I hope to be in London about the first of June, and to express more fully my acknowledgments in person.

Yours most faithfully
ELG

1. The editor is congratulating Sir Charles on his much-praised speech in defense of Charles Parnell before the Parnell Commission, convened to determine the truth of the London *Times*'s charges against the Irish leader.

To The Reverend Henry Codman Potter [1]

April 28, 1889 (Ogden 2:184)

MY DEAR BISHOP POTTER: I have treated myself by a reading of the whole sermon since you went away, and I must, before I go to bed, sit down and thank you for it from the bottom of my heart. I think it is the bravest, timeliest, and most effective piece of pulpit oratory which this generation has heard, and a noble use of a great occasion. If it hurts any one it will show that he is very sick and finds in you his physician. I have little doubt, too, it will loosen thousands of clerical tongues all over the country, and rescue many a grieving layman from the slough of despond. Many a great field has been saved by the ring of one manly voice at the right moment—"the psychological moment" —when even brave men begin to think of giving up the fight.

Sincerely and gratefully yours

ELG

1. Godkin is congratulating Henry Codman Potter (1835–1908) on the sermon he planned to deliver in St. Paul's Chapel, New York, marking the Federal Centennial. The Episcopalian bishop, who was active in Mugwump causes, had asked Godkin's opinion about the propriety of some of the political criticisms he intended to make.

To Henry Holt

April 28, 1889 (Ogden 2:129–30)

DEAR HOLT: The only "business purpose" for which I can conceive of the house being used is a boarding house or a lager beer saloon, and if you foresee the possibility of my letting anybody turn in into either, you must be a more nervous and more imaginative man than I supposed you.[1] You may depend upon it that any offer coming from anybody who is likely under any stress of circumstances to start any commercial undertaking with my furniture between June and October, will be peremptorily rejected. More than this, I will bind myself, if I hear of my tenant starting any business of any description, to have him expelled *vi et armis* with the utmost violence and even cruelty. I try to make a specialty of not being in any way disagreeable to my neighbors, and trust I have succeeded thus far. I cannot give you the name of my tenant because he has not shown himself. I have ordered Brown to go to work to dig for the meter and make connection on my own responsibility. I leave the ultimate responsibility for the cash to be settled by negotiation or arbitration on those great principles of equity by which men as well as nations ought to be governed.

Yours sincerely,

ELG

1. Godkin, at last, was making his long-deferred journey to England, and he was seeking owner Holt's permission to sublet Bon Repos during his absence.

To Former President Rutherford B. Hayes

Evening Post Editorial Rooms   New York, May 16, 1889
(Hayes Papers, OFH)

R. B. Hayes Esq.
DEAR SIR: . . . The greater portion of your speech will appear
in the *Evening Post* today or tomorrow.[1] I will have a copy
sent you.

Yours sincerely
ELG

1. Former President Hayes had given an address at a dinner commemo-
rating the Centennial of the organization of the United States under the
Federal Constitution.

To Mrs. William F. Smith

May 23, 1889 (Ogden 2:20)

. . . I shall be in London all through June, staying most of
the time with Harry James.[1] I feel a little sinking of the heart at
going back after so many years, for death has been very busy
among all whom I knew in my youth. . . .

1. The novelist Henry James was now living permanently in England.

To his wife

On board the *Augusta Victoria*, May 30, 1889 [1]

. . . I wrote a few lines by the pilot, which I hope you got.
. . . The passengers, except our table, are a sorry lot. Daisy
Miller from Milwaukee with her sister and mother are at the next
table. . . .[2] I finished "Risler Aîné" today. It is a wonderfully
powerful book. Why have I not read it before? Poor little
Desirée's fate brought tears to my eyes. What a wonderful
genius Daudet is! I am now working away at James' book. "London Life," as far as I have got, is very good, but very Jamesy.
He ought to write something without an American in it. . . .

"Ridgemount," Basset, Southhampton, June 1, 1889

. . . William Darwin met me on the wharf, hurried me through the Custom House and brought me out at once to this delightful house, with the warmest of welcomes.[3] After lunch, we drove over to Winchester, and spent the afternoon wandering through the Cathedral and College and the streets of the old city. . . . After a late dinner I turned in very, very tired, and, my dear, when I woke at half past four what should I hear for a good half hour but the cuckoo! The cuckoo of my boyhood, not a note of which I had heard for forty years! . . .

34 De Vere Gardens W., London, June 3, 1889

. . . On Sunday we went to Salisbury by train, took a trap over Salisbury plain to Stonehenge, lunched among the great stones, listening to the larks . . . drove back to the city and spent an hour in the Cathedral. . . . These English sights and sounds, Home-Ruler though I be, make me drunk with pleasure. . . . This morning I came up to London. James met me at the station full of cordial welcome, and we drove home to his apartment through streets roaring with the crowd of the season. A nicer apartment you never saw, full of pretty things, well lighted, handsomely furnished, a good cook and man-servant. I have a charming bedroom and a little library to myself. I found Russell and Bryce and Dicey and Bonham-Carter had already called. . . .[4] I have engaged to go for Saturday and Sunday, with James, to the Charles Roundells near Crewe. . . . The Salisbury day was full of heartache at thinking how you would have enjoyed it. Some day we must attempt it together, before I am too old. When we sat at lunch among the great stones on that beautiful sod, I was constantly wailing to myself over your absence. I am getting various smaller pleasures in England, about which I fear I must muzzle myself, if I am to maintain my standing as a "Good American". . . .

Athenaeum Club, London, June 4, 1889

. . . The people here are so polite, and there are so many well dressed, educated men, and life is so well ordered, I am thinking I am not worth a cent as a "good American." *This is confidential.* . . .

Devonshire, June 6, 1889

. . . James and I lunched at the Athenaeum Club and dined at the Reform Club in the evening, with our old friend Robartes. In the afternoon I called on Miss de Rothschild and found there Mrs. Morton.

. . . James and I called yesterday on my old friend Mrs. ——— but this business of meeting women after thirty years, whom you have known young, is a dreadful one. She is still very bright, but old, wrinkled and has a wig. . . .[5]

34 De Vere Gardens W., London, [8?] June 1889

. . . I went to the Epsom races with Russell on Thursday. He drove me down twenty miles, to a charming old Queen Anne house he has, two miles from the course, and after lunch drove over to the course in an Irish jaunting-car. There he had got me into the jockey-club enclosure and we had a long hot day of racing. I saw and had a long, pleasant talk with Lord Spencer, and short one with Lord Roseberry, and the famous "Jimmie" Lowther. The Prince of Wales was there with his son. In the evening we had Lord Dunham, an attractive man, to dinner and stay all night. He is given up to sporting, but I wish Lawrence could hear his English and see his clothes. . . .

Dorford Hall, Cheshire [9 June 1889]

. . . [I] came back to town early and after some hurried "errands," during which met Alfred Pell for a moment in the street, started with Henry James for this place. . . . There is a party here, among them Rhoda Broughton, the novelist, a connection of theirs, who lives at Oxford. She is very lively and amusing. . . . and a Mr. Fortescue, who lives in Ireland, and hates Home Rule, and Lady Cammilla Fortescue his wife, who is sweet and gentle. James and I occasionally meet in our rooms and have an old-fashioned American roar. To-morrow morning I go to Oxford to stay at All Souls and dine with the Fellows in the evening. I have received other invitations there to stay over Wednesday, but must go back to town on Tuesday in order to start for Devonshire on Wednesday. I shall mourn all my days that you have not seen this house; it is a model seventeenth century manor-house. It is only now that I am able to find my way to my room without advice. . . .

All Souls' College, Oxford, June 11, 1889

. . . I came on here yesterday and found a room and, what is very important in this weather, a fire awaiting me. I went as soon as possible to see Dicey who lives in the suburbs, and after a long visit we started out together and walked and talked for two mortal hours, partly in the cloisters and partly in the Magdalen Meadows. You doubtless know their beauty, even in a cold drizzle. I got back here just in time to dress for dinner in the Hall, a beautiful old room, where I sat next and much enjoyed meeting Lord Acton, a Catholic of very old family and one of the most learned men in England.[6] After dessert off old mahogany, in another room, and coffee in still another, and cigarettes and gin and soda in still another, I got to bed very tired. . . .

Heath's Court, Ottery St. Mary, Devon [12 and 13 June 1889]

. . . Yesterday at Oxford I wandered about the colleges until it was time to go to Miss Shaw Lefevre's garden party, at the Somerville Lady's College, the Oxford equivalent of the Cambridge Girton and Newnham. It was a damp drizzly day, but the way the English cling to the idea that the weather is always fine is really pathetic. The company was mostly collegiate and looked it, but I saw my old acquaintance Broderick, now warden of Merton, Thorold Rogers, the political economist, Freeman the old ruffian, who was very crusty, and Max Müller, whom I had never met, and was glad to see. . . .[7]

This afternoon I arrived here at Lord Coleridge's in the heart of Devonshire, a lovely spot. . . . Lady C. is pretty and charming and so is her sister. The house is full of company, but I have seen no one but Otto Goldschmidt, Jenny Lind's widower; the others with Lord Coleridge are out driving. . . .

June 13th.

I have not closed the letter. We have had a delightful morning at Exeter, twenty miles from here, visiting the Cathedral under

Lord Coleridge's guidance. . . . We had a large dinner last night without special interest, and in the evening in the library—a glorious room—lots of reminiscences of Newman, whom Coleridge knew well. . . . Lady Coleridge is really a beautiful woman and dresses *selon moi*, very well, but I do so miss the chance of talking things over with you at the close of the day, to hear what you think of the women and their clothes. I specially miss your botanical help to prevent my being brought to grief, as I constantly am, about trees and flowers. . . . Coleridge is about sixty-six and looks seventy, while his wife seems under thirty! She calls him "the chief." I think some of his children are older than she. . . .

34 De Vere Gardens W., London, June 17, 1889

. . . I closed my last letter at Lord Coleridge's in Devonshire. I had a charming visit there. Anything lovelier than Devonshire at this season you cannot imagine. The most attractive visitor there with me was Sir Alfred Lyall, a retired Indian Governor. We came back in the train together and had some terrible laughs, although he is ordinarily a silent, grave man. I got a cordial welcome home from James, and after a quiet dinner we went out in the rain to one of the "music halls," which are now a feature of London life, and which I had a curiosity to see. But except as a social phenomenon, they do not amount to much.

Yesterday, Sunday, I went to see Kate at St. John's Wood. I have also heard from Georgina. . . .[8] To-day I lunch with Ferdinand Rothschild, the only thing he has been able to get me for after several invitations to Waddesden. . . . As far as seeing people goes, the Whitsuntide holiday—a most silly feast—has worked badly for me, but I have been fully compensated by my country visits. . . .

34 De Vere Gardens W., London, June 19 [1889]

. . . on Monday I lunched with Rothschild and he urged me to try to arrange with Farrer to leave me free to go to Waddesden on Saturday next, and to Farrer some other Saturday.[9] I have accordingly done so, and am going down to Waddesden on Saturday for Sunday, with a large party, including Mrs.

Humphry Ward. . . . On Tuesday I went to see Miss Ashton, as per the enclosed note.[10] I was charmed with her. A very attractive face, fine eyes, a vivacious but sweet manner, a delightful voice, and a good talker, very cultivated and refined—in fact, Bryce is a lucky man. In the evening James and I went to Alma Tadema's wonderful new house.[11] I can give you no idea of it on paper. It is a marvel of art and money, but must be the devil to live in and has cost enormously, and must be unsalable at his death. We had music—piano by Sir Charles Halley and violin by Lady Halley and monologues—the old New York ones—by Coquelin, *père et fils*. . . .[12] In the . . . morning I had a long séance with Robinson of the *Daily News*.[13] Macmillan, the publisher, took me for a ramble through the New Law Courts (since my day) and I went down to the Temple in search of my old rooms in Garden Court, to which I came in 1851, a sanguine eager lad of twenty. . . .[14] I also took a walk along the wonderful Thames Embankment, a splendid work, and I sighed to think how impossible it would be to get such a thing done in New York where there is fifty times as much need for it. The differences in government and political manners are in fact awful and for me very depressing. James and I talk over them sometimes, "des larmes dans la voix." We have to console ourselves by remembering all the good Americans we know and love. From the embankment I went on to the city and saw Howard Potter, had a little chat and promised to visit him in his country house at Windsor. At Alma Tadema's I had a long talk with George Lewis, the famous attorney, who is managing the Parnell case, and with his wife, who wanted me for a night at their country house on the Thames. . . .

To-day (Wednesday) I went to the Commission . . . and visited the Grosvenor Gallery . . . and spent an hour with Turner in the National Gallery. Nothing will ever persuade me that Turner's *later* works are not arrant humbug. . . . Later in the P.M. I called on Mrs. Yates-Thompson, who has made several unsuccessful attempts to get me to dinner; found her alone and sat for an hour nearly. She is pretty and they have a pretty house. I forgot to say that last night I dined *en famille* with———'s [15] old lover, or "alleged lover," who has since married a rich girl. . . .

34 De Vere Gardens W., London, June 20 [1889]

. . . To-day James and I went down to Ascot and saw the Cup race—the principal one—driving through Windsor Park in lovely weather. We got back in the evening in time for a dinner at Macmillan's, the publisher, who has a pretty little American wife. The person of most interest present was Mrs. Green, the widow of the historian. To-night I dine with Bryce and expect to meet the G.O.M.

Your two letters of the 10th and 11th came together yesterday. I have moments of homesickness when it is a great comfort to see your handwriting, and know you are waiting for me beyond the sea. . . .

34 De Vere Gardens W., London, June 22 [1889]

. . . [Yesterday evening] I went to Bryce's to dinner. . . . I found, on going in, Sir Alfred Lyall, whom I knew, Sir George Trevelyan, whom I did not know, but was glad to meet, Wemyss Reid, the biographer of Forster, whom I had been trying to meet ever since I came, and Lord Aberdeen, Mahlon's friend.[16] But the G.O.M. was not there and I was afraid to ask whether he was coming. Suddenly "Mr. and Mrs. Gladstone" were announced, and there sure enough he was, and my eyes fastened on him as they have never fastened on any man since I was twenty. The first words he said to Bryce on shaking hands were, "Is Mr. Godkin here?" and then he began apologizing to me for not having sooner taken any notice of my card, pleading pressure and loss of voice since he came back from his stumping tour in the West. I sat by him at dinner and had a most delightful talk with him. He is younger in appearance than I expected, as young as I am in play of mind, with a charming little vein of humor and endless interest in all sorts of things. . . .

34 De Vere Gardens W., London, June 24 [1889]

. . . I came back from Waddesden this morning. There was a large party of whom the principals were Mr. and Mrs. Humphry Ward, Mrs. Green, widow of the historian, Lord and Lady Pembroke, Sir Philip Currie, under secretary of foreign affairs—

very pleasant—Lord and Lady Burton—he the great brewer, and the Harcourts. The place is splendid but bare and new looking. I was glad to see it.

To-night I dine with the Leslie Stephens.[17] I begin to long for home unspeakably. . . .

1. This letter and the letters to Godkin's wife that follow may be found in Ogden 2:140–54. Because of Ogden's inaccuracy with dates, the letters herein do not always bear the dates that he assigned them.

2. Mrs. Godkin, a sufferer from sea sickness, did not accompany her husband to England. Later she overcame her fears and went with him on his annual holidays to England and the Continent. Daisy Miller, of course, is the unconventional heroine of Henry James's novel of the same name.

3. Southampton banker William Darwin was the son of the great naturalist, Charles Darwin. His wife was the former Sara Sedgwick, sister of Arthur and Theodora Sedgwick and sister-in-law of Charles Eliot Norton. For a delightful recollection of the William Darwins, see Gwen Raverat, *Period Piece* (New York: W. W. Norton, 1952).

4. Sir Charles Russell, James Bryce, Albert V. Dicey, and, probably, Dicey's brother-in-law, Sir John Bonham-Carter.

5. Ogden omitted the woman's name, but she was undoubtedly Mrs. Frank H. Hill, Godkin's old Belfast friend, to whom he occasionally wrote during the 1880s. The fact that Mrs. Hill's husband never alluded to her in his letters to Godkin prompts speculation that he resented their friendship.

6. The distinguished historian Lord Acton (1834–1902) had just been voted the D.C.L. by Oxford University.

7. Godkin had become acquainted with Edward Freeman during the historian's American lectures in 1881–82. The day after writing this letter Godkin declined an invitation from Freeman to spend the weekend with him. F. Max Müller was the celebrated philologist who tilted with William D. Whitney and Addison Van Name in the *Nation* over their reviews of his *Chips From a German Workshop*.

8. A reference to two of Godkin's sisters, Kate and Georgina. Georgina lived in Italy with their widowed mother and wrote minor works of history and fiction. Their father, James Godkin, had been dead ten years, and a younger brother, Anthony, went to Australia and was lost sight of. Edwin, although he had a certain talent for friendship, did not get along with his father, and he showed little interest in his mother or in his sisters.

9. The Cobdenite politician, Sir Thomas Farrer (1819–99) had recently retired as secretary of the Board of Trade.

10. Marian Ashton was the fiancée of James Bryce.

11. The successful painter, Sir Laurence Alma-Tadema (1836–1912), had a lavish new house in St. John's Wood that was a fashionable meeting place for the gifted and important.

12. The great French comic actor Benoît Coquelin (1841–1909) had re-

signed from the *Comédie Française* after a dispute and was playing single engagements with his son.

13. Sir John R. Robinson (1828–1903) managed the *Daily News* of London during its halcyon days, 1868–87.

14. Godkin is referring here to the Middle Temple in London where he went in 1851 to study law. Ironically, it was his failure in the law that made possible his fame as an editorial writer.

15. Ogden, no doubt complying with the wishes of the Godkin family, omitted the woman's name. See also July 5 letter below.

16. The former Indian civil servant, Sir Alfred Lyall (1835–1911), was then winning praise for his *Verses Written in India* (London: Kegan Paul and Co., 1889). The historian Sir George Otto Trevelyan (1838–1928) was serving in Parliament. Editor and writer T. Wemyss Reid (1842–1905) was attaining prominence in Gladstonian Liberal circles; he began and edited the *Speaker*. Lord Aberdeen (1847–1934), grandson of an earlier prime minister, was also active in the Liberal party, and his friend "Mahlon" was Katharine Godkin's recently deceased brother, Mahlon Sands. Lady Aberdeen was known for her activity in social and family planning.

17. Writer Leslie Stephen (1832–1904) was in ill health from his heavy labors in launching the *Dictionary of National Biography*. Godkin met him during his 1870 visit to the United States and there was introduced by him to James Bryce.

To an unnamed correspondent

34 De Vere Gardens W., London, [ca. 27 June 1889]
(Fragment, Godkin Papers, MH)

. . . Bryce has been sued for libel by Oakey Hall, on account of an allusion to him in the history of the N.Y. ring furnished by Goodnow of Columbia to his book, and has retained George Lewis, the famous attorney.[1] He does not think the case will be pushed to trial but fears a good deal of expense. James and I are going down to spend Tuesday night with Lewis in the country. He is a small ferretty looking Jew, but has an extraordinary reputation here as a "solicitor," especially in "delicate" cases. He is probably consulted oftener I am told, in blackmail cases which are very numerous here, than all the other London lawyers put together, and I learn to my surprise, that he generally advises settlement in money where it is practicable, his dread of the scandal is so great. But how he keeps this class of business I can't imagine, he blabs about it so much.

I have got my winter's supply of clothes . . . and the fit is excellent. . . . The whole people, rich and poor, strike me as *much* better dressed here than in America, and the absence of saliva from the side walks and public stairways is the great solace to me.

I had a delightful morning with the Gr.O.M. besides sitting beside him at a dinner. He is not a bit old, and one doctor here says he may live to 150. Many Tories say they look eagerly for his death every morning when they open their paper, and one I saw in Cheshire, said he would "gladly hang him with his own hands". . . .

Yours ever
ELG

1. Writer and political leader A. Oakey Hall (1826–98) was acquitted of charges of complicity in the Tweed Ring during his term as mayor of New York, 1868–72.

To his wife

34 De Vere Gardens W. London, June 27 [1889] [1]

. . . When I got back from Waddesden on Monday, I drove straight to Gladstone's by appointment and had nearly two hours very interesting talk with him. He is much less old than I expected, and the flexibility and vivacity of his mind are something astonishing, to say nothing of his fluency. He talked of the Episcopal Church in America, recalling with curious fidelity things I had said about it at dinner on the previous Friday; talked of our and the English schools, education in general; Newman's views of the conscience, which he demolished; the effect of scepticism on morals, which he said was in England very bad, particularly as regarded the conjugal tie; about the Liberal Unionists, whom he denounced with curious fire, his eye glowing, his hand uplifted, and his face close to mine; talked of Ireland and the Irish members, whose conduct considering everything he thought very good; of Alan [Thorndike] Rice, of whose humbug he gave me a fresh illustration; of the *North American Review*, and of Reviews in general; of Ingersoll;

finally of Minnie of whom he spoke with great friendliness. We
had two interruptions from Mrs. Gladstone during the interview.
It was most interesting and I think would alone have repaid me
for coming to England. That is, I should not have died happy if
I had not had it.[2]

In the evening I dined with Leslie Stephen, meeting Admiral
Maxse and Mr. and Mrs. Holman Hunt, the painter. Poor
Stephen is in wretched health through over work. On Tuesday I
received a telegram from Sir Charles Russell asking me to go to
court to hear the great Durham-Chetwynd betting case, in which
he is counsel, and I had hardly got there when in walked Robinson, full of eagerness about English fashionable life. At two P.M.
I lunched with Harry. In the afternoon I went up to Oxford
with Dicey, dined in the Common Room of All Souls, with two
prigs, and slept at Dicey's; went to Commemoration in the
Sheldonian Theatre and saw several men get the D.C.L. [Doctor
of Civil Law], Bryce presenting them in Latin speeches, one of
them my attractive friend, Sir Alfred Lyall. Then came a most
delightful lunch in the Library of All Souls, the band playing on
the lawn outside, in the brightest sunshine ever seen in England.
The company assembled in the quadrangle, and included many
celebrities. I was introduced and had a long but *not* interesting
talk with Jowett of Balliol, a chubby-faced man with a small
mouth, very disappointing in appearance. Also with Max Müller,
and with many others, and took into lunch a Mrs. Willett, a connection of the Darwins. About three hundred sat down in the
glorious hall, where we were beautifully served—such a terrible
contrast to the Harvard and Yale Commencement dinners—flowers, old silver, hock and claret cup, and all the rest of it. The
scarlet robes of the numerous doctors, one of whom was Brown-
ing, lighted up the scene. I had to miss a very attractive garden
party in Worcester College, in order to catch the train for
town. I came down with Bryce and Dicey and had just time to
dress for dinner at Admiral Maxse's, where I met Stead, the editor of the *Pall Mall Gazette*. Maxse has a charming daughter and
niece. James called for me at eleven and we went to the annual
reception of the Royal Academy, an immense crowd of all the
swells in the place. From there we went to a party at Lord
Hartington's in Devonshire House, where the crowd was still

greater, but the rooms splendid, and where I saw a great many old acquaintances—Francis Buxton, Leonard Courtney, the deputy Speaker of the House, who visited us in New York twenty-three years ago, and others. They all showered invitations upon me which, alas! I cannot accept.

This morning I lunched at the Harcourts, meeting at last after several disappointments, John Morley, the good, delightful, wholly-satisfactory John Morley. The rest of the company—Lady Frederic Cavendish, Hartington's sister-in-law, and our hostess of last night, and a son of Chamberlain's.[3] Morley tried to get me to dinner, but I am engaged ten days ahead, so I am going to lunch with him next week. After lunch I spent an hour at the Royal Academy Exibition, among the pictures. The collection is chiefly remarkable for Herkomer's and Shannon's portraits, some of which are very fine. In fact the British are shining in portraits just now. . . .

Near Richmond Park, June 30 [1889]

. . . On Friday, Robinson of the *Daily News* gave a very good dinner in my honor at the Reform Club, about twelve men, among whom were Andrew Lang, the well-known critic and so forth, whom I was very glad to meet; Black the novelist, and Wemyss Reid and some others of less note. Very pleasant. Afterwards I called for James at another dinner and we went together to a party at Lady Russell's, but only to show ourselves as it was a dance. There I had some talk, however, with Sir Charles, and arranged to go hear him examine Davitt at the Parnell trial on Tuesday. Yesterday I came down here to this lovely spot near Richmond Park to spend Saturday till Monday with the Bensons, whom you remember. A family party, walked in the woods and drove to Hampton Court with Benson. . . .

34 De Vere Gardens W., London [July 1889]

. . . Last night, after writing to you, I dined with Lord Coleridge at the "Literary Society," a club which comes down from and is the successor of that which Johnson and Burke and Goldsmith formed at the Coffee House. The company was Lord Justice Bowen, a charming man, Sir Grant Duff, a well-known politician and late governor of Madras, Theodore Martin, the silly biographer of the Prince Consort, the Dean of Westminster, Sidney Colvin, the curator of the British Museum, Spencer Walpole, the oldest man who has sat in the House of Commons, Harry James and others. They never sit at the table more than two hours, and after drinking my health in a solemn old-fashioned way, we broke up and I went down to the House of Commons for a couple of hours, where I saw Bryce and Shaw-Lefevre. . . . On my way to Liverpool I want to spend a day or two with my delightful friend Albert Pell, as per the enclosed note. To go over the field of Naseby where Cromwell won his greatest battle, has been one of the dreams of years. . . .

34 De Vere Gardens W., London, July 4 [1889]

. . . On Monday I had a note from G[race Kuhn] telling of her arrival, and I went to her rooms the next morning early, and carried her off to Russell's chambers in Lincoln's Inn, and he took her over to the gallery in the Court room of the Parnell Commission, while Hamilton and I sat with him in the bar below, hearing him examine Davitt—one of the field-day occasions. We went and lunched afterwards, G[race], H[amilton] and I at the Criterion, and when I found I had missed my train for George Lewis's, I came back and dined with them. She is very attractive, animated, interested and seems very well. She gave good accounts of you. The next day I took G[race] and H[amilton] to the Parnell Commission, but left early myself to lunch with John Morley, but found a note putting me off, so I went and called on Lord and Lady Hobhouse—old acquaintances—and sat half an hour with both; they had vainly asked me to dinner last week; and also on Macmillan, the publisher, with whom I had dined the week I arrived.

Last night we dined at Sir Charles Russell's, the principal company being Lord Spencer, Lord and Lady Coleridge, the Lord Mayor, Lewis the solicitor and his wife, Miss Trevelyan, etc. I took in Miss Drummond. I had a charming Mrs. Lucy on the other side, and Lord Spencer at the corner of the table, with whom I had much good talk. He had already vainly asked me to dinner. . . .

To-day we lunch with Harry. . . . To-night I dine with the Miss Trevelyans. . . .

34 De Vere Gardens W., London, July 5 [1889]

. . . I had a pleasant visit at Mrs. Humphry Ward's yesterday afternoon in a large pleasant house in Russell Square. If we could only have such houses in New York! I don't think the rent is over $700 or $1,000! She has a very attractive face, sweet, gentle, serious and sensitive, with such nice manners. Everybody says she has no humor, but I did not detect the want of it.

In the morning I spent an hour with the Darwins in the Grosvenor Gallery, and then went to lunch at H[ill?]'s with James. There was Hamilton Aidé—the *pièce de résistance*—Lord and Lady G——— and young Herbert.

I dined in the evening at the Miss Lefevres, where I met a party of Home Rulers. Mrs. Kay—*née* Drummond—the daughter of the famous Irish secretary of former days, Barry O'Brien his biographer, whom I was glad to meet, Osborne Morgan, a member of Parliament, who asked me whether I had heard of a book called the "American Commonwealth," written by a friend of his, Mr. Bryce. "You bet," was my prompt answer.

I came home early and James and I sat up late talking, with many "bouffées de rire". . . .

The Athenaeum, London, July 6 [1889]

. . . I think I brought you up in my last to my going to lunch at Lord Spencer's. It was very pleasant. Mr. and Mrs. Gladstone, Lord Granville, the Marchioness of Aylesbury, a wonderful old relic, Mr. Leveson-Gower, and a very bright Miss Margo Tennant, and one or two others. I sat at one side of Lady Spencer, who is very pleasant, but distinctly *grande dame*, and Mr. Gladstone on the other, and he talked incessantly, but he is distinctly deaf. After the lunch, which lasted long, I went to G[race] K[uhn]'s and we went to the National Gallery and some print shops, and then James and I visited the Darwins, dined in the evening at the Oxford and Cambridge Club, with Robartes, who had Channing, one of the Boston Channings, who is now a member of Parliament and a naturalized Englishman, and a very amusing Dr. Yeo and a man named Praed, the husband of the novelist, who has just recovered $2,500 damages against a man for libel, for saying he had asked a young lady to dine alone with him at a restaurant. We had a very amusing evening, and then James and I walked home, through streets crowded with people, waiting to see the Shah, about whom London is going wild in a silly manner. The way well-dressed women will stand for hours in the hot sun, on the sidewalks, to see him pass is beyond belief.

This morning I breakfasted with Shaw Lefevre, a very pleasant party. . . .

I forgot to say that before going to Spencers, I spent a pleasant hour in the British Museum, going over the library and print collections with the Director, Sidney Colvin. The historical arrangement of the engravings, etchings and mezzotints is such that one could get instructed in the most wonderful manner by a few days study of them, with a handbook they furnish. There is nothing like it, he tells me, in the world. The Japanese department is especially remarkable. After he left me, I spent an hour or two on my own account among the statuary, Greek and Roman. . . .

Abinger Hall, Surrey, July 7 [1889]

. . . I came down here to Sir Thomas Farrer's—a delightful house in the most charming part of Surrey—yesterday. The party is Mrs. Green, the historian's widow, Mr. and Mrs. Paul, she is a sister of the Ritchie who has married Miss Thackeray, and a very charming woman, he a literary man, a very good fellow, Mr. and Mrs. Sidney Buxton, she very sweet and humorous, he a member of Parliament and good Home Ruler, and Mr. and Mrs. Yates-Thompson whom you know. But the gem of the occasion is Lady Farrer, who is a granddaughter of Sir James Mackintosh and a delightful woman, bright as a button, a charming talker with delightful manners. She is a credit to her grandfather. The house is large and handsome, full of that wonderful English completeness. But the scenery is what is best. You can imagine no more delightful picture of English rural peace than I have from my windows . . . the flowers, the hedges, the trees, the ferns, the heath, the lanes, the rolling hills, the old farmhouses, would set you nearly crazy. . . .

Later. I have just come back from the walk, which was mainly with Mrs. Green and was mostly through woods and over heath and furze-covered hills, and past *old, old* farmhouses, all of which you would have enjoyed so much that it gives me a heartache to think it was not with you. My talk with Mrs. Green was mostly of Ireland—she is Irish—and was rather hopeless. I am getting rather tired, and shall be glad when I get into the train for Italy, on Wednesday.

To-morrow (July 8th) I lunch with John Morley, go to the House of Commons in the P.M., and dine with the Roseberys.[4] On Tuesday I lunch with the Whites, tea with Mrs. Green, dine with the Buxton's, which closes the campaign. All efforts to get hold of Parnell, to meet me, have been in vain. He is undergoing one of his periodic eclipses, when no letters reach him and nothing is heard from him. Everyone says he is an extraordinary man, but very queer. . . .

34 De Vere Gardens W., London, July 10 [1889]

. . . I am leaving for Italy in an hour. I breakfasted with Bryce yesterday, after a dull aristocratic dinner at Rosebery's, where I took in Miss Ferguson, whom you remember in New York, a very pleasant girl. I lunched with the Whites to meet Lincoln, the new minister, Lord and Lady Ribblesdale and others; took tea with Mrs. Green; called on Lowell and dined with the Buxtons. So I had a pretty busy day. My visit to London has been crowded with impressions, and of Harry James's kindness and *niceness* in all ways, I cannot speak adequately. He is a delightful creature, too good for either England or America.

I spent an hour yesterday with G[race] K[uhn] at the miniature exhibition, with the Yates-Thompsons. She had just been to a sympathetic doctor with Mrs. ———— who said the whole trouble is neither husband nor children, but liver! . . .

Milan, July 12 [1889]

. . . Here I am since last evening at five o'clock. . . . James came with me to the station and said the thought of what I was going to see made it very difficult not to come with me. The climb of the train up from Lucerne is a wonderful piece of engineering, as it does not enter the tunnel till very near the top, and there all along was the delightful old carriage road that I had walked up as far as the Hospice in 1862, Fanny riding most of the way; now I fear greatly spoiled by the railroad.[5]

As soon as I could change my clothes I hurried out to the Cathedral. It made my poor English cathedrals seem small affairs. It is a marvellous building and I spent an hour walking about or sitting, lost in admiration and in sorrow, too, I must say, that there is not something real behind such a splendid expression of faith, something that all men, perforce, acknowledge, and that it is not in more fitting hands than these wretched priests.

After dinner I went back to the great square, which was flooded, cathedral and all, with full moonlight. Think of that! Got a little table in front of a café and drank my *limonade* like the rest and enjoyed the wonderful spectacle. There were crowds of people promenading and listening to the band, and among the officers I saw the uniform of my dear old friend Crespi's regiment, the "Cavalerie Légère d'Aosta," which is quartered here and was in the Crimea. The sight of it filled me with memories of thirty-five years ago, when he and I used to travel across the Balaclava Plain. *Sempre avanti Savoia!* (the motto of the regiment), I used to call out in joke when we rose into a gallup. . . . It is too bad that you are not with me; shall we ever travel together before I am too old for enjoyment? . . .

Palazzo Gritti, Venice, July 14 [1889]

. . . I spent the morning of Friday wandering about Milan although it was very warm, but gave my last hour to the cathedral, from which I tore myself away with difficulty to go to the train at one P.M. The journey across Lombardy was most interesting to me and I devoured the country with my eyes, the mountains in the background the whole way and the Largo di Garda coming on me with a sudden burst. At Peschiera we came on familiar historic ground to me. It was of the rising of the people against the Austrians in 1849 that Clough wrote that fine piece, "Tis better to have fought and lost than never to have fought at all." A bit of philosophy the unsuccessful find it hard to swallow. An Italian captain of Artillery got into the carriage with me here, with whom I had a great deal of interesting talk as far as Verona. The day was hot, the train slow. You may guess with what joy toward sunset I saw the land dwindling and the sea growing, and looking out of the window saw Venice rising from the water in the distance, and the desire of forty years gratified.

In a few minutes we ran into the station. I found Georgina waiting for me with a gondola and we came home through the smaller canals in the twilight to save time, and finally issued on the Grand Canal and this house, which is just opposite the Salute Church.[6] I cannot give you an idea of the impression of that first sail. To crown all, the moon, very full, was just rising and the water, after a hot day, was alive with gondolas and bathers. . . .

On Saturday morning we went to St. Mark's and the palace which you know all about. I was taken aback by St. Mark's, much as I was prepared for it. It is a wonderful artistic display, such as a wealthy aristocracy might like their church to be, but not in my eyes a good place of worship—in which I see I differ from Howells as well as from greater men. I went again in the P.M. and again this morning, but the first impression remains unchanged. For solemnity and religious suggestion it can't be compared to Milan, which almost persuades one to be a Christian. St. Mark's excites my curiousity and aesthetic admiration, but the gods and saints to which it turns my thoughts are Ruskin and Charles Norton. The Doge's Palace, as you may guess, made the deepest impression on my young mind. . . .

I am very well and bearing the heat beautifully. You need not be in the least troubled about the healthfulness of Venice; it is growing every year as a summer resort. There is nothing in the world like it, and it deepens my admiration of the wonderful Italian race. Think of having built Rome and Venice and Florence, and founded the Roman Empire and the Catholic Church! . . .

Northern Italy [ca. 16 July 1889]

. . . By the way, I had a delightful little Crimean reminiscence again yesterday. I came in a narrow street on other old friends, the Bersaglieri or riflemen of the old Piedmontese army, little men, with cocks' tails in their hats and dark green uniforms, who march always quick-step to the bugles. They were forming up to relieve the guard, and I followed them out into the piazza almost with tears in my eyes. I saw them go into action at the battle of the Tchernaya, to retake a bridge they had lost at daybreak. Govone and I were watching them together, our hearts in our mouths.[7] They took it, but lost heavily, and I rode among their dead in the white, dusty highroad in the afternoon, and see it all now through the mists of thirty-five years. . . .

1. This letter and the letters to Godkin's wife that follow may be found in Ogden 2:154–68; 1:21–22. Ogden removed the names "Grace and Hamilton Kuhn" from these letters. Mrs. Kuhn, of Lenox, Massachusetts, was for a time a close friend of the Godkins.

2. Later, between hearty laughs, Godkin would describe to friends his visit with Gladstone. The loquacious statesman was nearing eighty, and, according to Godkin, talked uninterruptedly for a full hour; then, rising to allow his visitor to take his leave, he told Godkin how much he had enjoyed "our conversation." The Liberal Unionists were old-line Liberals or, more correctly, Whigs who left the Liberal party chiefly because of their opposition to home rule for Ireland.

3. Sir William Vernon Harcourt (1827–1904) succeeded Gladstone in 1894 as leader of the Liberal party in Parliament. Lady Frederick Cavendish was the widow of the principal victim of the Phoenix Park murders. Her brother-in-law, Lord Hartington (1833–1908), was the leader of the Liberal Unionists.

4. Lord Rosebery (1847–1919) succeeded Gladstone as prime minister in 1894.

5. A reference to Godkin's two-year sojourn in Europe with his first wife.

6. Godkin's sister Georgina and his mother had come from Florence to be with him in Venice.

7. Guiseppe Govone was a Piedmontese officer with whom Godkin became friends during the Crimean War. Afterwards Italian minister of war, he committed suicide in the aftermath of a political scandal.

To Silas W. Burt

New York, August 8, 1889 (Burt Papers, NHi)

MY DEAR BURT: Many thinks for your note. I was most politely treated by the Custom house men, and wrote a note to Beattie thanking him for it. But I had nothing dutiable. . . .[1]

I had a most delightful time in England, and stayed there except ten days in Italy to see my old mother, who has been living there for a great many years. I wish most sincerely I could run down and see you for a day or two . . . but White and others here have been waiting for my return to get off, and I must now stick to the laboring oar for a while, though I confess I find returning to the discussion of Grant . . . and Harrison and Quay

weary work.[2] The milennium is dreadfully slow in coming—isn't
it? . . .

Ever cordially yours
ELG

1. Godkin is referring to his having received the "courtesies of the port"
exemption from customs inspection on his return from Europe, an interesting practice in the light of his and Burt's demands for integrity in public
officials. Thereafter Godkin, on his European junkets, bought most of his
clothing abroad, happily accepting the "courtesies of the port" at New
York and sometimes writing Burt to request them for his friends.

2. A reference to New York Mayor Hugh Grant, President Benjamin
Harrison, and Pennsylvania political boss Matthew S. Quay.

10. Battling the "Beasts of Tammany" in the 1890s

Godkin viewed compassion—like sentimentality—as weakness, and his fiery editorials normally spare neither friend nor foe. A recurrent theme in them during the 1890s is his mounting distaste for popular government. "This experiment in democratic government," he told his editorial protégé, Joseph B. Bishop, "is practically sure to fail. The trouble is I'm afraid I shan't be here to see it fail." An example of what disturbed him was Tammany Hall. The sins of that organization arising, as Godkin believed, out of universal manhood suffrage, irritated him quite as much as the corporate frauds and peculations of Tammany's respectable Republican opponents. Confronted with the alternative of co-operating with Tammany or with the conservative upstate Republican machine of Senator Thomas Platt, Godkin reluctantly chose Platt. Like other philosophical radicals who had found democracy useful for attaining bourgeois control, he saw the warts on it once the masses demanded a share of the power.

The reason Tammany flourished in New York, Godkin believed, was that most of the city's voters were "unendowed with the self restraint and discrimination of men bred to the responsibilities of citizenship." Especially was this true of recent immigrants. Whatever "a man's abstract right to vote may be, the fact is that he cannot vote without either benefitting or injuring his neighbor."

During the four years that Cleveland and the Democrats were initially in power, Godkin bowed to the exigencies of politics and refrained from attacking Tammany. But after the inauguration of President Benjamin Harrison in 1889 he and Horace White embarked the *Post* and the *Nation* on a relentless attack on the New York City Democratic machine. One of their tactics was the compilation of an anti-Irish Voter's Directory containing thumbnail biographies of the "Pats," "Barneys," and "Mikes" who dominated Tammany Hall. One after another those whom the *Evening Post* accused of malfeasance took Godkin to court; one after another the criminal libel charges against him were dismissed. Godkin almost hoped that one of his victims would assault him, but the closest he ever came to suffering physical retaliation was earlier—when a streetcar conductor that he was upbraiding shoved him from his car.

Some of the editor's charges against the Tammany leaders were true, others false. One of the irritating things about Godkin and his followers was their unreadiness to concede error or to engage in calm dialogue with those with whom they disagreed. Neither the *Nation* nor the *Evening Post* under Godkin were the market place of ideas they might have been.

In 1895 infighting broke out in the Reform movement in New York City. In the *Evening Post* and in the *Nation* Godkin attacked John Jay Chapman, a leader of the Good Government (Goo-Goo) faction. Although Godkin's Mugwump acquaintance Bishop Potter came to the defense of the Goo-Goos, Godkin did not desist in his public criticisms of them. Later, in his little magazine *The Nursery*, Chapman took his revenge. Comparing the two most famous New York editors, the "narrow and good" Godkin with the "cultivated and cynical" Charles A. Dana, Chapman came to the conclusion that each man hated the other because "each is the sort of hypocrite that the other most despises."

Yet to try to intimidate Godkin was, as someone said, like trying to stay the east wind. For his fearlessness in pointing out evil he gathered many admirers but few close friends. To some powerful acquaintances— J. P. Morgan and Andrew Carnegie, for example—he granted immunity to criticism, but others never knew when it might be their turn under his editorial lash. William Dean Howells acknowledged to Charles Eliot Norton his gratitude for Godkin's kind treatment of him (Howells) in the *Nation*, but Howells was puzzled at Godkin's continually abusing others "quite as deserving." William James grudgingly conceded that Godkin's editorial distemper was the reason half of James's friends were opposed in 1903 to the establishment at Harvard of the Godkin Lectures. One of these friends, Henry Lee Higginson,

dismissed to James the Godkin of the 1890s as a slanderer of enlarged "conceit, arrogance [and] evil temper." New Yorkers,
whatever their allegiance, chuckled appreciatively at the bon mot
that had Dana's *Sun* making vice attractive to New Yorkers in the
morning while in the evening Godkin's *Post* was "making virtue
odious."

Yet, none of this censure shook Godkin and his followers in
their conviction that stern voices were needed to arrest the moral
decay of their age. Admirers, while admitting that Godkin was
not always fair, lauded him as an honorable man fighting for the
survival of genteel values.

To James Bryce

115 East 25th St., New York, November 8, 1889
(Bryce Papers, Oxford University)

MY DEAR BRYCE: I cabled you yesterday asking you to wait, if possible until you heard from me, before selecting an attorney to take testimony etc. in the Hall case here. I did this as the result of a talk with Robinson, Carter and other lawyers. . . .[1] The man here who is of all men best fitted for this work is Albert Stickney, who was the attorney in preparing and pushing the case against Judge Barnard on which he was convicted. He is familiar with all the ins and outs of the Tweed Ring, and knows exactly where to go for everything. . . .

I had a letter from Wemyss Reid several weeks ago about the new paper, asking me to act as their American correspondent, and I agreed to do so, if I was not to be tied to fixed periods and to be left to my own judgment as to when a letter was necessary. I blew the horn for it a little in the *Evening Post* the other day.[2]

Garrison is looking after the procuring of newspaper files of 1870 for you. There has been little comment on Hall's suit here, because I think, most people look on it as a good joke, and then we are so used here to the bringing of libel suits for mere effect on the public mind, without any intention of pushing them to trial. There is no commoner device of a public rascal. We have three such hanging over us now, to which we pay no attention.

I hope you have seen a letter I wrote to the *Manchester Guardian* on Saturday last. . . . It contained the official figures of the amount of Sweeny's restitution. He also escaped like Hall because the money could not be traced to his bank account. He restored $444,000 on behalf of "his brother."

Yours ever
ELG

1. A reference to Oakey Hall's law suit against Bryce for inferences against him in Frank Goodnow's chapter of *The American Commonwealth* dealing with the Tweed Ring. The prominent New York lawyers, E. Randolph Robinson and James C. Carter, were close acquaintances of Godkin, Carter having served with him on the ill-starred commission appointed by Governor Tilden in 1875 to devise a system of government for the cities of New York, and Randolph having served with him on the civil service commission of New York City.

2. "A New English Weekly," *Evening Post*, 4 November 1889. This is an announcement of the appearance of the *Speaker*, a political journal launched by Wemyss Reid in behalf of the Liberal party. Although Godkin regarded himself as an Independent in American politics, he was a Gladstone Liberal in English politics.

To Grace Ashburner

115 East 25th St., New York, January 6, 1890
(Ashburner Papers, MStoc)

MY DEAR MISS GRACE: . . . [I] trust this will find you as well as anybody can be in this new African climate of ours.[1]

When I came back from England last August, I had a fixed resolve to run on to Ashfield and Cambridge before the winter closed in to tell you of my adventures during my trip, or rather experiences, for I had no adventures. But I found it impossible to get away after so long an absence. . . .

I wish I had more of our news to tell you . . . . No mill horse ever had a more regular and circular life than I do. . . . Lawrence is still with us, more and more absorbed in the law, and much improved in health, but shows no sign of marrying though he is in his thirtieth year. . . .

We had a delightful little glimpse of Charles Norton and Sally, one evening when they were here. How charming she is!

I sincerely hope Cambridge has not been desolated by the grippe as New York has. Half the men I know have been sick with it, and there have been a few very sad deaths from it. The city has steamed today like a tropical forest, making exercise impossible, and hot food repulsive. Tomorrow I go down town for the first time in ten days, after a dismal experience! We have alarming rumors here about the course of the gulf stream, but Cambridge is probably too scientific to pay any attention to them.

If you do not feel well enough to write us your news perhaps the indefatigable Theodora might find a moment for the purpose. But in any case, believe in the affectionate remembrance and good wishes for Miss Anne and yourself of your old friend

ELG
who sends Katharine's regards

1. The East Coast was experiencing an unseasonal warmth, with an epidemic of virus infection.

To James Monroe Taylor [1]

> 115 East 25th St., New York, January 14, 1890
> (Taylor Papers, NPV)

DEAR SIR: I ought sooner [to] have answered your kind invitation to address your college on the 21st. of Feb. I am of course much flattered by its repetition this year.

But I find some difficulty in accepting. I have undertaken some work for the reviews which just now keep me very busy. They pay me at a rate which I feel I ought not to ask as a lecturer, because I am really not a lecturer, having delivered but a few lectures[,] and these of the Collegiate sort, and am generally an oratorical disappointment. . .

> Very truly yours
> ELG

1. James Monroe Taylor (1848–1916) was president of Vassar College.

To Henry Holt

> January 21, 1890 (Ogden 2:130)

. . . I understand, of course, that you are free to sell between now and March 2, but if anybody bought, I should go after him with a shotgun.[1] Please make this known. I am not as law-abiding as I seem. . . .

1. A reference to Bon Repos.

To Silas W. Burt

> 115 East 25th St., New York, January 28, 1890
> (Burt Papers, NHi)

MY DEAR BURT: I send you herewith a bottle of some old port which was given me some weeks ago. It needs straining through muslin before use, as you will see, but has great excellence. Taken in large quantities it will make you happy as a king; a glass now and then will build you up, and increase your zeal for reform.

With best wishes for your health and prosperity.

Yours most truly

ELG

To Former President Grover Cleveland

Evening Post Editorial Rooms   New York, March 3, 1890
(Cleveland Papers, DLC)

MY DEAR MR. CLEVELAND: I have to acknowledge the receipt of your check for $856.82 being half the bill of Rogers Locke Milburn.

Let me add that we all here think your contribution to the expense of the suit ample and in all respects satisfactory to us. Allow me at the same time to congratulate you most humbly on the result of the trial, for it was a triumph for you as well as for us.[1]

Yours very sincerely

ELG

1. A reference to the inconclusive settlement of a five-year-old libel action against Godkin by the Rev. Dr. George H. Ball. During the bitterly contested election of 1884 the *Evening Post* accused Ball of lewd personal behavior when the Buffalo clergyman helped publicize the news of Cleveland's illegitimate child. The ensuing trial disclosed that it was a different clergyman of the same name who left Owensburg, Indiana, in haste after "insulting a lady," but Cleveland used his influence to get Godkin a clever lawyer and the court did not award Ball damages. Godkin is thanking Cleveland for paying half of his legal expenses.

To Samuel G. Ward

115 East 15th St., New York, March 30, 1890 (Ward Papers, MH)

MY DEAR WARD: I think the *Post* did kill the Blair bill, and I think we have smashed Grant, though I say it, who shouldn't.[1] Many thanks for your kindly recognition of the fact.

The Anti Catholic Movement in Boston is a ridiculous affair, but possibly also mischievous, for I see the *Sun* here is connecting it with the movement for ballot reform by pointing out that the same men are prominent in both. We are going to have some biographical sketches of the Tammany chiefs some day this week illustrating the kind of men who rule New York, which will amuse you. . . .

Yes, we are moving down to 10th. St. where we have bought a house, getting much more room down there for the same money we could uptown. . . . Our winter has otherwise been uneventful. The only novel incident is the appearance of Professor Royce of Harvard, as a drawing room lecturer on philosophy.[2] Sixty or seventy New York women and some men listening to a lecture on Kant in Whitney's ball room last night was an odd sight. How much they profit by it I don't know, but it is a sign of better things in New York I hope. . . .

Always faithfully yours
ELG

1. Godkin scathingly attacked the Tammany-backed Mayor of New York, Hugh J. Grant, in the *Evening Post* ("Our Mayoral Curiosity") on 24 March 1890.

2. Josiah Royce (1855–1916).

To Henry C. Lea

Evening Post Editorial Rooms   New York, April 9, 1890
(Lea Papers, PU)

DEAR MR. LEA: We shall ourselves in a few days issue a revised edition of the charges against Quay, and I propose printing these with your letter to the President received this morning, unless delay will injure it.[1] If so please let me know.

Yours very sincerely
ELG

1. Matthew S. Quay (1833–1904), the leader of the Pennsylvania Republican organization and a power in national party circles, was ultimately tried on a charge of misappropriating state funds but was acquitted. Lea belonged to the reform faction of the Republican party in Pennsylvania that wanted to throw out the Quay machine.

To Charles L. Brace

April 20, 1890 (Ogden 2:192)

MY DEAR BRACE: What with moving from Twenty-Fifth Street, and storing furniture and getting installed in a furnished apartment for a brief period here, and being occasionally arrested and getting ready to be arrested, I have neglected acknowledging the receipt of your book, "The Unknown God," for which a great many thanks. . . . I see it very favorably reviewed in the English papers. . . .

When do you go abroad? I was sorry to hear you say you needed the baths; I hope you are not ailing seriously. I keep wonderfully free from my rheumatism but live in fear and trembling, because we don't get hardier as we grow older.

Best remembrance to your little household; try and drop in before you go, any day, to lunch.

Yours ever most truly
ELG

To Richard Watson Gilder

Evening Post Editorial Rooms   New York, April 25, 1890
(Gilder Papers, NN)

DEAR MR. GILDER: It would have been difficult or impossible I think, to persuade the Tammany people and our Democratic contemporaries that your letter was not written in the office, if printed without your name. With your name it is very valuable, so as you permitted it I have used it, with your signature.[1]

I go before the grand jury today, but I don't think they will indict me; but do not greatly care if they do.

Yours very sincerely
ELG

---

1. During Cleveland's first administration, the *Evening Post* soft-pedalled its criticisms of Tammany Hall in deference to Democratic party wishes, but, with the departure of Cleveland from office, Godkin mounted an editorial offensive that included the circulation of a pamphlet scurrilously attacking Tammany leaders. A rumor arose that the editor was marked for physical retaliation, which, if true, Gilder assured the *Evening Post* in a

letter to the editor, would bring "a cyclone of civic wrath" against Tammany.

To James Russell Lowell

45 5th Ave., New York, May 12, 1890 (Autograph File, MH)

MY DEAR LOWELL: I did not imagine when I got your letter and the very droll verses that I should be lacking in thanking you for both. But when I tell you that I was about that time moving from one house to another, undergoing arrest about every second day and keeping bail ready for the next occasion besides editing a newspaper you will understand my procrastination. We are having a brief lull just now, but although three indictments against me have been dismissed, there is one still pending, a motion to renew one of the others is to come before the court tomorrow.[1] They would I think, try to "live down" a solitary newspaper attack, but the daily sale of the pamphlet keeps them in constant fury, which I must confess I enjoy. . . .

My wife . . . would almost feel easier if I were as you supposed "behind the bars," than as I am now, for I am followed about all day and night by a "shadow" a precaution which my friends insist on as necessary, but which is a dreadful bore, and fills her head with dismal forebodings. . . .

Affectionately yours,
ELG

1. Two Tammany Hall–backed public officials, Deputy Commissioner of Public Works Bernard F. Martin and Judge Peter Mitchell, had gotten arrest warrants against Godkin for libel. Two of Martin's complaints and one of Mitchell's had been dismissed by the time this letter was written; a second Mitchell complaint was dismissed by the Grand Jury two weeks later.

To Henry C. Lea

Evening Post Editorial Rooms   New York, May 14, 1890
(Lea Papers, PU)

DEAR MR. LEA: I have had a dozen of our Quay pamphlets forwarded to you today. If there be any of your friends who would like to circulate them in Pennsylvania—as I hope there are—we can forward them at $3 a hundred.

What is the outlook there about Quay and Delamater?

Yours very sincerely
ELG

To Henry Villard

The Country Club, Westchester, N. Y., July 2, 1890
(Villard Papers MH)

Dear Mr. Villard: We are going to Lenox for the Fourth of July tomorrow, so that I am afraid we shall not see either you or Mrs. Villard again before you sail. So I write to say a word of good bye to you and Mrs. Villard on behalf of my wife and myself. I have felt sorrier for you both, and especially for you than I can well express. I did not write to you after Hilgard's death, because ever since I went through it all myself, now seventeen years ago, I have felt as if words from anyone on such an occasion were idle.[1] It was a tremendous blow when it came to me, and was followed soon by a heavier one still and I know that under such calamities strength to bear it has to come from within.

Time makes such things easier; nothing else does. But you carry with you my deep sympathy and good wishes, and my thanks for all past kindnesses. We are beginning, in more senses than one to be quite old friends.

With cordial remembrances to Mrs. Villard from both of us[,] believe me always,

Most faithfully yours
ELG

1. Godkin, weeks later, is offering his employer sympathy for the death of one of his sons. Another son, Oswald, lived to become proprietor of the *Nation* after it was separated from the *Evening Post* and, pressed by his twentieth-century associates, converted it into a militant vehicle of social reform. Ever a Mugwump at heart, Oswald Garrison Villard (1872–1949) hypnotized himself—though not his associates—into thinking he was carrying on the *Nation* in the Godkin tradition.

To James Bryce

The Country Club, Westchester, N. Y., July 10, 1890
(Bryce Papers, Oxford University)

MY DEAR BRYCE: I confess I was somewhat relieved on getting your last note to find that you had declined the lecturing scheme. . . . Tyndall, Huxley, Freeman, Arnold, Farrer have all suffered through it in popular estimation here—though perhaps this is not so true of Tyndall and Huxley as of the others. The American lecture was, you doubtless know, never a first class performance. It relied largely on rhetoric and elocution and claptrap for its success, and to be successful you had to learn its tricks.

But I am delighted to hear you are coming over in August, and would be more so if we were settled somewhere. But we have let our house on the Sound this year my wife needs so much more bracing air, and are going up for part of this month, and the whole of August to the N East Harbor in Maine, a cold coast but now a favorite watering place. We have taken part of a house there, where we should be delighted to have you both visit us, in very primitive fashion. Gilman and Eliot are our near neighbors, and other pleasant men, and lots of pleasant women. Can't you come? My wife would join heartily in this prayer, if she were here. But she is visiting in Lenox, and I am staying here alone, going into town everyday (20 miles) until the 24th, when we leave for Maine. Besides this, you must remember, if you stay into October or November, we count on a visit from you in New York, if we can get into our house in time, as it is undergoing alterations. . . .

I have contradicted the lecture story in the *Post*.

I do not know whether you have heard that the Tammany rascals had me arrested four times for exposing them, and tried to get me indicted, but the Grand Jury made short work of them. My friends more than I were afraid of violence for a while, and had me "shadowed."

The *Speaker* is not satisfactory here. The tone is too shrill and screamy, not calm or judicial enough—too much like the ordinary newspaper. I hear disappointment expressed on this score and feel it myself. I hate to read—"We defy any one to point out etc."

The paragraphs too are not as pungent as they might be. But it does contain, nevertheless, a good deal of excellent stuff.

Yours ever
ELG

To his wife

The Country Club, Westchester, N. Y. [July 1890]
(Ogden 2:194–95)

. . . I had a good night at the Knickerbocker Club and came out here this afternoon, a lovely one. Every one puts on an air of joy in seeing me; the night is heavenly, a full Premium Point moon, making the coast as light as day. I wish you were here but I know that "my loss is your gain." The beauty of the night recalls many such at Premium Point, and makes me sorry that life should have passed away as an episode. I wish there had been something more continuous in our existence since our marriage, but I am going into the new house with the firm conviction that I shall only leave it for the "undiscovered country," of which I think a good deal, young and buoyant though I seem.

All is well at the office, every one glad to see me, and the paper prosperous.

I got on the weighing machine with some trepidation considering my *café au lait* and beer and cakes, but found I had only gained three pounds. My heart is still, as it had not been for many months before going away. I shall get to work at my article tomorrow, and the time will thus pass more rapidly till you come. . . .

To his wife

Evening Post Editorial Rooms   [July 1890] (Ogden 2:195–96)

. . . [You are] quite correct about "dread of men for vehement women." Dread is a mild word. I would myself go fifty miles to avoid one. . . . Poor R———. . . . It must be hard to have to make friends with "Fannie." All the Fannie-kind of women are jealous of R——— and are glad to pull her down and trample on her. Oh, my dear, cultivate sweetness and *kindliness* and *politeness*. In the hour of death and in the day of judgment even, they will help you. . . .[1]

1. Curiously, Ogden, no doubt in deference to the Godkins, omitted every name from this letter except "Fannie," a name that, in the context in which Godkin used it, could be construed as derogatory of the first Mrs. Godkin.

To Samuel G. Ward

Evening Post Editorial Rooms   October 2 [1890] *My Birthday*
(Ward Papers, MH)

MY DEAR WARD: . . . [That] you should have indicated my photograph . . . would give you most gratification is I think the greatest compliment I ever received. I send it today by Express.

Neither I nor my wife think it does me justice—you must make some allowance for this family vanity. She maintains I look far more genial than this, and I am disposed to agree with her, but such as it is I am much pleased to know that it will remind you of a man who has done some good in his day, and who remembers most gratefully the support he got from you in days when his claims to public confidence were not so plain as you are now pleased to consider them.

Ever faithfully yours
ELG

To Alfred S. Webb

45 Fifth Avenue, [6 October 1890] (Webb MSS, Cty)

Mr. Godkin has much pleasure in accepting General Webb's kind invitation to meet the Comte de Paris on Friday Oct. 17th 45 Fifth Avenue.[1]

1. Alexander S. Webb (1835–1911) was the president of City College, and the Comte de Paris (1838–94) was the exiled pretender to the French throne.

To R. U. Johnson

36 West 10th St., New York, November 27 [1890]
(*Century Magazine* Correspondence, NN)

DEAR MR. JOHNSON: [1] I do not know exactly what your "series on newspapers," is to be, for I have not seen the announcements, but I do not feel inclined to write anything on or about newspapers. As far as I am concerned the subject is exhausted, and I confess I have not for a good while seen anything new on it from anybody else.

   Thanking you all the same for the invitation, I remain

Yours sincerely
ELG

   1. Writer and pioneer conservationist Robert U. Johnson (1853–1937) was at this time associate editor of *Century Magazine*.

To James Russell Lowell

36 West 10th St., New York, December 14, 1890
(Copy, Lowell Papers, MH)

MY DEAR LOWELL: Thank you very much for the note you sent for the *Nation*. But what to say in acknowledgment of the praise you bestow on my humble labors in the Lord's vineyard I do not know, except that nothing more encouraging or more grateful has reached me during the last twenty-five years. . . .

Affectionately yours
ELG

To Mrs. William F. Smith

Millbrook Inn, Christmas Day [ca. 1890] (Ogden 2:21–22)

   . . . Here we are . . . spending Christmas in the fashion that grows more and more grateful, I think, to childless people as they grow older, in the solitude and silence of the country, with no better distraction than reflection and remembrance. . . . A long tramp over storm-swept roads is our main daily amusement, followed by books, interspersed with jokes in the evening. As usual, under such conditions, we foot up the people we wish were here, and I think your name, like Abou Ben Adhem's, "leads all the rest."

That is good news about Stuart, I congratulate you and him most heartily. His one danger now is of being too clever to work hard, for the world reserves nearly all its good things for the stupid drudges; it dearly loves an ass if he only keeps moving. . . .

To Charles Francis Adams, Jr.

> 36 West 10th St., New York, February 16, 1891
> (Adams Family Papers, MHi)

MY DEAR ADAMS: Many thanks for your kind proposal that we should dine with you on the 21st or 22nd. I know we are engaged on the 21st and as to the 22nd I am afraid we shall have to refer you to Mrs. Kuhn, as we do not know what arrangements she may have made for us, and are in her hands. If she has no objection to offer, it will give us great pleasure on the 22nd.

Do not postpone your Cuban trip on my account, as I can readily come again, when you come home.

> Yours sincerely
> ELG

To James Bryce

> 36 West 10th St., New York, March 5, 1891
> (Bryce Papers, Oxford University)

MY DEAR BRYCE: I have cabled you what we thought here about Hall's last proposal. You certainly should not agree to anything which would leave a cloud on the history of your book. . . .

For these reasons I telegraphed you to pay his costs, if [he] signed a withdrawal of all objection to your use of the omitted chapter. I feel very confident he will eventually accept this. . . .

What is all this fuss about Fitzjames Stephen? Is the poor fellow really insane?[1] If he is it will give a blow to the hammer and tongs philosophy of life.

I was greatly surprized by the result at Hartlepool and Northampton. . . . I should judge that Parnell was slowly losing ground. Lecky is writing feeble articles against Home Rule in the *N. A. Review.*

Do not forget your sketch of the G.O.M.[2]

. . . We have got rid of our rascally Congress, and carried the Copyright Bill at long last. It is by no means satisfactory but it stops open barefaced robbery. Cleveland's letter against the free coinage scheme has done him a world of good, and I think his nomination and reelection is now certain. The whiffs of economical doctrine however, we are now getting from Kansas and some other Western States are enough to make your hair stand on end. But they all show that the farmers are really moved and that they cannot be fooled any longer with the plan of "the factory beside the farm". . . .

You will be surprized to hear that Garrison—the ascetic, monastic, eremitic Garrison was married today, to an adopted sister of his first wife, who has been living in the house with him for some time—a widow, and no longer young, but a nice woman. I hope this will brighten him up a little. . . .[3]

I have sent as you have doubtless seen already, acting on your suggestion, an account to the *Speaker,* of an interview with a few representative Irishmen here, about Parnell etc.[4]

Ever yours
ELG

1. The English jurist and publicist, James Fitzjames Stephen (1829–94), had begun suffering from severe lapses of memory. A hard working, direct and open man, Fitzjames Stephen apparently had driven himself to collapse.

2. Contemplating the death of Gladstone, Godkin requested Bryce to write for the *Nation* a memorial to the statesman, for which he directed Wendell P. Garrison, who since 1881 had been titular editor of the weekly, to pay Bryce $400. James Bryce, "Gladstone," *Nation,* 26 May 1898, pp. 399–402.

3. A reference to Wendell P. Garrison, for some time a widower.

4. E. L. Godkin, "The American-Irish and Mr. Parnell," *The Speaker,* 28 February 1891, pp. 251–53.

To Former President Grover Cleveland

Evening Post Editorial Rooms   New York, March 24, 1891
(Cleveland Papers, DLC)
Private

DEAR MR. CLEVELAND: Mr. Phelps' performance in *Harper's Magazine* has mortified us greatly.[1] He was hardly known at all to the general public when you sent him to England, we did our best then and have done ever since, to trumpet his praises in every direction and certify to his intents and judgments. With this thick and thin endorsement of Blaine from such a quarter, we are plunged in confusion, and do not know how to account for what has happened. If it had been a dry legal argument we should not have minded it so much. But there is no law in the article— nothing but Blaineism of the most undiluted kind.

Yours very sincerely
ELG

1. Godkin had never forgiven Cleveland for making Edward J. Phelps (1822–1900), whom Henry Watterson called "a soppy little Yankee attorney," James Russell Lowell's successor as United States minister to England. Now, in *Harper's Magazine,* Phelps defended Republican James G. Blaine's conduct of the Fur Seal dispute with England.

To Charles S. Fairchild

Evening Post Editorial Rooms   New York, April 30, 1891
(Fairchild Papers, NHi)

DEAR MR. FAIRCHILD: Would it be asking too much, of you, to ask for occasional contributions long or short—that is paragraphs or articles, on the Treasury situation during the present crisis? If not, I should feel much indebted for them.

Yours very truly
ELG

To Moorfield Storey [1]

36 West 10th St., New York, May 23, 1891
(Copy, Godkin Papers, MH)

DEAR MR. STOREY: Do you think there is any possibility of getting the Democrats to nominate a first rate man on a first rate platform even as a forlorn hope with a certainty of being beaten, a man young enough to run again, and thus leave behind, the nucleus of something better than either of the existing parties—the party of decent and intelligent people, to belong to, and work for, hereafter?

Or, if this be impossible, are there not enough Independents left to form another organization, and name a candidate as the Barnburners did if only for the "immortal Gods." Why compel rational people to hide themselves in one or other of the existing odious organizations? Ought we not to proclaim to the world that however few in numbers, we exist, we are sane, and are fighting? All over the country there are tens of thousands waiting as the anti-slavery men waited for some organization to deliver them from "the body of this death."

Yours sincerely
ELG

1. The Boston Brahmin reformer Moorfield Storey (1845–1929) corresponded occasionally with Godkin during the 1890s.

To James Bryce

36 West 10th St., New York, May 25, 1891
(Bryce Papers, Oxford University)

MY DEAR BRYCE: . . . The Hurlbert case was received here with a mighty guffaw. He has been a foul, conscienceless creature from his youth up.[1] You should hear James Carter on him. He has cheated, as far as I can hear, every man and woman with whom he has ever had any relations. His success in England has been mortifying for Americans, for it looks as if Englishmen looked on them as cattle, between whom there were no moral differences. I refused to have [his] Irish book reviewed in the *Nation,* on the ground that I felt no certainty that he had ever been in Ireland. . . .

The changes in your political situation are bewildering. The Liberal ups and downs come wonderfully quickly. But even if you win the next election I don't see the way to the passage of a Home Rule Bill—do you? Here, everything is turning against the Republicans. The McKinley tariff works worse and worse, and the Treasury bids fair to be empty before Congress meets.[2] Blaine has made a mess of the Bering Sea matter, and the Secretary of the Treasury is an unsuccessful jingo.

I am very sorry to see that poor Leslie Stephen has had to give up the *Dictionary:* I trust he is comfortably off pecuniarily. James Stephen's retirement was pathetic. How I used to enjoy his pursuit of Harcourt twenty years ago in the *Pall Mall.*[3]

I am going to Sharon Springs in July for a month for rheumatism, which has come back on me this winter after four years' respite. . . .

Ever yours
ELG

1. The reason for Godkin's obsessive hostility toward Hurlbert is unknown.
2. A reference to the Republican-sponsored high McKinley Tariff and to the fact that the Republican Fifty-first Congress had established a new high in Federal spending.
3. The ailing James Fitzjames Stephen was the brother of Leslie Stephen. Between 1865 and 1879 Fitzjames Stephen contributed to the *Pall Mall Gazette* where he sometimes tilted with Vernon Harcourt in the *Saturday Review.*

To Wendell P. Garrison

North East Harbor, Maine, July 31, 1891 (Ogden 2:190–91)

MY DEAR GARRISON: I have read the article with great pleasure and interest. . . . [It] makes me regret for the fiftieth, if not the hundredth time, that you have not been able all these years to write more. I know no better political philosopher. I can safely say that in twenty-five years of perils by land and sea, there is nobody from whose advice and arguments I have got so much comfort and courage, in introducing novelties and oddities to an unappreciative world.

> Yours ever
> ELG

To Francis J. Child

North East Harbor, Maine, August 15 [1891]
(Child Papers, MH)

MY DEAR CHILD: Your letter which only reached me yesterday, was most welcome, although the news that all was over with poor Lowell had preceded it. . . . The loss to the country is immense. . . . I do not believe three months have ever gone by in these last twenty five years without my receiving a note from him praising the *Nation* for something or other, and descanting on its value to him, and so forth. He was a delightful creature, and full of wisdom, in spite of his poetic temperament; and I am afraid the social conditions which bred such men are gone by.

I hope Mabel's boys promise well, for she will have little other comfort now.[1]

I do not like, my dear Child, to think of the little circle into which I entered when I first knew Cambridge, and yet I am constantly recalling it, sadly enough. You and Norton and the two Miss Ashburners are all that is left of it, if indeed the two old ladies can [be] said now to be left. . . .

> Yours very affectionately
> ELG

1. Mabel Lowell Burnett, the poet's daughter, had a difficult marriage and had come with her children to live with the aging Lowell. Already she was afflicted with the tuberculosis that would kill her in a few years.

To Charles Eliot Norton

August 15, 1891 (Ogden 1:291)

. . . I cannot let Lowell pass away without expressing to you, through whom I first knew him, and who knew him so well, something of my sense of his loss to us all, and to the country. I am afraid his type is rapidly disappearing, and will soon be extinct. He proved to me for twenty-five years a most delightful friend—for he kept up a constant supply of what was most grateful to me, sympathy and encouragement. To you in Cambridge he must leave a terrible gap.

What is going to be done about his life and letters? I hope any memorial to him that may be resolved on will not fall into the hands of Dr. Holmes, and that it may devolve on you to write it. . . .

To Francis J. Child

36 West 10th St., New York, September 6, 1891
(Child Papers, MH)

MY DEAR CHILD: . . . Cambridge people and old Cambridge days have been much in my mind since Lowell's death. The disappearance of the Gurneys, and Jane Norton, and the Jameses, make my early acquaintance with the place seem infinitely remote.

I hope your gout is less troublesome, and your children are doing well, and your roses bloom to suit you, and that in fact, you have all the minor consolations in perfection. Remember us cordially to Mrs. Child. We were very unlucky about seeing you both when we were in Boston in February, but I spent three days of my week's visit in my bed, or in my room with the grippe!

Ever affectionately yours
ELG

To James Bryce

Evening Post Editorial Rooms   New York, September 9, 1891
(Bryce Papers, Oxford University)

MY DEAR BRYCE: I have just finished reading your Gladstone, with the greatest admiration. . . . We shall make the most of it in every way if we survive the G.O.M.

It has, however, one defect, which I should call serious, if it were not so easily supplied. I mean your failure to give a clear idea of him as a *legislator*, that is, as a former and passer of measures, particularly economical measures. One does not get an adequate idea of his contributions to the statute book, which I presume are more important than those of any of his predecessors, not excepting Pitt or Peel. Your discussion of him as a parliamentary orator, a literary man . . . is admirable, but I think it is extremely important to let his decriers here, who abound as well as in England,—know how much he did in the way of legislation to change the English system of taxation etc., and in fact transform English Society. You could do this in a paragraph or two.

I am just back from two months at North East Harbor, and we shall begin our winter life about Oct. 1st. Next spring we confidently expect to see you in England, if you are to be there. . . .

Yours affectionately
ELG

To Daniel Coit Gilman

Seabright, N. J., September 9 [1891?] (Gilman Papers MdBJ)

DEAR GILMAN: I am sorry about this. . . . I don't think gross fraud should ever be charged without positive knowledge.[1]

Yours
ELG

1. Godkin is expressing his regrets for a rash statement in the *Nation*.

To Henry Villard

Evening Post Editorial Rooms   New York, October 5, 1891
(Villard Papers, MH)

DEAR MR. VILLARD: The trouble is largely in the Democratic candidate. He is nobody in politics; has no known opinions on any leading subject; has undoubtedly bought for cash *all* his nominations, including this one; and has been nominated by Tammany, which for the first time since Tweed controlled the State Convention. If we could [clean] up the candidate, our path would be easy, but we cannot.[1]

Secondly, we are committed up to the chin to the doctrine that the State and city ought not to be sacrificed to Federal affairs. The State governments are being mired in corruption all over the country—witness Pennsylvania, by the practice of using their elections simply to influence Federal politics. The result is that each State government is more and more in the hands of worthless rascals, who get in and stay because people are afraid if they opposed them it would in some manner help or hurt at the presidential election and yet nine tenths of our interests are in the hands of the States. To go back in all this for a man like Flower and an organization like Tammany would give the influence of the *Post* a deadly blow with its peculiar constituency and the influence of the *Post* is of course our main concern from both the moral and financial points of view.

What confuses me in the matter is the worthless character of Platt and his course also, but I confess I think them saintly compared to Tammany. We must not sacrifice too much for the Presidential election because after all Cleveland cannot *legislate*. The tide is turning in every direction against Silver etc. [end of sentence] I do not believe for a moment that we need to help Flower and Tammany to save Cleveland, and if he should be nominated our support would be of little use to him if we had supported Boss Croker and his crew.

But I recognize the force of what you say about even neutrality and we try to keep it up. But consider our past attitude toward Tammany.

Yours ever
ELG

1. Godkin is paying his disrespects to Democrat Roswell P. Flower (1835–99), the Tammany-endorsed candidate for governor of New York, while explaining to Villard that he does not agree with him that the *Evening Post* ought to refrain from attacking the State Democratic ticket in order to help Cleveland in the forthcoming national election.

To Charles Eliot Norton

October 18, 1891 (Ogden 2:34–35)

. . . I received the *Dante* some days ago—a very pleasant surprise, because I had not heard of your being engaged in any such work.[1] As a sign of remembrance of me it is of course most grateful. As I know nothing of the original, I can express no judgment on the merits of the translation, but I can truly say that, to any one like myself who only knows Dante through metrical translation, a prose version which aims at exact rendering, and has had no sacrifices to make to metre or rhyme, is a veritable boon. So I have begun to read it as a fresh treat.

It recalls vividly one of the evenings at Longfellow's to which you took me twenty-five years ago when he was working on his version. Fields and Lowell were there, and some one else, at the supper. You and I are the sole survivors of the party, I am pretty sure. . . .

1. The first volume of Norton's translation of Dante's *Divina Commedia* had just appeared. In 1881 Norton, with Lowell and Longfellow, began the Dante Society of America.

To Moorfield Storey

36 West 10th St., New York, October 31, 1891
(Copy, Godkin Papers, MH)

DEAR MR. STOREY: Many thanks for the report of your address. It is excellent reading and I mean to make some use of it in the *Post*, when we get some room, after Tuesday.

What is in store for us on that day nobody is able to predict.[1] The pros and cons are so evenly balanced that I think most Independents are very indifferent as to the result. In so far as there had been any change in that body during the canvas the drift has been towards Flower. . . .

Yours very truly
ELG

1. State election day.

To Henry Villard

Evening Post Editorial Rooms   New York, November 23, 1891
(Villard Papers, MH)

DEAR MR. VILLARD: Mr. White tells me you think Fawcett's financial articles "very good" and wish them continued.

I now wish to assure you that Fawcett has brought discredit on the financial side of the *Post* for ten years by his gross blundering in *facts* and *figures*, especially figures; that he is considered by everyone I know one of the most unreliable men connected with the New York press; that a collation of his two last articles with our regular financial and commercial columns, shows both contradiction and repetition, as I have already pointed out to Mr. White; that they contain nothing which does not appear day by day in our financial department.

Secondly—He was removed last summer for gross and notorious incompetency and negligence, and that his return to the office after this as an *ex cathedra* writer in the same field, is very demoralizing to the whole staff, and I must say very disrespectful to me. . . .

Yours very sincerely
ELG. . . .

To Grace Ashburner

36 West 10th St., New York, November 23, 1891
(Ashburner Papers, MStoc)

MY DEAR MISS GRACE: . . . My fall, thank you, has left no ill effects, and I have not decided finally to give up riding. But I cannot now face the ordeal of finding another horse. A horse strong enough to carry me, and which has all the virtues besides is very hard to find. . . .

Lowell was, indeed a dreadful loss for the country as well as for his friends. . . . He belonged to what I am afraid is a vanished type. His death brought sadly to mind all the changes that have occurred in Cambridge, since first I knew it, now nearly thirty years ago. Henry James sent me his own and Alice's photograph a few weeks ago. He is becoming very middleaged and she looks sadly changed. I do not know how his play has turned out pecuniarily, but I know he counted on it for money a good deal. I do not think his works have been remunerative of late years. Plots he cannot make, and dialogue without plots are to the modern public, vanity. But he is such a nice fellow, and such a good fellow!

I made an attempt to take Cambridge on my way down from

N. E. Harbor in September, but I . . . was crippled with rheumatism, which made me a sorry spectacle coming home from a summer's outing. I have got over it, but it is a wonderfully adhesive complaint, and wanders all over one's frame with such impartiality and inscrutability. I am fighting it now with, long walks and Indian Clubs, but I fear it will get the better of me yet.

. . . We expect to go on to visit Mrs. Kuhn in Feb. and hope there may then be a chance of seeing you. I am delighted to get such good accounts of Miss Ashburner. I am sorry to tell her I think the Gladstoners will win at the next election, which Bryce says will be in the spring—sorry I mean on her account, not on my own. I am still faithful to my errors, but Tory or Radical or Home Ruler, I am always affectionately yours

ELG

To James Bryce

36 West 10th St., Christmas Day [1891]
(Bryce Papers, Oxford University)

MY DEAR BRYCE: I wonder if you could help me to get hold of (by purchase) the first *two* vols of Hodgskin's "Italy and Her Invaders" and the first of Gardner's Hist. of "The Great Civil War." I did not bethink me of buying either of them until the second vol. appeared and the first was then gone. This is what often happens with books of several vols. published at long intervals. You are expected to know it is going to be a great work as soon as the first vol. is issued. I have had half a mind to write to Hodgskin, whom I do not know, when I saw he had been lecturing against Home Rule, to say that he would be much better employed getting out a reprint of his first two vols. I have been trying to get the two somewhere for a year.

Things are in a great muddle here politically, but I would still bet on Cleveland against the field. Domestically we all have the grippe but it is lighter this year than last.

Things in Ireland are most disappointing and depressing. This fighting at elections is disgusting everybody here[.] What the *raison d'être* of the Parnellite party is, is not apparent at this distance. Surely English interest in Home Rule must be declining.

How is the *Speaker* getting on financially? The articles are, I still think, pitched in too high a key for a Weekly from which people expect somewhat more calm. But it is not too high certainly for Chamberlain. What a charlatan! I remember your predicting much of him to me in a letter about '84.

I hope Mrs. Bryce is well. Give her our kindest regards and best wishes for the New Year.

I would be willing to pay a premium for those three vols.

Yours ever
ELG

To Samuel G. Ward

36 West 10th St., New York, February 4, 1892
(Ward Papers, MH)

MY DEAR WARD: I have heard with real concern of your illness. . . .

You know very well I hope, how much I have for so many years valued your friendship and sympathy, and how sorry I was that circumstances took you away from New York; and I have been looking forward with great pleasure to seeing you in Washington next month when my wife and I go on with Mrs. Kuhn for a short visit. I will insist on believing with Seneca, that nothing can happen but good to a really good man, such as I believe you to be, and in this opinion I am sure I have the hearty concurrence of the gods. . . .

ELG

To I. Wayne MacVeagh

36 West 10th St., New York, February 4, 1892
(MacVeagh Papers, PHi)

MY DEAR MACVEAGH: I was composing a letter to you, in my mind congratulating you on being chosen by Harvard to make the address on Lowell, when I heard of your illness. I was going to say, and I now say it, that none of your friends could have wished you a higher compliment, and I must also add, honestly and without flattery, that I as an old friend of Lowell's could not have wished for his memory a fitter eulogist. . . It was as a patriot, a man who loved his country in a really noble way that I always most admired him, and to this side of him I protest I know no man so well qualified to do him justice as you, because I do not know of any other public man who has his standards and has the courage to apply them to the affairs of his own time.

I am therefore most glad to hear of your recovery, and earnestly trust that you be thoroughly "fit" when the time comes. "Let 'em have it," as St. Patrick said, when all his arrangements were made for the destruction of the Irish snakes. . . .

Yours very cordially
ELG

To Daniel Coit Gilman

36 West 10th St., New York, February 17, 1892
(Gilman Papers, MdBJ)

DEAR GILMAN: At the risk of not meeting with a sympathetic response, I am going to congratulate you on the departure of Ely for other fields. I think he has been for years a discredit to you and mischievous to the community in spite of his extraordinary industry, or rather because of it. Professors of Political Economy preaching their own philanthropic gospel as "Science," are among the most dangerous characters of our time, and Ely was one of them.

I have been itching to say this for years, but feared to do so. Now I shall feel easier.[1]

Yours sincerely
ELG

1. Godkin is congratulating President Gilman on the resignation of Richard T. Ely from Johns Hopkins University. Although this letter has been cited as evidence of Godkin's forbearance, Gilman, a regular reader of the *Nation*, was never in the dark as to Godkin's feelings toward Ely. Two years later Godkin, whom Ely regarded as one of his leading persecutors, aired in the *Evening Post* a charge by a public school superintendent in Wisconsin that Ely was unfit for his new post at the University of Wiscon-

sin. In an ensuing trial before the Board of Regents, historian Frederick Jackson Turner and other noted scholars came to the economist's defense, and he was acquited. "You must remember that the *Evening Post* has a black list," Dr. Albert B. Shaw tried to console Ely during the proceedings, "and has not the slightest desire or intention to be fair, that its assaults against a man of high character and standing usually help such a man more than they hurt him." Richard T. Ely, *Ground under our Feet* (New York: Macmillan, 1938), pp. 219–32.

To James Bryce

36 West 10th St., New York, February 29 [1892]
(Bryce Papers, Oxford University)

MY DEAR BRYCE: . . . You ask my opinion about two things—the Negro at the South and the Germans. I have read your article on the Negro, in the *N.A.R.* but the only good reason I know of for your discussing it further, is, as I told Garrison, that it excites interest in England. Here it excites none whatever—absolutely none. The Republicans cannot reconcile themselves to their failure to get votes enough from the Negroes to break the "Solid South" at Presidential elections, and consequently hanker after some sort of Federal interference, but I think the late "Force Bill" will be the last attempt in this direction.[1] As to the community in general outside the ranks of the political managers, and including the philanthropists, they are absolutely content with the improvement in the Negro's material condition, and with the enormous agricultural and manufacturing success of free labor. 8,000,000 bales of cotton against 3,000,000 before the war, and a tremendous increase of manufactures affects the American mind far more powerfully than the inability of the Negroes to vote the Republican ticket can ever do. In short the question is in my estimation, *dead*. The hotel is burnt down, and the proprietor has "gone into something else." I feel this way myself. The Negro is growing up to the suffrage through industry and not through argument.

As to the Germans, you are absolutely right and Von Holst very wrong.[2] The German influence amounts to nothing. They were a great failure in the field in the Civil War, largely I think through bad officering. The European needs far more officering than the American, and the Germans having largely left home to avoid fighting had no stomach for fighting here. Schurz and Sigel were their only generals and both were ludicrous failures. They have produced no public men of note except Schurz, who is a good orator, but has no originality of mind, or much mental force. His place in America is ludicrously overrated in Germany. They are unknown in literature, and also in the social life of the large cities, where they live almost entirely to themselves. This last is I think largely due to the condition of their women, who are mere *haus frauen* and are despised by the American women. But they are an excellent population as regards peaceableness and industry. In politics they are apt to go in the cities with the party which meddles least with their beer. . . .

Yours ever
ELG

1. The "Force Bill," sponsored by Godkin's one-time friendly acquaintance Henry Cabot Lodge, would use Federal power to protect the voting rights of blacks. It passed the House of Representatives in 1890 but died in the Senate. Godkin's comfortable acceptance of white supremacy distinguished him from his alter ego Wendell P. Garrison, who, despite the backsliding of many of the former antislavery people, never forgot his father's labors for the black people.

2. A reference to historian Hermann E. von Holst (1841–1904). Von Holst was the German correspondent of the *Nation* from 1874 to 1878, when Godkin dismissed him. For a letter complaining at length of Godkin's treatment of him, see von Holst to Godkin, 13 April 1878, Hermann von Holst Papers, ICU.

To Henry Holt

36 West 10th St., New York [March, 1892?]
(Godkin Papers, MH)

DEAR HOLT: Referring to our interview the other day, my counsel advises me that it would be more effective to produce my ammunition after [the] other man's story is all in, and discharge it in one broadside, rather than communicate it previously to individual members of the Grand Jury. Consequently I shall not trouble you to send the papers I spoke of to Mr. [Taber?]. But if the opportunity offers and you will say a good word for me personally to him, I shall be very much obliged.[1] The case will be in the hands of the G. J. probably tomorrow.

Yours very sincerely
ELG

1. Apparently Holt had agreed to intercede with a juror in Godkin's behalf in a pending libel suit.

To Henry Villard

Evening Post Editorial Rooms   New York, March 29, 1892
(Villard Papers, MH)

DEAR MR. VILLARD: I am going to take my vacation abroad on the 1st of May. I am not well, rather sleepless, rheumatic, and I begin to have that serious sign of fatigue—pains in the back of my head after any prolonged brain work. The doctor says I ought to have six months rest. I propose to compromise on four, so that I can be back here for the heavier work of the canvas.

I have passed my sixtieth birthday—a time of life when a man has to stop and rest a little if he is to make respectable time in the home stretch. . . .

I write to ask you first as the party most interested, whether you think it unreasonable to expect the *Evening Post* to stand this —by continuing my salary for the whole period. . . .

I am frank about this, as I feel I am speaking to a very kind as well as old friend.

Yours very truly
ELG

All this is contingent on the Grand Jury's not finding an indictment against me. In that case I must stay and stand my trial. I am to appear before them tomorrow.

To James Bryce

36 West 10th St., New York, March 29, 1892
(Bryce Papers, Oxford University)

MY DEAR BRYCE: We are sailing in all human probability April 30th for Havre [*sic*] and shall spend May and June most likely in France and Northern Italy. . . . I . . . am not fit for London just now. I am a good deal run down, and my one thing needful for a month or two is rest and quiet. So we are going to begin by roving about in Normandy and Brittany.

I have been having another brush with the Tammany fellows. They arrested me again last Sunday, and tomorrow I expose them again, before the Grand Jury who will, I expect, as before, throw out the bill. They are an awful lot, but I think their end is at last in sight.

I am going so much sooner than I expected, because the political tide has fairly turned. Hill is "done up," and since the defeat of the silver men in the House Cleveland's nomination is assured.[1] I think he will be nominated by acclamation on the first ballot, and I am equally sure will be elected. . . .

Yours ever
ELG

1. Former New York governor David H. Hill, a political rival of Cleveland, was trying to wrest the 1892 Democratic presidential nomination from him. Godkin pronounced Hill in the *Evening Post* "the worst man any political party in America has ever offered for popular suffrage."

To Wendell P. Garrison

Evening Post Editorial Rooms   New York, March 30, 1892
(Godkin Papers, MH)

MY DEAR GARRISON: . . . I write mainly to tell you what I fear will be unwelcome news to you, that I am going abroad April 30 for *four* months. . . . I have told Villard this, and added my opinion that the payment of my salary for the full period would be a not unsuitable tribute to a good man, from the *E. P.* What view he will take of this I have not heard. But I am going in any case.

. . . I think, that with Ogden, you can get on now without any additional *inside* help.[1] There would be plenty of outside contributors, if you wanted them.

You will have seen that I have been arrested again.[2] The old story. I go before the Grand Jury today. . . .

Yours as ever
ELG

1. An unhappy Garrison replied to this that Godkin's letter contained "nothing pleasant" for anyone except its author. "Sooner or later," complained Godkin's long-time assistant, "one's clientele discovers that the principal is gone and the officeboy in charge, and the business suffers." Rollo Ogden (1856–1937) at this time was an editorial writer for the *Evening Post*.

2. Those who suspected Godkin of hypocrisy were jubilant when he admitted offering a five-dollar bribe to the police officer who came to arrest him.

To Charles Eliot Norton

36 West 10th St., New York, April 12, 1892
(Godkin Papers, MH)

MY DEAR NORTON: . . . I got your note of lament over your inability to come in to the Saturday dinner, and shared in it deeply. I went, but it was rather a melancholy affair to me. There was but a small party, and several ghosts, and the talk of the two old men at the end of the table was almost all that broke the silence.[1] *Eheu, fugaces, labuntur anni!* . . . Our winter here has on the whole been rather dreary. . . . [To] wind up the season one of the Tammany people had me again arrested the other day, to have the charge again dismissed by the Grand Jury. The whole situation (politically) here is so odious, that it needs more love of country than I possess to make it tolerable. One does not need to be very vain, to think one's self born for better things than denouncing these wretches. . . .

1. A reference to a meeting of the Saturday Club of Boston to which Godkin belonged for many years and where he shared the company of Parkman, Howells, Lowell, Norton, Charles W. Eliot, and William James.

To Wendell P. Garrison

Aix-Les-Bains, May 22, 1892
(Ogden 2:207)

MY DEAR GARRISON: We had a perfectly smooth passage, but this did not prevent my wife suffering greatly. . . . A week in Paris was given mainly to recruiting. It is thirty years since I was last in it, and I saw no difference except an increase of brilliancy and activity and beauty. I am quite sure that as far as one can judge from the streets, it has lost nothing by the overthrow of the monarchy. But Laugel gives a sad account of the increase of political corruption, which really, according to his account, seems to be in the very warp and woof of democracy.[1] I went out with him one Sunday to lunch with the Duc d'Aumale at Chantilly, and had a very interesting morning with the old gentleman, who, I was sorry to see, is *old* in every way. Tell Horace White I had an interesting evening in the Eiffel Tower with a party of which Miss Maginnis was a member. She had a good pastel in the salon. Curiously enough, they absolutely refused to put her name down in the Catalogue as McGinnis or Maginnis; they insisted that it must be Ginnis, and wrote it so. Eiffel let us up to the very top, into which the public is not admitted, and where he has nice rooms and a kitchen.

We left Paris last Sunday night in the hideous "wagon-lit," and have been here ever since, where I am taking my cure, douches of hot sulphur water accompanied with massage. . . .

This is a lovely region. . . . We made a pilgrimage yesterday to "The Charmettes," near Chambéry, which was in honor both of Jean Jacques and you, and had a most delightful day. . . . I collected such photographs as can be had, and send them in a separate package, with the latest bit of Rousseau literature. This I do almost as a pious duty, for it is the first chance I have had, in twenty-seven years of real fraternity, of giving you a bit of pleasure at your request, often as I have longed for one.

I have been and am really sorry to be away this summer when you are so much perplexed by conflicting duties and cares; but I had, as I have told you, no choice. . . .

I hope all goes well at the office. I have seen no American papers but the Paris *New York Herald*, which I never take up without shame and disgust. Silliness and vulgarity stand out in every line of it. . . .

1. Auguste Laugel was still the Paris correspondent of the *Nation*.

To James Bryce

Hotel Belalp, Brieg, Valais, Switzerland, July 13, 1892
(Bryce Papers, Oxford University)

MY DEAR BRYCE: Your letter received this morning was rather dismal reading, but not unexpectedly so. I have been watching the election returns during the week, and had come to the conclusion that neither side would have a working majority, and that a terrible muddle was therefore at hand. Nor am I greatly surprised at what you say about Gladstone's waning influence. The positive and inevitable absence of future for him was sure to bring this before long. But more of this when we meet. . . .

We are enjoying and profitting [*sic*] greatly by the mountains. There [are] *seven* parsons in this small house, some of them in long cassocks! They cross themselves on sitting down to meals. The Bishop of Gloucester comes this week.

Our united remembrances to Mrs. Bryce.

Yours ever
ELG

To James Bryce

36 West 10th St., New York, October 16, 1892
(Bryce Papers, Oxford University)

MY DEAR BRYCE: I do not think the riots you enumerate indicate diminishing respect for law on the part of *Americans*. . . . As far as I have been able to learn, the great bulk of those who have been engaged in the disturbances of which you speak, are of foreign birth. . . . The Long Islanders who opposed our landing, are curiously enough, though of New England origin, a semi-barbarous lot, but their conduct I admit is hardly explicable, by me at least.

Our experience on the *Normannia* was horrible. . . . It was due to a panic got up and fostered by the newspapers here, simply to increase "sales" which found expression through an incompetent and somewhat ruffianly Tammany Health Officer, appointed solely because he married the sister of the Boss, Croker. A history of the affair would furnish an excellent illustration of nearly everything that is bad in the social and political life of this city. . . .[1]

The chances thus far seem decidedly in favor of Cleveland. . . . But the outward indications are not . . . safe reliances, so completely do the Republicans seem to be relying on bribery. Neither side can win *easily* without New York, and there are grave fears that they [are] arranging to buy votes in this city and state on a great scale. The manufacturers, in fact, are desperate, and feel that they are defending their property. Still I think we shall win. Some of the open desertions of the Republican party within a week or two have been remarkable, Wayne MacVeagh's and Judge Gresham's for instance. . . .[2]

Yours as ever
ELG

1. There were two sides to this dispute, which concerned the cholera epidemic of 1892. A generation earlier, during the cholera epidemic of 1865–66, Godkin resorted to diatribe in the *Nation* to chastise the New York Board of Health for not quarantining the Port of New York. But in 1892 Godkin found his personal circumstances reversed; returning from Europe in a ship on which several passengers had fallen victim to cholera, he and his fellow passengers were put in quarantine on their arrival at New York. Godkin-admirer Allan Nevins one-sidedly describes the editor's course: "His letters to the *Evening Post* were delightfully scorching, he kept up the attack till the quarantine officers were panic-striken, and he demolished their last defense in an article in the *North American Review* that is a masterpiece of destructiveness." (*The Evening Post*, p. 535.) Henry Villard objected to Godkin's editorial course in the *Normannia* incident, as did much of the public.

2. Having behind him two unsuccessful bids for the Republican nomination to the presidency in 1884 and 1888, Walter Q. Gresham (1832–95) defected, along with Wayne MacVeagh, to Cleveland and the Democrats. Cleveland rewarded Gresham with the post of Secretary of State and MacVeagh with the post of minister to Italy.

To I. Wayne MacVeagh

36 West 10th St., New York, October 22 [1892]
(MacVeagh Papers, PHi)

MY DEAR MACVEAGH: Nov. 4th is the Round Table dinner—the first of the season—which I think will be interesting, and which I think you too, ought to attend. All the men will want to see you particularly as the election will be on the following Tuesday. . . .

Your speeches have been really remarkable.—the first one a fine piece of writing of the best kind, the second one of the most *effective* as regards the audience I have ever listened to. And I was *thunderstruck* by your voice, which I expected to be weak, to give out in an hour, instead of which etc. etc.

Yours sincerely
ELG. . . .

To Moorfield Storey

Evening Post Editorial Rooms   New York, October 27 [1892]
(Copy, Godkin Papers, MH-Ar)

MY DEAR STOREY: I can not tell you, but must try, how much I have enjoyed your two addresses before the Democratic Convention, and the War College. It is political writing of the highest order. But it makes me despondent. The picture of what we ought to be compared with my own expectations of anything we can be, or are likely to be very soon, is depressing. But, *sursum corda.*

Ever yours
ELG

To Charles Eliot Norton

35 West 10th St., New York, January 24, 1893
(Norton Papers, MH)

MY DEAR NORTON: A talk with Sally about your Lowell work led me to look over his letters to me, of which I have a great many, all most delightful. I thought it possible there might be some which you would care to print. But I find they are nearly all so full of praise of the *Nation* and of me personally, that it would be impossible to use them. I send, however, three or four from which I think it possible you may like to extract something. . . .[1]

Affectionately yours
ELG

1. Norton and Horace Scudder were editing Lowell's letters for publication.

To Edward Atkinson

Evening Post Editorial Rooms   New York, March 1 [1893]
(Atkinson Papers, MHi)

DEAR MR. ATKINSON: Mr White has handed me a letter of yours containing a plan for the settlement of the Hawaiian question, which I fear we cannot print in the *Post*. The reason is not that it would make you seem a visionary, but that it would make us seem to think you were not. I do not say that you are, but we are fighting a hard battle for things far within your plans, far more feasible than what you ask for, and I am afraid our contention would suffer seriously, if we were thought to be looking now to complete neutralization and the abrogation of the existing treaty.[1]

Sincerely yours
ELG

1. In 1892 a band of white planters in Hawaii carried out a successful revolt against the rule of Queen Liliuokalani, a revolt assisted by United States troops brought ashore on orders of the jingoistic American minister. A treaty of annexation was rushed to Washington, but, before it could be gotten through the Senate, President Harrison left office. Edward Atkinson wanted the United States out of Hawaii, whereas Godkin, whose anti-imperialism has been misconstrued by Robert L. Beisner, wanted to retain an American sphere of influence there, simultaneously avoiding the expense of governing the islands.

To James Bryce

36 West 10th St., New York, March 17 [1893]
(Bryce Papers, Oxford University)

MY DEAR BRYCE: . . . I am following the discussion with keen interest, and think you came out well except as to the position of the Irish Members of Westminster. I have always felt it was rather weak on the part of the G.O.M. to yield on this point. . . . The Tory predictions of the things the Irish will do when they get loose resemble amusingly the Republican predictions here as to what would happen after Cleveland was elected in 1884. A very sensible man, a banker assured me that in the contingency he would gladly take "fifty cents on the dollar" for all his securities. Another said we should be knocked down and robbed in Broadway by starving workmen. The *Tribune* said the Democrats would divide $3,000,000,000 among the ex slaveholders and rebel soldiers. . . .

I am in my third week of confinement from a broken leg, acquired by simply missing my footing on the staircase of a friend's house in Boston; but if all goes well I expect to be about again in another week.

Politically we have entered on the golden age here. In truth Cleveland's course is rapidly breaking up the Republican party, but he does not seem able to manage the silver maniacs, who will, I fear, keep on baying.[1]

. . . We both long to see you again, by which we mean especially Mrs. Bryce, with whom I would give a good deal for half an hour's political gossip. She is more trenchant in her personalities than you are. . . .[2]

I am as a prophet swollen with pride over Balfour's failure, because I always said his success in Ireland was that of a Colonel of Cavalry, and that a hundred men could be found in the British army to achieve it, and that if he was ever called on for constructiveness and leadership he would fail. Is not this now demonstrated? . . .

Yours ever
ELG

1. By 1893 the money question, a thorny issue in American politics since 1873, had shaken down into a contest between the supporters of a single

gold standard and the supporters of bi-metalism who wanted to expand the
currency by continuing to mint silver dollars freely at the traditional value
of 16 to 1. Godkin, like most of the creditor class, was a "Gold Bug," a
position that led his one-time friend Henry Adams to assert that he confused
morality with his own personal interest. *The Education of Henry Adams*
(Boston and New York: Houghton Mifflin Company, 1918) 336.

2. Oddly, James Bryce kept no secretaries in his house—apparently he did
not trust them in sensitive matters—and his wife sometimes wrote his letters.
Somewhat more candid than he, she is said to have faithfully represented
his views.

To Silas W. Burt

36 West 10th St., New York, March 27 [1893]
(Burt Papers, NHi)

My DEAR BURT: . . . I write . . . to ask whether you can get
me "the courtesies of the port" for Mr. Frederick Martin, who is
the bosom friend and chum of my wife's brother and is coming
home to attend the wedding of his brother's (Bradley Martin)
daughter to [Lord Craven?] (a wretched business but he is not
to blame).[1] He is in the *Teutonic* which sailed last Wednesday
from Liverpool, and is due, I suppose, tomorrow . . . .

Yours very sincerely
ELG

1. Frederick T. Martin was a New York and London socialite who later
set aside his leisure long enough to write a book, *The Passing of the Idle
Rich* (New York: Doubleday, Page, 1911), in which he affectionately cited
the *Evening Post* as a newspaper published for the rich.

To President Grover Cleveland

April 5, 1893 (Cleveland Papers, DLC)

My DEAR MR. CLEVELAND: I am going to take the liberty, after
some years of steady and unflinching support of both yourself
and your principles to lay some considerations before you touching two appointments on which I learn, you are shortly to act.

One is Mr. Henry White in the London legation. I am informed whether truly or not I couldn't tell, that a strong effort is

being made to induce you to remove him. . . . I have never seen a more valuable man in a similar place. I do not believe there is any one in our diplomatic service to be compared to him. . . .

I am sure our late Ministers, Lowell, Phelps, and Lincoln would all give the same testimony about him. Mr. Lowell often spoke to me of the very great service he rendered him in steering the legation through all the intricacies and pitfalls of that very complicated machine known as "English Society." I am sure he cannot be replaced without great loss and damage to the very objects for which we keep an embassy in London.

I may add that I have had no communication with him on this subject, and he does not know that I am writing this letter.[1]

The other matter is the rumored appointment of Mr. Van Alen to the Italian mission. It has been a common report here in all the clubs ever since the election that he had been promised the mission in return for $50,000 in cash contributed to the campaign fund. . . . I have steadily refused to believe this, because I know that Mr. Van Alen has no qualifications under heaven for the Italian or any other important mission, and because giving it to him . . . would be . . . worse than the sale of the cabinet post to Wanamaker, because Wanamaker had at least some ability. I have, therefore, paid but little attention to the story till tonight when it reaches me in such very positive shape, as to cause me to call your attention most respectfully, to the very great pain and anxiety it is causing scores of those in this part of the world who honored, admired, followed you, and in their small way vouched for you.[2]

Excuse this intrusion on your already much burdened time seeing that I didn't ask you, and have never asked you[,] for any personal favor.

Faithfully yours, with great respect
ELG

The Honble. Grover Cleveland, President of the United States

1. Six months later the President asked for White's resignation. Returning home in March 1894, White encountered on shipboard young Lawrence Godkin who told White his dismissal was "the only regret [his] father felt in connection with the new administration." Interestingly, Godkin's opinion was shared by his enemy Theodore Roosevelt, who found Henry White the most useful man in the United States diplomatic establishment.

2. There is little to substantiate Godkin's charges against James J. Van Alen, a man of some culture and linguistic ability who was offered the post after Edward Cooper turned it down.

To Samuel R. Honey

36 West 10th St., New York, May 7 [1893]
(Cleveland Papers, DLC)

MY DEAR HONEY: All I know about the Van Alen matter is hearsay, but it is pretty good hearsay, originating in Van Alen's own talk at [the] Knickerbocker Club and elsewhere. In fact it has been a matter almost of notoriety here for weeks. The sum was put at $30,000 to $50,000. It has excited the reformers very much, and Cleveland was written to by several, mentioning the report, and protesting against the appointment on that ground, and *no denial has come from any official quarter*. This strikes me as very strange if the story be not true. . . .

Yours sincerely
ELG

To Henry Villard

Evening Post Editorial Rooms   New York [23 May 1893]
(Villard Papers, MH)

DEAR MR. VILLARD: I enclose you a specimen of the kind of thing of which I spoke to you at our interview the other day, which weights us in keeping up the position and character of the *Post*. . . .

Yours very truly
ELG

To Henry Villard

June 7, 1893 (Villard Papers, MH)

Personal and Private

DEAR MR. VILLARD: I had no idea of annoying you in any way by the clipping I sent you. . . . I wished to show you, by a con-

crete example that I had shared in the disagreeables of your position for long years, without blaming you in the least, or wishing
to deny that I knew all about the connection of the *Post* with
the Northern Pacific perfectly well when I went into it. Things
like this cutting, have been laid on my desk about once a week
for twelve years, all going to show that I was editing a railroad
organ under your orders for dishonest purposes. . . .

I can well understand your regretting the investment of so
much money in newspaper property, and it is true you have
effaced yourself to a remarkable extent as an owner. But allow
me to observe that you owe it to this effacement that the *Post*
is as good a piece of property as it is. Without it the *Post* would
have shared the usual fate of the personal organs of financiers, in
being ridiculous and unprofitable. . . . I believe that the suspicion
that you did *not* efface yourself was a hindrance to it in the
earlier years. . . .[1]

The one complaint I have to make relates to this very matter. I
was surprized and annoyed that you should have allowed them
to suppose during the late Canvas at the Democratic headquarters,
that Harrity had only to send down [a] messenger to me to direct
me how to edit the *Post*, what to put in and what to keep
out. . . .[2] I would have expected you to protect us against this
sort of thing, to have told them at the outset that I was not that
kind of man, nor the *Post* that kind of paper. . . .

What you mean exactly by this last paragraph in your letter, I
do not know. You say that "your experience with many fair
weather friends during the past few years etc. has been such
your faith in the existence of chivalrous sentiment among them is
very much shaken, and that no lack of loyalty among them any
longer surprizes you."

. . . I have put into the *Post, that is into your stock mainly*,
twelve of the best years of my life and all my faculties of mind
and character, when during some of the time I was harassed
painfully by financial embarrassment caused by losses on your
railroad. It is not immodest to say that it is owing to my exertions
mainly that the *Post* has at last reached its present position. In
fact, when I think of all I have done for it, I feel that I have occupied in all these years the worst paid place of its kind in the
United States, but I have never asked for an increase of salary,

or an increase of anything, except vacation, and this only when
the state of my health made it absolutely necessary. . . .[3]

Yours very sincerely

ELG

1. The statement made by the historian of the *Evening Post*, Allan Nevins,
that Villard made the editors of that paper "wholly independent" is only
partly sustained by the Henry Villard Papers at the Harvard Graduate
School of Business Administration, which are rife with directives from Villard about *Post* editorial policy.

2. William F. Harrity (1850–1912) was the chairman of the Democratic
National Committee.

3. By 1893 the increasing demands of Godkin for extended paid vacations
had become an irritant not only to the proprietor but to the whole staff.
Eventually Wendell P. Garrison, after conferring with Horace White, advised Villard to pay the temperamental editor for the past but to "rigidly
define the future."

To Henry Villard

Evening Post Editorial Rooms   New York, June 21 [1893]

(Villard Papers, MH)

DEAR MR. VILLARD: . . . As to my share in the success of the
Post, I am very far from wishing to depreciate Horace White's
services, which in his field I appreciate as much as you do.[1] But
mine have not consisted simply in my writing of which you
take such a flattering view. . . .

It is true "the masses are beyond my reach," but I do not
understand the relevancy of this observation, as the *Post* has not
got the masses. *Your dividends do not come from the masses.*
They come from a class of advertizing which you would not get,
if the *Post* did not reach the very class *I do reach also*. If you
tried to make the *Post* a paper for "the Masses" today you would
land it in bankruptcy.

Finally, no money would have induced me to "serve under"
Pierpont Morgan or anyone else. The proposed plan of purchase
involved no such risk. . . .[2]

Sincerely yours

ELG

P. S. I am going to Europe with my wife July 1st for my two

months vacation. As we have no house in the country, this seems the healthiest and most refreshing thing we can do every year, if her remedy for seasickness proves a success. But I should like much to have the two weeks spent on the ocean in the years we go there, added on to my allowance, if you do not think this unreasonable.

ELG

1. Villard was aware that, without the management of Horace White, the *Evening Post* would probably fail financially. Godkin was a great editorial writer but he was a poor editor, and some of his staff writers he did not even know by sight. At work in his office, if at all, only in the morning, characteristic of him was his joking dictum: "I see no one before one and at one I go home." White, who in the 1870s had lifted the undistinguished *Chicago Tribune* briefly to Gilded Age stature in American journalism, was the man who held the *Evening Post* on course.

2. A reference to the editor's unsuccessful attempt to get J. P. Morgan to help him buy the *Evening Post*.

To Silas W. Burt

Waterloo Hotel, Bettws Y Coed, North Wales, July 16, 1893
(Burt Papers, NHi)

My dear Burt: My wife's mother and brother (Mrs. A. B. Sands, and Henry Sands) are going over in the *Campania*, due in New York the 28th July. They will have nothing dutiable, and she is an old lady. If you can do anything towards getting "the courtesies of the port" for them I shall be greatly obliged.

We are rusticating a few days in this lovely spot to enable my wife to get over the voyage. I ran down to London for two or three days last week, and saw the G.O.M. who is as lively as a cricket, full of fight, and evidently means to live as long as any of them. He has beaten them thus far at every point.

Yours ever
ELG

To Wendell P. Garrison

36 West 10th St., New York, October 5, 1893
(Godkin Papers, *Nation* Business Records, MH)

DEAR GARRISON: . . . I agree to the proposed rule as to absence and pay for Mr. White you and myself with certain qualifications.

1. I cannot accept the theory that the value of any one of us to the paper, ceases when he leaves the office. The radiance of a blameless life and high intelligence is reflected in the office, no matter where he may [be] in the flesh, and has a money value.

2. Under the rule, strictly construed, whenever I run off to Washington or Boston or the like in winter for a few days, as I have been in the habit of doing, it would cost me $154 besides railroad fare. This you will admit would be slavery, a peonage. The lot of an *adscriptus glebae* would be preferable. Some modification is necessary here.

I do not expect to be more than one summer more in harness. So the whole matter is of comparatively small importance to me, but I want to be right in the record. I am older and probably less "fit" than either of you, and look on myself as an emeritus, and feel entitled to freedom of movement in my last years of work.

Please lay this before Mr. White.

Yours sincerely
ELG

To Moorfield Storey

Evening Post Editorial Rooms   New York, October 18, 1893
(Copy, Godkin Papers, MH)

DEAR MR. STOREY: I am having a list of the new consuls made out and find there is no information about them on file at the State Department except the recommendation of the "influence." I want to compare this with Quincy's statement that he had improved the service by asking him what he knew about a single appointment he made, before going any further.[1] I would like your advice about the most effective manner of doing this.

Henry White, who has just come back, says the English appointments are the worst ever made. The secretaryship there has been sold to Roosevelt for $10,000 I am told.

Yours very truly

ELG

1. During his second term, Cleveland made Bostonian Josiah Quincy (1859–1919) first assistant Secretary of State with the task of filling consulate posts made vacant by the change of administration, but Quincy resigned soon after this letter was written.

To James Bryce

36 West 10th St., New York, November 19 [1893]

(Bryce Papers, Oxford University)

MY DEAR BRYCE: I ought to have written you long ago, if for no other reason, by way of acknowledging your great kindness to us while in London. But immediately after getting home, we were in a measure compelled to go to the Chicago Fair, at which we spent ten days, with a fair amount of discomfort, although we had a furnished house with Sheldon, and were thus saved the enormous misery of the crowded hotels. The buildings of the Fair were really wonderful—the contents except the pictures and some few curiosities, were I think much below the average of the European exhibitions.[1] But the general success was an enormous gratification to Chicago pride. The mayor I am glad to say, was shot at the close by one of his own followers. He was a great blackguard and dangerous demagogue. I hope some other one will dispose of the Governor. Violence seems the only way of getting rid of these creatures.[2]

We have just escaped here from what had become a really alarming state of things. The Ring have had possession of the city and the legislature for two years, and waxing bold, nominated for the Court of Appeals, a man who had been convicted of the grossest fraud at the election last year. This was the last straw. The Bar rose up, and the public indignation was great enough not only to defeat him, but to win the legislature and the consitutional convention which is to sit next year. . . .[3] You will have seen what a good thing Cleveland did in Hawaii. . . . Otherwise Cleveland has been disappointing us very much. He pushed through the Silver repeal bill manfully, but he has permitted the old license about the offices, which have been distributed right and left as "spoils." . . . These things in his case make one feel as if it was useless any longer to look for moral sense among public men in this part of the world, for certainly no man has since Washington, had so clean a field for the play of his moral faculties as Cleveland in this last term.

. . . Our old friend Villard, sailed for Egypt a week . . . ago, I may say, in disgrace. He has been kicked out of every enterprize he was connected with here, and is universally denounced as a visionary, if not worse, who has made money at the expense of other people. Unfortunately he has given color to these things by very expensive living all this summer. I am told the Germans are now as furious with him as the Americans which accounts for his going to Egypt, and, I am told, "round the world." The unfortunate truth is that of six companies of which he was the forefront, every one has either gone to smash or depreciated enormously in value, and the losers naturally ask how it is that he has so much money? How vain is human greatness!

Kindest remembrances from us both to Mrs Bryce.

Yours ever sincerely

ELG

1. The World's Columbian Exposition of 1892-93. Godkin's admiration for the buildings was not that of an architectural sophisticate; except for Louis Sullivan's Transportation Building, the design of the fair represented a setback for American architecture. Godkin omitted comment on the grounds, which were designed by his old friend Olmsted.

2. Godkin, with characteristic extravagance, is expressing a wish for the assassination of Governor John Peter Altgeld of Illinois who had incurred the anger of conservatives by pardoning three of the surviving Haymarket anarchists.

3. A reference to Judge I. H. Maynard, a supporter of former Governor David B. Hill, accused of stealing election returns in 1892. Maynard was defeated in the election for the New York Court of Appeals after the city's Bar Association formed a Committee of Fifty to oppose him.

To Charles Francis Adams, Jr.

36 West 10th St., New York, December 2 [1893]
(Adams Family Papers, MHi)

DEAR ADAMS: Many thanks for your attempt to depreciate your ancestors. You are a first rate iconoclast, and I have enjoyed much your play among the Pilgrims. I am surprized you did not work in the observations of Lucretius on "Religio." He "got onto" Religion in its intolerant aspect before anybody else. I am a little sorry for the Puritans, because they have had their reputation for toleration and liberalism, thrust on to them by recent generations, and now suffer somewhat unfairly in being stripped of their illegitimate fame.

Come on here when you come to town.

Yours sincerely
ELG

To William James

Evening Post Editorial Rooms   New York, January 22 [1894]
(James Family Papers, MH)

MY DEAR JAMES: . . . [Harry's failure] was all very unfortunate, but judging from the way he talked to me about the theatre last summer, he cannot have been wholly unprepared for it.[1] I have read the plays he has published, and wherein he fails, is simply *plot*. His dialogues are masterpieces, but nothing particular happens. The characters don't cut each other's throats, or jump into a well, and the regular play goer, particularly the blackguards in the gallery, insist on this.

The whole thing has pained me much, for if I love any man in the world it is H. J. I never see him without wanting to hug him, and neither time nor distance makes any difference. He always remains in my memory the most loveable of men.

I wish you would put into execution your boasting intentions of coming to stay with us. You will never be more welcome anywhere. Many thanks for the nice things you say about me. I have had many tough years, and am glad at last of a little recognition, but I long for a place like Heaven, in which there is no "popular government." I think Satan invented it, as indeed all other governments yet tried by man.

Kindest remembrances to Mrs. James, and I remain

Always yours
ELG

1. When the intended London producer of Henry James's play "Mrs. Jasper's Way" voiced objections to the play, James heatedly withdrew it.

To James Bryce

36 West 10th St., New York, January 29, 1894
(Bryce Papers, Oxford University)

MY DEAR BRYCE: . . . I can give you no idea of the political confusion which reigns here. Cleveland under Whitney's influence —a bad fellow closely connected in business with the Tammany ring—seems to have begun his reign by supposing he could come to some kind of terms with the Hill gang, and restore "harmony in the party." [1] It has after a year of trial totally failed, and as he had already turned the cold shoulder to the "Anti-Swappers" and reformers he is in a singularly friendless condition. . . . The politicians all hate him, and he has had the singular folly to snub his old supporters.

The defeat in Massachusetts at the last election was, I think, largely due to his bringing on young Quincy from that state, to make a clean sweep of the Consulships.

. . . Villard has gone abroad utterly discredited, and much reviled, having been kicked out of everything. I wish he had some defence, but he has not. . .

Yours ever
ELG

1. Relations were cooling between the *Evening Post* and the White House as Cleveland turned for advice to William C. Whitney, the New York City transit promoter whom Godkin had asked to help him buy the *Evening Post*. The "Hill gang" was a reference to the faction backing former governor David H. Hill.

To Sir Charles Russell

36 West 10th St., New York, May 5, 1894 (Godkin Papers, MH)

MY DEAR RUSSELL: I do not know whether I should congratulate you in going on the bench or not. The bar and the House of Commons will miss you terribly. . . .[1] This quarrelling among the Irish again, is terrible for any Irishman who like myself, has been maintaining their capacity for better things than they have yet had. I suppose whatever may be said, Home Rule has been pushed a good way into the background. The Irish rule in the cities here has wholly destroyed any popularity they may once have had, fifty years ago. The way they take to low political intrigue and jobbery is something extraordinary and to me inexplicable. But the Americans are just as bad. The way they pretend that the Irish have got ahead of them in this matter is very funny. Philadelphia, where the government is American[,] is worse than New York.

We are going over June 30, to the Tyrol. . . .

> Ever sincerely yours
> ELG

1. Sir Charles Russell had just been appointed Lord Chief Justice of England. As a child, the Irish-born Russell lived at Newry, County Down, not far from the Godkins.

To his son

Henley, Yorkshire, July 12 [1894] (Godkin Papers, MH)

MY DEAR LAWRENCE: We had a triumphant passage. The sea was smooth as a millpond, and Katharine was not sick at all, and was on deck every day. She landed in excellent condition on Saturday morning, where we were met by a maid sent up from London by Mrs. Yates-Thompson, and came on here the same day where we have delightful rooms, and the best table I have ever had in a hotel in either hemisphere. The scenery is lovely and we are surrounded with ruined castles and abbeys among which we have spent the last four days, completely forgetting your struggles with "Labor," in which, as well as I can judge, Cleveland has been behaving very well. . . .[1]

Judge Gary was very pleasant on the passage. The others were . . . Scribner the publisher, McCabe, Simon Sterne (terrible), Baring the banker, and others less known to fame. We had a fourth of July celebration, at which McCabe made a "ringing speech". . . .

England looks lovely in spite of the hard times.

Yours ever
ELG

---

1. The Panic of 1893 had brought commercial distress and a consequent reduction of wages which eventuated in labor troubles, centering in the Pullman Strike in Chicago. Godkin endorsed Cleveland's militant position against the strikers.

To Henry Villard

Almond's Hotel, London, September 12, 1894
(Villard Papers, MH)

DEAR MR. VILLARD: We have been for a month in the Tyrol, where I have been hoping we might fall in with you, but in vain. . . .

What I wanted particularly to say to you was, that though I have no immediate intention of quitting the *Post*, yet in the ordinary course of human events, there is a possibility of my doing so, before I am superannuated. But I find it practically impossible among my friends to dispose of my (4) shares of stock if I mention the likelihood of my leaving, or in fact do not guarantee my remaining.[1] Now it would ease my mind somewhat if I could be certain that you would buy them, and pay me a fair price for them. . . . Would you mind giving me any promise or guarantee on this point? . . .

Yours sincerely
ELG

---

1. Godkin held a 2 percent interest in the *Evening Post*, a million-dollar concern.

To Frederick Sheldon

36 West 10th St., New York, September 25 [1894]
(Godkin Papers, MH)

MY DEAR SHELDON: . . . I saw no American newspaper for
three months, and up in the mountains no Americans. But in
the town and down on the plains they must have been as numerous as the hordes who overthrew the Roman empire. In the
steamer which followed us out, there were *100* women in one
band "personally conducted" by a woman, who served out their
chewing gum to them every morning. In Rome they are rapidly
ousting the Romans. Villard, whom I saw in Cortina, told me he
had been invited somewhere to talk or "conference" with a great
American editor named "John Bennett Gordon" on public affairs
but[,] when they met[,] "Bennett Gordon" was so drunk, that
conference was impossible. . . .[1]

Yours ever
ELG

1. Presumably the proprietor of the New York *Herald*, James Gordon
Bennett, Jr.

To Henry Villard

36 West 10th St., New York, October 28 [1894]
(Villard Papers, MH)

DEAR MR. VILLARD: . . . I simply thought that as you had
decided to keep the *Post*, you might possibly be willing to
acquire more of the stock. No one that I know of, considers he
has any claim on you.

Yours truly
ELG

To Brander Matthews

36 West 10th St., New York, November 5 [ca. 1894]
(Matthews Papers, NNC)

DEAR MR. MATHEWS [*sic*]: I am afraid on reflection that my colleagues on the Committee will think two professors from the same College too much. I am sorry, but I fear I shall be compelled to admit that there is something in this.

All this apropos of Nicholas Murray Butler, an excellent fellow.

Yours truly
ELG

To Daniel Coit Gilman

36 West 10th St., New York, November 8, 1894
(Gilman Papers, MdBJ)

MY DEAR GILMAN: . . . Nothing more crushing has occured [*sic*] in my time. It beats the Tweed rising hollow, because there is so much of it.[1] The passage of the Constitutional Amendment, which we did not expect, is the crowning mercy. The wicked have never been so sorrowful in this city. . . .

Yours sincerely
ELG

1. A reference to the sweeping defeat of Tammany Hall in the 1894 New York City elections after an investigation by the Lexow Committee of the State Legislature.

To James Bryce

36 West 10th St., New York, November 9 [1894]
(Bryce Papers, Oxford University)

MY DEAR BRYCE: . . . You have seen what a triumph we have had, and we got your congratulatory cablegram.

. . . [What] brought on the crisis was the revelations made by a committee of investigation of the State Senate—the "Lexow

Committee," of the shocking corruption of the police. It appeared they were levying tribute from almost every kind of criminal, besides extorting money from all the small shopkeepers and street vendors, that the privilege of joining the force was sold by the Commissioners, and also all the promotions on it—as much as $10,000 being paid for a Captaincy. The Commissioners are of course Tammany "heelers."

The explosion of public wrath was very great, and the various rascalities of Hill the Democratic candidate for governor helped to swell the tide. We have carried the city by majorities ranging from 37,000, to 50,000, and the state by 183,000. In addition to this all the amendments to the State Constitution, framed by the recent State Convention, some of them most valuable have been carried. In fact the Democrats have been swept off the face of the earth.

Much the same result has occurred all over the country owing to the general disgust with the conduct of the Democrats over the silver bill, and the tariff bill, last winter in Congress. I think it would be a great mistake to suppose that this means any return to the McKinley bill or a protective policy. . . .[1] The Republicans are generally convinced that the McKinley venture was a mistake. . . .

What I think is not unlikely is the drifting back of the Republican party to its old position of the championship of order, sound currency, and national unity—or in other words of conservatism. The Chicago labor riots and the growth of "populism" have frightened people a good deal.

. . . We have settled down for the winter, now that the excitement of the election is over. . . . If Tammany had won, I was going to let our house and go abroad. Life here would probably not have been safe, and certainly not comfortable. But my previsions as to what democracy will have to go through here and every where before it gets clarified have not changed in the least. . . .

Yours ever
ELG

---

1. When the Democrats returned to power under Cleveland in 1893, the McKinley Tariff was replaced by the Wilson Tariff, which lowered some duties and removed others. Yet, because some Congressional Democrats

were lukewarm to tariff reform, the Wilson Tariff represented a compromise pleasing to no one.

To Samuel G. Ward

36 West 10th St., New York, November 13 [1894]
(Ward Papers, MH)

MY DEAR WARD: . . . We have, indeed had a glorious, wonderful overwhelming victory, and the City and State lie at our mercy. I am much flattered by your opinion of my share in it, and I do think I have in some degree contributed to it. But if you knew the small amount of recognition my labors receive you would wonder more than you do at my persistence. In all this canvas, not a single mention has been made by anyone in pulpit, press, or platform, of the *Evening Post's* having had anything to do with the overthrow of Tammany, although the fullest acknowledgments are made to me by every man I meet, *in private*. Yet I began this fight six years ago. I carried it on for four years singlehanded, before Parkhurst engaged in it.[1] I was five times arrested by these ruffians. . . .

What will become of the victory depends now on the Legislature and Martin and Strong. The new Mayor is I hear everything that is good, but I am told he is narrow and a fierce Republican. . . .[2] Where I think the new regime will come to grief will be in finding new men of a better class for the offices. . . . A first rate man will not go into the service of the City for two or three years. . . . Politicians of course take offices for any term, however short, as they live from hand to mouth and their whole existence is a sort of gamble. The problem, in fact, is an intellectual rather than a political one. Whenever the public gets hold of the idea that a city must be managed like a bank, the thing will be done. . . .

ELG

1. The Reverend Charles H. Parkhurst (1842–1933), through his sermons and affidavits about the connection of Tammany Hall with vice, sparked the legislative investigation that led to the downfall of Tammany in the 1894 New York City elections.
2. The millionaire merchant William L. Strong (1827–1900) had been elected mayor of New York City. One of his official acts was to appoint Godkin, Everett P. Wheeler, and Randolph Robinson to a five-man New

York City civil service supervisory board on which the editor served for eighteen months.

To Charles Dudley Warner

Evening Post Editorial Rooms   New York, November 19 [1894]
(Warner Papers, CtTr)

DEAR MR. WARNER: I have made some enquiries about the Brockway matter since seeing you, and find the course of the *Post* was due to the impression made on Mr. Horace White who was in charge of the paper during my absence in Europe, by that very excitable and unreliable but excellent lady, Mrs. C. R. Lowell.[1]

Thanks for your pamphlet.

Yours very truly
ELG

1. Zebulon R. Brockway (1827–1920), a nationally prominent penologist, had been suspended from his post as superintendent of the Elmira, New York, reformatory after charges were made against him of cruelty to prisoners. Josephine Shaw Lowell (1843–1905) was active in New York reform movements, including prison reform. Brockway was reinstated by the governor after a gubernatorial commission cleared him.

To Emma Brace

December 12, 1894 (Ogden 2:193)

MY DEAR EMMA: Many thanks for your letter. . . .

Of course it was I who wrote it. I would not let anyone else talk of your father's memory in my paper, and I am very glad your mother and you liked what I said.[1] With more space I might have done better. He was a very kind friend of mine, long ago, when I was young and needed friends. I do not think I ever had a more sympathetic one, but now "clouds o'er the evening sky more thickly stand."

With kindest remembrances to your mother,

Ever sincerely yours
ELG

1. A reference to the editor's favorable review of *The Life of Charles Loring Brace* (New York: Charles Scribner's Sons, 1894), edited by Brace's daughter.

To The Reverend Henry Codman Potter

January 2, 1895 (Ogden 2:182)

MY DEAR BISHOP POTTER: I received yesterday morning your most kind note, and the list of women who have subscribed to the cup which you presented to me on New Year's Eve.[1]

I feel much more deeply than I can express, the great honor which these ladies have done me. I value it mainly because it indicates strong interest in the causes I have had at heart for so many years, no less than approval of my manner of supporting them. It makes me feel, too, that we shall in this city have less battling to do hereafter, of which I am all the more glad because I have reached the time of life at which, Matthew Arnold somewhere says, we begin to care less about regulating other people's lives, and more for the infusion of grace and peace into our own. . . .

1. In recognition of Godkin's role in the overthrow of Tammany Hall, seventy New York women bought him a silver loving cup at Tiffany's and inscribed it: "From friends in grateful recognition of fearless and unfaltering services to the City of New York." Bishop Potter presented it to the editor, with appropriate speeches by New York lawyer Joseph H. Choate and others, at a New Year's Eve gathering at the home of Mr. and Mrs. G. E. Kissell. The cup today is in the possession of the New York Historical Society.

To Charles Eliot Norton

January 12, 1895 (Ogden 2:199)

MY DEAR NORTON: It was a great pleasure to hear from you, and especially to be congratulated by you. . . . Nearly every one here whose good opinion I care for came forward to cover me with praise and felicitation, the press very characteristically remaining studiously silent; and there is a fair prospect of good government in the city for a few years at all events, possibly for my time. But with a villainous press—venal and silly,—and somewhat frivolous and distinctly *childish* public, it is difficult to be sure of more than a few years. . . . Think of old Dana being asked to Cornell University to deliver the address on "Founders' Day"![1]

But enough of this writing. You see I am not sanguine about the future of democracy. I think we shall have a long period of decline like that which followed the fall of the Roman Empire, and then a recrudescence under some other form of society. Our present tendencies in that direction are concealed by great national progress.

. . . In my little address the other night when they presented me with the cup, I recalled the day you came to New York thirty years ago to propose the *Nation* to me. The world has been going round very rapidly since then, and it is a great gratification to me to think that you have nothing to regret concerning that enterprize.

We have been a good deal troubled here—some of us—about the proposed withdrawal of the Harvard examinations for women in New York. They have been a great source of pride and profit to many young women, and their place could not be taken as yet in the public eye by Radcliffe examinations, Radcliffe being much less known and respected. We sent a letter to Eliot about it, signed by Bishop Potter, Edward King, Lyman Abbott, and myself, but as he was just starting for Europe he turned it over to Martin Brimmer.[2] If it comes under your notice, and you have not heard of the matter, will you look into it?

Affectionately yours
ELG

1. A reference to Charles A. Dana, proprietor of the New York *Sun*, with whom Godkin feuded in the *Evening Post*.

2. Martin Brimmer (1829–96), sometime secretary to the President and Fellows of Harvard College, was one of the original Boston stockholders in the *Nation*.

To Carl Schurz

Evening Post Editorial Rooms   New York, January 14 [1895]
(Schurz Papers, DLC)

DEAR MR. SCHURZ: I have no knowledge of Phillips since I left office. He never came near me under the Tammany regime for

which I did not blame him, as it might have injured him. . . .
He came to me, however, immediately after the election in considerable alarm about his position, and then I inquired how he stood with the C[ivil] S[ervice] reformers. Potter said, badly, but McAneny and Wheeler stood up for him on the grounds you mention, and when I received from Wheeler a certificate of good behavior *during one term of office*, I signed it, not thinking I could well refuse. When I had a talk with Strong (the mayor) the other night he seemed disposed to retain Phillips, and as I had no knowledge to rely on against him, I said nothing. This is my condition now. I agree entirely with what you say about the desirableness of having a man above suspicion in the place, and will submit your letter to the sub committee.[1]

Very truly yours
ELG

1. Apparently a reference to the Reform Club of New York City, of which Godkin was the past chairman of the civil service reform committee.

To James Bryce

36 West 10th St., New York, January 30, 1895
(Bryce Papers, Oxford University)

MY DEAR BRYCE: . . . I have judged for some time that things were not looking well for the Ministry . . . I never believed Rosebery would succeed, in spite of your good opinion of him. His speeches were to me most bewildering.

I cannot give you an idea of the state of things here. It amounts almost to a breakdown of popular government. The ignorance and imbecility of Congress passes belief. We may pull out of the financial muddle by some sort of fluke, but it will be a fluke.

In the city we are fighting Platt who controls the legislature through the Republican majority, to extract from him the reform legislation which our victory at the polls called for, and find it thus far impossible to get it without promising him offices for his "heelers." [1] But I think he will be beaten in the end.

. . . When I see how things are going here in the way of

legislative deterioration I am really surprized at your cheerfulness over there as you are pushed down the incline. . . .

Your new chapters read very well, but as you say you will need to bring out a new edition every six months, if you mean to keep up with the march of American democracy. . . . I hope the American tide is not flowing as fiercely in you, as it used to. Garrison has written an article in the *Nation* on your Southern Chapter, which is tinged of course with the old Abolitionist flavor.[2] One of the saddest things in the change down there is the very inferior quality of the Whites who are coming to Congress. They are a wretched substitute for the old slaveholders. . . . If I told you more of the fight which mere civilization is having here you would be wearied. . . .

Yours ever
ELG

1. Godkin is conceding that, by overthrowing the New York City Democratic machine, the Republicans and their Mugwump allies traded the rule of Tammany Hall for that of the state Republican machine headed by Thomas C. Platt. The Mugwumps now found themselves making deals with the Platt forces, whom Godkin admittedly found preferable to Tammany Hall.

2. Wendell P. Garrison, "The South and the Black Man," *Nation*, 31 January 1895, pp. 86–87. Garrison had long undergone criticism from his Abolitionist relatives for his unquestioning loyalty to Godkin, but he could occasionally follow his own principles, as when in 1895 he rebuked *Nation* contributor Goldwin Smith for a passage abhorring miscegenation as contrary to nature. "This I do not believe in," Garrison informed Smith in explaining why he was deleting the passage, "I think we ought to be very careful not to foster race and color prejudice."

To Daniel Coit Gilman

36 West 10th St., New York, March 30, 1895
(Gilman Papers, MdBJ)

My dear Gilman: I was exceedingly sorry to have missed your address and reception last night. . . . There is no man to whom the country is more indebted. Scribner and Co. are going to publish this summer a volume of old *Nation* articles, and I had great pleasure and pride in putting in my forecast made twenty years ago, of what you would do.[1] Long may you wave!

Faithfully yours
ELG

1. Edwin Lawrence Godkin, *Reflections and Comments, 1865-1895* (New York: Charles Scribner's Sons, 1895). Godkin is referring Gilman to a *Nation* editorial on pages 164-72 therein suggesting to the trustees of the newly founded Johns Hopkins University what direction the University ought to take. Gilman was not mentioned.

To R. U. Johnson

Evening Post Editorial Rooms   New York, May 13 [1895]
(*Century Magazine* Correspondence, NN)

DEAR MR. JOHNSON: Many thanks for your invitation, but I really do not care to write anything more about newspapers, and besides this, do not care for any extra work before sailing for Europe June 15th.

Truly yours
ELG

To Senator George F. Hoar

Evening Post Editorial Rooms   New York, May 31, 1895
(Hoar Papers, MHi)

Senator Hoar

DEAR SIR: As we would like to comment on your interesting address yesterday, with intelligence, will you kindly inform me what the book is, and who "the liar" to whom you refer in the following passage.[1] We are unable to identify the work in question through your description.

Truly yours
ELG

1. In a Decoration Day address, United States Senator George F. Hoar (1826-1904) declared that a beloved American man-of-letters (James Russell Lowell) had once dedicated a book of verse to "the most unscrupulous liar

connected with the American press." To Godkin's sarcastic query, Hoar promptly replied that, by the liar, "I meant you." Godkin kept the Massachusetts lawmaker's letter for several years, then sent it back to him marked "Returned to an old blackguard."

To Senator George F. Hoar

36 West 10th St., New York, June 5, 1895 (Hoar Papers, MHi)

Senator Hoar

Sir: I wrote to you for the purpose of securing under your own hand, evidence of the depths of blackguardism, and absurdity, which a modern Senator can reach. The blackguardism is readily explained by the character of a good many of your colleagues with whom you pass a large part of the year. The absurdity is your own.

Mr. Lowell did not dedicate a "book" to me. What he did dedicate was "Three Memorial Poems." Nor were they lamentations over the country and its public men.[1] They exulted in its glories. Your ignorance of this shows the muddle-headed way in which you prepared your Decoration Day attack on the critics. I have heard a good many attacks on your intelligence. Indeed I have cast aspersions on it myself. But even those who think most lightly of it, were not prepared for your accusing the most "beloved' literary man of the country, of dedicating patriotic odes to a notorious liar, in an address meant to be peculiarly American. No one would have been more disgusted with this, than he, were he living. I do not think you are worth disgust. The worst charge that can be made against you is silliness, and of this you have been long suspected.

> Yours truly,
> ELG

1. James Russell Lowell, *Three Memorial Poems* (Boston: James R. Osgood and Co., 1877). The dedication to this ninety-two page book reads: "To E. L. Godkin, in cordial acknowledgment of his eminent service in heightening and purifying the tone of our political thought." Despite Godkin's denial, the little volume consists of three hortatory odes lamenting the political manners of the Gilded Age. Senator Hoar, who had been on terms of mutual respect with Lowell, felt, perhaps with reason, that Godkin was primarily responsible for the poet's defection to the Mugwumps.

To James Bryce

Hôtel Victoria, Montreux, Switzerland, August 21 [1895]
(Bryce Papers, Oxford University)

MY DEAR BRYCE: Our letters have crossed. I was delighted to hear from you, and to get your explanation of the disaster.[1] I agree with you in thinking the Liberals are out until there is some great change—such as a more vigorous democratization of the lower middle and working class. But of course great Tory blunders are among the possibilities.

. . . [Your] South African trip will be interesting I am sure, but when one has lived as long as I have in "a new country," one does not care to see another.

Have not the Tories begun well in keeping Gully, and making Wolseley Commander in Chief? Poor Morley! Where and how is he. . . .[2]

Bon Voyage!

Yours ever
ELG

1. The Liberals had suffered a crushing defeat in the recent English general election.
2. William C. Gully (1835–1909), a Liberal, was allowed to continue as Speaker of the House of Commons after the Liberal defeat. The new government represented a coalition of Conservatives and Liberal Unionists. Godkin is expressing sympathy for John Morley because he had temporarily lost his seat in Parliament.

To Mrs. William F. Smith

October 4, 1895 (Ogden 2:22)

. . . I received your congratulatory telegram and thank you all for it, but it is not pleasant to be sixty-four, and condolence would be more appropriate than congratulation. . . .

Old age is a subtle poison, and it is sad to feel it in one's veins, but this makes it all the more necessary to get all we can out of life before it floors us. This is about what I am doing. . . .

To Charles Eliot Norton

October 12, 1895 (Ogden 2:200)

. . . Scribner and Co. have induced me to publish a volume of. my articles in the *Nation* on non-political topics during the past thirty years. It will appear in a month or so. I am desirous of inserting in it a word of inscription to you, who more than any other man was instrumental in founding the *Nation*, and to whom I owed so much sympathy and encouragement in early and gloomy years. If you do not forbid it, it will appear.[1]

Yours ever

ELG

1. Godkin, *Reflections and Comments* (New York: Scribner and Co., 1895). The dedication reads: "To Charles Eliot Norton, to whom the foundation of 'The Nation' was largely due, in grateful acknowledgement of a long friendship."

To Lloyd McKim Garrison

Evening Post Editorial Rooms   New York, October 26 [1895]
(Autograph File, MH)

DEAR LLOYD MC GARRISON: I wish you would say to those crazy fellows, that Bishop is in no way to blame about the Davison letter.[1] He wished and advised its publication, but I decide in the last resort what shall go into the *Post* and I decided that this should not. All promises to print things in the *Post* are conditioned on my approval. I will not allow the roof to be taken off this building.

Yours sincerely

ELG

1. A reference to the infighting within the New York City reform movement. Joseph B. Bishop was a protégé of Godkin—he imitated the editor's style so successfully that some of their editorials are indistinguishable—who had been hired at Godkin's request in the aftermath of the 1883 Godkin-Schurz feud. "Those crazy fellows" were the Good Government men (Goo-Goos), chief among them the socially prominent young lawyer, John Jay Chapman. The Goo-Goos regarded the *Evening Post* as a corporation

organ and the anti-Tammany Committee of Fifty as a group of self-serving plutocrats eager to make deals with the state Republican machine.

To John Jay Chapman

36 West 10th St., New York, October 27 [1895]
(Chapman Papers, MH)

DEAR MR. CHAPMAN: I learned yesterday that there was a good deal of abuse of Mr. Bishop, and a good many charges of bad faith against him among Good Government men because Mr. C. S. Davison's answer to Mr. Garrison did not appear in the *Evening Post.*

A little enquiry or consideration would have saved Mr. Bishop from this. He desired and advised the publication of Mr. Davison's letter. It was *I* who excluded it. Nothing appears in the *Post* without my approval. . . .

Yours sincerely
ELG

To John Jay Chapman

November 12, 1895 (Chapman Papers, MH)

DEAR MR. CHAPMAN: I wrote to you some time ago, as I heard from Mr. Garrison you had been abusing Mr. Bishop, to relieve him from responsibility that did not fairly belong to him. But I did not expect any answer, nor invite an expression of your views on journalism and other matters. Consequently I was rather surprized by the receipt of your letter last night, and as I find it somewhat impertinent I return it herewith, thinking you may wish to use it elsewhere.

Yours truly
ELG

To Silas W. Burt

36 West 10th St., New York, November 27 [1895?]
(Burt Papers, NHi)

MY DEAR BURT: All this seems to me excellent. I have marked one place that of meteorologist, which I think ought to be classified.[1] But I think it has no defects that can be ascertained otherwise than by experience, when they begin to try to "beat the law."

Yours ever
ELG

1. A reference to the classification of state jobs under civil service. Burt was serving on the state civil service commission, and Godkin was on the civil service advisory commission of New York City. This letter, plus other heretofore unpublished correspondence of Godkin, shows that he was more active in public affairs than his biographer Ogden was aware.

11. Jingoes, Bryanites, and a Shattered Dream

By 1895 Godkin had lost much of his energy and zest for combat. He was writing fewer editorials each year, and during the constantly lengthening vacation periods in Europe he wrote nothing. The events that in the last two years of the century catapulted the United States into the world arena saw him take an editorial back seat to his associates. It was not so much his pen as that of his younger colleague, Rollo Ogden, which moved President McKinley in 1898 to consider charging the *Evening Post* with treason. Yet the war with Spain, as the letters that follow attest, aroused Godkin's deepest and, some contend, finest sentiments. In the *Evening Post* he blasted American navalism, jingoistic patriots, and the thirst for colonies, not comprehending that they were unavoidable trappings of the imperialism he favored. For it was not expansion that the censorious Godkin objected to so much as the men who were leading it. In an 1899 article in *Forum*, "The Conditions of Good Colonial Government," he tendered his prescription for governing the new American empire, but he had no hope that his advice would be heeded. "The one thing which will prevent expansion being a disgrace," he complained to a woman acquaintance, "is a permanent colonial civil service, but who is doing or saying a word about it?"

By now the captiousness of Godkin and his colleagues on the *Evening Post* had become legendary. One popular after-dinner story described a timid lady living in the country, who, instead of getting herself a watch dog, arranged to have the *Evening Post* delivered each evening to her doorstep. "It just lay there and growled all night."

The initial letters in the section that follows relate to the Venezuelan Boundary Dispute of 1895, which brought to an abortive end the cooperation between the *Evening Post* and

President Cleveland. In December 1895 Cleveland in a special message to Congress asked for an appropriation to send a commission to Venezuela to determine the facts of a dispute between Venezuela and British Guiana. In effect, Cleveland proposed that the United States draw the boundary line and require England to abide by its decision. Godkin at first responded to the Administration's "twisting of the Lion's tail" with mild editorial disapproval, but he abruptly changed course when opposition to the President appeared in financial circles. In a tirade in the *Evening Post* and the *Nation,* the editor branded Cleveland "the greatest international anarchist of modern times," a president "morally impeached of high crimes and misdemeanors." Ultimately, voices of moderation appeared and the dispute was settled peacefully, but Cleveland, whose chronic mistrust of the press was swelled by the course taken by Godkin, never expressed confidence in him again.

Godkin's stand on social issues during the later 1890s reflected his deepening gloom and reaction. Having many years earlier parted company with John Stuart Mill, he now was immersed in Edmund Burke; in 1899 he wrote the preface to the American edition of Burke's *Orations and Essays* (New York: D. Appleton & Co., 1900). Privately and in his editorials Godkin fulminated against social capitalism (which he confused with Marxism), William Jennings Bryan (whom he termed an "Anarchist"), and mounting worker unrest. In England he chaffed at Joseph Chamberlain's social welfare program, and at home he admonished genteel readers of the *North American Review* that to attempt to alleviate discontent among the poor "is as hopeless a task as to abolish poverty." Despairingly he told an acquaintance: "I came here fifty years ago with high and fond ideals about America, for I was brought up in the Mill-Grote school of radicals. They are now all shattered, and I have apparently to look elsewhere to keep even moderate hopes about the human race alive."

Central to the problem that the editors of the *Evening Post* and the *Nation* faced was that they had never been firm in their liberal moorings. Ever since Godkin and White took editorial control of the *Evening Post,* intolerance had been growing in that paper. Undaunted by their failure in 1894 to help obtain the dismissal of Richard Ely from the University of Wisconsin because of his rejection of classical economics, Godkin and White continued to support academic purges, such as the dismissal two years later of the pro Silver Professor E. Benjamin Andrews of Brown University. White voiced the sentiments of both men when to a friend he exulted over Andrew's dismissal: "In Colorado I am credibly informed that [Andrews] wore a silver pin in his shirt front and called attention to it, as an indication of his soundness, like a demagogue politician."

To Charles Eliot Norton

Pellwood, Highland Falls, N. Y., December 29, 1895
(Ogden 2:201–2)

. . . We are up here spending two or three days with the Pells. I was rather used up by the excitement of the past week, which was the most anxious I have known in my career.[1] I was thunderstruck by Cleveland's message, and have seen so much Jingoism even among intelligent people, and so much cowardice in the face of Jingoism, that the prospect which seemed to open itself before me was a long fight against a half-crazed public, under a load of abuse, and the discredit of foreign birth, etc., etc. It was in this state of mind we opened our batteries on that Friday morning, and I am bound to say relief came promptly. We were literally overwhelmed with laudatory and congratulatory letters. . . .

But the sureness of our own position, of course, does not do away with anxiety about the country. The Jingoes are still numerous and powerful and absolutely crazy, and Cleveland's submission to them, with the aid of a serious Boston lawyer like Olney, is a terrible shock. . . . An immense democracy, mostly ignorant, and completely secluded from foreign influences, and without any knowledge of other states of society, with great contempt for history and experience, finds itself in possession of enormous power and is eager to use it in brutal fashion against anyone who comes along, *without knowing how to do it,* and is therefore constantly on the brink of some frightful catastrophe like that which overtook France in 1870. The spectacle of our financial condition and legislation during the last twenty years, the general silliness and credulity begotten by the newspapers, the ferocious optimism exacted of all teachers and preachers, and the general belief that we are peculiar or chosen people to whom the experience of other people is of no use, makes a pretty dismal picture. . . . The present crisis is really a fight between the rational business men, and the politicians and the newspapers, and the rational business men are not getting the best of it.

The press is the worst feature in the situation, and yet the press would not be what it is without a public demand for it as it is. . . . I am just now the great object of abuse, and the abuse is just what you would hear in a barroom row. . . . I have had a delightful and characteristic letter from William James urging me not "to curse God and die," but to keep on with "the campaign of education." [2]

Ever affectionately yours
ELG

1. A reference to the crisis between England and the United States over the Venezuelan boundary.

2. Godkin unfortunately did not trouble to read all of James's letter, which contained some stern advice. While complimenting the editor on his courage in standing up against evil, James cautioned him against using expletives, and he urged him in the future to be more "patiently explanatory." Singling out for criticism Godkin's allusion to Cleveland and the public as "howling savages," James offered the opinion that jingoism was caused not by savagery but by ignorance.

To William James

Pellwood, Highland Falls, N. Y., December 29, 1895
(James Family Papers, MH)

My dear delightful James, probably the only man in the world capable of writing me such a soul stirring letter:

Our crisis here passed quietly as far as I am personally concerned. We began our fight on Friday week in a more dismal frame of mind than I have known for thirty years, but my anxiety was at an end in a few hours. The intelligent public[,] business men, bankers, clergy, professors, came to our support almost with a roar of applause and showers of letters, and our circulation (of the *Post*) ran up 1000 a day. . . .

But my dear fellow, the trouble is not over. We are now dealing with a generation which has grown up under the newspapers, and the "Americanism" of the schoolbooks. It thinks history began in 1776, that we are a peculiar people and are strong enough to do what we please, whip England, and make silver circulate at 16 to 1 all over the globe, and looks on instructed or thoughtful people, people who are influenced by human experience, as "bad Americans," or pessimists. The newspapers stand between this generation and the light and make it very hard to get at them, and the danger is that we shall have some frightful catastrophe before we settle down to the plain and rational living arranged for the republic by the Founders.

. . . The spectacle of incapacity, not to say imbecility, and credulity which you see in Washington today, in the dealing of Congress with the finances, shows a state of things which will not be cured in ten years or in thirty. Democratic government everywhere, has in my poor opinion, to go through many crises and much sorrowful experience before humanity will be able to get into ecstasy over it. The press is now the great enemy of good government and of rational views of human affairs. Everybody I see here agrees about this, but no one is able to see how improvement is to come. I cannot, myself, imagine a better field for patriotic millionaires than the establishment of good newspapers, free from party bias. Highly as I value colleges, I really think in our present condition money spent in this way would do more for our civilization than donations to Harvard or Yale or Chicago. College culture somehow does not get down among the masses quickly enough to affect politics. We are unfortunate, too, in being so far removed from contact with other societies, and types of government. The credulity about foreign politics which I meet with would disgrace any European peasantry. . . .

ELG. . . .

To James Bryce

36 West 10th St., New York, January 9, 1896
(Bryce Papers, Oxford University)

Private

MY DEAR BRYCE: . . . No one knows, who is willing to tell, the origin of Cleveland's extraordinary performance. My belief, on the best information I can get, is that the Republicans having more than a year ago, taken up the Jingo policy as the winning card, so badgered and hounded him about the feebleness and "Un Americanness" of his foreign policy . . . and being[,] as he heard[,] about to introduce a resolution in the House forcing his hand in the Venezuela matter, he determined to . . . steal their thunder. As a political move it was most effective, for they all rallied to him. . . . I think he was dismayed when he saw the effect of his message on the Stock market. . . .

I have seen this Jingo policy coming, among the Republicans for a year and a half and have been pounding away at it in the *Evening Post,* but I was utterly unprepared for Cleveland's action. . . .

Now let me say something more, *which you will not quote.* The opponents of Jingoism, and of Cleveland's performance are the business men, clergy, professors, and the like of the eastern coast. The hatred of England in the west and Southwest is rabid, bitter and ferocious, and would welcome war tomorrow. There are a few newspapers, here and there *rari nantes,* which condemn Jingoism, but the great mass are frantically for war. Washington is furious for war. The West would not mind if New York were laid in ashes. The children have been taught in all the schools for twenty five years to hate England, and to believe that we can thrash her, and that we did so in 1812. They do not know why they should fight England, except that she is "grabbing" and insolent. They resent English contempt for American manners and customs, and envy her greatness, and think America ought to make as big a figure in the world as she does. A clique of politicians, too, has sprung up, who call for war—any war— as a good thing for character and trade, but by war, they always mean a war with England.

You greatly, in England, overrate the popular intelligence here. A generation has come into the field which has since it left school been fed on a very vile and silly press. It is cut off from all other communities. It knows nothing of Europe, and knows nothing of any history before 1776. It does not read books at all. It is made perfectly drunk by the knowledge that it is 70,000,000 strong, and has a large revenue. Its morals are very low, and it has no religion to speak of, and no public men who act the part of teachers, or exert any influence or authority. It has a curious Chinese contempt in fact, for the rest of the world, and thinks it can do without Europe, and has a superstitious, mediaeval dislike of bankers, and dealers in money, and knows nothing about credit. If I could illustrate all this for you, you would be astonished. Sumner of Yale said to me the other day, your [*American*] *Commonwealth,* was fast becoming a "political romance."

I think, that when the enormous disparity of force on the sea, is brought home to this half insane multitude, they may quiet down for a while. But they are building a large navy, and I am very certain will have a war with you when they get it ready. *You must be prepared for this.* Civilization on the political and moral side, is I assure you, running down rapidly in this country. The colleges are becoming the sort of intellectual refuges the monasteries were in the Middle Ages, but their influence on government amounts to nothing. At this moment there is a complete breakdown of the government in Washington. Congress is no more able to deal with the financial problems than a company of children, and nearly every state of importance is in the hands of a conscienceless and shameless boss. Nothing will, in my mind, bring this mass of barbarians to reason, but a severe check at the hands of Europe, that is, actual experience of the sufferings and losses of war.

. . . Much of the abuse of you, and threats against you, is due to a popular belief that England "will not fight." In fact a great many Jingoes defend their wild talk in this way. So I am sure a firm policy clothed in conciliatory language, but copious in argument and explanation, is the best one for you. You have nearly all the intelligence, and business interests of the country on your side, and your talk should back them up, by its reasonableness. . . .

Ever yours
ELG. . . .

To Carl Schurz

Evening Post Editorial Rooms   New York, January 10, 1896
(Schurz Papers, DLC)

DEAR MR. SCHURZ: Can you be induced to address the Commercial Club of Providence,—composed of Merchants and Manufacturers—on the Venezuela question and the Monroe Doctrine—on Saturday night, Jan. 20. All expenses literally paid. It is very desirable to preach the gospel wherever it is asked for. If you can let me know tomorrow, I shall be much obliged.

Yours sincerely
ELG

To James Bryce

36 West 10th St., New York, February 3 [1896]
(Bryce Papers, Oxford University)

Confidential

MY DEAR BRYCE: . . . Before leaving for Washington for a week or two, there are two or three things I want to impress on you, and which you may use as you think best, as long as you don't "give me away."

This Jingo outburst has been preparing for a year as a bit of party policy on the part of the Republicans. Morton of *the Cabinet*—a good man—has confided to us, that Cleveland and Olney broke out as a counterstrike, to anticipate the Republicans. . . .

Secondly, my solemn belief is that had it been successful, that is, had it not produced such a terrible business shock, a quarrel with some foreign power would have become a regular feature in every Presidential canvas. I fear this may be the case as soon as the Jingoes get a big navy.

Thirdly, this abuse and threatening of England has gone on so long without coming to anything serious that the politicians no longer consider it dangerous. There is a firm belief among the masses in the West etc. that England "will not fight," and may be insulted with impunity. . . .

Fourthly, the only chance of success, we here who are fighting for international law, have, lies in *your* standing by it. If Salisbury is weak, and gives ground, we shall be covered with ridicule, and contempt. . . .

Fifthly, you cannot overrate the ignorance of the rest of the world of these Western men, and indeed of all the politicians, their conceit, and immorality. . . .

The Professors and Clergy, and all the thinking educated class stood firm as far as I see. But there is not a statesman left in public life, and you may consider yourselves dealing with a semi-barbarous Power. I leave you to the deductions from all this yourself. But it is "God's truth."

Yours
ELG

To Charles Eliot Norton

36 West 10th St., New York, June 2, 1896 (Norton Papers, MH)

My dear Norton: I am twice asked to subscribe to a scheme for a Memorial to Lowell in the shape of a park formed with his own land. I do not see your name among the promoters. What sort of scheme is it? Is it genuine? and credible?

I do not quite like these real estate Memorials. . . .

Ever affectionately yours
ELG

To Charles Eliot Norton

North East Harbor, Maine, July 7, 1896 (Norton Papers, MH)

My dear Norton: . . . The enlargement of the *Post is* a sign of prosperity, and I do not think it will entail any more labor or anxiety on me, but in two years more, I shall retire from active management. I am pretty tired both of it, and of American politics. I think very evil times are in store for democracy which we shall not live to see but while we are we must do the best we can. . . . I was amused by Lodge's declaration at the dinner. To be responsible to nobody but his own conscience is certainly the best arrangement he could make for himself, but an odd one for a public man.[1]

Ever affectionately yours
ELG

1. Senator Henry Cabot Lodge's adverse estimate of Godkin is found in *Selections from the Letters of Theodore Roosevelt and Henry Cabot Lodge, 1884–1918* (New York: Charles Scribner's Sons, 1925).

To Charles Eliot Norton

North East Harbor, Maine, July 13 [1896]
(Norton Papers, MH)

My dear Norton: . . . The political outlook is dark enough. The American optimism is amusingly illustrated by the cheerful way people are now turning to the wretched McKinley. . . .[1]

I want you to note one thing: All our recent "crazes," silver and labor etc. are either started or nourished by men of education who either want to "support the government" or "get close to the people." The currency craze was supplied by the Supreme Court, giving Congress the power to turn even leather into money. The silver craze has been kept going by the bimetallists, professors and instructed cranks. They kept telling the Silverites that they were right in principle, but they could not go it alone. The European rascals could not agree. This finally developed into positive hatred of England for not changing her standard (See Lodge *passim*). Then the labor craze formed and promoted by "ethical professors" and clergymen ended in the Chicago riots, and the production of Altgeld. . . .[2]

Affectionately yours
ELG

1. William McKinley had received the Republican nomination for the presidency.

2. A reference to the Pullman Strike of 1894 and to Governor John Peter Altgeld, who had incurred the hatred of conservatives by opposing Cleveland's use of Federal troops to quell the strike.

To James Bryce

North East Harbor, Maine, July 28 [1896]
(Bryce Papers, Oxford University)

MY DEAR BRYCE: Russell has made a mistake and a great one but he must keep it as little as possible by getting away from his patronage as soon as possible. Carter ought to have told him, but Carter is very careless about such matters, and was only too glad to get someone to do something for Russell at this deserted season.[1] V. has no position at all, and I think no character. He has ruined many people and made a failure himself, and is a recognized and astounding liar.

We are in an astounding position politically. . . . Nearly all the public men have flattered, cajoled, or gone half way with the Silverites, and legislated to please them. There is not a single *sincere* gold man in the field, though many now frightened ones. Curtis has himself frightened the Supreme Court in his argument on the income tax—a most outrageous thing. In fact honest vigorous opposition ten or fifteen years ago from educated men would have arrested this thing. It is very like the French Revolution.

My own impression about investments is, that McKinley will probably be elected, that stocks will be low and a good purchase till the election, that then there may be a short spurt of cheerfulness such as men feel after a great escape; that then more dulness [sic] will set in for three or four years, when American investments will be bad. I would sell promptly after McKinley's election. . . . there will be no revival here till after complete reform of the finances, of which there is no immediate prospect. All will depend on the Congress to be elected in November. Since the French Revolution no people was ever so given over to folly.

We did not go over this summer owing to the situation and are here, among the same set. . . . Eliot, Gilman, Low, Fisher and others are all here. . . .[2] We expect to go over in the spring, January or February, for four or five months, when I hope you will be in London. I do not know whether you have seen an article of mine in the June *Atlantic* on Lecky's book.[3] It is (the book) an extraordinary production, especially the second volume.

The Tories are making an awful mess of it, and my early estimate of Balfour is exactly fulfilled. Salisbury is very unsatisfactory in American matters. . . .

Yours ever
ELG

1. A reference to a visit to the United States by the Lord Chief Justice of England. Apparently Godkin is disturbed that his friend James Carter did not caution Lord Russell against accepting the hospitality of Henry Villard, with whom Godkin was suffering increasingly strained relations.

2. Presidents Eliot of Harvard, Gilman of Johns Hopkins, Low of Columbia, and Professor George P. Fisher of Yale.

3. E. L. Godkin, "The Real Problems of Democracy," *Atlantic Monthly* 78 (July 1896): 1–13, a mildly critical review of Irish historian William E. Lecky's *Democracy and Liberty* (London: Longman's and Co., 1896). Lecky, an admirer of the writings of Godkin and Bryce, was finding an adverse reception for his book on both sides of the Atlantic because of its criticisms of democracy. Theodore Roosevelt found Lecky's views "ludicrous," he told John Morley, "because they were largely derived from Godkin and the *Nation*."

To Theodora Sedgwick

Seabright, N.J., September 14, 1896 (Child Papers, MH)

MY DEAR THEODORA: . . . The Campaign is simply disgusting. We shall win, but what victory! [1]

Yours always
ELG. . . .

1. The *Evening Post* was supporting McKinley for president in his race against Democrat William Jennings Bryan. Although Godkin disliked Bryan, he was nearly as contemptuous of Bryan's Republican opponent.

To Richard Watson Gilder

36 West 10th St., New York, October 26 [1896]
(*Century Magazine* Correspondence, NN)

MY DEAR GILDER: I am not of course discussing the merits of any particular war. . . .[1] I am discussing what might be, were we different and our customs different. I am, as it were, talking to South Carolina duellists about the year 1855. Society without duelling seemed to them impossible. Call the war of the rebellion anything you please[,] were the Southerners rational business men they would have offered to give up slavery for a round sum, and I am convinced they would have eventually got it, and have prevented unnumbered woes.

Yours truly
ELG

I have made some alterations in describing the war to make matters plainer. That is, war decides which can kill most people; not what is right, or under the circumstances expedient.

1. Gilder, who was proud of his brief Civil War service, objected to parts of Godkin's manuscript article, "The Absurdity of War," which Godkin submitted to him for publication in the *Century Magazine*. Godkin was not consistent in his attitude toward war, which he occasionally praised.

To Lord Farrer

36 West 10th St., New York, [9?] January 1897
(Farrer Papers, London School of Economics)

DEAR LORD FARRER: I trust you will use your influence to prevent very serious attention being paid, or encouragement given to Senator Wolcott who has gone over to talk about another international conference about silver. He is himself a good deal of a bimetallic humbug from one of the Silver States, and this talk of another conference which was thrust into the Republican platform, is intended simply to hoodwink the Silver men into the passage of another high tariff. It is exciting general dismay and disgust here now, and is simply a continuance of the game of imposture which the Republicans have been carrying on for fifteen or twenty years, and which has now landed us in Bryanism. The encouragement given to these emissaries in England has been a great hindrance to us here in bringing the country back to sanity. People cannot distinguish between Englishmen, and when they are told that Balfour is a bimetallist, or somebody belonging to the Bank of England, they fancy the consummation is at hand. Do say, or have said, something about his mission while there, that we can quote. . . .

Sincerely yours
ELG

The Right Hon. Lord Farrer

To Richard Watson Gilder

36 West 10th St., New York, January 23 [1897]
(*Century Magazine* Correspondence, NN)

DEAR MR. GILDER: This man is too vituperative to reply to him. There is no use in arguing with an excited patriot.[1] Besides he has totally mistaken the purport of my article. I did not seek to determine who began any quarrel, but the absurdity of trying to settle the dispute by cutting and stabbing. Even if Germany was wholly in the right, her quarrel with France is not settled. It has resulted in the creation of an enormous French army, to be used when the time comes, in getting back her two provinces. There is wide difference of opinion in both countries today as to the origin of a war which killed or disabled half a million men! Think of this.

This German thinks I am a liar; I think he is an *ass!*

Yours sincerely

ELG

1. Godkin is deigning to reply to a reader's criticism of his "The Absurdity of War," *Century Magazine*, O.S. 53 (January 1897).

To Henry Villard

36 West 10th St., New York, February 13, 1897
(Villard Papers, MH)

DEAR MR. VILLARD: One last word.[1] You are naturally surprised to hear me boast of myself, because I have never had to do it to any one but you.

. . . It is not my writing in the *Post* on which I plume myself most, and which made me say the stockholders are indebted to me, but my editorial management. Every feature in the *Post* which distinguishes it from its contemporaries is due to me. Its high character, its independence, its veracity, its influence in this community as a moral force, are due to me. . . .

I told you in 1892 that what I prevented was nearly as valuable as what I did. . . . [I believe] that but for me the *Post* would now be known simply as a personal or party organ, and be about as profitable and influential as the *Mail and Express* or the *Commercial Advertiser*. . . .

I am quite content with the action about my absence, but I am sorry that I had to fight for it. I am sorry, too, as I have often been previously, that I have not had more of your sympathy and appreciation in doing work, which I look back on with pride, and which the rest of the community greatly values.

Yours sincerely

ELG

1. This letter is in reply to one from Henry Villard answering Godkin's request for full salary during a five-month vacation abroad. A heated exchange took place in which Villard, though giving in to Godkin, rebuked

him for the "extraordinary self-appreciation" that he alleged kept Godkin from giving due credit to his co-workers for the success of the *Evening Post*. The semiretired Godkin was now writing fewer than one-fifth of the *Evening Post* editorials, while—so associate editor White informed Villard —accepting credit for editorials that Joseph B. Bishop wrote, and collecting a full salary for duties that White and Wendell Garrison shouldered in his absence.

To James Bryce

Florence, May 21 [1897] (Godkin Papers, MH)

MY DEAR BRYCE: You were kind enough before I left London, to offer to put me up at the Athenaeum on my return, or some other Club. . . .

We shall be in England about June 7. As we shall be in the country a Club in town would be very convenient for me, and if a month would exhaust my privileges at the Athenaeum, I suppose I could then get into the Reform. But you must do as you think well about it. . . .

I am delighted to see the Old Turk bothering the "Powers." How Ireland sits heavy on your souls. Salisbury was an utterly discredited Foreign Secretary, when you brought up Home Rule. Now he is one of the wisest of men. Balfour and Chamberlain have all been lifted into eminence by opposition to home rule simply. One is more and more convinced that every country— almost except the very small and weak, deserve their government.

Yours ever
ELG

To Louise Dawson

Monte Generoso, May 24, 1897 (Ogden 2:23)

MY DEAR LOUISE: We have been in Italy for the last six weeks and are slowly making our way back to England. . . .

We expect to be in Surrey for three months, barring a visit to Scotland to the MacLeods at Dunvegan in the Isle of Skye. I keep calm about American politics by not reading the papers. The English are gone mad about the "dear Queen." [1]

Salisbury has shown himself what he is in the Turko-Greek affair, and Providence, I am satisfied, is keeping an eye on your friend Chamberlain. . . .

1. Godkin is referring to the Diamond Jubilee in celebration of the sixty-year reign of Queen Victoria.

To James Bryce

Paris, June 3 [1897] (Bryce Papers, Oxford University)

MY DEAR BRYCE: Your news was delightful and gratified me beyond measure. It is the only honorary degree I care for and one I prize considerably more than the Bath or the Garter. Many years ago, I am afraid twenty five, Harvard gave me an M.A. but never has taken any further notice of my combats with beasts at Ephesus: The fact is, they are all in America afraid of the black-guard press, which makes Oxford's recognition of my labors, such as they are, doubly welcome. . . .[1]

Yours as ever
ELG

1. At the instigation of Bryce and Albert Dicey, Oxford University had voted to award Godkin the D.C.L. (Doctor of Civil Law).

To Thomas Wentworth Higginson

Ewhurst Place, Nr. Guildford, Surrey, June 16 [1897]
(Higginson Papers, MH)

DEAR HIGGINSON: I have just received your two notes from the Athenaeum . . . and am glad to hear of you in England. I left New York at the end of March, after a severe attack of grippe, and my wife and I wandered about the continent till June 8. I have taken a house here in the country for three months, as I wanted a quiet life while doing some work I have in hand for the *Atlantic Monthly*.[1]

On Monday we go to town for the jubilee and shall be at Henry James' apartment 34. De Vere Gardens till Thursday. On

Wednesday week, I shall hope to see you at Oxford, where as you so kindly say, I am to be honored as I "deserve."

My political "sin" must be forgiven on the ground of "invincible ignorance."

Yours cordially
ELG

1. Godkin was doing a series of five articles for the *Atlantic Monthly*, later to be published as a book, *Unforeseen Tendencies of Democracy* (Boston and New York: Houghton, Mifflin, 1898).

To Frederick Sheldon

Ewhurst Place, Nr. Guildford, Surrey, June 16, 1897
(Godkin Papers, MH)

My DEAR SHELDON: . . . I got your note this morning, about the recent occurrences in the *Evening Post* office. . . . There is no question, Seymour has behaved in a rascally manner, but he was offered a bonus of $20,000, by Stillman and Hubbard, who have that Searles money and have been spending it lavishly without effect in the *Comm. Advertiser*, which refuses to live.[1] They have then determined to make one grand effort, by offering prodigious bribes to two of our best men. Besides the bonus, Seymour is to get a large salary, and Wright, I am told [is] to edit the paper, at a large salary also. . . .

Of course it is all rather rascally, and shows the power of money in this community, but this is all the significance I think it has. It might not have occurred if I had been at home, but I am really not sorry to be rid of men capable of doing such things. I heard before leaving that Seymour has been lately obliged to take opium to quiet his nerves, which made me rather uneasy. . . .

Whitelaw Reid "Special Ambassador."! ! ! . . .[2]

Always cordially yours
ELG

1. *Evening Post* publisher J. S. Seymour, together with city editor Henry J. Wright and two star reporters, Lincoln Steffens and Norman Hapgood, had accepted an offer to resurrect the moribund New York *Commercial Advertiser*. Their departure from the *Post* was the result of a widening split

over editorial policy. Managing editor Linn wanted the *Post* to continue representing Godkin's aristocratic tastes, whereas the others wanted to boost circulation by a wider coverage of the news, including human interest stories and crime. Later, Joseph B. Bishop, disgruntled because he was not chosen as Godkin's successor on the *Evening Post,* joined the *Commercial Advertiser.*

2. Reid, who was influential in the Republican party, was appointed special ambassador of the United States to Queen Victoria's Diamond Jubilee.

To Mrs. William F. Smith

Ewhurst Place, Nr. Guildford, Surrey, June 18, 1897
(Ogden 2:22–23)

MY DEAR FRIEND SARAH: We have just settled here in our hired house, which is delightful, in a lovely region, after six weeks wandering on the Continent. Immediately on our arrival I received news of an event which is not the greatest which has happened since the birth of Christ, but still is very agreeable to us; namely, that Oxford is to give me an honorary D.C.L. at the Commemoration on the 30th of June. I tell you that you may rejoice with us on that day; it is, you know, the "blue ribbon" of the intellectual world, and very gratifying; K. is, I think, even more gratified than I am. I wish you were over here to be present.

The Jubilee is something awful. Miss de Rothschild has invited us to see it from her windows in Picadilly, but we would not have gone for want of a place to sleep the night before if Harry James had not lent us his rooms. . . .

To Sally Norton

Ewhurst Place, Nr. Guildford, Surrey, July 4 [1897]
(Fragment, Norton Papers, MH)

DEAR SALLY: . . . I cannot, of course, help thinking they did right in giving that "one degree," you speak of, but I disagree heartily with what you say about their way of allowing the ceremonial to be marred by the silly and *vulgar* interruptions of the undergraduates. . . . What you say about Charles Eliot is quite true. He is superb on such occasions.

We met Mrs. Kuhn and Hamilton at the Station—she from London, and they are now here. We all leave on Wednesday, we for Scotland. . . .

It was very kind of you and the Darwins to come to Oxford on my account.[1] I include the Darwins in the circle of dear friends I call "Little America". . . .

1. William Darwin and his wife came to the Oxford Commemoration Day with Mrs. Darwin's niece, Sally Norton, to see Godkin receive his honorary degree.

To Richard Watson Gilder

The Royal Hotel Portree, Isle of Skye, July 17 [1897]
(*Century Magazine* Correspondence, NN)

MY DEAR GILDER: I have seen General Porter's last "Campaigning with Grant," some time ago, and have just been reading Baldy Smith's answer to the part which relates to him, and it appears so conclusive . . . that I cannot help expressing surprize that you should have let Porter, under the colour of "reminiscences" of one officer make attacks which he could not prove, on the character of another.[1] Porter, I am told, has been for some time on unfriendly terms with Smith. This, with men of gentlemanly feeling, ought to have made him very particular ꞏot to indulge in any insinuations about him, or depreciation of him, when he was not sure of his facts. But even if he was wanting in delicacy, you ought to have kept a watch on him.

It is a liberty to write this to you, but everyone you know thinks he may remonstrate with an editor. . . .

Yours faithfully
ELG

1. Godkin is remonstrating with the editor of *Century Magazine* about General Horace Porter's attack in that magazine on the war record of General William F. Smith.

To Charles W. Eliot

Ewhurst Place, Nr. Guildford, Surrey, July 21 [1897]
(Eliot Papers, MH-Ar)

DEAR PRESIDENT ELIOT: I think you may want to know that James Bryce is sailing for America next week. . . . I suppose you will want to see something of him. . . .

I am sorry the news we get of the McKinley administration is not more cheering. The last, really ruffianly despatch about the Seals, is producing a very painful impression here. . . .[1]

I remain
Sincerely yours
ELG. . . .

1. Godkin's Anglophilism was affecting his judgment. Morally the position of the United States in the sealing controversy was hardly "ruffianly," even though an international tribunal had decided against it in 1893. The indiscriminate slaughter at sea of the seal herd that bred on the United States–owned Pribilof Islands had reduced the herd to a fraction of its former size, and it was threatened with extinction.

To Charles Eliot Norton

Ewhurst Place, Nr. Guildford, Surrey, July 21, 1897
(Godkin Papers, MH)

MY DEAR NORTON: I need hardly tell you that no one's pleasure in the Oxford honour to me, gives me more, or indeed so much, pleasure as yours. You know you were one of my earliest friends, when I had to be largely taken on trust. . . . I have never forgotten the loyalty and courage with which you supported me in those early days of the *Nation* when I was young, unknown, and mistrusted by so many crazy people. . . .

The daily news from home is more and more distressing. The weakness and stupidity of the President is more and more apparent. I did *not* vote for him. I said I would not do it, no matter what happened. I voted for the gold Democrat.[1] The last blackguard despatch about the seals, has I fear been prompted by the success of Cleveland's Venezuela escapade. I saw Hay yesterday, and he is greatly distressed by it. . . .

Ever affectionately yours
ELG

1. John M. Palmer (1817–1900) was the aged presidential candidate of the "Gold Democrats" in the Election of 1896. Although Godkin states that he voted for Palmer, the *Evening Post* and the *Nation* supported McKinley, and Palmer received no electoral votes. The day after the election Ellery Sedgwick heard Godkin remark, "We've worked and worked and *worked* to get McKinley in. Now we must work and work and *work* to get him out again." Ellery Sedgwick, *The Happy Profession* (Boston: Little, Brown and Co., 1946), p. 324.

To Frederick Law Olmsted

Ewhurst Place, Near Guildford, Surrey, July 23 [1897]
(Copy, Godkin Miscellaneous Letters, MH [1])

MY DEAR FRED: I had sent you a cutting of the doings at Oxford before I got your letter. . . . The honour that Oxford has done me is considered a very great one, but I assure you there is no gratification it gives me personally, greater than the fact that it is likely to gratify old friends in America like yourself.

I do not forget that it is forty years since you and I met, and that no break in our friendship has ever come in that long period. I have been since then through some very deep waters, and there has never been any one to whom I turned for sympathy with more confidence than to you.

. . . We saw the jubilee procession splendidly from Miss de Rothchild's windows in Piccadilly, but after this were only too glad to be out of London. You never saw anything like the crowd and confusion during the whole week. Lawrence arrived the day after here in the country and was present at Oxford at the great ceremony. The weather has been splendid, hardly any rain. We have just come back from a fortnight in Scotland, with out having had a single drop.

. . . What do you think of McKinley? Thank God I did not vote for him.

Yours ever
ELG

1. This copy contains the only example this writer has encountered of Godkin addressing one of his adult male friends by his first name, raising the speculation that Godkin's heirs, besides their usual practice of revising Godkin's spelling and punctuation, changed the salutation as well.

To William James

Ewhurst Place, Nr. Guildford, Surrey, July 30 [1897]
(James Family Papers, MH)

My dear James: I have been reading your essays, with great pleasure—your vocabulary is delightful—but the first one puzzles me.[1] What *do* you mean by "religion?" This term covers the fetichism of the African savage, as well as Emerson's pantheism, the Cotton Mather Methodism of the Tennessee farmer, as well as your philosophy. There is in fact nothing in the world called religion, in which theories of the Universe are not mixed up, with scientific theories, and historical facts. I cannot swallow Christianity, or "will to believe" it, without also willing to believe an immense mass of tradition, gossip and "evidence" of all sorts about a certain man alleged to have lived 1897 years ago. Can it be that I have a "living option," to believe all this, or not? What *I* believe about the universe, for instance, is not called "religion" at all by religious people. Believe me you must define "religion," to make your essay really effective. But you are nevertheless a most interesting and successful thinker, and I am

Yours very faithfully,
ELG

1. Godkin is gratuitously proffering his opinion of James's famous essay, "The Will to Believe." (William James, *The Will to Believe and Other Essays in Popular Philosophy* [New York, London, Bombay: Longman's, Green and Co., 1897].)

To Charles W. Eliot

Ewhurst Place, Nr. Guildford, Surrey, August 12, 1897
(Eliot Papers, MH)

DEAR PRESIDENT ELIOT: I have never believed that we should get rid of this tariff incubus, without a complete experiment. . . . Now a complete experiment requires as conditions that the Republicans should be in power in all branches. . . . Everything is now ready, and I believe there will be miserable failure before the end of McKinley's term. They have broken faith with the Democrats shamefully, and they will, you may be sure, be very extravagant, and there will be increased deficits and they will be unable to blame Cleveland or the Wilson tariff, and so the problem will be worked out. But I am afraid there is a more serious one before us. Are the men we now send to Congress competent to govern a great *commercial* country, with a vast foreign commerce, with a great, and very delicate structure of credit? Consider their terrible financial ignorance, their contempt for foreign trade, and for credit and their inability to understand it, and their readiness to destroy it by bill or resolution. . . .

Yours sincerely
ELG

To Arthur G. Sedgwick

Adhurst St. Mary, Peterfield, August 16, 1897 (Ogden 2:214–15)

MY DEAR SEDGWICK: . . . There are many things here which reconcile me to America, but there is no country in the world to-day in which you can be very happy if you care about politics and the progress of mankind, while there are many in which you can be very comfortable, if you occupy yourself simply with gardening, lawn tennis and true religion. This is one of them. I think I could prepare for heaven far more easily here than in America. . . .

To Charles Eliot Norton

36 West 10th St., New York, September 23 [1897]
(Norton Papers, MH)

MY DEAR NORTON: I telegraphed you from Stockbridge, and
ought to have written to you immediately on getting back here
yesterday, but I have found so many things waiting for me! . . .
I have been absent now five months, and the men here are sigh-
ing for a little relief. . . .

It is not very cheering, however, to get back to my work. The
state of the country, and its prospects are not exhilarating. Happy
you who can live in the still air of delightful studies, and only
now and then relieve your soul. The government really begins
to look a little like a burlesque. But some of the phenomena in
England too, are depressing. . . .

Ever yours affectionately
ELG

To Louise Dawson

New York, October 10, 1897 (Ogden 2:24)

. . . We are having a fierce canvas here, but I am far less excited and interested than I used to be. I am more and more inclined to the opinion of the old Englishman who said to me "he
was in favor of letting every nation go to the devil in its own
way." The way our leading citizens drop off under a little
temptation is almost amusing. Look at Tracy! [1]

K. desires me to say that your letter to her was very "nice." I
simply add that you are very nice also, and that I am very sorry
for the unknown man whom you ought to have married. . . .

1. Former Secretary of the Navy Benjamin F. Tracy (1830–1915) declined
to back Independent New York mayoral candidate Seth Low and instead
ran against him with Platt's endorsement on the regular Republican ticket
with the result that the Tammany candidate, Robert A. Van Wyck, was
elected.

To Emily Tuckerman

New York, October 13, 1897 (Ogden 2:217)

MY DEAR EMILY: . . . I wish, I must confess, that you were more interested in men and less in trees. As far as I can see, the great interests of civilization in this country are being left pretty much to the women. The men have thrown themselves pretty much into simple money-making. . . . It is the women who are caring for the things which most distinguish civilized men from savages. But the best women are leaving no descendants. They train no men. The best I know do not marry, so that society gets but little from them. . . . You are one of them. You think apparently you are serving the state sufficiently by attention to forest and infant schools. *Erreur, erreur [com]bien douloureuse!* . . . I do not think things are going well with us in spite of our railroads and bridges. Among the male sex something is wanting, something tremendous. . . .

To James Bryce

36 West 10th St., New York, October 22 [1897]
(Bryce Papers, Oxford University)

MY DEAR BRYCE: Low's chances seem to improve every day, as the situation seems to become more serious, and the character of Tracy's candidacy becomes plainer. Platt has been singularly indiscreet in revealing his reasons for running a separate candidate, which are chiefly a desire to retain the nominating power. . . . Then, we hear every day of more and more Republicans going over to Low, on becoming quite satisfied that he will not retire, and that there will be no "deal" or fusion.[1] Moreover, the Plattites have made another great mistake in confining their canvas, especially of late, to attacks, generally rather frivolous on Low, while saying little or nothing against Tammany. Tracy is . . . heavily weighted, too, by his business connection with Platt. . . .

Tammany has displayed similar imprudence. Croker is more than usually bold in the exercise of his despotic power. . . .[2] They say they will dismiss Waring, and put old Pat. Brennan

back in charge of the public hospital etc. a dreadful old rascal.[3]
A most disreputable rascal has been nominated for the district
attorneyship, Gardiner, and he has shouted from the platform—
"To hell with reform!"

Putting all these things together, I am growing more hopeful
of Low's success. Prolonged discussion is producing the effect it
so often does in America, of greatly helping the right thing. But
I am less hopeful every year about things here owing to the
want of courage. . . .

Yours

ELG

1. Seth Low (1850–1916), the millionaire merchant who was president of
Columbia University, had received the blessing of the Mugwumps and
many regular Republicans in his bid for mayor of New York. In a rare
moment of agreement with the *Evening Post,* Theodore Roosevelt told
Godkin that he hoped for a Low victory.

2. Richard Croker (1841–1922), the leader of Tammany Hall.

3. George E. Waring (1833–98), prominent sanitary engineer and street
commissioner of New York City, was a long-time acquaintance of Godkin.

To Louise Dawson

November 6, 1897 (Ogden 2:24–25)

MY DEAR LOUISE: . . . One night, the night of the election, was
pretty bad. A small party of gloomy people came to our house
to hear the returns, but did not stay very long. I awoke in the
morning in better spirits and on going down town found that
every one was disposed to be pleased with what they had accomplished and "to continue the fight," which I think they will do.

But, for my part, being "nearer to the wayside inn" I am
"weary" thinking of their load. . . . I am tired of having to be
continually hopeful; what I long for now is a little comfortable
private gloom in despair. It seems in America as if man was made
for government, not government for man.

These views are all for your private ear; don't give me away.
As an editor I am bound to keep cheerful and expect grand things.

I am glad to hear that "he" is not "impossible." I want all the
nice women I know to marry and have large families for the sake

of the country,—the trash of the earth, alas, is so prolific! K. joins me in all sorts of sweet things.

I am delighted to hear she has persuaded you to come and see us some time this month. I shall then express to you in purest Tuscan how nice you are and what a pleasure in knowing you is taken by

Yours most faithfully

ELG

To James Bryce

36 West 10th St., New York, November 19 [1897]

(Bryce Papers, Oxford University)

MY DEAR BRYCE: You may guess from my last letter about the election, that I was much disappointed in the result. All the outward indications were decidedly favorable, but Tracy's candidacy and George's death ruined all.[1] His followers drifted back to Tammany from Low the aristocrat and rich man. Then Platt was, undoubtedly, in relations with Croker, and used all his influence to defeat Low in any event.[2] For many weeks, his people said nothing against Tammany on the stump, and abused Low steadily. . . . The victory of Van Wyck, leaves, they think, the City in the hands of a man with whom they can "deal" about offices. The affair is an immense catastrophe, however any way we look at it.

In the first place it has hoisted Low with his own petard. He deliberately repudiated the chapter he contributed to your book, by sitting on a Commission with Gilroy, the rogue who was our last Mayor, and Tracy who was Platt's son's partner, to draw up in haste a charter for a "Greater New York," . . . . in contemptuous defiance of everybody representing the property and intelligence of the City. After he (Low) had done the deed, he publicly eulogized Tracy and Gilroy both. . . .[3] Nearly the whole of the newly annexed district contains only a poor ignorant Tammany population, among whom there is to be an enormous expenditure of money, which is sure to be expended corruptly. The expansion of the City, considering the mess that had been made of the original smaller one, was one of the maddest schemes ever undertaken by civilized man. . . . .

In short, the trouble, my dear Bryce, is, as I told you when writing about the Venezuela matter in 1896. The fundamental, *vera causa*, of bad government here is that the majority do not seek what you and I, and the likes of us, mean by "good government". . . . There are a hundred signs—too numerous to put into a letter—that we are rapidly approaching the South American type of statesmanship. McKinley is a farce, and instead of trying to reform the currency, he is pardoning criminals, and distributing offices, so as to secure his own renomination. Such illustrations of want of character and self respect, as Tracy, and Cornelius Bliss, and Frank Scott, a candidate (Tammany) for a judgeship, tell the whole story. The ideal of "a gentleman," which you have managed to keep alive in England, is worth any money to you.

Don't quote *me* about any of these things. . . .

Yours ever

ELG

1. The death of reformer Henry George in October 1897 after his nomination for mayor in opposition to Low, Tracy, and Van Wyck, caused some of his followers to shift to Tammany candidate Van Wyck.

2. Godkin is suggesting that there may have been an understanding between the Platt forces and the Tammany forces similar to that of 1886 when Henry George was beaten for the mayorship by a Republican-Tammany coalition backing Democrat Abram F. Hewitt.

3. In 1897 the State Legislature enacted a new charter establishing the modern-day New York City of five boroughs, with a president for each and a mayor for the whole. Thomas F. Gilroy was the Democratic mayor of New York, 1893–94.

To Henry Villard

Evening Post Editorial Rooms   New York, December 17 [1897]
(Villard Papers, MH)

DEAR MR. VILLARD: There is no warrant whatever in the writing for the paper for the "resolution" you sent me. Nobody but Wright who is no longer here, has ever been shown guilty of want of caution. What you mean by "personal responsibility" I do not [know], but the best and only kind of responsibility, is sense of duty. No caution will prevent corrupt judges or officials from pursuing us if they are so minded.[1]

I do not think the "resolution" is a kind of thing to address to gentlemen. A civil note would have been far more effective and becoming.

Yours truly
ELG

1. Concerned over the continuing threat of libel suits, the trustees of the *Evening Post* adopted a resolution calling for more editorial responsibility. The resolution was aimed chiefly at Godkin, whose relations with his fellow editors and Villard had now deteriorated to the point where he declined to meet with them at Villard's home to discuss *Post* policies.

To Theodore Roosevelt

[1897] (Roosevelt, pp. 221–22)

. . . I have a concern, as the Quakers say, to put on record my earnest belief that in New York you are doing the greatest work of which any American to-day is capable, and exhibiting to the young men of the country the spectacle of a very important office administered by a man of high character in the most efficient way amid a thousand difficulties. As a lesson in politics I cannot think of anything more instructive. . . .[1]

1. Godkin and Theodore Roosevelt briefly relaxed their feud while Roosevelt was gaining national recognition for his work as police commissioner of New York City.

To Moorfield Storey [1]

Evening Post Editorial Rooms   New York, January 19, 1898
(Copy, Godkin Papers, MH)

Dear Mr. Storey: I hope you Boston people who are disposed to make a great statesman of President Low will remember that he aided the Bosses in inflicting on us the new charter, the greatest misfortune, except armed sack and pillage that ever overtook a city; sat on the Commission beside Gilroy, the ex-mayor, a swindler and thief, and Tracy, a boss's partner in iniquity, reported in favor of a two chambered Municipal Assembly (89 blackguards) and a bi-partisan police board, pretended he was creating "home rule" for New York, and generally showed himself a complete dupe, or "duffer" in constructive legislation.

He was put up as a candidate for the new mayoralty by the reformers because we could do no better, but although the triumph of Tammany is a terrible thing for the city I am satisfied *his* triumph would have been bad for the cause of Good Government. It would have made "reform" ridiculous.

These views are for your judgment, but you can readily see why this letter should be *confidential*. I enclose a letter of Low's written to the *Post*, when we were fighting the Charter for dear life. It, the Charter, was an undoubted "deal" between the Bosses, but he felt so sure of being the first mayor that he saw nothing of the real character of the measure. Please send these cuttings back.

                                        Yours Sincerely
                                        ELG

1. None of the letters to Moorfield Storey herein are true copies, having been altered by Godkin's heirs to correct Godkin's punctuation.

To James Bryce

                 36 West 10th St., New York, March 22 [1898]
                                        (Godkin Papers, MH)

MY DEAR BRYCE: Your letter about the county council was very interesting. I confess I enjoyed Joseph's discomfiture keenly. . . .[1] You are in a great deal of hot water in England, but you have the great advantage of being in earnest, which, I do not think, we are here. . . . We are busy preparing for war, and McKinley has got fifty millions to spend as he pleases. He will, if he can keep the Cuban matter dragging along till November, be renominated and reelected. Public attention has, in this way, been wholly turned from the currency and the deficit in the yearly revenue which is rolling up in alarming proportions. McKinley was elected on the currency issue, and yet nothing whatever has been done

about it. . . . Everything in the domestic affairs of the country,
is at sixes and sevens. . . . As it seems to us, Hanna, McKinley's
manager appeared on the scene at this juncture, and gave a fillip
to the Cuban trouble. Somehow or other I think this will be made
to drag along until the fall and the next election. The scheme is
working admirably thus far. We keep edging towards war fast
enough to keep the jingoes quiet, and yet not fast enough to
frighten or alarm the good people, and we owe it all to the good
and great McKinley. *Justum et tenacem propositi virum.* The
newspapers are filled with promises, although everybody ac-
knowledges in private that he is an intriguing ass. . . .

Ever yours
ELG

1. Joseph Chamberlain (1836–1914), the one-time radical ally of Gladstone now colonial secretary in Lord Salisbury's Unionist cabinet, had long
been under fire from Cobden Club Liberals. At the moment, his advocacy
of social legislation was troubling Godkin.

To James Bryce

36 West 10th St., New York, April 1 [1898]
(Bryce Papers, Oxford University)

MY DEAR BRYCE: . . . Congress seems to be getting away from
McKinley's control and to have determined to have war at any
cost. It looks now as if we might have it next week. They are
persuaded—particularly those from the West—that the people
want war, and that their own seats would be in danger if they did
not give it to them. McKinley has behaved extremely well, and
has done everything that a man in his position could do, for
peace, partly because he sincerely dislikes war, and partly because
the effect of war on his fortunes would be very uncertain. I believe he had arranged to keep the negotiations going slowly on
during the unhealthy season, until after the next election of Congress. I do not believe you have any idea of the state of savagery
of the popular mind about war there is, in some parts of the
country, particularly the West. Many newspapers have openly
advocated it as a means of promoting business. I think the influ-

ence of the intelligent and really civilized grows feebler every year, and their voice fainter, but their "patriotism" will not permit them to acknowledge the fact. The complete indifference to the state of the finances, is to me, a most alarming symptom, but they seem to care less and less about it. Financial reform is not now spoken about, though there is a huge deficit in the revenue every year, and although on the outbreak of war the Treasury will be promptly stripped of its gold, and I fear, there will be a terrible panic. . . .

Ever sincerely yours
ELG

To Louise Dawson

Woodlands, Cobham, Surrey, May 29, 1898 (Ogden 2:25–26)

My dear Louise: . . . We are counting, you know, on endless visits hereafter, but just now, seeing you *sur le champs* would be useful.

My portmanteau went overboard at New York, leaving me with one suit. The tailor will, after the bank holiday, begin to clothe me gradually; I am still decent. . . .

To Louise Dawson

Woodlands, Cobham, Surrey, June 22, 1898 (Ogden 2:26)

My dear Louise: . . . Lord Russell has invited me to stay with him at Winchester, and I am going down on Sunday night or Monday morning. I am going to sit with him at the Assizes, and if you are brought up for manslaughter, as you readily may be, I will do what I can for you. You are distinctly a dangerous person. . . .

To C. P. Scott [1]

Woodlands, Cobham, Surrey, June, 1898
(Villard Papers, MH)

DEAR MR. SCOTT: Of course the alliance, or *entente cordiale*, with England would fulfil [*sic*] my strongest desire, but I hope you all here will not count too much on its steadiness or permanence. A great change has occurred in America. The power has passed to the valley of Mississippi; from the old states of the Seaboard, that is, from the hands of the statesmen, and more cautious, tradition ruled politicians, to a population profoundly ignorant of the rest of the world, of extraordinary volubility, and completely ruled by a vile press, and with an immense consciousness of strength. I think there will eventually be a moral union of the two countries, but you may have some trying experiences before it comes, and if you ever levelled yourself down to American politics, it would be an awful misfortune for mankind.

Sincerely yours
ELG

1. Liberal M.P. C. P. Scott (1846–1932) was editor of the *Manchester Guardian*.

To Frederick Sheldon

Woodlands, Cobham, Surrey, July 5 [1898]
(Godkin Papers, MH)

MY DEAR SHELDON: That share offered for sale, I should think, was Wright's, the city editor who went over to the *Commercial*. I do not suppose he wants to hold [stock] in the *Post* now.

The people I have in mind to buy ours are White and Villard. I have spoken to them about them. I have impressed on them the necessity of not letting my going seem to make a difference, and they concurred.

We have a house down in Surrey, which is very pleasant, but we think of spending our last sad month in Cumberland. I was at the "American dinner" last night. Much rejoicing over Sampson's victory; many blackguards, including Croker, and Brice.[1] One orator eulogized Croker, and made him grin from ear to ear. I cannot help thinking this triumph over Spain seals the fate of the American republic.

The news about Honey's grogshop is amusing. Where we were simple, was in supposing, that Honey would ever let that fund remain indefinitely in our hands, with no benefit for himself. . . .

Yours ever
ELG

Sail (alas!) Sept. 3

1. A naval squadron under the command of Captain William T. Sampson had triumphed over the Spanish squadron at Santiago Bay, Cuba. The "blackguards" to whom Godkin refers are former Tammany leader Richard Croker and, probably, Calvin S. Brice, railroad builder and former United States Senator from Ohio.

To James Bryce

Woodlands, Cobham, Surrey, July 23 [1898]
(Godkin Papers, MH)

DEAR BRYCE: . . . Can you furnish me with the facts about "Joe" and the old age pensions? [1] I do not mean anything long, but a reliable summary. The Americans ought certainly to hear the truth about it. He wins them over by his hospitality when they go to see him, with the aid of his American wife. And then, he lies awfully. The calm with which the public accepts him, makes me feel that you are travelling our road. The news from America is, as you know, that the fellows who were most active in hurrying McKinley into war, are now working hard to get him to make peace. This is preparation for fall elections, and confirms what I told you about the objects of the war. Their impression was that it would not last more than a week or two, and that they would be able to meet the constituents with a beautiful peace. You cannot conceive what depraved scoundrels they are. . . .

Yours as always
ELG

1. A reference to Joseph Chamberlain.

To Louise Dawson

July 25, 1898 (Ogden 2:26–27)

MY DEAR LOUISE: We have just returned from our visit to Mrs. [Kay] to lunch. . . . We took a charming walk by the river with Miss Drummond, and the place was full of your associations.

Here Louise walked, here she sat and read, here she strolled and mused, here she loved and lost, here she prayed and wept, here she saw the dawning of a better day, and so on. It was all delightful, but it was sad to be reminded of you so much when we compare the present date with June first. Then everything was full of hope and promise. . . . The 3d of September is hanging over us like an awful doom. I do so hate to go back and brag and lie and "get nearer to the people."

We went with the Bryces to spend Sunday at Farnham Castle with the Bishop of Winchester, and it is wonderfully grand and romantic. . . . Thence . . . Monday to Fulham, to the Bishop of London's dinner party; Stanleys of Alderly, Major-General Schab and wife, Sidney Colvin. Bishop in purple; house full of portraits of bishops, mostly old rascals, I am sure. Delightful lunch at the Farrers' on Thursday. . . .

We got your letter; sorry you had to carry the coffeepot; a lamp and milk-heater has also gone after you. Be sure to put plenty of coffee in. I think of using coffeepots as presents for nice girls. . . .

To Charles Eliot Norton

Ravenstone, Keswick, Cumberland, August 4 [1898]
(Norton Papers, MH)

MY DEAR NORTON: I have just seen the correspondence between you and old Hoar, which Emily Tuckerman, who is visiting us, brought with her. Otherwise I should have missed it, as I have refrained all summer from seeing any American Papers. I do not know in the public life of any country a more incompetent and unprincipled old rascal, and his abuse is a great boon to you. Ever since the Blaine canvas, in 1884[,] I have known that he was utterly unscrupulous and mendacious, and every succeeding year has supplied fresh proof of his ignorance. . . . The old humbug is bellowing *for* England now. Last March he was denouncing England, and he produced in a speech, as proof of her hostility to America, her having selected *me*, for a degree at Oxford! What use is there in God's earth for such creatures.

I am delighted that you still hold high the flag of rationality and decency. When I think of what I hoped from America forty years ago, and see what is coming, I see that we all expected far too much of the human race. What stuff we used to talk! . . .

Always affectionately yours
ELG

To his son

Ravenstone, Keswick, Cumberland, August 5 [1898]
(Godkin Papers, MH)

MY DEAR LAWRENCE: I got your letter yesterday. Two things I want you to remember. One is, that my trade is that of a commentator, by which I earn my bread and make my reputation. Consequently . . . if I only said what would please the blatherskites, and "patriots," I would only be fit for slaughter. But if you will provide me with a decent income, I will joyfully promise not to open my mouth about American politics as long as I live. . . .

The second is, that I would feel sure that, if the U. S. conquered the whole of this continent, it would set up a better government in the Spanish American states, than they now have. But I should feel very certain that the larger their extent of conquered territory the worse government they would have *at home*. . . . I do not care a "two penny damn" for the happiness of the Spanish Americans, and do not feel in the least responsible for it.

If you keep these two things in your mind, you will understand my position better. . . .

The English are gleefully putting the Americans up to be Conquerors, and have "a foreign policy". . . . It is like getting a child to drive a four in hand. The subjugation of the Spaniards was a sad business. They were slaughtered without resistance. "Gunning" them was like shooting a monk. That I in my lifetime

would see America engaged in such a business would, when I was
your age, have seemed a ridiculous supposition. But I am glad
you take the position you do. It will make your life happier,
and enable you to succeed in your profession. The principal thing
in the world is to succeed in one's own business, and your success
is my principal source of happiness.

My book has done well here. . . .[1]

Good bye. "Whoop-la!"

Affectionately yours
ELG

Hearst, Bennett, Reid are a grand trio, to settle the terms of
peace.

---

1. Godkin's *Unforeseen Tendencies of Democracy* was printed in both
an American and an English edition.

To Louise Dawson

Ravenstone, Keswick, August 26, 1898 (Ogden 2:27–28)

MY DEAR LOUISE: . . . No; we have not given a coffee-pot to
Miss Tuckerman, although I feel we ought to have given her
something, for she paid us a delightful fortnight's visit. You, on
the contrary, never gave us more than three days at a time, and
if you had not been so very agreeable and so kind in finding us
a house, we could not have given you a coffee-pot, much less a
coffee-pot and milk-heater. . . . If girls expect coffee-pots they
must stay longer with their friends.

I am . . . dreadful sorry to hear about the "evil eye". . . .
Whenever I hear of such stuff I bless and prize England more
than ever. These tomfooleries vanished from her more than a
century ago. . . .

To his son

Ravenstone, Keswick, August 29 [1898]
(Godkin Papers, MH)

DEAR LAWRENCE: . . . Do not get too joyful over the war, but
just enough. The victories were not quite equal to Trafalgar, but

would have approached it, if a few more men had been killed on our side. That was a bad business, not losing more men.

There is great amusement here over our entering on a warlike career just as the Czar is trying to draw out of it. McKinley's advisers, too, Paul Dana, Hearst, and Whitelaw Reid, are just the men for an "imperial policy." Whoop-la! . . .

Your peace loving parent
ELG

To James Bryce

Ravenstone, Keswick, August 29 [1898]
(Bryce Papers, Oxford University)

MY DEAR BRYCE: Alas! it is too true. We sail on Saturday, after a delightful month here. We have had a most comfortable house, on the very side of Skiddaw, with an enchanting view, and no heat to speak of, and only three rainy days. Was not this luck? We had a very delightful four days of Pell. They are [touring?] in America—one of their bursts of childish joy, which I hope they will have got over by the time I reach home. . . .

Since seeing you we have paid another ecclesiastical visit—this time to the Dean of Hereford—Madame is a daughter of Fanny Kemble. They were very pleasant. But the more I see of the church, the more amused I am. . . . What a wonderful thing, this proclamation of the Emperor of Russia is. Is it sincere, or "a put up job?"

The "imperial policy" in America will not begin till Congress meets. Then you will see fun. The finding out what kind of people the Cubans are, is the first act in the Comedy. I think in McKinley's case bewilderment is taken for deep meditation. The Peace Commission shows, what the new regime is to be. They are all except White, pretty ignorant, and some rascals.[1] Nothing can be worse for anything except dogstealing than Whitelaw Reid. You have had a grand escape from Hoar, as Minister.[2] A more absurd old creature does not exist, or a more virulent England hater. He denounced England like a mendacious fish wife, no longer ago than last March. Another[,] Commissioner Frye[,] proposed, during the Venezula [*sic*] business, to wait for two years, till our navy was large, and then go "declare war against England, without giving any reasons!!" [3]

It is good, too, to get rid of that buffoon, Depew. . . .[4]

Yours ever

ELG

1. The commission that McKinley appointed to conclude a formal treaty of peace with Spain was heavily composed of expansionists.

2. Senator Hoar and Godkin joined in their opposition to the Spanish Treaty, but they remained otherwise at odds.

3. William P. Frye (1831–1911) Republican Senator from Maine.

4. Republican political leader Chauncey M. Depew (1834–1928).

To James Bryce

Ravenstone, Keswick, August 31 [1898]
(Bryce Papers, Oxford University)

DEAR BRYCE: I forgot in writing to you yesterday, to say I should be very glad to make Brassey's acquaintance on board, but I am a bad hand at introducing myself, especially to an English peer. . . .[1] If therefore, you feel at liberty to send a note to Brassey in the *Campania* Liverpool, saying I am on board, and worth knowing, I shall make up to him sweetly. . . .

Yours as ever

ELG

I cannot keep pointing out to you the class of "statesmen" which the imperial policy is bringing on the scene, apropos of poor Sam Ward's pension, of what the new responsibilities would do for our politics. A more ignorant and corrupt gang than the new "peace Commission," except Judge White, does not exist. And they are all of the Rep. party, whose aim is more and more moneymaking. Congress has agreed with the silverites to coin a million and a half per month, of silver, for nothing, except to keep the price up. Here is "patriotism," wisdom, and, the new era. "Whoop-la!"

1. Naval authority Lord Brassey (1836–1918) was at this time governor of Victoria.

To Emily Tuckerman

Ravenstone, Keswick, September 1, 1898
(Godkin Miscellaneous Papers, NN)

Goodbye dear Emily. We leave this lovely place tomorrow. It's heartrending to go back to the "patriots" for me. Mrs. Sands bought the Dwight house, where I shall meet you, soon after your return, as I cannot go up there for a fortnight after my return, owing to Dicey, who comes to our house for a couple of nights on his arrival. We lunched on Tuesday at Isel Hall, Norman Keep (10th Cent) long low house, walls ten feet thick, charming hostess, parsonage nearbye giving parishioners an idea of heaven. Had you seen it, you would not only have thrown your arms around Katharine's neck through delight, but possibly even around mine.

Your visit has been the pleasantest episode of our summer— all the pleasanter for creating the hope that it will be repeated some other year soon, under similar circumstances. . . .

Au Revoir,

Yours affectionately
ELG

To James Bryce

New York, September 17 [1898]
(Bryce Papers, Oxford University)

MY DEAR BRYCE: . . . I told the men in our office what Hay told you about the Senate and they were convulsed. As to its [rascals] being all . . . of the new western states, look here—Mass. Lodge; New Hampshire, Chandler, one of the worst; New York Platt, a most scoundrelly, ignorant boss and Murphy, a completely illiterate Irishman, a collarmaker by trade; Penn, Quay a double-dyed rascal and Penrose, a worse; Maryland, Gorman, a perfectly unscrupulous boss; Ohio, Foraker and Hanna; South Carolina that awful blackguard Tillman—there are ten first-class scoundrels from states which far later than Tocqueville's day, sent men of the highest standing and character.

The public here is in a most comic condition about the war. To make a long story short, the Republicans are likely to lose the house at the next election on account of indescribable fraud and mismanagement during the war.

In other words, things have turned out exactly as I predicted. There is not honesty or character enough left in public life to carry on a war. The Secretary of war was dismissed from the army by sentence of court-martial, for cowardice in 1862.[1] Being rich, wealthy, and as usual, shameless, he got the place by a bargain with McKinley, at the last presidential convention, by which he agreed to throw certain votes from Michigan for him. Depend upon it the only limit to the wickedness of these fellows, will be their corruption and incapacity. . . .

Yours as ever
ELG

Hay has married a rich wife, lives in style in Washington, and belongs to the rich Republican coterie who dine together, and divide the tariff. He could not live there, or get an appointment, if he said the Senate had declined. Hoar will not go; is naturally an old ass.

1. Godkin's target was Secretary of War Russel A. Alger (1836–1907), who joined the Union army in 1861 as a captain of volunteers and rose in rank until he was brevetted major-general of volunteers in 1865.

To James Bryce

New York, October 20 [1898]
(Bryce Papers, Oxford University)

MY DEAR BRYCE: . . . Roosevelt[,] a rather ridiculous war hero, has been nominated by the Republicans for the governorship of the state, and has been going about attended by a company of what he calls his "rough riders" to the disgust of the judicious. The general opinion now is that he will be badly beaten. . . . But not only this, but there is a widespread expectation of what is called a "democratic landslide" all over the country. . . .

I write you this, lest some of the wandering Americans have been persuading you that the country is wild for annexation, and that McKinley is a wise statesman. He is a hypocritical ass. . . .

We have had a very funny time with Dicey. . . . He is now in Cambridge with Eliot. They are busy humbugging him as they would humbug you if they could get a chance. . . .[1]

I forgot to mention that the Governor of Illinois, an awful scamp is in open armed rebellion, but old McKinley takes no notice of it the state being Republican and the election near.[2]

> Yours ever
> ELG

1. A reference to the 1898 lecture trip of Professor Albert V. Dicey to the United States, during which he stayed for nearly two weeks with the Godkins. His unpublished impressions of Godkin—the most lucid and penetrating that this writer has seen—are somewhat critical of the editor.

2. An allusion to Governor John R. Tanner's expulsion of black miners whom the mine operators imported from Alabama to break the coal strikes at Pana and Virden. Subsequently, manslaughter indictments were obtained against the mine operators for killing some of the local strikers.

To Andrew Carnegie

November 1 [1898] (Carnegie Papers, DLC)

DEAR MR. CARNEGIE: You are doing the best work of your life.[1] God prosper you! I will let you know about the subscription.[2]

> Yours sincerely
> ELG

Keep it up; we will copy you every time.

1. Evidently Godkin is praising Carnegie for his stand against the acquisition of the Philippine Islands.

2. Carnegie had offered to contribute to a subscription for the widow and children of Godkin's just deceased friend, George E. Waring.

To James Bryce

36 West 10th St., New York, November 10 [1898]
(Bryce Papers, Oxford University)

MY DEAR BRYCE: The elections have ended in cutting down the Republican majority in the House to about 8 from fifty. . . .

Roosevelt has been elected in this state by a small majority—18,000. . . . The anti-annexationists think they are sure to defeat the Phillipine [*sic*] scheme in the Senate. . . .

Roosevelt's failure here was terrible, as long as he confined himself to his military exploits and the war. It was not until he betook himself to state affairs that his star began to rise above the horizon. The silver lunacy seems almost to have disappeared. But Quay's candidate has been again elected in Pennsylvania. . . .

Yours ever
ELG

To Charles Eliot Norton

36 West 10th St., New York, November 29 [1898]
(Norton Papers, MH)

MY DEAR NORTON: . . . I agree with you about democracy; the childishness, has been a subject of remark to me and every intelligent man I know, for some time. Nearly all foreigners speak of it to me. I have pretty much given [it] up as a contributor to the world's moral progress. We have ceased to give *consideration* to anything any more than boys at school. I too tremble at the thought of having a large navy and the war making power, lodged in the hands of such puerile and thoughtless people—100,000,000 strong. It is an awful prospect for the world, and I am glad to be so near the end of my career. McKinley is probably one of the silliest and most ignorant creatures in America, well known to be such, yet we have a man like Choate praising him to the skies. Morals in this community, except sexual morals, are entirely gone. I fancy that the press has had a good deal to do with this awful decline—the greatest in human history. But then the people make the press. So I simply tumble down on "the world's great altar stair."

Our love to your girls. We expect Sally before long.

Affectionately yours
ELG

To William R. Thayer

36 West 10th St., New York, December 29 [1898]
(Thayer Papers, MH)

MY DEAR SIR: I should like extremely to do what you ask about David A. Wells, but I am very busy indeed just now, and would be very glad if you could get it done by somebody else. I have to address Columbia College or some of it, about Colonial government, Jan. 24, and have to prepare something.[1] But if you are still without any suitable person, by Jan. 8 and will let me know at that date, I will try to have 2500 words for you by the 20th.[2] This is an appeal *ad misericordiam*.

Very sincerely yours
ELG

1. Godkin is referring to his paper before the Academy of Political Science of Columbia College, 24 January 1899, published under the title, "The Conditions of Good Colonial Government." The paper was published in *Forum* 27 (April 1899): 190–203, after *Forum* editor Walter Hines Page, a former *Evening Post* writer, made Godkin change what Page called its "hopeless" tone.

2. Thayer had asked Godkin to write an obituary of David A. Wells for the *Harvard Graduates' Magazine*, a request that he complied with. See E. L. Godkin, "David Ames Wells," *Harvard Graduates' Magazine* 7 (March 1899): 351–55.

To Emily Tuckerman

New York, February 4, 1899 (Ogden 2:217–18)

DEAR EMILY: I ought long ago to have acknowledged your very kind letter conveying to me Sir Wilfrid Laurier's appreciation of me and the *Nation*.[1] My feeling that he must be a very level-headed man increases my appreciation of you as one of the kindest of women. . . .

We are all waiting anxiously here for the news of the treaty on Monday.[2] I expect it to be confirmed, if not in this Senate then the next. . . . I am diverted every day by the number of people who are ready to take the "responsibility" of expansion, but do nothing but "take it." The one thing which will prevent expansion being a disgrace, is a permanent colonial civil service, but who is doing a thing or saying a word about it? . . . We "took the responsibility" of the Indians one hundred years ago, but what has happened? . . . Theodore Roosevelt told us recently that he introduced into a speech a recommendation of this sort, simply to "frighten McKinley." This shows how far it is from the thoughts of all politicians. . . . But they think in England we are sure to have it! . . .

1. Sir Wilfrid Laurier (1841–1919), Prime Minister of Canada.

2. The peace treaty with Spain, signed in Paris the previous November, was encountering opposition in the United States Senate from the Democrats, as well as Republican Senators Hoar of Massachusetts and Hale of Maine.

To William James

Evening Post Editorial Rooms   New York, March 2, 1899
(James Family Papers, MH)

MY DEAR JAMES: . . . The only fault I found with Salter was the disgracefully complimentary way in which he spoke of old McKinley, whom I think one of the worst men this continent has produced.[1] I feel as [if] I were living in a brigand's cave, and sail for England May 20.

Yours for righteousness, honesty, and justice and decency, and in fact all the virtues.

ELG

1. William M. Slater (1853–1931) was an occasional contributor to the *Nation*.

To Robert C. Ogden

36 West 10th St., New York, April 11 [1899]
(R. C. Ogden Papers, DLC)

Robert C. Ogden, Esq.
DEAR SIR: I have to acknowledge your favor of Saturday last: Putting together what I know myself and what you tell me, I

do not see clearly what has caused all this trouble. There was no editorial policy behind the reporter's article of the 8th March and no mistakes in it that could not have been corrected in a few words: Moreover, the *Post* is now, as it has been for eighty years, an open forum for opinions and statements on all subjects, including prices: We are sorry to offend any one but we cannot admit that there are for us any "forbidden subjects:" [1]

> Sincerely yours
> (signed) ELG

1. This letter arose out of the *Evening Post's* attacks on the New York clothing houses that were supporting what Godkin labeled the Customs "baggage abuse," the searching of the luggage of returning American tourists for dutiable foreign clothing. When the *Post* interviewed a New York matron who charged that "a woman cannot get as good wearing apparel in New York as she can in London and Paris for the same price, with the duty added," Robert C. Ogden of the firm of John Wanamaker objected, and Godkin responded to him as above. Thereupon Godkin editorially repeated his charges, and Congressman Wanamaker directed his lawyer to sue the *Evening Post* for libel. Angry New York dry goods merchants were withdrawing their advertising from the *Post*, and the paper's deficits were mounting. The controversy ended when Wanamaker's lawyer advised him not to sue, but not before relations between Godkin and *Evening Post* proprietor Henry Villard, who objected to Godkin's course, had undergone severe additional stress.

To James Bryce

> 36 West 10th St., New York, April 23 [1899]
> (Godkin Papers, MH)

MY DEAR BRYCE: . . . I have had a custom house row of grand dimensions on my hands. The tailors and milliners of New York succeeded in getting an atrocious provision almost secretly into Dingley's bill two years ago directed against European travellers. . . . [When] I exposed them the travellers began to boycott them. The "drygoods dealers" as we call them who secretly sympathized with them, then began to withdraw their advertizing from the *Evening Post*, causing a loss of about (at the rate of) ten thousand pounds a year. . . . It all gives you an idea of our civilization.

Politically things grow worse. It begins to be generally recognized that McKinley's Phillipine enterprize is a failure, but the wretched creature does not know how to get out of it. . . . The war department scandals, too, are dreadful. Did they occur with you, all concerned would seek safety in flight. In every direction is corruption and disorder. . . . Worst of all, Reed the Speaker, the one man of capacity and understanding left at Washington has announced his intention to quit public life for the practice of the law in New York. . . .[1] I am as many others amused by the beautiful belief of Wemyss Reid and the *Spectator* and *Daily News* that we are preparing a high-souled colonial service for our new possessions. We are doing nothing of the kind. . . . Judging from what I see in the papers, you are laboring under an immense delusion in England about this American colonial business. I have never, presumptuous as it may seem, felt more confident of anything in my life, than that you will have a rude awakening, and that if the American anti-imperialists fail to stem the present tide of barbarism and rascality, you will, before many years, have to deal with a new and more formidable America, without either religion or morality, under a government better fitted for predatory purposes. Have you read the accounts of the negro burning and mutilation in Georgia? Was there anything worse than that in Paris in '93? . . .

Yours ever
ELG

1. Speaker of the House of Representatives Thomas B. Reed (1839–1902) had broken with the Administration over its imperialistic course.

To Hamilton W. Mabie

36 West 10th St., New York, May 12, 1899
(Papers of the National Institute of Arts and Letters,
National Academy of Arts and Letters)

DEAR SIR: I approve of the Constitution of the National Institute, but think Sept. an unsuitable time for the Annual meeting. [Many] members will not have got back from their summer holiday. I suggest a day later in the fall.[1]

I further suggest that a majority of *all* votes be necessary for the election of members. Otherwise, you will have "packing" for the benefit of particular candidates, a thing which goes on at all the Clubs.

Yours truly
ELG

1. Writer Hamilton W. Mabie (1846–1916) was helping Dr. Holbrook Curtis organize the National Institute of Arts and Letters, the first members to be chosen by a committee from the parent organization, the Social Science Association, of which Godkin had long been a member.

To Charles Eliot Norton

Vichy, July 1 [1899] (Godkin Papers, MH)

MY DEAR NORTON: I am here for my sins to drink these waters for rheumatism, which had become intolerable. . . .

Passing through Paris, I sought out and made the acquaintance of Gustave Le Bon, to whom my attention was drawn by his book on the *Psychologie des Foules*, which struck me as extremely remarkable, as it explained so many of the phenomena of our war and the period immediately preceding it. His thesis, is that the mental and moral apparatus of a crowd differs, in *toto*, from that of an individual, and explains many of the oddities of popular government. He has recently published another which I consider a very remarkable explanation also of the present condition and immediate future of the western world—*La Psychologie du Socialisme.* . . . Do get hold of it, if you can. . . .

I spent a fortnight in London and found the two most interesting subjects were war and athletics, and that there was a steady indisposition to believe my accounts of McKinley and his government. It looks as if Chamberlain would succeed in what he is trying for; a war with the Transvaal. . . . France is travelling fast on the American road, in some places faster, in others slower, but always in the same direction. Not only liberty and order, but even rationality, seem to have taken refuge in England.

Ever affectionately yours
ELG

To Louise Dawson

Villars, Switzerland, July 24, 1899 (Ogden 2:28–30)

MY DEAR LOUISE: . . . I spent two weeks in London, out of which two Sundays had to be taken for Oxford and the Bryces' country-house, and a Wednesday for my friend Pell in Northampton. I dined at the House of Commons, meeting Balfour, saw the "trooping" of the colors from the treasury windows, but I was miserable with rheumatism and had no enterprise about anything and saw none of the races, matches, or shows. . . . I am very well, but stiff, and now figure as a *"vieux respectable."* My youth is utterly gone, and I am about the right age for a "sage," a business I intend to take up when I get home. I have equal vents of smiles and tears over the way you are getting on with your great civilizing and evangelizing war.[1] I was particularly delighted, as comedy, with the proclamation of Platt, certifying to the good conduct of McKinley and Alger. This has been observed to draw laughter from several worn-out cavalry horses. . . .

1. A reference to the war being conducted by the McKinley administration against Filipinos who declined to accept American rule.

To E. B. Smith

[Summer 1899] (Ogden 2:219)

. . . You know how much I am with you, how much I am, heart and soul, an American of the *vieille roche.* American ideals were the intellectual food of my youth, and to see America converted into a senseless, Old World conqueror, embitters my age. Don't despair, however. . . .

To Emily Tuckerman

Adhurst St. Mary, Petersfield [7 September], 1899
(Ogden 2:219–20)

DEAR EMILY: We are staying another fortnight, and will not sail until the 23rd. I have not courage to face the New York heat.

The doctors have warned me so solemnly against heat and fatigue that I have agreed to retire from hard work.

After suffering terribly on the way home from Paris, we reached England Aug. 27, and went at once to stay with H. James at Rye, where he has bought a delightful old house, in a decayed mediaeval town, oak panelling, king's room, sweet garden and lawn, and all the requisites for the "long home" of a bachelor tired of the world. Four delightful days, then here in Sussex, with an American hostess, Mrs. Bonham-Carter, married to a very intelligent English squire. . . .

We leave on Monday for Ethel Sands' in Oxfordshire. There one fortnight, and then back to "holy wars," patriotism, and buncombe, arriving in New York about the 1st Oct.

. . . England in spite of the drought is as lovely as ever. We paid a visit yesterday to one of the loveliest of its ruins, Cowdray, but these ruins fill me with melancholy when I think of what is succeeding them. *Ay de mi,* as Carlyle said. . . .

To Henry Villard

36 West 10th St., New York, October 2 [1899]
(Villard Papers, MH)

DEAR MR. VILLARD: I was much gratified by your letter yesterday, and by that of Garrison and White, and the resolution of the Trustees.[1] They are kind and nice, and very welcome to an old Warhorse, who seems to be turned out to grass. I am glad you think the arrangement a good one. It suits me very well. I shall be able to do some work in the next three months, when I get set up a little. I have just seen the doctor here, and he thinks a little rest and the avoidance of fatigue, will make me as well as a man of 68 can expect to be. But I shall not die happy without witnessing McKinley's downfal [*sic*]. . . .

Yours very sincerely
ELG

1. After debate, the trustees of the *Evening Post* concluded to pay Godkin his full salary for an additional three months leave of absence, with the understanding that he would give up the title of editor-in-chief at the end of the year.

To Charles Eliot Norton

36 West 10th St., New York, October 3 [1899]
(Godkin Papers, MH)

MY DEAR NORTON: I came back on Saturday, pretty tired with travelling and not very well. . . . So I withdraw from the editorship of the *E. P.* Jan. 1st and in the meantime do little or nothing. I shall continue to contribute when I feel disposed, and always to give "advice." But I have made my last change, and if I am not hereafter a "sage" I shall simply be a "vieux respectable."

I think it but becoming, my dear and early friend, to communicate this first to you, who witnessed and encouraged my beginnings. I hope all is well with you, and am glad we both survive to finish our careers. But you need not noise it abroad.

Ever affectionately yours
ELG

To Thomas Wentworth Higginson

36 West 10th St., New York, October 11 [1899]
(Higginson Papers, MH)

DEAR COLONEL HIGGINSON: Forty years ago, that is June 1859, I read with great delight an article of yours in the *Atlantic Monthly* —"A Charge with Prince Rupert." It kindled much my youthful imagination, but I have never seen it since. It was recalled to me vividly by walking over Chalgrove Field in England, a few weeks ago with my wife. We were staying in a house a mile and a half away, and I urged her to read it. But on returning to New York, my publisher reported to me, that it was out of print. But I have since received it from Boston and it renewed my old pleasure. I got in London, a new life of the Prince, which has just appeared. I thought you might like to hear what memories you had created.

Eheu, fugaces labuntur anni!

Faithfully yours
ELG

To Everett P. Wheeler

Ridgefield, Conn., October 17 [1899]
(James W. Brown Collection, NHi)

MY DEAR WHEELER: I have relinquished the office management of the *Post* mainly because of my health; but I have had nothing to do with city affairs, since the last election. I have been engaged in the business of "rescuing the city from Tammany" for forty years, and am tired of it. My belief is that the mass of the people prefer Tammany government to any you can provide for them. And then, think of the conduct of such "intellectuals" as Low, and Roosevelt, and Tracy and Root. I am out of the Sisyphus business. Bishop is now in charge of it.[1] I do not print my views because I do not wish to discourage more hopeful men like yourself. In my opinion nobody can save the city of New York but God almighty, who will do it in his own way and in his own good time. . . .

Sincerely yours
ELG

1. Infighting in the *Evening Post* editorial offices was now keen, Joseph B. Bishop seeking to supplant associate editor Horace White, whom Godkin and he contemptuously called "Uncle."

To R. E. Leupp

[ca. 8 November 1899] (Ogden 2:237)

. . . I am of course sorry to retire, but nature has a very imperative way with men of my age. Then our present political condition is repulsive to me. I came here fifty years ago with high and fond ideals about America, for I was brought up in the Mill-Grote school of radicals. They are now all shattered, and I have apparently to look elsewhere to keep even moderate hopes about the human race alive. . . .

To The Reverend William R. Huntington [1]

New York, November 13, 1899 (Ogden 2:237–38)

DEAR DR. HUNTINGTON: There is no man in the United States whose *Ave et vale* I value more than yours. The doctors have told me it is time to take in sail, and I have had insinuations to that effect from even surer sources. The last two or three years, too, have been very trying to me, as rowing against the tide always is. And then I have suffered from seeing the America of my youthful dreams vanish from my sight, and the commencement on this continent of the old story; and I must confess I think I have seen great decline in both morals and politics, within my forty years. Arthur Balfour told me last summer in London that "he heard I was a pessimist." I said "what would you think of me if I were satisfied and made cheerful by all I see?". . .

My thoughts often recur to you as one of the public teachers who "stand fast." The disposition of the church almost everywhere to take pains not to rise above the morality of the crowd has been one of the afflictions of my later years. . . .

Yours grateful friend
ELG

1. William R. Huntington (1838–1909), Protestant Episcopal clergyman and author.

To Mrs. James Bryce

New York, November 14, 1899 (Ogden 2:238–39)

MY DEAR MRS. BRYCE: . . . I am on the whole not sorry for your experience.[1] You now know what we have been through, seeing a perfectly avoidable war forced on by a band of unscrupulous politicians, the permission of whom to exist and flourish on the part of the Almighty always puzzles me; and behind them a roaring mob.

We are dragging wearily in the old way, killing half a dozen Filipinos every week, and continually "near the end." The folly of ignorance and rascality we are displaying in the attempt to conquer and have "subjects" would disgrace a trades union. You do not see a quarter of it in England.

I have resigned from the *Post*, as you will see by the enclosed slip. The work had become not only more and more disagreeable in the present state of our politics, but more and more wearing to my health. My wife had become absolutely peremptory. I am receiving shoals of lamenting letters. . . .

1. The outbreak of the Boer War.

To Daniel Coit Gilman

36 West 10th St., New York, November 15, 1899
(Godkin Papers, MH)

MY DEAR GILMAN: Your kind letter would be very grateful, if only because it is over forty years since first "we were acquent." But, I have ever since been taking pleasure in the fact that you were yearly achieving success by doing what I thought "the right thing" in a very great field of activity, and then you know, I am your wife's "oldest friend" as she has often remarked. You both carry me a long way back up the stream of time, to the "jours charmantes de la vie". . . .

Ever sincerely yours
ELG

To Mrs. James Bryce

November 18, 1899 (Ogden 2:239)

. . . In writing to you in the beginning of the week, there were some things I forgot to say.

The election is over with a heavy majority all over for the Imperialists. This is a great change from the beginning of the summer, and is undoubtedly due to your war. You know they are very childish, and think, as you have "a war of civilization," they must have one too. We are much amused but somewhat sickened by your professions of love for America as soon as she abandons what constituted her ancient fame, and launches on a career of lawless brutality, and serves your purpose. These professions are a popular joke here. You are hated just as much as ever, and it is a common remark how the stumps would resound with denunciations of your attack on the Boers, if we were not in the same business ourselves.

A few days ago I dined beside Reed, the Speaker of the last Congress, and the one statesman remaining in Washington. Said I, "What do you think of McKinley; You must know him pretty well. Some people tell me that, although he has made mistakes, he is a good man." Said he, "What do *you* think of a man who gets his debts paid by other people and rewards them with missions in the public service?" I need not comment on this. But we are making money gloriously. . . .

To Mark A. DeWolfe Howe

36 West 10th St., New York, November 28 [1899]
(Copy, Godkin Papers, MH)

DEAR SIR: It so happens that I never liked Horace Greeley, had hardly any acquaintance with him, and from my point of view thought his equipment for journalism wretched. His stock of general knowledge was deplorably small; his great merit in my eyes was his sincerity, though his prejudices and self-conceit made him ridiculous.

You will thus see that I am about the unfittest man in America to write his life.

I am, however, obliged and flattered by your offer, though compelled to decline it.[1]

Yours sincerely
ELG

1. Mark A. DeWolfe Howe (1864–1960) approached Godkin to write a short biography of Horace Greeley for the *Beacon Biographies* series of which Howe was the editor.

To Emily Tuckerman

Thanksgiving Day [30 November], 1899 (Ogden 2:240–41)

DEAR EMILY: . . . Nothing has happened since you went except Bell's "Feat of Arms" in the Philippines. It's high time for another childish craze, and I feel the need of one. We had a very agreeable visit last night from ex-Speaker Reed. He came very kindly on my invitation to advise us about the "Traveller's Defence" Bill. He makes a distinct impression of power, and is full of sardonic humor, which suits his face very well. It is so pleasant to meet a mature rational man.

I am going to look forward to a day at Mt. Vernon with you. When last there, fifteen years ago, it quite *m'attendrissait*. It will be delightful to see it with a dear sympathetic friend. . . .

To Charles W. Eliot

36 West 10th St., New York, December 5, 1899
(Eliot Papers, MH-Ar)

DEAR PRESIDENT ELIOT: . . . I know I have seemed to many a professional fault finder, but I have hated the business, and I have always made it the rule of the office to praise where praise was at all possible. But in forty years of journalistic life in New York, I remember only two measures, the reform of the Civil Service, and the reform of the election law, which were avowedly passed for the good of the community. . . . I have not discussed constructive work much, because there was little or no constructive work to discuss. . . . We had a charter suited to our needs two years ago, when one boss introduced a new and absurd one, drafted by a University President, sitting beside an ignorant thief in the person of our late Mayor (Gilroy) and containing provisions against which he had himself argued in Bryce's book, and in the Magazines. Under it the City was handed over to Tammany. . . . *C'est tout dire.* George Rives said to me the other day that he did not see how we were ever to mend our ways, as long as people steadily refused to believe that any thing could be wrong, as long as they were making money.

But judging from the kind farewells which have poured in

on me from various parts of the country, I cannot complain that my little efforts to make things better, have not been appreciated. . . .

Very sincerely yours
ELG

To Louise Dawson

December 23, 1899 (Ogden 2:30–31)

. . . I do not like to talk about the Boer war, it is too painful. To think of England, which I love and admire so much, and which is so full of beauty, being filled with mourning at this season! When I do speak of the war my language becomes unfit for publication, and I therefore will not write of it to you. Talking of the Philippine war has the same effect upon me, and I have therefore ceased to write about McKinley. Every one who believes in the divine government of the world must believe that God will eventually take up the cases of fellows who set unnecessary wars on foot, and I hope he won't forgive them. . . .

Kipling has long been to me a most pernicious, vulgar person. I only admire one thing of his, "The Recessional." He may have written other things as good, but I don't read him. I think most of the current jingoism on both sides of the water is due to him. He is the poet of the barrack-room cads. Of course I don't venture to set my judgment of him up against many good people.

Thank your mother as the author of such a delightful work as Louise, and say "Tchok Salaam" [sic] to her on our behalf. Dublin will be delightful because you are. . . .

To Emily Tuckerman

December 26, 1899 (Ogden 2:241–42)

. . . I cannot accept the office of godfather without knowing distinctly what are its obligations. For what am I responsible? What have you forsworn? Doubtless you have abandoned the devil and all his works, and "the flesh," but how about "the world?" I never accept an office for which I think I am not thoroughly fit. As your uncle, I would feel easy and would not care what you did; but as your godfather, I would feel uneasy constantly. Had I not better be simply your uncle, and thus be able to allow you complete moral freedom? It is probably because you are a Unitarian that you take the office of godfather so lightly. I, on the other hand, having never left the Episcopal church, still have a certain reverence for it, and like to see its duties faithfully fulfilled. Think of these things. . . .

To his sister

December 28 [1899] (Copy, Godkin Papers, MH)

MY DEAR GEORGINA: . . . As you know I have resigned from the *Post*. . . . I am for all ordinary purposes of life very well, but I have damaged my nervous system by overwork and the doctors threaten me with serious things if I do anything that can be called labour any more. So I am simply enjoying life by means of the *dolce* [*farniente*]. I have not found life so agreeable for many a year. My library is more delightful than ever. We are staying in the country till next autumn when I think we shall go to Italy or Southern France for the winter. . . .

I have written for the last day of the old year for the *Post* a sketch of my whole career since I went to the Crimea.[1] I will cut it out and send it to you. . . .

I hope you are all well.—My mother specially. I would write to [Kate] if I had her address. Will you send it to me when you write. Tell me also if Tim Healy is still living. If he is I should like to send him some little remembrance. . . .

A happy New Year to you both!

Your affectionate brother
ELG

1. E. L. Godkin, "Random Recollections: A Retrospect of 40 Years," *Evening Post*, 30 December 1899.

12. Retirement, 1900–1902

Late in 1899 Godkin was sixty-eight and in poor health. Although he still had some of his hearty sense of humor, he was not meeting gracefully either his advancing years or his responsibilities, and dissatisfaction with him was increasing in the *Evening Post* editorial rooms. At last, the paper's embarrassed attorney, Lawrence Godkin, son of the editor, fell to conspiring with the editor's long-time lieutenant, Wendell Garrison, to put the "tempery" old warrior on the shelf. Their opportunity came in September when Godkin returned from his annual three-month junket to Europe broken down with rheumatism and other infirmities of age. With his reluctant consent, the trustees of the *Evening Post* relieved him at once of his editorial duties but permitted him to keep the title of editor until January 1, 1900. Thereafter, it was agreed, he would be free to contribute to the paper signed pieces of his own choosing.

Scarcely had his retirement been announced in the press than Godkin was back in the news for another reason. One Christmas-time evening, late in December 1899, he left his comfortable home in the Village and set out uptown. Walking to the elevated station at Eighth Street and Sixth Avenue he moved his stout frame up the steps to the platform. While awaiting his train his keen eyes fell on an unpleasant spectacle below: two police officers halted on their beats, heads together in amiable conversation. Taking out his watch, Godkin timed the exchange of pleasantries, then descended the stairs, took the names of the officers and filed a formal complaint against them for malingering. Three days after Christmas he appeared on his own motion to testify against them before the Police Commissioner. Retirement obviously had not dulled Godkin's notion of civic duty.

Godkin's published writings after his retirement, as well as his personal letters, reflect his continued misgivings about the men who were charting the new imperial course of the United States and his sorrow over the passing of the genteel tradition. In February 1900 he suffered a stroke in New York while working on his intended memoirs and did not lift his pen again for six months. The next year the *Evening Post* rejected one of his signed pieces on the grounds that it was too "extreme and pessimistic" and would make readers think its author was "dwelling in the past."

By the middle of 1901 Godkin's health and mental facilities, which had been declining for several years, would not permit even the slight exertion of writing. Convinced, he said, that he could not prepare for heaven in the United States, he sailed with his wife and an attending physician to his beloved England where, on May 21, 1902, he died.

To Edward W. Ordway

36 West 10th St., New York, January 3 [1900]
(Ordway Papers, NN)

E. W. Ordway Esq.
DEAR SIR: I shall be happy to accept the Vice presidency of the Anti-Imperialist League, if the gentlemen you name, are likewise to act.

Yours truly
ELG

To Moorfield Storey

January 19, 1900 (Ogden 2:242–43)

MY DEAR STOREY: I was mortified to have missed your visit. . . .

I am, as you know, a gentleman of leisure. . . . The nearest I come to work is a letter once a week to the *Post* on anything that occurs to me,[1] and I have agreed with the publisher to amplify my recollections into a good-sized volume to be ready next fall. . . .

I agree with you that things look very black. . . . the indifference to what happens, as long as "prosperity" continues, is . . . appalling, and the military spirit has taken possession of the masses, to whom power has passed. But for the extraordinary power of self-deception possessed by Americans, the changes would have been perceptible long ago.

Do try and come in some day, even mutual lamentation would be pleasant. . . .

1. See "Ignoble Peace," 3 January 1900; "The Mills of God," 10 January 1900; "Optimism and Pessimism," 17 January 1900.

To Charles W. Eliot

36 West 10th St., New York, January 24 [1900]
(Eliot Papers, MH-Ar)

DEAR PRESIDENT ELIOT: A year ago at the Saturday Club, you asked me what I thought of Roosevelt's theory that it was a good plan to jump into politics and practice with the bosses, in order to accomplish something. There was not time then to give you my full mind about the notion. I thought it an illusion. I have spoken about it more at length in the *Post* this week, and if you will do me the honor to read the enclosed article, you will, I think find some reason, for believing that the whole Lodge-Roosevelt creed is humbug.[1]

> Very truly yours
> ELG

1. E. L. Godkin, "The Education of Example," *Evening Post*, 24 January 1900.

To John Brooks Leavitt

> January 26 [1900] (Copy, Villard Papers, MH)

My dear Sir: . . . at the time in question I was under a delusion, from which I have recovered, that deliverance might come for this City from our respectable classes, and that your "Goo-goos," were ruining a movement which had some chance of success. Since [then] I have seen the President of your University sitting beside a notorious thief, Gilroy, to draft a ridiculous and unnecessary charter, and then going down to Princeton to eulogize him, also unnecessarily, and well knowing that he was living in luxury on stolen money, and Roosevelt entertaining that scoundrel Platt. . . . Thank God, I am "out of it." Such a condition of things among the instructed classes needs at least a generation to be reformed.

> Truly yours
> ELG

To Charles W. Eliot

> 36 West 10th St., New York, January 27 [1900]
> (Eliot Papers, MH)

Dear President Eliot: I perhaps did not make myself sufficiently clear about Roosevelt and Platt. He comes down to New York, ostentatiously to meet him for "conference." He has had him staying at his house. He practically shares the governorship with him in its most important function, to Platt's great benefit. . . .

Yours very truly
ELG

To R. U. Johnson

36 West 10th St., New York, January 28 [1900]
(*Century Magazine* Correspondence, NN)

DEAR MR. JOHNSON: Writing once a week for the *Post*, and preparing my "Recollections" for publication, are really as much work as I now feel equal to, or inclined to. Otherwise I should be very glad to embrace your obliging proposal that I should do something for the *Century*. . . .[1]

Yours very truly
ELG

1. A few days after writing this, Godkin suffered a moderately severe cerebral hemorrage.

To James Bryce

36 West 10th St., New York, April 23 [1900]
(Bryce Papers, Oxford University)

DEAR BRYCE: I am making a little use of my first returning powers to thank the friends, who, during my illness expressed any concern about me. I have come back to life and am improving steadily. . . . I am, of course out of American politics, which appears to me more than ever the game of ill taught schoolboys. . . . I am amused by your belief in England that there is a regular government here. The government consists of an old mixture of the fool and knave, called McKinley. Don't deceive yourself the trouble is "democracy." There is a mixture of equal parts of political knavery and Christian Missions. . . .

Your affectionate friend
ELG

To James Bryce

Lenox, May 11, 1900 (Ogden 2:244–45)

MY DEAR BRYCE: . . . I am here on my way upward, I hope, but my handwriting is not yet fit for letters. I am much obliged for your English news. The disappearance of conscience from public affairs has long been visible to us, but there is always enough hypocrisy kept on hand to impose on foreigners. In spite of a very valiant "remnant," our prospects are far gloomier than yours.
. . . I have read about the Queen's visit to Ireland, and am amused to see how Salisbury managed to throw cold water on it and prevent its having any good effect—one of his finest "blazing indiscretions" and one of the worst. A man like Salisbury needs a man like Chamberlain to do his dirtiest work. I suppose he has as little objection to Chamberlain as he had to Disraeli, and the future historian will have difficulty in fairly dividing between the two whatever rascality there is in English politics. . . .

To James Bryce

Lenox, May 16 [1900] (Bryce Papers, Oxford University)

MY DEAR BRYCE: . . . Of course I cannot help sympathizing with you over the Imperial sorrows, but they are inevitable. I have no doubt you will come out of them well, as England generally does.
  English madness, except about Ireland, is apt to be brief. . . . What makes me now write is the desire to do something towards arresting the American humbug, which seems to grow greater every year. We have no statesmen to utter words of stern exposure, such as were uttered in the recent debate in Parliament on the Spion Kop dispatches. Both parties are here maneuvering for position in the Presidential campaign. Each trying to deceive different people, and all trying to deceive somebody, while one of them is engaged in slaughtering a distant and defenceless people. I don't know in History a more sickening spectacle than our politics present just now; there is not even one decent public man left, and political literature consists chiefly of the exposure of frauds. What I told you when in England, was certain to happen,

the commission of frauds on an astounding scale in Cuba, has begun, and all the leading Post Office officials have just been arrested, other exposures have still to follow. The only interest in the Boer War seems to be due to calculations as to the extent to which it may be made to damage the British; most of the pro-British sentiment is due to the desire to get into London society. . . . Give our love to your wife, her letters are a great pleasure to me—and remember that nearly everything you hear from this side of the water is *humbug!*

> Faithfully yours
> ELG

To Wendell P. Garrison

> Lenox, Mass., June 3 [1900] (Godkin Papers, MH)

DEAR GARRISON: I have read your article with interest, and hearty approval. . . . What you say about McKinley is all true. He is not only unfit for the Presidency but unfit for decent society. I have never changed my opinion of him, since he received and read the Spanish Minister's letters before the war.

I am doing pretty well here; I am already able to compose a little daily, and am progressing, I walk over a mile every day. I hope you are getting on well, and that the *Nation* is maintaining its ancient fame.

> Yours ever faithfully
> ELG

To Charles W. Eliot

> Monadnock, N. H., July 8 [1900] (Eliot Papers, MH)

DEAR PRESIDENT ELIOT: I am here, as you possibly know, to aid in the restoration of my health; it is a fine air, but rather a remote place, as regards accessibility. Books I find difficulty in getting. Charles Norton, when visiting me in May last in New York, suggested to me to solve this difficulty by applying to you for permission to use the Harvard College Library to a moderate extent, I paying the express for anything that could be sent to me. Will

you kindly let me know if this is practicable? The newest books
of biography travel and history, would meet my case, if this is
not asking too much.

With kind regards, very sincerely yours

ELG

To Charles Eliot Norton

Monadnock, N. H., July 31, 1900 (Ogden 2:246–7)

MY DEAR NORTON: . . . I rise early, take a longish walk after
breakfast, over rough ground, as an exercise in locomotion, read
an hour or two in books kindly sent to me by Eliot, in accordance
with your suggestion, mainly biography and travels, always an
hour or two, and am now beginning to write about fifteen minutes for the *Post*. . . . I take a drive with my wife every afternoon in a one-horse wagon, she driving, through country pic-
turesque but monotonous. I find I am a "homme très policé," and
only thoroughly enjoy scenery treated and improved by man.
Nature, except Switzerland, tires me. The summer resorters here
are few, but respectable and intelligent. The westerners are rich.
I am amused by their political hopefulness. . . .

I was . . . not surprised by what you say of England. If the
Lord means to save modern nations now is his time. The fall of
England into the hands of a creature like Chamberlain recalls the
capture of Rome by Alaric. . . .

I congratulate you on the D.C.L. I presume you would have
got it long ago but for the personal-presence condition. . . .

To Professor George P. Fisher

Monadnock, N. H., August 12, 1900 (Ogden 2:248)

DEAR FISHER: . . . I was very glad to hear your North East
Harbor news. . . . I have been slowly toiling up the hill since
February last, cheered by the fine promises of the doctors, who
say that before long I shall be as well as ever. . . .

I have retired from the active elevation of mankind; man must get on now by his own unaided exertions! . . .

To Wendell P. Garrison

Monadnock, N. H., September 28 [1900] (Godkin Papers, MH)

MY DEAR GARRISON: There is no one with whom I have so long "clambed the hill thegither" as with you, and naturally now on returning once more, even for a brief period, to life, I am exceedingly glad to hear from you. . . .

I had intended paying no more attention to American politics, but the habits and interests of forty years cannot be dropped in a minute. McKinley has excited my hatred and contempt more [than] any man I have ever known, and I could not therefore close my career, without giving him one more dig, even if it were, as John Holmes of the Irish bar, said, "the last voice of expiring nature. . . ." [1]

Yours ever affectionately
ELG

1. Godkin is referring to his letter, "The Clergy and War," which appeared in the *Evening Post* 26 September 1900. In it Godkin proffered the thesis that "it is the eager support of the clergy which has launched McKinley on his career of conquest."

To Wendell P. Garrison

Monadnock, N. H., October 7, 1900 (Godkin Papers, MH)

MY DEAR GARRISON: I saw only yesterday, in the papers, the sad news of your son Lloyd's death. I shall spare you the usual reflections on its sadness. I am sincerely sorry for you. . . . going to the Virginia Hot Springs for a few weeks by th recommendation.

Your faith
ELG

To F. W. Gookin

[26 October 1900]
(Copy of fragment, Godkin Miscellaneous Letters, MH)

. . . My name closely resembles yours, and my friend, the late
James Russell Lowell, used to try to persuade me that yours was
but a corruption of mine, due to the Puritan scruples of the Massachusetts Gookin about using the syllable God in his name. But
I have never heard that our name underwent any change since
the settlement of a small colony on the coast of Wexford in the
twelfth century, in what was called the Barony Forth. It was a
small settlement of Englishmen, distinguished for their piety and
industry, and they became Protestants at the Reformation. They
spoke a dialect of the Anglo-Saxon, peculiar to themselves, not
unlike the Lowland Scotch, down to the beginning of the present
century. The names of the two first settlers are Ram and Godkin.
There was still a Godkin among the landed proprietors in the
Barony as late as 1870, I saw by the Doomesday Book. The others
have all disappeared long ago. My father, James Godkin, died
30 years ago, and I have no brothers. I myself have now been
over 40 years in America. . . .

To W. McKinstry

[21 November 1900] (Ogden 1:10–11)

. . . I received your letter of the 5th Nov., and as I am only
just recovering from a severe illness, I am sorry not to be able to
answer in my own handwriting. I regret to say my recollections
of Queen's College have dwindled considerably, but I can very
vividly recall the announcement of the first scholarships, of which
1 one in law, the occupant of that chair being then William
cock, now long deceased.
ontemporaries were "Tom" Ingram, the brother
Trinity College, who is, I think still living;
the then President of the college; Dunlop,
byterian minister, and of whom I
nes Ross, who was afterwards a

judge of the Irish Common Pleas, and who died in that position; and Sir Robert Hart, now Controller of the Customs in China, and who entered the year I left. These are all I can at present remember.

I was the first President of your Society, and was considerably puffed up by reading a paper on Lord Eldon before a crowded audience in one of the college rooms.

The professors whom I best remember were Hancock of Political Economy and Jurisprudence, Molyneux of Law, and MacDonough of Latin, and Craik of English Literature. These are all I can remember at this moment; others may come to me later. I am glad to hear the Society is still not only in existence, but prospering. . . .

To Charles J. Bonaparte [1]

36 West 10th St., New York, November 25 [1900]
(Autograph Collection, NRU)

DEAR SIR: I am unfeignedly sorry that the state of my health will render it impossible to take any part in the proceedings of the League next month.

Yours very faithfully
ELG

1. Charles J. Bonaparte (1851–1921) was active in public causes, including the Anti-Imperialist League to which this letter apparently refers. Later he served in Theodore Roosevelt's cabinet.

To his son

36 West 10th St., New York, November 27 [1900]
(Godkin Papers, MH)

DEAR LAWRENCE: The last I saw of those bonds was at my office. . . . If they have disappeared I am *planté*. I find that talking over the matter addles me and I wish you would, like a good fellow take charge of the whole Olmsted affair and settle it. . . . I will send you my cheque the first of every month, and ask you to meet

my liabilities. All I owe in the world is to the Olmsteds, if anything, and Sheldon. . . . But please don't talk business to me as
yet. It stirs up my wretched head badly. . . .

> Your affect. father
> ELG

To Charles Eliot Norton

December 31, 1900 (Ogden 2:248–49)

MY DEAR NORTON: . . . I have intended to write you ever since
Christmas began to loom on the horizon, through the typewriter,
which Katharine works for me. . . .

My dear fellow, no anniversary ever comes round without recalling most vividly the happy days passed with you in the sun-
niest years of my life, and how much of the sun of those years
was due to your kindness and friendship! In fact, all you say about
my work is simply a compliment to your own goodness of heart.
. . . We are both nearing the end of our career, and certainly
the sweetest memories of mine are clustered around you and your
sisters. . . .

To James Bryce

36 West 10th St., New York, March 18 [1901]
(Godkin Papers, MH)

MY DEAR BRYCE: . . . I have been completely disabled since
February, by a recurrence of my old disability, and am now
writing from Lakewood a health resort near New York to which
I have come in the hope of getting rid of extreme weakness and
getting back my power of locomotion. Here I have luckily found
Goldwin Smith and his wife, and some other friends. . . . We are
going to England early in May. . . . We . . . intend to stay
abroad, if possible, as long as old McKinley is President. As I was
not born in this country, I do not want any one to suppose that
I came here voluntarily to live under this caricature of civilized
government, composed of McKinley and his blackguard Senate.

The mere reading of their doings ever morning, I verily believe, keeps me from recovering my health more rapidly.

. . . Our whole community here seems utterly rotten, and Smalley is their chronicler. What a lying blackguard he is! [1] Things are going here from bad to worse. Do read Mark Twain in the *North American Review*. He is doing excellent work. . . .

The old ruffian in Washington, and his gang: I will not any longer share their [responsibility?]. . . .

ELG

1. George W. Smalley (1833–1916). As London correspondent of the New York *Tribune*, Smalley had long excited Godkin's animosity. Once, in a vain effort to heal their squabble, *Tribune* proprietor Whitelaw Reid got Godkin to publish a piece by Smalley in the *Nation*.

To William James

Castle Malwood, Lyndhurst, July 9 [1901]
(James Family Papers, MH)

MY DEAR JAMES: You have little idea how much pleasure the receipt of your letter gave me. The former letter I never received. I must leave it to my wife to explain it. . . .

I am delighted to hear of your recovery. . . . Like other people, I mourn the loss of my aggressive years, of youth, but confess that I enjoy my leisure, my peace, and the English landscape, on which I gaze with delight. My years of combat have been so unsatisfactory that I do not care to protract them, and I have long felt the need of friends' society, and am now bent on enjoying it. I am greatly gratified on finding that you are again in the field, would I could think that old McKinley would again feel your rod. I am looking forward to your stopping here on your way back through England. . . .

Affectionately yours,
ELG

[P. S. to the above by Katharine Godkin]

Dear Mr. James

The burdens, as well as the privileges, of wives are various, and one of mine is the responsibility of your letter referred to herein.

When it came Mr. Godkin was not well enough to receive it and later I dreaded explaining to him fully. So he was told of your writing and it was reported "mislaid."

He greatly enjoys this place, and we *count upon* showing it to you when you all return to England.

Yours most sincerely

KG

To James Bryce

Castle Malwood, Lyndhurst, July 18 [1901]
(Bryce Papers, Oxford University)

MY DEAR BRYCE: My opinion of Rosebery has never wavered for 20 odd years, from my first seeing him as a young man in New York, down to his late letter on Liberal dissensions. It was confirmed by hearing a speech from him at the Eighty Club, after a dinner at your house, along with Asquith, I thought then I had never listened to anything so like a whine of excuses, for being useless and incompetent. He was the person principally to blame, and he blamed every body else.

It was further confirmed by a dinner at his house, where he appeared once more as a slight, flighty young man. When I saw him again in New York, he devoted himself to the society of Sam Ward and William Henry Hurlbert, two of the greatest scamps I have ever known.[1] That anyone should have supposed that he had force enough or persistence enough, or weight enough to lead a party, has always seemed to me absurd. . . .

The best thing for him to do now, is to live jauntily on his Jew money! [2] I feel all this so strongly, that I can't help disburdening myself to you.

My wife and I want to know whether you have got us down for another visit, and a longer one, in August, or sooner. . . .[3] I found myself distinctly the better for your visit.

Our love to you both.

Yours ever faithfully

ELG

---

1. Godkin is referring here to the so-called "wicked Sam Ward," not to his old friend Samuel G. Ward.

2. The prejudiced Godkin is calling attention to the long marriage of former Liberal prime minister Rosebery to the daughter of Baron de Rothchild. Lord Rosebery had incurred the wrath of the "Little Englanders" in his party by his support of the Boer War.

3. Despite Godkin's progress reports, his friends knew he was dying, and one by one they responded to his entreaties to visit him in the New Forest. In August came William James, Henry James, and Henry D. Sedgwick. For Sedgwick's recollections, see Simon Nowell-Smith, comp., *The Legend of the Master* (New York: Charles Scribner's Sons, 1948) pp. 5, 29.

To the Evening Post

Hatley St. George, Torquay, November 1 [1901]
(New York *Evening Post*, 16 November 1901, p. 6)

I regret that I cannot do more than send a line of Godspeed to the paper that I put so many of the best years and best endeavors of my life.[1] My recollections of the *Evening Post* go back to the days of the administration of Mr. John Bigelow, when I wrote one or two articles for it—one, I remember, upon the East India Company, which was then expiring. The press was then very different from what it has since become. But that the *Evening Post* has, through all its changes of ownership stood for righteousness and decency is my recollection, and that it may so continue, my hope.

1. Godkin, unable to be present at the luncheon in observance of the one hundredth anniversary of the *Evening Post*, sent this note to the paper from England.

To Wendell P. Garrison

Hatley St. George, Torquay, November 29 [1901]
(Godkin Papers, MH)

MY DEAR GARRISON: I have received your account of the *Evening Post* anniversary. . . . It is some return for the way in which we all spent ourselves. . . . I missed from the list of names at the luncheon those of Geo. Rives, Marshall, Arthur Sedgwick, Col. Burt. I shall write to the latter myself, directly. He has been for years my model American. . . . I have read what you saw fit to say of me with emotion, it is certainly most gratifying. The dearest thing I recall in it all, is my thirty years association with you. . . . Some day, I believe Civil Service reform will have become as obvious in America, as it is here. . . . The antislavery fight seemed even more hopeless, yet it was won, and now people wonder that there ever was any fight at all.

I am progressing here slowly, I have back everything but my hand-writing and walking, I do a little of that on a good terrace we have, but nothing to boast of yet.[1]

. . . I have been reading a life of my poor friend Russell, by Barry O'Brien, and have enjoyed it very much, I hope you will have it well reviewed in the *Nation*. . . .[2]

Yours always
ELG

1. Death approaching, Godkin met his decline with fortitude. His final contribution to the *Evening Post* had appeared the previous August, a piece that Wendell P. Garrison declined to reprint in the *Nation* on the grounds that it showed marks of his former chief's "mental decay."

2. Former Lord Chief Justice Russell died in August 1900.

To Charles Eliot Norton

Hatley St. George, Torquay, January 22, 1902
(Ogden 2:252–54)

MY DEAR NORTON: Your letter, received two or three days ago, gave me great pleasure, but I still have not confidence enough to answer it, as it ought to be answered, in my own handwriting.

. . . I am sickened to see how closely we are following the Tories, and also to see how we are flattered here, in place of the abuse which was heaped upon us of old. The grand place we promised to occupy in the world seems to be completely out of sight. . . . Chamberlain is a capital specimen of the rise of an unscrupulous politician, and we have not yet seen the end of him. America is hereafter to play a large part in European politics; our means of resistance to bad influences is less than it used to be. American methods are much more in favor over here than they once were, and the art of lying is much more popular. Our army in the Philippines is repeating the practices of the

Spanish and other older despotisms. The worst of it is that the cheap press has become a great aid and support in all these things. It has by no means turned out, as it was expected to, a teacher of better manners and purer laws.

. . . I am somewhat reassured by you about Roosevelt, of whom I have had grave doubts.[1] I quite agree with you in what you say as to the improvement over McKinley. . . .

Always my dear old friend, yours with real affection,

ELG

1. Theodore Roosevelt had assumed the Presidency four months before.

To William James

Hatley St. George, Torquay, February 21 [1902]
(James Family Papers, MH)

DEAR JAMES: . . . We have moved down from the New Forest to Torquay, a model watering-place in its way; situated on a series of hills on the edge of the sea. The inhabitants it is true, are all Jingoes, but that does not disturb me, I can bear Jingoes of any material except Americans. It seems to suit every other nationality better. . . . I had a short fit of sickness caused by it here, but that is all. The Jingoe [sic] is just the same ass that he was when I was fifteen years old. It is most curious how the great lessons of Liberalism of my youth seem to be forgotten, fairly decent men have been turned into roaring blatherskites. . . . McKinley's example shows how easy it is for even the most de-graded members of the class to become sainted Jingoes.

It will be a great pleasure to us to see you and your wife here. . . . [And] you must arrange to be more liberal of your time than you were last summer. We are expecting Harry here as soon as he is able to come, he was laid up when he last wrote with a passing ailment. I am glad he has a good woman in his house to take care of him. . . .

Always, my dear fellow, yours affectionately

ELG

To James Bryce

Greenway House, Brixham, R. S. O., May 13 [1902]
(Bryce Papers, Oxford University)

DEAR BRYCE: I am glad to think the election at Bury has turned out so well, I am sorry old Gladstone has not lived to see it, it is the turning of the tide, *style* has got a black eye! Luckily I have been seeing the *Manchester Guardian*, which keeps its head straight, taxing bread will turn all the country liberal, as it did before.

We were hoping Whitsuntide would bring you to us again, and I assure you we are still more worth a visit at Greenway, than at Hatley. . . .

Mrs. Whitman and Emily Tuckerman come down on Thursday, additional attractions. . . .

We regard this place as a bit of perfection, and count on showing it to you and Mrs. Bryce sooner or later. . . .

Our love to you both, and best congratulations on the capital speech with which you [led] off the Education Bill. I wish I could have heard you.[1]

Affectionately yours
ELG

1. This is probably Godkin's last letter. Eight days later he died.

Index

Godkin, Georgina Sarah (sister), 390n, 400, 401n; Godkin's letter to, 530

Godkin, James (father), 1, 77, 173, 390n

Godkin, Katharine Sands (second wife), xiii–v, 166n, 303n, 306–7, 312, 314, 330n, 351–52, 357n, 364, 366, 367, 380, 390n, 414, 437, 455, 490, 496, 499, 512, 523, 542; note to Henry James, 543–44; Godkin's letters to, 303, 349, 416

Godkin, Lawrence (son), xiii–v, 165, 166, 211, 219, 237, 251, 279, 297, 307, 328n, 330, 331n, 350, 350n, 354, 362, 366, 367n, 385, 493; tendered political appointment, 328; campaigns for Cleveland in 1888, 372–73; legal career, 408, quoted, 445n, differs with father on Spanish-American War, 508, 509; encourages father's retirement, 531; Godkin's letters to, 211, 214, 455–56, 508–9, 509–10, 541–42

Godkin, Maria (sister), 69

Godkin, Sarah (mother), 401n

Godkin Lectures, 310n; J. P. Morgan and, 348n

Godkins of County Wexford, 540

Godwin, Parke, 114; Godkin tries to sell *Nation* to, 114n

Gold Democrats, 492; in election of 1896, 493n

Gold Standard: Godkin's inflexibility toward, 482; *See also* Currency Question

Goldschmidt, Otto: meets Godkin, 386

Goldsmith, Oliver: mentioned, 394

Goodnow, Frank J.: writes chapter on Tweed Ring for Bryce's *American Commonwealth*, 362

Gookin, F. W.: Godkin's letter to, 540

Gordon, C. G. "Chinese,": pronounced "half cracked" by Godkin, 312, 313n

Gorman, Senator Arthur P.: branded an "unscrupulous boss" by Godkin, 512

Gould, Jay: 374; and Erie Scandal, 129, 130n

Govone, General Giuseppe: friendship with Godkin, 92, 400; suicide of, 401n

Grace, Mayor William R., 358; Godkin's praise of, 346; dubbed "the pirate of Peru," 347n

Grace Lines, 347n

Granger Movement: Godkin's distaste for, 195

Grant, Mayor Hugh J., 402n; Godkin's aversion to, 401, 411n

Grant, Ulysses S., 135, 136n, 183, 185, 186, 190–91, 239, 247, 293, 324n; estimate of his generalship, 15, 18; Godkin's support of his presidential candidacy, 126, 145, 190; Godkin's opposition to his renomination, 170–71, 177; Godkin's support of his reelection, 192–93; Godkin's renewed opposition to, 201, 202, 239; financial failure, 313

Granville, Lord: and Isthmian Canal dispute, 281, 282n; meets Godkin, 396

"Greater New York" Charter, 500n; denounced, 499

Greeley, Horace, 187n, 527n; Godkin's aversion to, 186–93 *passim*, 527

Green, Alice Stopford (Mrs. John Richard Green), 389, 397–98

Gresham, Walter Q.: deserts Republican Party in 1892, 440

Grey, Albert, 4th Earl: makes Godkin's acquaintance, 302, 330, 331n

Grey, 2nd Earl: mentioned, 302

Grey, 3rd Earl: on Irish disturbances, 338

Grosvenor, William M.: branded a "charlatan and adventurer" by Godkin, 201